TPS-Lean Six Sigma: Linking Human Capital to Lean Six Sigma

A New Blueprint for Creating High Performance Companies

Advance Praise for TPS-Lean Six Sigma:

Hubert Rampersad and Anwar El-Homsi combine the power of Lean Six Sigma with an approach that stresses the importance and need of developing an organizational structure and philosophy that combines the goals of and aspirations of the individual with those of the company.... During my 38 years of business experience, I've seen many well developed management concepts being applied without success and that have failed to recognize the importance of aligning the needs and aspirations of employees with those of company objectives. The TPS-Lean Six Sigma concept offers a systematic process of continuous improvement and development of personal and organizational performance with potential for breakthrough results. —**Ricardo A. Gonzalez Director Worldwide Purchasing, EASTMAN KODAK COMPANY, USA**

Successful implementation of Lean Six Sigma relies on people up and down the organization working together to achieve quality. Despite best intentions, the importance of the human element in the overall implementation scheme can be overshadowed by a focus on the tools. Hubert Rampersad and Anwar El-Homsi have written the most important book yet on creating a culture of Lean Six Sigma. It clearly spells out how to address the issues and challenges associated with implementing a comprehensive and effective Lean Six Sigma program. —**Stephen Haight, Vice President Global Quality, Bausch & Lomb**

Hubert Rampersad and Anwar El-Homsi continue their superb integration of business, project, and personal life in their new book. Their disciplined, logical, and scorecard approach to melding business and personal lives will be a major benefit to companies, leaders, and employees. The new book is full of examples, tools, and exercises that will help individuals discover and align their personal vision and mission to the company where they work. This book links the lean six sigma profession with human capital in a fully integrated and through way.—**Dave Ulrich, Professor of Business, University of Michigan, and Partner, The RBL Group. He was ranked as #1 management educator and guru by Business Week, #2 among management thinkers by Executive Excellence, and listed by Forbes as one of the "world's top five" business coaches.**

This book packs a big punch. Any company interested in improving their quality processes fast needs to incorporate its message. —**Paul Bracken, Professor of Management, Yale School of Management**

TPS-Lean Six Sigma puts heart in the (Lean) Six Sigma process. It's designed for human beings and integrates both process and people to achieve maximum results. —**Marshall Goldsmith is a world renowned executive coach and the author of the *New York Times* best seller *What Got You Here Won't Get You There*. He is recognized by the American Management Association as one of 50 great thinkers and leaders who have impacted the field of management over the past 80 years.**

See back matter for more advance praise

TPS-Lean Six Sigma: Linking Human Capital to Lean Six Sigma

A New Blueprint for Creating High Performance Companies

by

Hubert K. Rampersad

and

Anwar El-Homsi

Information Age Publishing, Inc.
Charlotte, North Carolina • www.infoagepub.com

Library of Congress Cataloging-in-Publication Data

Rampersad, Hubert K.
  TPS-Lean Six Sigma : linking human capital to Lean Six Sigma / by Hubert Rampersad and Anwar El-Homsi.
    p. cm.
  Includes bibliographical references and index.
  ISBN 978-1-59311-825-9 (pbk.) -- ISBN 978-1-59311-826-6 (hardcover) 1. Total quality management. 2. Six sigma (Quality control standard) 3. Employee motivation. 4. Goal setting in personnel management. 5. Organizational effectiveness. I. El-Homsi, Anwar, 1951- II. Title.
  HD62.15.R364 2007
  658.4'013--dc22

                                                                        2007033622

ISBN 13: 978-1-59311-825-9 (pbk.)
         978-1-59311-826-6 (hardcover)
ISBN 10: 1-59311-825-2 (pbk.)
         1-59311-826-0 (hardcover)

Printed in the United States of America

CONTENTS

FOREWORD

The root of both Lean and Six Sigma, go back to the time when the greatest pressure for quality and speed were on manufacturing. Lean rose as a method for optimizing process speed and efficiency in automotive manufacturing; Six Sigma evolved as a quality initiative to eliminate defects by reducing variation in processes within the semiconductor industry. It is not surprising that the earliest adopters of Lean Six Sigma arose in the service support functions of manufacturing organizations like GE Capital, Caterpillar Finance, and Lockheed Martin.

Recognition by practitioners and business executives that you cannot do "just quality" or "just speed" without overlooking opportunities has led to the effective use of this balanced process over the past years as a business improvement methodology. It has often led to maximizing shareholder value, fast rates of improvement in customer satisfaction, cost, quality, process speed and invested capital. However, Lean Six Sigma as a concept alone will not deliver meaningful results, unless it is enthusiastically supported by the organization's human capital and its application aimed at key organizational objectives. Success or failure in applying Lean Six Sigma largely depends on how it is sold to an organization and the degree to which its members adopt it. In this book, Hubert Rampersad and Anwar El-Homsi combine the power of Lean Six Sigma with an approach that stresses the importance and need of developing an organizational culture and philosophy that combines the goals of and aspirations of the individual with those of the company. They call this approach "Total Performance Scorecard" (TPS). It links the driving force and motivation of individuals within the organization (using a "Personal Balanced Scorecard") with the organizational vision, mission and critical success factors to achieve competitive advantage for the company. This is referred to as the Organizational Balanced Scorecard (OBSC). TPS is an all-encompassing management approach that leverages the motivation and capabilities of corporate associates and applies them to the realization of the highest corporate objectives. During my 38 years of business experience, I haven't seen many well developed management concepts being applied without success and that have failed to recognize the importance of aligning the needs and aspirations of employees with those of company objectives. The "Total Performance Scorecard" concept presented here, used in combination with Lean Six Sigma (TPS-Lean Six Sigma), offers a systematic process of continuous improvement and development of personal and organizational performance with potential for breakthrough results.

Ricardo A. Gonzalez
Director Worldwide Purchasing
EASTMAN KODAK COMPANY

PREFACE

The companies that survive longest are the one's that work out what they uniquely can give to the world, not just growth or money but their excellence, their respect for others, or their ability to make people happy. Some call those things a soul.

—Charles Handy

We have been deploying Lean Six Sigma in various large and medium size companies for many years and have realized excellent results in most instances. We found that while Lean Six Sigma does a great job addressing the primary concerns of manufacturing and service, we felt that there was something missing in the deployment of Lean Six Sigma programs at many companies. Something that could help foster sustainable breakthroughs; something to realize durable performance and sustainable quality enhancement based on a happy and engaged workforce, something to create a real learning organization in which people are working smarter, are committed and improve themselves continuously. That something is human capital. We found that the results could be enhanced if the importance of human capital is considered as an integral part of the process. We learned that Lean Six Sigma, in itself, does not sufficiently address human capital at many companies. While expected results from Lean Six Sigma alone will be good, we believe that adding the human component to Lean Six Sigma has the potential to realize sustainable, long-term growth and produce a transformation into a lean, learning, prosperous organization with a highly engaged workforce.

Research has shown that the lack of engagement is endemic, and is causing large and small organizations all over the world to incur excess costs, under perform on critical tasks, and create widespread customer dissatisfaction. Gallup statistics show that unhappy workers cost the American business economy up to $350 billion annually in lost productivity, and that earnings per share increase 2.6 times more if employees are engaged. (Gallup Poll, 2005). Gallup's research also indicates that 70% of U.S. employees are not engaged at work. Companies with such a large number of dissatisfied employees have more absenteeism and lower productivity—as well as 51% higher turnover rates than those with engaged employees. Improving organizational performance and controlling business processes requires a highly engaged and delighted workforce. Research on happiness in the workplace suggests that worker well-being plays a major role in organizational performance and that there is a strong relationship between worker happiness and workplace engagement. The *Gallup Management Journal* (Krueger & Killham, 2005) surveyed U.S. employees to probe their perceptions of how happiness and well-being affect their job performance. Gallup researchers examined employee responses to see which factors differed most strongly among engaged employees and those who were not engaged or actively disengaged. These findings suggest that while most workers experience varying degrees of happiness and well-being at work, engaged workers get the most from these feelings. They reported higher levels of overall life satisfaction.

Lean Six Sigma primarily addresses quality issues, manufacturing issues, transactional issues, customer issues, speed and variability issues. However, unless your organization is run by robots, you still need engaged people to make it all work. There was nothing in Lean Six Sigma that systematically addresses the very real needs of the people who are the heart and soul of any business. Let's face it—you can design the best Lean Six Sigma program in the world, but if the people running it and working within it are not happy and engaged, how effective do you think the program will be? Let's consider the corollary—what if you had employees that are highly motivated running your Lean Six Sigma initiative? Wouldn't that be the best approach? Would you have to force feed the program to your employees, or will they grab on and move the program along even further then originally envisioned? That is what we have included in detail in this book and in our related training and certification programs; How to design, develop, and implement the most powerful Lean Six Sigma program in the world, TPS-Lean Six Sigma. We have combined all the powerful tools and methodologies of Lean and Six Sigma with personal power optimization of Total Performance Scorecard (TPS). The result is a revolutionary, holistic, and breakthrough program, called TPS-Lean Six Sigma, that increases speed, reduces waste, motivates the workforce, satisfies customers, and drives up profit in a sustainable way. Lean is about working *faster*, Six Sigma is about working *better*, and

TPS is about working *smarter*. TPS-Lean Six Sigma is about working *faster, better, and smarter.*

Combining the complimentary TPS processes actively brings human involvement into Lean Six Sigma in a manner that not only stimulates commitment, integrity, work-life balance, and passion, enjoyment at work and employee engagement but also stimulates individual and team learning in order to develop a happy workforce and sustainable performance improvement and quality enhancement for the organization.

TPS-Lean Six Sigma is a continuous voyage of discovery involving continuous personal and organizational improvement, development, and learning. The starting point in this concept is a journey to understand personal goals and ambitions of the workforce. Then we take the organizations goals and ambitions and marry them with the workforce, and find the best people for the job. Using our structured approach for aligning the personal scorecards with the organization's scorecard, we are able to create a symbiotic relationship between employees and organizational desires through the establishment of TPS-Lean Six Sigma project teams that will enthusiastically drive positive results.

TPS-Lean Six Sigma is like a "turbo-charged" Lean Six Sigma program. All of the proven, sound methodologies of traditional Lean Six Sigma are charged with highly motivated team members. The result is a powerful people driven Lean Six Sigma program that leads to a high performance culture and allows employees to realize their full potential and contribute creatively while the organization benefits from increased profitability, market share, and customer satisfaction. TPS-Lean Six Sigma is the perfect marriage of Lean Six Sigma and the Total Performance Scorecard. With TPS-Lean Six Sigma, your business, your project your customer, and your employee's personal goals are all realized in concert with each other. By integrating human capital into the Lean Six Sigma equation, organizations have the opportunity for exponential, quantum levels of improvement and success. Your customers will be happy, shareholders will be happy, management will be happy, employees will be happy, processes will be optimized, waste will be eliminated, and profits will soar. It is quite possible that now, with TPS-Lean Six Sigma, we actually have reached nirvana. It is the only program of its kind that incorporates the element of human capital as a structured part of a Lean Six Sigma program.

People are happiest when they are given freedom, challenges, and control over their lives. TPS-Lean Six Sigma also offers a systematic and integrated approach and a road map to the transformation of people in organizations, and to impact business strategy, culture, organizational effectiveness, and the controllability of business processes. It entails a learning process, which transforms people into happy, inwardly involved, and committed employees. This will not only allow them to contribute exceptionally but will also persuade them to support, defend, and promote their organization and their project. This approach lies at the heart of successful organizational and cultural change. After all, it is difficult to change the organization, but if we change ourselves, the organization will change with us. This unique TPS-Lean Six Sigma system is based on several new models, guidelines and tools that have been proven in practice. It integrates the individual's aspirations with the shared ambition of the organization, balancing the personal with the shared ambition, embedding ethical behavior in the individual's mind and links individual capabilities with an effective talent management process. It links human capital to Lean Six Sigma. This concept and the related new tools provide an excellent and innovative framework for creating sustainable breakthroughs in both the service and manufacturing industries.

We would like to express our thanks to Rodney Rampersad, Madeleine Anne Cuciti, Heather El-Homsi, Carolyn and Michael Ganley, Leslie Henckler, Susan Kadray, Michael Lemieux, Jeff Slutsky, and Nick Usher who have given constructive feedback.

We are very grateful to our vice-president of customer relations at TPS-Lean Six Sigma LLC, Charles D. Hardy, for his valuable contributions to the realization of this book. We also would like to express our thanks to Ricardo A. Gonzalez (Director Worldwide Purchasing, EASTMAN KODAK COMPANY), Dave Ulrich (Professor of Business at University of Michigan), Paul Bracken (Professor of Management, Yale School of Management), and Marshall Goldsmith who have given encouragement.

Writing this book has been a challenge to us, as well as a learning process. A special word of thanks to our families and friends, who inspired and stimulated us to take this challenge. We hope you enjoy TPS-Lean Six Sigma as much as we love bringing it to you. We wish you lots of success on your voyage toward enhancing personal and company value via TPS-Lean Six Sigma. Feedback is welcome at h.rampersad@TPS-LeanSixSigma.com, a.el-homsi@TPS-LeanSixSigma.com and www.TPS-LeanSixSigma.com

Hubert K. Rampersad
President, TPS-Lean Six Sigma LLC Sigma, LLC
Anwar El-Homsi
CEO, TPS-Lean Six Sigma, LLC
New York/Florida, August 15, 2007

CHAPTER 1

INTRODUCTION

A customer is the most important visitor on our premises; he is not dependent on us. We are dependent on him. He is not an interruption in our work. He is the purpose of it. He is not an outsider in our business. He is part of it. We are not doing him a favor by serving him. He is doing us a favor by giving us an opportunity to do so.

—Mahatma Gandhi

Your most unhappy customers are your greatest source of learning.

—Bill Gates

With today's growing global economy, business Executives face many challenges; rising competition, retaining and satisfying customers with increasing demands, pricing pressure, profit growth, improving productivity, stimulating innovation and creativity, speed, flexibility, and adaptability to change. Today's market does not have the patience to wait for companies to develop, if you are in the game, you need to remain competitive or get out of the way since there are other companies breathing down your neck who can. Let's face it, the world has changed and it's never going to go back to "the way it used to be." This *is* the new reality—the status quo is just not going to cut it. You must embrace the new reality of change. Change in the way you think, change in the way you work, and change in the way you run your business. While most organizations have not had the guts to enthusiastically embrace dramatic change, some have, and are succeeding. How are they doing it? Lean Manufacturing and Six

TPS-Lean Six Sigma: Linking Human Capital to Lean Six Sigma: A New Blueprint for Creating High Performance Companies, pp. 1–11
Copyright © 2007 by Information Age Publishing

1

Sigma. That's how. Lean and Six Sigma have transformed companies such as GE, Xerox, and Motorola to name a few. These are all organizations that were backed against the wall, they were basically forced to change or face certain demise. While the answer for these companies was Lean and Six Sigma, is there a better, more sustainable way?

We have been deploying Lean and Six Sigma (also known as Lean Six Sigma) for over the past 5 years, don't get us wrong, there is absolutely nothing wrong with Lean Six Sigma; in fact, it is the best tool we have ever seen until now. What we found is that while Lean Six Sigma does a great job addressing the primary concerns of manufacturing and service, there was something missing, something to keep the momentum going. That something is human capital. That's right, Lean Six Sigma primarily addresses quality issues, manufacturing issues, transactional issues, customer issues, speed and variability issues. However, unless your organization is run by robots, you still need people to make it all work. There was nothing in Lean Six Sigma that systematically addresses the very real needs of the people who are the heart and soul of any business. Total Performance Scorecard-Lean Six Sigma (TPS-Lean Six Sigma) is the only program of its kind that incorporates the element of human capital as a structured part of a Lean Six Sigma program. Let's face it—you can design the best Lean Six Sigma program in the world, but if the people running it and working within it are not happy themselves, how effective do you think the program will be? Let's consider the corollary—what if you had employees that are highly motivated running your Lean Six Sigma initiative? Wouldn't that be the best approach? Would you have to force feed the program to your employees, or will they grab on and move the program along even further then originally envisioned?

So what is TPS-Lean Six Sigma? Hopefully by now you are wondering how this approach can work for you and your company. That is what we are going to share with you in this book. How to design, develop, and implement the most powerful Lean Six Sigma program in the world, TPS-Lean Six Sigma. But before we lay out how you can implement this powerful program, we think it's important to have an understanding of how we arrived here. It's important to understand the underlying principles of Lean Manufacturing, Six Sigma, and the Total Performance Scorecard. But prior to getting into the specifics of that, let's take a look at how quality has evolved from inspection to TPS-Lean Six Sigma (see Figure 1.1).

As Albert Einstein said "We cannot solve our problems with the same thinking we used when we created them." Organizations need to have new and innovative ways to help them to be more efficient and effective to succeed. We believe that Total Performance Scorecard-Lean Six Sigma (TPS-Lean Six Sigma) is the methodology which will provide the

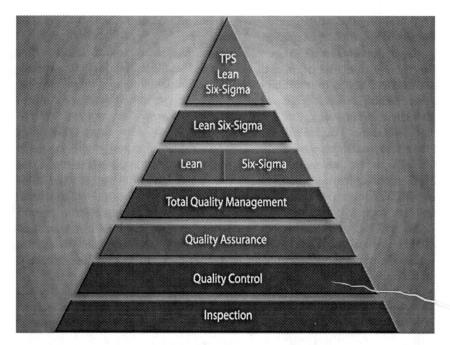

Figure 1.1. Evolution of Quality and TPS-Lean Six Sigma.

efficiency and the effectiveness needed today for an organization to design and provide more reliable, cost effective products and services while adapting to a changing world.

Quality concepts and applications have changed continuously over the years. In the beginning of the quality evolution, inspection was the method used to assure quality. In the earliest examples, it was one of the duties of the manufacturing operator to inspect the part and make a decision to accept or reject it. As companies and operations became larger, so did the time needed for inspection, and the first full-time inspection job was created. Companies began to have full-time inspection positions created in various locations around the manufacturing floor. In order to maintain continuity between inspectors, the quality control department was created. The quality control department became a completely independent department that was operated by its own manager. The quality control manager was responsible for training, standards, and the recording of data. Soon it was discovered that some of the problems that arose were too technical for inspectors alone to handle. Furthermore, manufacturing Foremen wanted to prevent defects from occurring in the first place. In the 1920s, statistical theories were being applied to manufacturing and quality. In 1924, Walter Shewhart[1] created the world's first control chart.

As the technical aspects of quality control evolved, so did the idea that the quality function needed to be applied not only to finished product acceptance, but as part of the in-process, and development stages as well, hence quality assurance was created. Quality assurance developed process checklists, procedures, and started to check the product against the customers needs. Through the 1940s, while it was true most companies employed quality control and quality assurance functions, there was little available in the area of quality training, not only that, but most could not apply these functions effectively. In the late 1940s and through the 1950s, American companies hired (among others) industrial engineers and statisticians to run their quality departments. Two of these experts, Joseph Juran and William Deming became prominent members of the American quality scene. Both Deming and Juran helped companies supplying the U.S. military during World War II to increase production and manage quality.

After the war with the trade markets reopened, Japan became known for supplying the world cheap products. While their products were inexpensive, they were also made of poor quality; Japan was in an economic crisis. In 1954, Dr. Juran was invited to come to Japan to help them improve quality. At the same time, Dr. Deming working independently of Juran, came to Japan to start teaching courses in quality management. By the 1960s, the Japanese were preoccupied with the quality movement. Japanese products became known for increased quality and in the 1970s everyone around the globe wanted to know how the Japanese were turning things around so fast. Japanese companies like Toyota were exporting cars around the world that were cheaper than any other, yet were also of higher quality of all others. How they were doing it was total quality management. Total quality management, or TQM, was actually born back in the 1951, but not until Japanese demonstrated success with it was TQM practically embraced in the 1960s.

> TQM is a management approach for an organization, centered on quality, based on the participation of all its members and aiming at long-term success through customer satisfaction, and benefits to all members of the organization and to society. (International Organization for Standardization, 1972)

The quality revolution moved slowly to the west and it was not until the 1980s that American companies introduced their own total quality programs to counter the Japanese success. As the Western world was playing catch up, international bodies formed registered standards. The British had been using BS 9750 with success for several years. This document merged with international organization for standardization to become the ISO 9000 the series of standards in 1987. As the standards evolved, so did the needs of the company. The worldwide marketplace continued to grow. There was no longer room for waste and inefficiencies which mean loss of profit and productivity—a clear formula for failure. It was out of these market conditions that the concepts of Lean Manufacturing and Six Sigma came into focus.

Lean manufacturing deals predominately with the reduction of waste, and increasing efficiency, and Six Sigma deals with reducing variation and increasing quality. Lean was the driving principle behind the Toyota production success in Japan. Lean is a set of tools that assist in the identification and then steady elimination of waste (*muda*), driving improved quality, and production time and costs are reduced. Tools include continuous improvement process (*kaizen*), "pull" production (by means of *kanban*) and mistake-proofing (*poka-yoke*). In this way, it can be seen as taking a very similar approach to other improvement methodologies.

Six Sigma, is a system of practices, originally developed by Motorola to systematically improve processes by eliminating defects. The process was pioneered by Bill Smith at Motorola in 1986 and was originally defined as a metric for measuring defects and improving quality, and a methodology to reduce defect levels below 3.4 Defects Per Million Opportunities (DPMO).

Lean and Six Sigma continued down parallel paths through the 1990s and into the new century until they eventually melded into what is known as Lean Six Sigma, a combining of Lean Manufacturing and Six Sigma methodologies. The powerful concept has been applied by companies in a two-step approach. Lean is first applied to reduce or eliminate waste, and then Six Sigma comes in and optimizes the process. While there is real benefit from Lean Six Sigma to improve the bottom line, there is another aspect of the business that is ignored.

Let's look at an example. If we said to you that we knew a company that implemented Lean Six Sigma and successfully improved cycle time, reduced inventory, improved customer satisfaction, and improved their bottom line by threefold, you might think this is fantastic! What else could they have done, or what else is there to do? Let's take a deeper look. The company improved their equipment, their processes, their stakeholders, and their bottom line, what is missing? How about the people? Mary Kay Ash said: People are definitely a company's greatest asset. It doesn't make any difference whether the product is cars or cosmetics. A company is only as good as the people it keeps. Without *engaged* people to run the equipment through the processes, there would be no product to deliver; in fact, there would be no company at all without the people, the employees, to make it work. The impact of engaged employees on the company performance can be illustrated with the following research data. There are 22 million actively disengaged employees in America, according to Gallup (2005). Their dissatisfaction is manifested in employee absence, illness, and a variety of other big and small problems that occur when people are unhappy at work. Gallup statistics show that unhappy workers cost the American business economy up to $350 billion annually in lost productivity, and that earnings per share increase 2.6 times more if employees are engaged. Active engagement of employees in their jobs and work is mandatory if U.S. businesses are to enjoy high productivity in our global economy. However, Gallup research indicates that 70% of U.S. employees are not engaged at work. Companies with such a large number of dissatisfied employees "have more absenteeism and lower productivity —as well as 51% higher turnover rates than those with engaged employees," says James Harter, chief scientist for Gallup's international management practice.

Employee disengagement is a global epidemic. According to the latest Gallup poll information:

- Sixty-one percent of the British workforce, 67% of the Japanese workforce, and a whopping 82% of the workforce in Singapore is not engaged.
- Disengaged employees cost Singapore $4.9 billion; the country's workforce ranks among the lowest in the world in employee engagement.
- Twenty percent of Australian workers are actively disengaged at work and this costs the economy an estimated $31.5 billion per year; the survey of 1,500 Australian workers, found that only 18% are engaged at work and providing their employers with high levels of productivity, profitability, and customer service.
- The percentage of engaged employees in organizations is less than 20% in Europe.
- The highest recorded levels of engaged employees are in Brazil (31%) and Mexico (40%). The lowest recorded levels are in Asia.

Furthermore, a recent conference board study showed that 53% of American workers are unhappy in their jobs. In seven countries (United Kingodn, United States, Sweden, Netherlands, India, Hong Kong, and Australia) SHL, the world leader in providing psychometric assessment techniques, asked hundreds of managers how much time they spent managing "poor performers." In its 2004 research study, it was found that the cost of bad performance by employees costs as much as U.S.$32 billion in the United Kingdom. New research shows that poor performance of disengaged employees can actually "infect" their coworkers and put a drag on an entire company's morale. Sirota Survey Intelligence (Salary.Com Research, 2006) found that many managers fail to realize the tremendous impact that poor performance of a few employees has on the entire company's operations. Out of 34,330 employees polled for this study, 33% of managers and 43% of nonmanagement employees think their companies aren't addressing poor performers in an appropriate manner. This has a tremendous negative impact on motivation and productivity, says David Sirota. "It has to do with employees being frustrated by coworkers. It's indicative of management that's really not managing. People want management to care about performance. If somebody's not working, it's a real detriment to everyone's performance." Consequently, when companies do address poor performance, employee engagement and productivity increase. According to Sirota research (Salary.Com Research, 2006), nearly three-quarters (73%) of employees who think their company is doing a good job of addressing poor performers identify themselves as "favorably engaged" at work. To take advantage of these findings, companies need to make lagging employees understand that performance is taken seriously, offer training and let them go if they do not improve with coaching.

What is being done about it? A new blueprint and road map for creating a highly engaged and happy work force is needed, whereby personal and organizational performance and learning mutually reinforce each other on a sustainable basis. This is where TPS-Lean Six Sigma steps in and this is the reason we created the TPS-Lean Six Sigma approach. TPS-Lean Six Sigma is the perfect marriage of Total Performance Scorecard (TPS) and Lean Six Sigma. Total Performance Scorecard and the related Personal Balanced Scorecard were launched by Hubert Rampersad in 2003.

TPS-Lean Six Sigma is a business management program that takes into account human capital. We believe that improving the person, will improve the company.

> Human capital issues are at the top of the agenda for today's CEO. Enlightened Executives have realized that human capital represents a real sustainable competitive advantage. Yet, organizations continue to treat human capital as a non-strategic asset. In fact, many continue to witness employee goals misaligned to the business strategy, training initiatives yielding only incremental improvements and skill gaps prohibiting the successful execution of strategy. Today, with knowledge workers accounting for over 50% of the workforce, the challenge for most organizations is how to ensure their employees have the right capabilities and are motivated to execute their strategy. (Palladium, 2007)

By aligning the Personal Balanced Scorecard with the Organizational/ Project Balanced Scorecard (OBSC), both the organizational/project goals, and the personal goals of the employee are realized concurrently. This is the power of TPS-Lean Six Sigma; Quality's final evolution (see Figure 1.1.)

TPS-Lean Six Sigma is now at the pinnacle of all these concepts and we believe, will be the method of choice for decades to come. The evolution of quality to finally arrive at TPS-Lean Six Sigma has been a long road. The choice is yours, continue with the status quo and face the consequences, or transform into a continually improving, learning organization with a happy and engaged workforce that can climb to the top of the market.

LEARNING OBJECTIVES

After reading this book and applying its concepts, as an individual employee or project team member, you will:

- be able to execute your TPS-Lean Six Sigma project successfully and be more committed and engaged
- understand the history and principles of Lean Manufacturing, Six Sigma, and Total Performance Scorecard
- understand and be able to create personal, organizational, and project balanced scorecards
- realize the benefits of integrating Total Performance Scorecard with Lean Six Sigma
- understand yourself better, and be able to achieve your personal goals in life
- strengthen your sense of self-responsibility and act more proactively due to this heightened awareness
- increase your personal effectiveness and learn to utilize the Plan-Do-Act-Challenge cycle, to systematically seek out new challenges and develop new related skills
- increase the effectiveness of your project with the help of the TPS-Lean Six Sigma Project BSCsoft and TPS-Lean Six Sigma Personal BSCsoft software

As a leader or TPS-Lean Six Sigma Champion/Master Black Belt/Black Belt/Green Belt/Project Manager, in addition to the above, you will:

- be able to create sustainable breakthrough in both the service and manufacturing industries
- be able to successfully address the primary concerns of manufacturing and service in a sustainable and a more holistic way.
- be able to successfully design, implement, and deploy customer and human focused TPS-Lean Six Sigma initiatives in your organization
- be able to manage your TPS-Lean Six Sigma project successfully
- learn techniques to increase employee/project member's engagement and develop a happy workforce of committed employees/ project members
- create conditions for a real learning organization and a high performance culture
- improve your coaching skills to maximize the personal development of your employees/project members and to manage, develop and utilize their talents effectively
- improve their ability to work productively and harmoniously together as a team and create quality results
- be able to stimulate their personal integrity, work-life balance, passion, and enjoyment at work
- be able to stimulate individual and team learning and sustainable performance improvement and quality enhancement.
- drive transformational change in your organization and business results due to the transformation in employee's motivation and engagement.

This book provides you a unique instrument that will transform your workforce and your organization into a lean, customer driven, profitable, learning organization through the breakthrough power of TPS-Lean Six Sigma. In chapter 2, the essence of the Total Performance Scorecard concept is described. You will make sense of what drives you and learn how to create your company and your own personal balanced scorecard to enable personal and organizational growth. In chapter 3, you will learn the foundation of Lean Six Sigma by studying the history and methodology of Lean Enterprise and Six Sigma. By studying these quality approaches independently, it will become clear why some success has been realized with each approach, and why the combination becomes even more powerful. In chapter 4, we will integrate TPS with Lean Six Sigma and introduce our TPS-Lean Six Sigma model in its entirety for the first time. This is the most comprehensive chapter of the book, and we provide details of the program fundamentals. Chapter 5 is totally dedicated to design for TPS-Lean Six Sigma. Here, you will learn the steps necessary to design and develop new products and services that meet Six Sigma quality in reliability and performance. You also learn how this method applies to both the service and the manufacturing industries. Chapter 6 is devoted to implementing a successful TPS-Lean Six Sigma program. We will discuss how to overcome resistance, and provide you with some tools, such as the TPS-Lean Six Sigma Implementation Quick Scan that will help you decide if you are ready to go. In chapter 7, we will outline how to select winning TPS-Lean Six Sigma projects and the importance of early success to breed sustainable success. Managing and tracking TPS-Lean Six Sigma projects will be the focus of chapter 8. We will also recommend components of tracking software you might find helpful to use. Chapter 9, 10, 11, and 12 introduces you to some different types of certifications and training programs offered by our Academy for TPS-Lean Six Sigma Certification based on some unique tools (such as the new holistic TPS-Lean Six Sigma Life Cycle Scan and personal/executive coaching framework). TPS-Lean Six Sigma Certification include: Black Belt, Green Belt, Coaching, Consultant, and Company certifications. In chapter 11, we are also introducing a TPS-Lean Six Sigma coaching process for a coach, which is based on a Ten-Phase PBSC coaching framework. This focuses on life and career coaching and Executive coaching. Appendix A summarizes some of the TPS-Lean Six Sigma tools referred to in the improving phase of the TPS-Lean Six Sigma Cycle throughout the book. It also covers an overview of TPS-Lean Six Sigma Personal BSC-soft, an interactive software system that will assist you with the successful formulation and implementation of your Project Balanced Scorecard (Project BSC), and TPS-Lean Six Sigma Personal BSCsoft, an interactive software system that will assist you with the formulation and implementation of your Personal Balanced Scorecard (PBSC). Appendix B covers extra tools for effective interpersonal communication and for team evaluation. Appendix C describes the TPS-Lean Six Sigma Team Evaluation which can be used to enhance the performance of TPS-Lean Six Sigma meetings. Appendix D describes the TPS-Lean Six Sigma Knowledge Management Quick Scan to be used to increase the learning ability of organizations.

NOTE

1.   Walter Shewhart—Dr. Shewhart, born in 1891, created the basis for the control chart and the concept of a state of statistical control by carefully

designed experiments. Shewhart stressed that bringing a production process into a state of statistical control, where there is only chance-cause variation, and keeping it in control, is necessary to predict future output and to manage a process economically.

CHAPTER 2

THE FOUNDATIONS OF TOTAL PERFORMANCE SCORECARD

Doing the right things right the first time is determined by enjoyment, passion, love, courage, self-responsibility, self-confidence, self-knowledge, self-learning, and personal integrity.

—Hubert Rampersad

Management deals with doing things right. Leadership deals with doing the right things. Leadership comes first and then follows management.

—Anwar El-Homsi

The Total Performance Scorecard (TPS) concept was developed by Hubert Rampersad and published by Butterworth Heinemann in 2003. His related book *Total Performance Scorecard: Redefining Management to Achieve Performance with Integrity* (2003) has been translated into 20 languages. TPS is a holistic management approach, which refers to the maximum personal development of all corporate associates and the optimal use of their capabilities for the realization of the highest organizational performance. It encompasses an amalgamation and expansion of the concepts of Personal Balanced Scorecard (PBSC), Organizational Balanced Scorecard (OBSC), Talent Management and Total Quality Management. Figure 2.1 illustrates the correlation between these four TPS modules. The TPS philosophy includes a synthesis of these four closely related management concepts to form a harmonious whole. There are overlaps between these concepts, as

TPS-Lean Six Sigma: Linking Human Capital to Lean Six Sigma: A New Blueprint for Creating High Performance Companies, pp. 13–26
Copyright © 2007 by Information Age Publishing
13

illustrated in Figure 2.1. The shaded area in the center illustrates the similarities between the four management concepts.

TPS is defined as a systematic process of continuous, gradual, and routine improvement, development, and learning that is focused on a sustainable increase of personal and organizational performances. Improving (improvement of personal skills and business processes), developing (job-related talent development of employees), and learning (internalizing and actualizing knowledge in order to change behavior) are the three fundamental powers in this organic management concept. They are closely interrelated and must be kept in balance. Balancing the three fundamental elements is essential for achieving successful personal and organizational change. Improving, developing, and learning together represent much of the common area in Figure 2.1.

TPS = Process of Continuous [<Improvement> + <Development> + <Learning>]

The TPS concept consists of the following four elements:

(1) The Personal Balanced Scorecard (PBSC) encompasses the personal vision, mission, key roles, critical success factors, objectives,

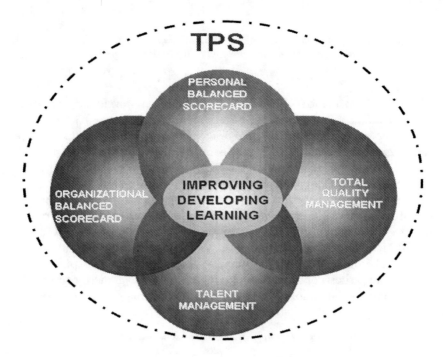

Figure 2.1.   The interrelated modules of the TPS concept (Rampersad, 2003).

performance measures, targets, and improvement actions. The PBSC was developed by Hubert Rampersad. His related book *Personal Balanced Scorecard; The Way to Individual Happiness, Personal Integrity and Organizational Effectiveness* (2006), has been translated into 15 languages. This concept impacts your personal well being, and success at work and in the rest of your life. Here personal vision, mission, and key roles are called personal ambition, which allows you to express your intentions, identity, ideals, values, and driving force, as well as, to gain more insight about yourself. The elements of the PBSC are divided among four perspectives, which are of essential importance to your self-development, personal well-being, and success in society. They are, namely (see Figure 2.2):

1. *Internal*—your physical health and mental state. How can you control these in order to create value for yourself and others? How can you feel good in your skin at work, as well as, in your spare time?
2. *External*—relations with your spouse, children, friends, employer, colleagues, and others. How do they see you?

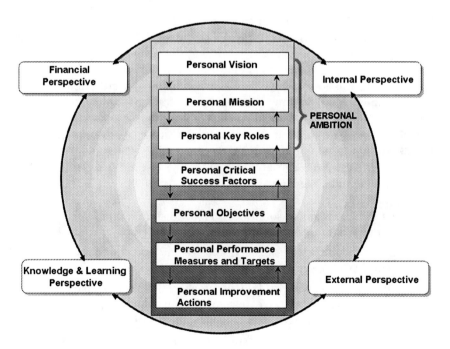

Figure 2.2. The PBSC model (Rampersad, 2006).

3. *Knowledge and learning*—your skills and learning ability. How do you learn, and how can you remain successful in the future?

4. *Financial*—financial stability. To what degree are you able to fulfil your financial needs?

The PBSC can be defined as the following formula—

PBSC = personal vision + mission + key roles + critical success factors + objectives + performance measures + targets + improvement actions (divided along the four perspectives: internal, external, knowledge & learning, and financial).

Personal ambition = personal vision + mission + key roles

The emphasis here is on *personal management* (personal strategy development and implementation). The implementation of the Personal Balanced Scorecard is done according to the Plan-Do-Act-Challenge cycle (Rampersad, 2006), see also Figure 4.15.

(2) The Organizational Balanced Scorecard (OBSC) is a top-down management instrument that is used for making an organization's strategic vision operational at all organizational levels. It includes the overall (corporate) organizational vision, mission, core values, critical success factors, objectives, performance measures, targets and improvement actions. The OBSC is a participatory approach that provides a framework for the systematic development of business strategy. It makes the shared ambition measurable and translates it systematically into actions. Here, organizational vision, mission, and core values are called shared ambition. The OBSC entails an adaptation of the balanced scorecard concept developed by Robert Kaplan and David Norton (2003); it offers a means to maintain balance between financial and nonfinancial measures and to connect strategic and operational Standards. As with the PBSC, the following 4 basic perspectives have been chosen for the OBSC; however, the contents have different meanings (see Figure 2.3):

1. *Financial*: Financial soundness. How do shareholders see the company? What does it mean for our shareholders?

2. *External*: Customer satisfaction. How do customers see the company? What does it mean for our customers?

3. *Internal*: Process control. How can we control the primary business processes in order to create value for our customers? In which processes do we have to excel to continuously satisfy our customers?

4. *Knowledge and learning*: Skills and attitudes of the employees and the organizational learning ability. How can the company remain

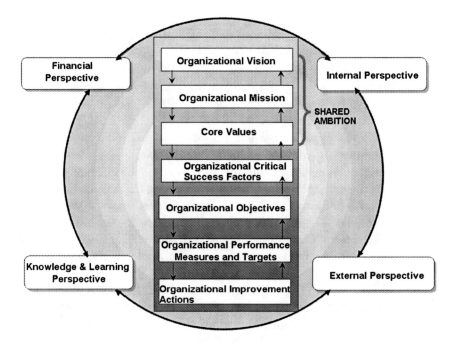

Figure 2.3.   The OBSC model (Rampersad, 2006).

successful in the future? How should we learn and improve, and through this continuously realize our shared ambition?

These four basic perspectives also cover the consequences for the community.

The OBSC can be defined as the following formula—

OBSC = organizational vision + mission + core values + critical success factors + objectives + performance measures + targets + improvement actions (divided along the four perspectives: internal, external, knowledge & learning, and financial).

Shared ambition = organizational vision + mission + core values.

Selected TPS-Lean Six Sigma projects are part of the organizational improvement actions, resulting in Project BSC's.

The emphasis in the OBSC is on *organizational management* (organizational strategy development and implementation).

(3) Talent Management encompasses the process of the continuous development of human potential within the organization. The goal of talent management is continuously delivering top performances with a motivated and developed community. It focuses on the maximum development of employees and makes optimal use of their potential in order to achieve the goals of the organization. The talent development cycle is central here, which consists of the following phases: *result planning, coaching, appraisal,* and *talent development* (see Figure 2.4). The emphasis here is on job-related *talent management.*

(4) Total Quality Management (TQM) is a disciplined way of life within the entire organization whereby continuous improvement is central. Defining problems, determining root causes, taking actions, checking the effectiveness of these actions, and reviewing business processes are accomplished in a routine, systematic, and consistent way. TQM emphasizes the mobilization of the entire organization in order to satisfy the needs of the customer continuously. It is a philosophy, as well as, a set of guidelines that forms an ever-improving organization on the basis of the Plan-Do-Check-Act (PDCA) cycle (see Figure 2.5). The emphasis here is on *process management.* The implementation of the OBSC is done according to Deming's Plan-Do-Check-Act (PDCA) cycle and the implementation of the PBSC is done according to Rampersad's Plan-Do-Act-Challenge (PDAC) cycle (see Figure 4.20). The PDAC cycle focuses on

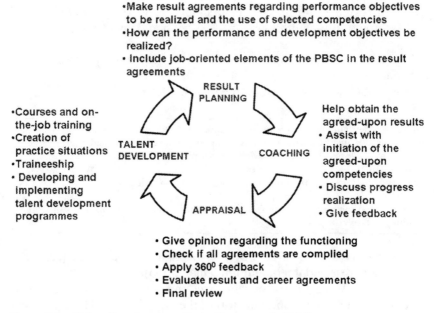

Figure 2.4.   Talent Development Cycle (Rampersad, 2006).

DEVELOP AN IMPROVEMENT PLAN
- Define the problem
- Formulate critical success factors related to the vision
- Formulate objectives
- Define performance measures and targets

Plan

IMPLEMENT THE VERIFIED IMPROVEMENTS
- Document them in standard procedures
- Train those involved
- Repeat the cycle

Act

Do

IMPLEMENT THE IMPROVEMENT PLAN ON A LIMITED SCALE
- Collect data
- Train those involved
- Describe the business processes
- Formulate project teams

Check

CHECK IF IT WORKS
- Evaluate the trial project
- Provide feedback
- What have we learned?

Figure 2.5.   Plan-Do-Check-Act cycle (Deming, 1985).

TPS =   PROCESS OF CONTINUOUS [<IMPROVEMENT> + <DEVELOPMENT> + <LEARNING>]

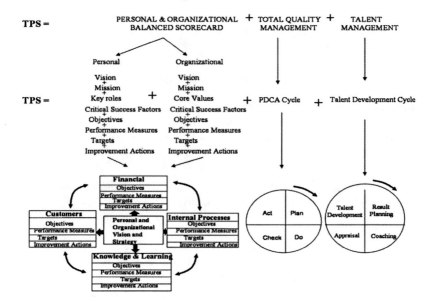

Figure 2.6.   The TPS concept.

human beings and the PDCA-cycle focuses on processes (processes don't have challenges).

Figure 2.6 illustrates the correlation between the different Total Performance Scorecard modules. Table 2.1 illustrates the six principles on which the TPS philosophy is founded and that form a stable basis of real learning organizations. The TPS concept will be integrated with the Lean Six Sigma concept, which will result in a new business management model, called TPS-Lean Six Sigma. This revolutionary holistic model will be introduced in chapter 4. In the next chapter, we will discuss the Lean Six Sigma concept.

Following are some praises for Total Performance Scorecard and Personal Balanced Scorecard.

PRAISE FOR TOTAL PERFORMANCE SCORECARD

Hubert Rampersad takes the balanced scorecard and other management ideas and puts them in a framework of personal integrity. By unifying organizational change strategies with individual ethics, he has written an outstanding synthesis, which is addressed to the corporate challenges of managing in the 21st century.

—Paul Bracken, Professor of Management, Yale School of Management.

Dr. Rampersad's latest book makes a most useful contribution to the never ending challenge of aligning individual motivations and behaviors with enterprise performance aspirations.

—Jon R. Katzenbach, coauthor of the international bestseller *The Wisdom of Teams* and editor of *The Work of Teams,* a Harvard Business Review compendium.

This book should be read by anyone interested in affecting organizational improvement and change. By expanding and integrating concepts such as the Balanced Scorecard, Total Quality Management, Performance Management and Competence Management into one overall framework, which he calls the Total Performance Scorecard, Dr. Rampersad gives us a new blueprint for creating a learning organization in which personal and organizational performance and learning mutually reinforce each other.

—Cornelis A. de Kluyver, Henry Y. Hwang Dean and Professor of Management, Peter F. Drucker Graduate School of Management, Claremont Graduate University.

Hubert Rampersad has amassed and synthesized a huge amount of material... The book serves as a practical guide, in that there are numerous exercises and business illustrations.

—From the Foreword by Dorothy A. Leonard, The William J. Abernathy Professor of Business Administration, Harvard Business School.

Table 2.1. The TPS-Principles

Focus on Customer Satisfaction

- Customer orientation is an essential part of the Personal and Organizational Balanced Scorecard
- Customer oriented behavior is one of the competences by which employees are judged
- Employees and customers are mutual partners
- We are acquainted with and understand our customers
- Customer needs are integrated in our daily activities
- More is done for the customers than the customer expects
- Satisfied customers have a high priority
- Changes in customer needs are systematically collected and improved upon
- Preventing complaints rather than reacting to complaints is our goal

Love, Passion, and Enjoyment

- The organizational environment is characterized by love, passion, enjoyment, motivation, commitment, inspiration, and enthusiasm
- People are acting with love and passion
- Fear and distrust have been chased out
- Voluntary and active involvement of everyone is a priority
- Teamwork, open communication, and mutual trust are valued
- Investment in people (training) is emphasized
- Employees are empowered
- Entrepreneurship and leadership is encouraged in all business units
- People are open to change, improvement, and renovation
- Making mistakes is permitted, for we learn constantly from mistakes
- Feedback is given regarding the improvement actions accomplished by employees

Consistent Personal and Organizational Objectives

- Managers and employees have formulated their own PBSC and use this as a compass for personal improvement, development, and learning
- A shared and inspirational organizational ambition is developed and propagated decisively at all levels of the organization
- Critical success factors, objectives, and performance measures are formulated and communicated to all associates
- Managers' behavior about the formulated BSCs is consistent
- Guidance is provided to performance improvement
- Top management is committed to change and improvement
- Managers act as coaches, are action-oriented and encourage a fundamental learning attitude

Ethical and Fact-Based Behavior

- The shared organizational ambition is guided by ethics
- The organization cares about ethics and corporate social responsibilities
- The behavior of people is based on high moral standards
- Performance measures are linked to targets
- Work is done based on facts and performance indicators
- The causes and consequences of problems are analyzed based on the principle "measuring is knowing"
- Data is purposefully gathered and correctly interpreted
- Measurements are taken and adequately improved on all business levels
- Measurements are based on figures and targets
- Assessment of individual associates is based on concrete competences and results, which in turn, are related to performance measures and targets
- The organizational culture is characterized by simplicity, self-confidence, teamwork, and personal involvement

Table continues on next page

Table 2.1. The TPS-Principles Continued

Process Orientation	Focus on Improvement, Development, and Learning
• Processes are guided based on performance measures	• Formulation of the PBSC results in the personal improvement of individuals and is aimed at their personal well-being and success in society
• Internal customers are also satisfied	
• The effectiveness of business processes is measured	• Formulation of the OBSC results in improvement and control of the business processes is aimed at achieving a competitive advantage for the organization
• Suppliers are seen as long-term partners	
• Process variation reduction takes place continuously	• Formulation of the competence profiles and performance plans of individual employees results in job-related competence development and is focused on effective job fulfilment
• Errors are regarded as an opportunity for improvement; they are considered an opportunity to become better	
• Improvement, development and learning are seen as a continuous and gradual process	• Employees improve themselves continuously and help others improve themselves
• Knowledge is constantly implemented and incorporated in new products, services, and processes	• Emphasis is on continuous process improvement based on the PDCA-learning cycle
• Improvement teams are created in which different learning styles are represented	• Emphasis on the continuous development of human potential based on the plan-do-act challenge cycle and 360° feedback
	• Emphasis is on continuous learning that is based on self knowledge
	• Emphasis is on prevention instead of correction
	• Improvements are based on a cross-functional approach, and are continuously documented
	• A working climate exists where continuous improvement, development, and learning are routinely done and are a way of life

Hubert Rampersad's Total Performance Scorecard is management technology for the enlightened age. Rampersad beautifully explains how anyone can apply principles of motivational alignment and individualistic scorecard techniques to engineer an organization for continuous learning."

—Dr. James O'Toole, Massachusetts Institute of Technology.

Total Performance Scorecard is a thorough, systematic, and integrated approach to individual and organization success. It synthesizes and extends personal, leadership, and organization theories of change and success. It offers Managers tools to do a complete physical for their organization and it offers individuals an encyclopedia of knowledge about personal success.

—Dave Ulrich, Professor of Business, University of Michigan.

"For organizational leaders looking to achieve outstanding results through the Balanced Scorecard, this book by Dr. Hubert Rampersad is essential reading. Through his exceptional framework of the Total Performance Scorecard (TPS), Dr. Rampersad takes the ideas of the Balanced Scorecard to even greater heights. His system creates a completely new vision for bringing individual, team and organizational performance to higher levels, through a comprehensive set of tools that can easily be applied to a broad range of organizational systems. The TPS goes beyond individual behaviour to the more challenging goal of measuring and then changing organizational processes that limit and even impede individual performance. In this sense, it goes to the heart of a learning organization in which measuring systems facilitate the personal development of employees. Peter Senge broke the mindset barrier and showed how systems thinking and system change are essential to support individual development. The strength of TPS, however, is that it measures personal development in the context of organizational development. This highly interactive process creates the foundation for dynamic change where everyone can benefit from constant learning and improvement. Dr. Rampersad's brilliance lies in bringing Peter Senge's ideas of system symbiosis into alignment with ideas of personal ambition, vision and mission. When leaders can accurately measure true performance—low, average or outstanding—it is possible for the ideal to become a reality.

—George A. Kohlrieser, Professor of Leadership & Organizational Behavior IMD, Switzerland.

I am amazed with the fact that the Total Performance Scorecard (TPS) concept is spreading like gospel. Dr. Hubert Rampersad's innovative and pragmatic approach to combine organizational and personal performance agendas into one line of thinking helps organizational participants to come up with tangible solutions to current performance and leadership issues.

Padmakumar Nair, PhD, D.Sc., MBA, Organization, Strategy and International Management, School of Management, University of Texas @ Dallas.

There is often a disconnect between organizational goal-setting and the way individuals establish individual objectives and are reviewed. Total Performance Scorecard fills the gap with a complete system that unites individual and organizational performance scorecards, linking continuous improvement efforts with individual learning and development programs. If you are looking for a comprehensive toolkit for improving results in your company, this is the book to buy.

—Philip Anderson, Professor of Entrepreneurship, INSEAD Alumni Fund Chair in Entrepreneurship, Director, 3i Venture lab.

The United States Air Force is trying to become more accountable for performance using the Balanced Scorecard method, but I like the way Dr. Hubert Rampersad has tied the BSC to a Personal Balanced Scorecard. It's almost like Kaplan & Norton meet Stephen Covey"

—Bob Marx, United States Air Force.

Successful companies are High Performance Systems, something that is true today even more than ever. A condition to make these levels of High Performance possible is the alignment of personal and organizational targets and interests, irrespective of company levels or sectors. The Total Performance Scorecard (TPS) is a new management instrument that introduces this alignment and creates value based, ethical acting on a sustainable foundation. Dr. Hubert Rampersad has achieved a large and very important jump forward with the presentation of this concept.

—Professor Dr. Kuno Rechkemmer, Director DaimlerChrysler, Germany.

Praise for Personal Balanced Scorecard

Personal Balanced Scorecard offers individuals a sense of hope and a pathway to get there. Ultimately, all change is individual and personal and this book offers a practical guide for helping people turn personal missions into personal improvement actions. The frameworks and questions focus attention on the right issues in the right way.

—Dave Ulrich, author HR Value Proposition, partner The RBL Group, and Professor Ross School of Business, University of Michigan, USA.

Personal Balanced Scorecard offers a useful framework to help translate organizational strategies into personal development and improvement plans. By providing the tools to help turn strategy into action, this book can help any manager enhance his or her personal and professional success.

—Mark Huselid, Professor of HR Strategy, Rutgers University, USA, and coauthor of the international bestsellers *The HR Scorecard* and *The Workforce Scorecard*.

Unlike so many other business books, this one presents a truly unique method that touches on every aspect of human nature: spiritual, physiological, mental, emotional, moral and ethical. All of these are integrated into the context of producing optimal organizational efficiency, through proper alignment of our personal ambition and objectives along with organizational vision and mission

—Jeannette Lee, founder of Sytel, Inc., winner of the national Entrepreneurial Excellence Award in the field of innovative Business Strategies, Working Woman magazine and listed as the 2001 Washingtonian Magazine's "100 Most Powerful Women in Washington."

Personal Balanced Scorecard is excellently on time and on target. It is one of the first tangible and usable means to provide for a person the opportunity to create, follow, measure and improve his own agenda. With PBSC, we start the long way towards a society in which the person will become the central focus point, with a responsibility that will be larger than ever before. In a world that will be more complex and tougher than seen and experienced so far. PBSC will make the current but more so the next generation better and stronger for the "personal age" that is about to arrive to all of us.

—Professor Roel Pieper, former Vice President of Philips Electronics and Compaq Computer Corp.

Personal Balanced Scorecard provides a roadmap for the organizations of the future! Hubert Rampersad is one of the great thought leaders who are both helping organizations increase effectiveness and helping people have better lives. He is helping make the world a better place, and is one of the few consultants who look at the entire picture—not just a small part.

—Marshall Goldsmith, recognized by the American Management Association as one of the 50 great thinkers and leaders who have impacted the field of management over the past 80 years. He has appeared in: *The Wall Street Journal*—as one of the top ten executive educators, *Forbes*—as one of the five most-respected executive coaches and *The Economist*—as one of the most credible thought leaders in the new era of business.

Personal Balanced Scorecard is an outstanding contribution to the field of self- mastery and personal transformation. Written from a pragmatic viewpoint, this book is likely to help set your agenda for a radical shift from systems-driven change to self-led change. I often ask, if livelihood is for life, what is life for? Dr. Hubert Rampersad's work explores that question deeply and comes up with startling answers.

—Professor Debashis Chatterjee, Head, Centre for Leadership and Human Values, Indian Institute of Management, Lucknow, India and author of *Leading Consciously.*

In the world of organizational development and organizational change, many theorists have provided models and guidance on attempting to change the culture through leadership development and instilling a sense of personal responsibility in all employees. However, no theorist has provided an infrastructure such that the process that will change the culture is embedded in the organization.

> *The Personal Balanced Scorecard process is integrally linked with organizational goals within individual performance plans for every employee to ensure change actually occurs and far richer outcomes are realized. It is critical in this time of globalization to take advantage of the intelligence of every employee and find ways of engaging them as a whole human being. We have used the PBSC ourselves and we have used it with clients and we've seen it work.*

—Regina M. Bowden PhD and Eleanor Lester ABD, Organizational Change Managers, Michigan.

In the following chapters Total Performance Scorecard and Personal Balanced Scorecard will be linked to Lean Six Sigma. This has been illustrated in Figure 2.7.

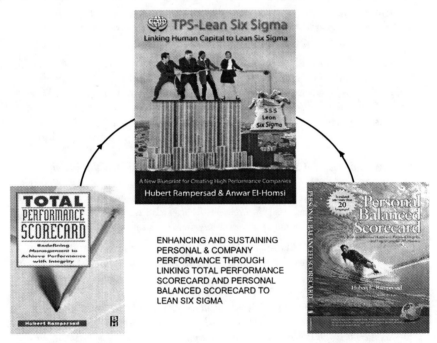

Figure 2.7.   Total Performance Scorecard and Personal Balanced Scorecard linked to Lean Six Sigma.

CHAPTER 3

THE FOUNDATIONS OF LEAN SIX SIGMA

*Six Sigma is the only program I've ever seen where customers win,
employees are engaged in and satisfied by, and shareholders are
rewarded—everybody who touches it wins.*

—Jack Welch, past Chairman of GE

*Quality is a state in which value entitlement is realized for customer and provider in
every aspect of the business relationship.*

—Mikel Harry

This chapter emphasizes the foundations of Lean Manufacturing and Six Sigma. We will go into detail reviewing the history of Lean and how it became a prominent model for business improvement. After discussing Lean, we will move onto Six Sigma, detailing its history and the building blocks that make a successful Six Sigma program. Then, we will look at the recent phenomenon called "Lean Six Sigma," a *good marriage* of these two complementing methods. Finally, at the end of the chapter, we will introduce you to what we feel is the ultimate business improvement model called TPS-Lean Six Sigma which is the integration of Total Performance Scorecard with Lean Six Sigma to form "the *perfect marriage.*"

*TPS-Lean Six Sigma: Linking Human Capital to Lean Six Sigma: A New Blueprint for
Creating High Performance Companies*, pp. 27–53
27

3.1 LEAN—THE PATH TO EFFICIENCY

The introduction of lean was thoroughly described in the book, *The Machine That Changed the World* (1990) by James P. Womack and Daniel Roos. This book was the actual result of a research project that studied the world of automotive manufacturing. The authors investigated the ways in which Japanese companies had completely rewritten the rules of doing business. This groundbreaking book explained how companies could dramatically improve their performance through the "Lean production" approach pioneered by Toyota Motor Corporation. It also clearly articulates the production techniques that can breathe new life into any company.

Toyota knew that they could not compete with other industrialized economies on costs, volume or quality using typical mass production techniques. Most companies in Japan had limited recourses, especially after the devastation of World War II. They had very little capital to build modern factories or to buy modern equipment. Many Japanese manufacturers had to "make do" with what little they had. These limitations actually promoted and created the ideal environment for the true conditions for Lean to operate. For many years, Toyota has proven the success of this system by producing quality products and promoting cost reduction activities. A further study of Toyota will reveal that the foundation of Lean is derived from a combination of different tools and techniques.

Kiichiro Toyoda,[1] Taiichi Ohno,[2] and Shigeo Shingo,[3] are considered the fathers of many Lean operational methods. Their pioneering thinking with a focus on low-tech, pull systems became the foundation of the Toyota Production System. The total elimination of waste evolved as the purpose of the system. Other generic names for Lean production include; cellular, flexible, one-by-one, synchronous, demand-flow manufacturing and pull manufacturing. Most common, however, are the terms *just-in-time* and *kaizen*. Since the mid-1980s, the large automobile manufacturers have adopted many of the basic principles of Lean manufacturing. Additionally, many of the lean principles had previously been covered in the book *World Class Manufacturing*, by James Schonberger in 1996. However, the term Lean manufacturing first appeared in *The Machine That Changed the World* (1990) by James Womack, Daniel Jones, and Daniel Roos.

In a subsequent book, *Lean Thinking* (1996), by James P. Womack and Daniel T. Jones the two authors revealed to Executives and Managers the benefits of Lean thinking. This thinking had its roots in manufacturing but could be applied by anyone championing a lean transformation. Readers discovered that Lean thinking will help to solve their business problems with a simple use of five dynamic steps. The steps start with the critical starting point of defining value. Womack and Jones believe that value can only be defined by the ultimate customer and is only meaningful when expressed in terms of a specific product (a good or a service, and often both at once). This must also meet the customer's needs at a specific price at a specific time. After defining value, comes value stream, flow, pull, and perfection:

- Specify the **value** desired by the customer
- Identify the **value stream** for each product providing that value and challenge all of the wasted steps (generally 9 out of 10) currently necessary to provide it
- Make the product **flow** continuously through the remaining, value-added steps
- Introduce **pull** between all steps where continuous flow is possible
- Manage toward **perfection** so that the number of steps and the amount of time and information needed to serve the customer continually falls

After 1996, *Lean Thinking* became the next generation of lean terminology and was heavily promoted by the authors. Their book provided a call to action for managers at all levels. They point out that many business leaders have lost sight of what true value is for their customer. They challenge all leaders to consider these five basic steps to increase the value added to their customers. Although basic, they are powerful and embody a new way of thinking. Besides outlining the steps to follow, the book also provides examples of companies that gave it a try and succeeded.

Lean thinking has been proven and can be a groundbreaking mindset for those that are willing to try it. The book is considered a "must read" by top Executives in any industry. Truly, when applied correctly, Lean thinking has revolutionized today's business world. Although Lean has its origination in manufacturing, all industries including service and nonprofit have successfully adopted some form of a Lean strategy. These strategies have included the service industry introducing a "Quick Lube" for your automobile. A "once and done" for the help desk, streamlining aid to disaster zones, and processing "made-to-order" computer system shipped directly to your home. These few examples show that leaders who understand the value to the customer and have implemented a Lean system that beats their competitors and have led to sustainable growth and higher profits. After decades of downsizing and reengineering, many companies have been successful embracing this new way of thinking.

3.1.2 ELIMINATION OF WASTE

Eliminating waste, or *muda*, from processes is a core concept of *Lean*. The Japanese word *muda* is often used rather than an English word. Japanese language tends to be more three-dimensional and its words tend to paint pictures or tell stories. In Japanese, *muda* is much more than 'waste." It translates literally as "to flog a dead horse; go on a fool's errand, uselessness, pointless, vain efforts and, to waste money on." Many U.S. companies have continued to use the word *muda* as it sends a stronger vision of how terrible the activity really is.

Many have learned seven types of waste. However, being able to spot these wastes on the shop floor or office environment is the challenge. This is because the wastes are often hidden by a common symptom that has often become accepted as normal in the workplace. We often can see the symptom; however, it takes a trained eye to recognize it and to identify the true waste that hides beneath. The benefit comes from eliminating the underlying waste and thus resolving the symptom once and for all. In this illustration, the symptom is clearly inventory. You can see that there are a number of problems that cause companies to create and store excess goods. These goods are tying up valuable cash on a company's balance sheet that could be used for other important investments.

1.   Waste of Overproduction—Producing more than the exact amount of goods that the customer (internal or external) requires. This

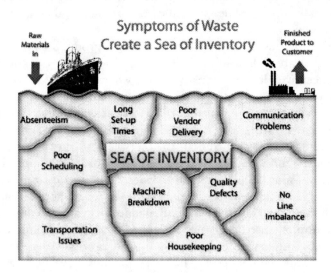

Figure 3.1.   Symptoms of waste.

challenges the Western premise of the Economic Order Quantity (EOQ) which was built on acceptance of fixed ordering costs, built around set-up times, and thus the need to spread these fixed costs over large batches.

2. Waste of Inventory—Any type of material (raw, work-in-process, finished goods). Any level of stock can hide problems.

3. Waste of Defects—Anything more than the ideal state of zero defects. The simplest form of waste is components or products that do not meet the specification.

4. Waste of Motion—All unnecessary operations, movement and steps of humans. Workers spending time moving around the plant is equally wasteful. The time a machine operator takes walking to the tool room or the stores for a fixture or a component.

5. Waste of Waiting—Delays and downtime because of machines or people. Time not being used effectively thus incurring the cost of wages and all the fixed overhead costs.

6. Waste of Transportation—Movement of material and the repeated handling of the same parts through the factory. Items being moved incur a cost such as the electricity absorbed by a forklift truck.

7. Waste of Over-Processing—Working a product more than necessary throughout it's manufacturing cycle. The most obvious example of inappropriate processing is over packaging.

Overproduction is most known as the root cause of other forms of *muda*. Think about what happens when a process over produces. People are busy making or doing things that nobody ordered—waste of motion. Unneeded finished goods must be moved to storage warehouses—waste of transportation. Over production creates unnecessary raw materials, parts and work in progress—waste of inventory. Additionally, over processing occurs when organizations build in more complexity or specifications than are required by the customer. These are several examples of extra costs that occur as a result of over production. Overproduction is a source of waste for most firms and is referred to as the batch and queue mode of operation.

This large-batch processing mode is an outdated paradigm. The main problem with large batches is that there is no connection between the pace of production and the pace of demand. Lean tools can help with reduced lot sizes with quick set-up capability. These are the new paradigm of the twenty-first century. Producing various models in small lots improves responsiveness to customers and flexibility to respond to changes in demand. The smaller the lot, the smoother the process flow. Lean manufacturing views continuous, one-piece flow as the ideal and emphasizes optimizing and integrating systems of machines, materials, people and facilities. Continuous flow follows the ideology of produce one-by-one as efficiently as possible.

An eighth waste has recently emerged and is getting much attention. *People waste* or the waste of human capital can also arise from disengagement of employees and failure to harness the potential that exists in all work groups. There is a loss of value that arises when management and employees at all levels are not consistently aligned to address critical issues. Problems are not resolved because resources are focused or aligned on different priorities. This type of waste is considered to be more important than the other wastes and companies are just starting to recognize the huge potential. Peter Drucker (the father of management) said: "The first sign of decline of an industry is loss of appeal to qualified, able, and ambitious people." This is the reason TPS-Lean Six Sigma is the breakthrough the world has been waiting for, TPS-Lean Six Sigma is the only Lean Six Sigma initiative that fully integrates human capital into its program.

Examples include institutional knowledge from change implementations such as Lean, robust information systems, introducing or designing a new product, and making continuous improvement a way of life for every employee. The freeing up of employees creativity when other wastes are removed provides many benefits for companies from a larger source for new ideas, improved employee morale, lower turnover, and a culture of continual improvement.

3.2 LEAN FOCUSES ON INCREASING VALUE

Figure 3.2 shows examples of how much waste exists in typical modern organizations. Even for companies with a concerted focus on reducing waste, there is still room for continued improvements. Breaking down the chart shows the following:

Typical Company: Companies traditionally first started with improvement activities that often focused on the value-added activities as seen in the top bar. Historically, Engineers were busy determining how to do the process quicker with improved quality. They tended to focus on the value-adding activities only and often left out large opportunities. Unfortunately, many cost accounting systems promoted this type of behavior. Routings on the shop normally showed the "build" time and did or could not capture the total cycle time to make the product. It was very common for waste or nonvalue added activities to be over looked, when this was easily 99% of the total lead-time to the customer.

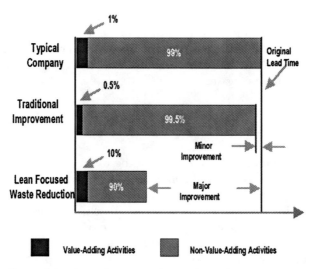

Figure 3.2.   Lean focuses on increasing value.

Traditional Improvement: As illustrated with the middle bar, only small improvement of increased value to customers was often achieved (0.5%). Occasionally, breakthrough improvements occurred as new innovative methodologies were introduced, such a Six Sigma tools pioneered by Motorola. These tools typically focus on minimizing the variation in the steps of the process that causes errors leading to defects.

Major improvements can only be achieved when the focus is on waste and nonvalue added steps of the system.

Lean Focused on Waste Reduction: As the waste is identified and eliminated, the percent of the value-added activities automatically increases. In this example, it goes to 10%. Proportionally, eliminating and reducing wasteful activities, becomes a tremendous increase in value to the customer. Companies can often achieve up to 50% reduction of lead-time as seen in the third bar. Lean tools and techniques such as continuous one-piece workflow and reducing change over to reduce inventory lots sizes often prove this to be true. Recent challenges to our cost accounting systems have promoted companies to build only the quantity that the customer is ordering. When waste is categorized (as earlier defined) and the proper Lean tools are applied, the elimination or minimization of wasteful activates can be staggering.

Many Lean tools and principles have been proven out in the manufacturing environment. Today, companies have taken these same principles and applied them to administrative areas of the company with great success. Lean techniques have also been proven out in the service industry, as well. You can now read about Lean improvements in industries such as health care, software, and logistics, just to name a few. Regardless of the application, the basic approach remains the same. That is, to focus on reducing areas of cost, improved quality and delivering value by the relentless elimination of waste.

3.3 LEAN PRINCIPLES

Value must be maximized in every facet of the value stream. Instilling the discipline to reduce costs while combined with providing a fair market price will achieve this. Typically, value-added activities are those that the customer is willing to pay for. Anything that the customer is *not* willing to pay for is nonvalue added or waste. For the most part, a value-added activity is one that changes the fit, form or function of the product. For example, a customer is willing to pay for the actual time spent making the product, but they are not willing to pay for time spent waiting for supplies, rework or repeated physical movement of the product without any real change to its appearance. Some nonvalue added work is necessary such as machine change-overs, tax accounting, and sales and marketing. The goal is to eliminate all forms a waste and to reduce nonvalue added unnecessary work the best possible.

The value stream of a business is the sequence of steps that a company performs in order to satisfy a customer's need (see Figure 3.3). A value stream is used to identify all steps needed to deliver value to the customer (order to cash). By documenting this, activities are evaluated through the customer's eyes, and then actions are taken to eliminate those steps that do not create value to the customer. Flow is promoted to ensure the value creating steps occur in the right sequence. To provide smooth flow, a number of processes must be linked together to provide customers with little or no disruption. One-piece flow is the most popular choice for *Lean manufacturing* experts. This concept allows products to flow at the rate in which customers are buying them often called *takt* time. Throughout the value stream, customers pull value from the next upstream activity, which in turn authorizes the process responsible to build another one. When necessary, the customer may need to pull from prepositioned inventory stock locations. Ideally, these locations are close to the customer and are only used as a counter measure until flow is established. The pursuit of the perfect value stream is the ultimate objective.

Lean is a fundamental enterprise conversion that must be approached as a total organizational and cultural transformation. An important step a company must take to change a value stream is to determine its Lean status. Value stream mapping is a good tool and will train leaders to find waste in the system. Once waste is identified, the root cause of the waste must be examined to implement proper counter measures. Value streams typically includes the study of cycle and lead times. They also document the total number of people needed, tools, technologies, and information loops. When mapped out on paper, the goal is to clearly see information and material flow of the business. Each step on the map includes a data box with all the specifics associated with that step in the process. These numbers provide a qualitative means of measuring the magnitude of the waste and the success of the countermeasures in driving the numbers from the current state to the future state. Once opportunities are identified, plans are laid out to close the gap between the current and future state maps. A large number of activities are typical in a strategic plan and should include both long-term and short-term actions. There are currently many project planning tools that can help manage the improvement activities. The ultimate goal is to keep it simple and to manage and use.

The value stream map is a technique that enables leaders to see the waste in the system. This pictorial representation of material and information flow differs from process mapping which tends to only represent the material flow. In a process, many things happen concurrently. The map gives you a picture that shows the various process levels within the whole value chain. Standard icons are used to create a common language that all can understand. This allows the map to be read by anyone familiar with the icons and can be used as communication tools across organizations to share current state situations. Additionally, the future state vision and the countermeasures plans are also shared with any functional teams associated with the value stream. A very good reference for developing current and future state value stream maps is in the book, *Learning to See* by Mike Rother and John Shook (2003)

3.1.4 LEAN AS A BUSINESS SYSTEM

Lean principles works together as a business system. Understanding the current state of the material and information flow is the starting point. When you have stable, predictable, and repeatable processes, we begin to focus on speed and quality improvements. This is always done with the customer in mind. The goal is to ensure that the elements of the system are working together to include the tools and people. At times, *Lean leaders* must teach others how to think with a continuous improvement mindset. The culture and climate brings change for the better, specially, when improvements made are sustained.

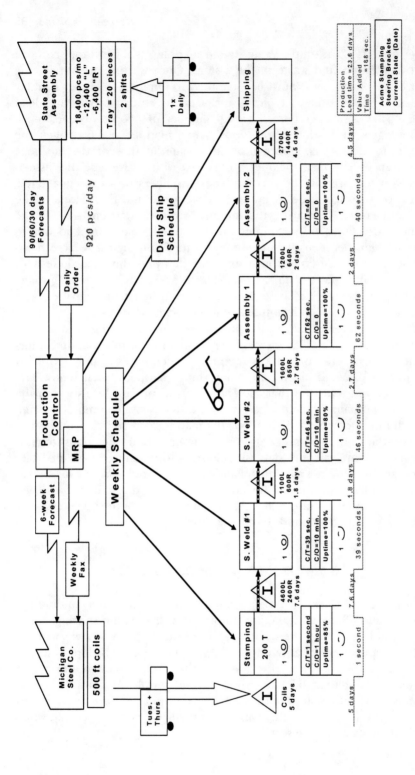

Figure 3.3. Example of value stream from *Learning to See* (Rother & Shook, 2003).

The ability to think Lean in every decision must be made with an understanding the impact to the customer. The goal is to create processes in the least waste way. Having steps that are value adding from the end customer's perspective does this. By focusing on what the customer's needs and wants, you can clearly determine what clearly the value-adding steps. The Just-in-Time pillar directly links output to customer consumption with little or no inventory. This should be the future state of any manufacturing company. Remembering, that inventory is simply a counter measure to a perfect flow to your customer. Ideally, a "make to order" system is the best vision to achieve. The Jidoka pillar typically represents the quality side of the house. At Toyota, this comes in the form of automation in which machinery automatically inspects each item after producing it. When defects are detected, the process automatically stops additional abnormalities and then notifies the worker in creative ways that a defect was detected. Together, these two powerful pillars must work together in satisfying our customers.

3.5 BENEFITS OF LEAN

Implementing "Lean" can create superior financial and operational results. Many companies are turning to Lean manufacturing in an effort to become more profitable. Lean is a management system for satisfying

Figure 3.4.   House of Lean, a business system.

customers on delivery, quality and price. When understood, Lean can become a business system that enables:

- Quicker response to customer needs promoting better satisfaction
- Reducing inventory & increasing cash flow
- Understanding and simplifying the Value Stream to reduce allocated coast structures
- Solving problems sooner to reduce quality defects
- More efficient flow of the process to reduce cycle time
- Increasing capacity throughout to avoid additional capital expenditures
- Reducing waste significantly and taking cost out of the bottom line
- Eliminating bottlenecks with improved scheduling
- Extending the life of machines and equipment

As a system, *Lean* becomes a philosophy of how to run a business. It is comprised of many tools and techniques. Without the picture of the whole value chain, people will tend to apply the tools and the techniques with no real end goal in mind. By having a current and future state map, clear plans can be developed. Process checks can be used as tools to monitor the successful implementation of these techniques. Applied in the proper order and at the right points in the chain, minimizing the waste and maximizing the value to the customer is achievable. Other areas that benefit from Lean include: cost, quality, delivery, safety, and morale.

As a Lean business system, success comes when every single person in the organization understands the philosophy. Not only do they understand, but they practice it as they go about their daily jobs. The system promotes individuals and teams to be involved looking for waste and suggesting for better ways. Success often comes from how people are treated and thought about in the Lean journey. Promoting a no "blame" environment where employee's suggestions and ideas are heard and participated. This requires that each and every day, employees at all levels look for ways to eliminate waste. Identifying opportunities is critical as you begin to train yourself and others to "see" waste. However, this is just the start; the ability to execute change is the true test. Lean cultures engage everyone in identifying and implementing improvements everyday. These improvements are more than continuous improvement, they are *kaizen* (Imai, 1986). *Kaizen* is a Japanese word. *Kai* means to take apart and make new. *Zen* means to do so in a way that helps others. So the *kaizen* improvement, not only eliminates the waste but it makes the person's work better.

3.6 LEAN SUMMARY

When you look for companies that have successfully used Lean to deliver business results, Toyota comes to mind as perhaps the best example. Toyota embraced Lean principles after World War II, when there were limited resources available. Taiichi Ohno (1990) is considered to be the father of Toyota Lean strategy—the Toyota Production system. Over the years, many companies have gone to Toyota to try to learn and emulate what Toyota achieved. Toyota has opened its doors to anyone interested, even competitors, because the Toyota Production System or Total Production System foundation for success was not based on techniques like "5S", that is a tool clearly seen on the shop floor. Instead, it's based on a way of thinking. This thinking is a value system adopted and shared by everyone at Toyota.

Taiichi Ohno describes the Toyota Production System as, "All we are doing is looking at the timeline from the moment the customer gives us an order to the point when we collect cash and we are reducing that time-line by eliminating non-value adding wastes." No where does he mention the use of *Kanban*, 5S or visual controls or all the other techniques that we use when equating with Lean. Taiichi Ohno is defining the system as a way of thinking about Toyota's business. The true focus is collapsing the timeline to get as close to what the customer wants and when they want it as possible. He defines an evolving journey during which a company constantly is comparing its capabilities to its customer values.

Many organizations' failures with lean are derived from a "tool shopping". Rather than designing a step-by-step implementation Lean strategy, they attempt to pick low hanging fruit. For example, *kanbans* and lot size reductions will always reduce inventory, but they often generate more waste of waiting unless standard work is followed. Additionally, error-proofing efforts will eliminate only a small portion of waste such as defective goods. Another example involves set-up reduction procedures. They will dramatically reduce machine downtime and increase capacity in any traditional plant. The economic benefit is the cash saving of reduced inventory levels by installed *kanbans* and work leveling. Simply stated, the full profit and quality impacts of Lean can only be achieved by implementing Lean as a total business systems approach.

As we have seen, Lean success depends upon more than just tools. Don't be fooled between Lean tools and Lean thinking. Lean thinking has a framework centered on the Plan-Do-Check-Act (PDCA) cycle (see Figure 2.5) developed by Walter Schewhart in the 1930s. This was later refined by W. Edwards Deming. We have discussed some Lean tools and techniques. But it's the thinking, not the tools that promotes waste elimination and increases a value of flow to the customer. Tools such as value stream alignment were process layouts are replicated and distributed throughout the plant and organized so that products can flow sequentially through the processes is neither a means nor the end. Additionally, inside specific production flow cells, you will find tools like single piece flow rather than batch flow. These tools are easy to understand and apply in any specific instance. However, that is not the Lean challenge. Tools fix problems here and there but will not be pursued for any length of time without structure and ownership. Tools will not create a new culture of Lean. That is why; there are so few world-class organizations. In order to create a Lean culture that will apply appropriate tools when necessary over the long-term, a leadership team must provide focus, structure and ownership at all levels of the organization, every day. For organizations in the manufacturing and operations arena, there is no alternative to Lean for long-term survival and success. Every successful plant or site in the world is/or will be implementing some form of Lean technique methods and approaches as needed for survival. Organizations that understand the thinking and improve their cultural inter-relationships will be the best in their industry.

Today, you can find a number of books on Lean. This chapter was not to give a comprehensive overview of the Lean principles. Rather, a view of the history and some ideas to succeed. Many have read the book "*Lean Thinking*" and consider it the foundations of Lean. However, if you were to stop by at Toyota Plant, they may reference the book, *Henry Ford's Today & Tomorrow*. Never the less, the concepts are thought provoking as the thinking challenges our way of life in industries that have been built around mass manufacturing concepts. Creating a strong vision such as Henry Ford conceptualizing the idea of mining ore on Monday, then melting, processing and forming it for use in a car assemble plant on Thursday is clearly Lean thinking. Henry Ford's vision is described in chapter 4. He was the first to introduce the assembly line in 1914, and to mass produce cars, which made them affordable for the general public. He was a technological genius who followed his vision/ passion/dream and was the creative force behind an industry of unprecedented size and wealth that, in only a few decades, permanently changed the economic and social character of the United States. Other successful companies such as the Wiremold Company of West Hartford, CT featured in *Lean Thinking*, realized that it's not about the tools—it's a way of thinking. It must be a value or belief system through which a business is led and decisions are made. A Lean strategy then could be called a strategic value system. One could also argue that this puts into perspective all of the technique debates on the true meaning of Lean. We consider that Lean philosophical approach to a path of effectiveness. It is more about the people and less about the actual tools and techniques. Implementing a Lean strategy is primarily about changing the way people think about business processes specifically the status quo. Successful Lean companies who have adapted and survived "back sliding" have learned to think with their hearts, minds and hands before their checkbooks.

3.6 SIX SIGMA—THE PATH TO EFFECTIVENESS

In the 1980s, Motorola was struggling to compete with foreign manufacturers, especially Japanese companies. This struggle became apparent, after an Executive meeting held in Chicago chaired by Robert Galvin, Motorola's president. At the end of the meeting, Art Sundry, a senior sales vice president stood up in front of 75 Executives and admitted that "Motorola's quality stinks," This forced Motorola to benchmark other companies and they recognized their need to improve the quality of their products. Robert Galvin challenged his people to improve the quality level by tenfold. Six Sigma was the method these executives presented as the way to meet his challenge.

Bill Smith,[4] a quality engineer at Motorola is called the father of Six Sigma. He first introduced a Six Sigma statistical approach, which was aimed at increasing profitability by reducing defects. Dr. Mikel Harry[5] and Richard Schroeder later took this concept and transformed it into an enterprise-wide strategy. By combining change management and data-driven techniques, Six Sigma was transformed from a simple quality measurement tool to a breakthrough business excellence methodology.

In 1986, Six Sigma implementation began at Motorola began with a plan to close the quality gap. Goals were set to achieve 10 times quality improvement in 2 years, 100 times quality improvements in 4 years and to obtain a Six Sigma Quality level in 6 years. Motorola position in the global market today, demonstrates the benefits of the Six Sigma methodology. Initially, at Motorola, Six Sigma was used as a process improvement method primarily in manufacturing. Since those early days, Six Sigma has been shown to be beneficial in a wide range of nonmanufacturing settings. Today, it is used in all company functions in many industries such as purchasing and IT. It has also demonstrated powerful results in service industries as diverse as financial services, software development, and health care to mention a few. It has become a business initiative used to grow market share, improve customer satisfaction, develop new products and services, accelerate innovation, and manage ever changing customer needs. Six Sigma has changed the definition of quality. According to Six Sigma, quality is achieved when both the organization and its customers benefit from it. Most previous quality programs addressed quality only with regard to the customer. They did not address the business aspect of it.

After the success that Six Sigma demonstrated at Motorola, three other companies adopted it. They were Eastman Kodak Company, Allied Signal, and Texas Instruments. Larry Bossidy, Allied Signal's former CEO, introduced Six Sigma to Jack Welch, General Electric's former CEO. Welch convinced Bossidy who was also an ex-GE senior executive to talk to the GE leadership team about Six Sigma initiative and the successes achieved at his company, and how this approach would benefit GE as it transforms itself. The GE leadership team was convinced that Six Sigma was the tool needed to improve GE's business. In 1995, Jack Welch directed the company to undertake Six Sigma as a corporate initiative with a corporate goal to be a Six Sigma company by the year 2000.

The success achieved by Motorola and GE through their Six Sigma programs has secured the popularity of this business improvement methodology. Today, there are thousands of companies; including household names like American Express, Chrysler Company, DuPont, Eastman Kodak, Sony, Toshiba, and Xerox, which have been using Six Sigma successfully.

3.2.1 WHAT IS SIX SIGMA?

Six Sigma's definition has evolved since the late 1980s. Six Sigma has many meanings to many people. As with "beauty is in the eye of the beholder" each person sees it differently. Motorola University defines Six Sigma at three different levels; as a metric, as a methodology, and as a management system. It is all three, at the same time.

In this book, we define Six Sigma as a management driven, structured, and data based methodology for product and process improvement, which provides breakthroughs in financial performance and customer satisfaction. It focuses on both strategic business goals and customer needs.

Six Sigma is based on a solid foundation of tools and methodologies, an infrastructure that is designed for success, and processes that are capable to meet the business and customer's needs. Through Six Sigma, there will be a greater focus on the customer, the entire organization will be involved, processes will be improved, employees will be empowered, and as a result, the company will retain loyal customers, and increase profit margins. We call this, the building blocks of Six

Sigma (see Figure 3.5). Without a strong foundation, the whole initiative will collapse.

3.7 DMAIC MODEL

The Six Sigma methodology is a structured process aimed at understanding customer's needs, identifying key processes linked to these needs, applying statistical and quality tools to reduce process variations of those key processes and finally sustaining this improvement over time.

Every improvement project follows the define, measure, analyze, improve, and control (DMAIC) model. In the define phase, the team seeks to understand what the problem is. In the measure phase, the team assesses the current process performance. In the analyze phase, the team needs to find out the root cause of the unacceptable or undesired process performance. In the improve phase, the team seeks solutions to improve the process performance. In the control phase, the team looks for ways to sustain process improvement achieved in the previous phase. The steps and activities for each phase are outlined in Figure 3.6. The tools used for each phase is explained in detail in Appendix A (TPS-Lean Six Sigma tools).

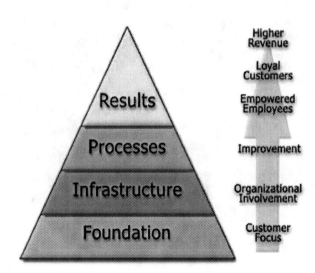

Figure 3.5.   Building blocks of Six Sigma.

The DMAIC steps and activities are discussed in detail in chapter 4, under the Continuous Process Improvement section. The related tools in each step in this model are included in the Appendix. Below is a summary of the steps for each of DMAIC phases:

Define Phase Steps

- Understand the Voice of the Customer (VOC)
- Define the Business Case
- Establish Business Goals
- Map Critical Processes
- Estimate the Cost of Poor Quality (COPQ)
- Develop the Team Charter

Measure Phase Steps

- Specify key Critical to Quality characteristics (CTQs)

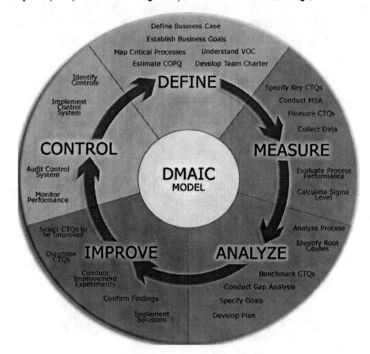

Figure 3.6.   DMAIC model.

- Conduct a Measurement Systems Analysis (MSA)
- Collect Data and Measure the Quality characteristics (CTQs)
- Evaluate Process Performance
- Calculate the Sigma Level

Analyze Phase Steps

- Conduct Gap Analysis
- Specify Goals
- Develop Plans
- Analyze the Process
- Identify Root Causes
- Benchmark the Quality characteristics (CTQs)

Improve Phase Steps

- Select Quality characteristics (CTQs) to be Implemented
- Diagnose Quality characteristics (CTQs)
- Conduct Improvement Experiments
- Confirm Findings
- Implement Solutions

Control Phase Steps

- Identify Controls to be used
- Implement Control System
- Audit Control System
- Monitor Performance

3.8 SIX SIGMA METRICS

Six Sigma is a statistical unit of measurement that allows you to measure the quality of your products or services. The higher the sigma level, the lower the number of defects in your product or services. Six Sigma quality level means that a product, with a single critical requirement, is produced with only 3.4 Defects Per Million Opportunities (DPMO). An opportunity is an estimate of the number of chances to create a defect. It will be explained in more detail in this section. Traditionally, quality level in most North American companies has been measured at the 3 or 4 sigma level (66,807 DPMO – 6,210 DPMO).

Delivering innovative products or services without defects, when promised, at high value will satisfy customers. These criteria are met by reducing and eliminating defects in the process, in other words, reducing process variation. To reduce process variation, the process must be centered, on target and within customer specifications (see Figure 3.7). As shown in Figure 3.7, a process with too much variation or off-target can lead to excess defects. It is not until you use Six Sigma tools to reduce the variation and center the process about the mean that you will have a process that is capable and on-target. A process that is capable and on-target is one that will meet the customer's needs.

3.9 SHIFT HAPPENED

Motorola's studies and other independent research suggest that a typical process shifts and drifts over time to the right or to the left of the target by about 1.5 sigma (σ). Sigma is a measure of process variation. A typical process spreads for about 6 (σ). Figure 3.8, shows this process shift. The process should be well centered between the specifications with minimum variation in order to be capable of meeting customer requirements. This shift represents the average amount of change in a typical process over many cycles of that process. There are many possible causes that could result in process shift. Some of these are:

- Production Shift Changes
- Changing Operators
- Machine Life
- Tool Wear over Time
- Equipment Breakdown or Repairs
- Equipment Calibration
- Ambient and Operational Temperature Changes
- Humidity Fluctuations
- Variation in Quality of Incoming Material

3.10 METRICS USED IN SIX SIGMA

Six Sigma contains many types of metrics through its collection of tools. Some metrics are specific to an organization, and others are universally

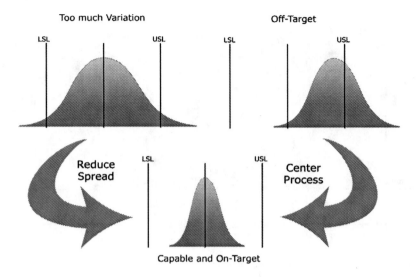

Figure 3.7. Reduce process variation and center process, leading to fewer defects.

practiced. Be careful when selecting metrics that they are well defined and understood, as these same metrics may have different meanings for different organizations. The following is a list of some universal metrics used in Six Sigma:

Defect Per Unit (DPU)

DPU is one of the most common Six Sigma metrics. Unit can be a component, piece of material, line of code, administrative form, time frame, distance, and so forth. It reflects the average number of defects found during the manufacture of a unit.

DPU = Number of defects observed/Number of units

Motorola uses the product DPU metric as "the universal measure of quality" which reflects the number of defects per unit found in the entire manufacturing process is directly proportional to delivered defects, average cycle time of the manufacturing process and latent defects.

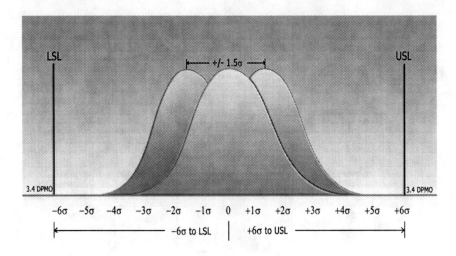

Figure 3.8.   Typical process shift of 1.5 sigma.

Rolled DPU

Rolled DPU is the total average number of defects for the product being produced, combining the DPU for each process step across the entire flow.

$$\textbf{Rolled DPU} = DPU_1 + DPU_2 + DPU_3 + \ldots\ldots\ldots\ldots DPU_{last}$$

Defect Per Million Opportunities (DPMO)

DPMO reflects the average level of defects found during the manufacturing of a product. An opportunity is an estimate of the number of chances to create a defect.

Motorola defines an opportunity as any action performed or neglected during the creation of a unit of work, where it is possible to make a mistake which may ultimately result in customer dissatisfaction.

DPMO = (Rolled DPU/ Number of Opportunities per Unit) *1,000,000

DPMO is normalized through the use of opportunities. It allows comparison of products or services of varying complexity. DPMO is converted to Sigma level using Table 3.1. The table lists two types of

Sigma level. The first is the short term Sigma (Sigma $_{ST}$) that is calculated based on data gathered over a few manufacturing cycles. The second is the long term Sigma (Sigma $_{LT}$) that is calculated based on data gathered over many manufacturing cycles (3 to 6 months, depending on the process).

To demonstrate how to convert DPMO to sigma level, let's use an example of a process to fill in an application form. The form has six sections where required information needs to be entered. For example, the information could be someone's name, address, birth date, social security, phone number, and e-mail address. There are six possibilities to make a mistake when completing this form. We have one form and six opportunities.

Let's assume, we entered three sections wrong. Here is what we have:
Unit = 1 form
Number of defects = 3
DPU = (3 defects) / (1form) = 3

Table 3.1.   Sigma Level Conversion Table

DPMO	Sigma $_{ST}$	Sigma $_{LT}$
500000	1.50	0.00
300000	2.02	0.52
200000	2.34	0.84
150000	2.54	1.04
100000	2.78	1.28
68000	2.99	1.49
25000	3.46	1.96
10000	3.83	2.33
5000	4.08	2.58
1000	4.59	3.09
500	4.79	3.29
233	5.00	3.50
50	5.39	3.89
40	5.44	3.94
30	5.51	4.01
20	5.61	4.11
10	5.76	4.26
3.4	6.00	4.50
1	6.25	4.75
0.1	6.70	5.20

Since the Number of opportunities = 6,
Defect Per Opportunities (DPO) = 3/6 = 0.5
Defect Per Million Opportunities (DPMO) = (DPO) * 1,000,000 = 0.5
* 1,000,000 = 500,000

Using Table 3.1, the short term Sigma Level is equal to 1.5 and the long term Sigma Level is equal to zero.

3.11 COUNTING OPPORTUNITIES AT KODAK

Counting process opportunities is a challenging task. The Six Sigma deployment team needs to agree on a universal method of counting opportunities prior to applying Six Sigma methodologies. For example, they could agree to counting opportunity for each product delivered, each step in the process, or each activity performed.

Kodak, for example, defined 3 opportunities for each part or component assembled into a product. The 3 opportunities are:

- The part is "to spec" or "not to spec"
- The part is or is not assembled or not installed properly
- The part does or does not function in the product

Opportunity count is then calculated by multiplying complete Bill of Materials (BOM) by 3. Whatever method the company chooses, it must be simple and uniform throughout the organization.

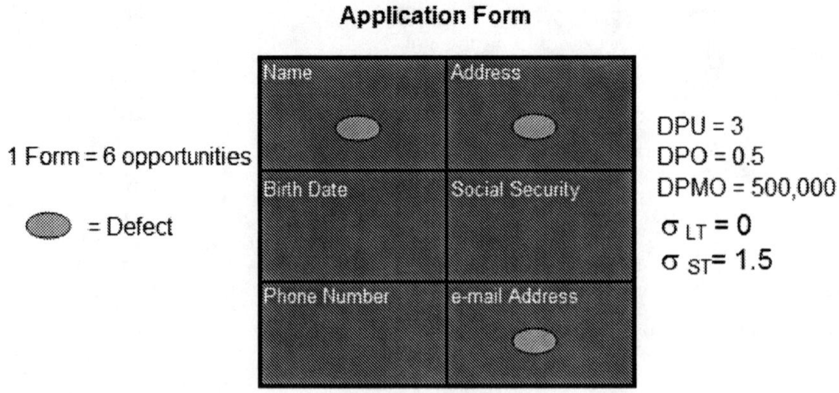

Figure 3.9.   Converting DPMO to Sigma Level.

3.12 LEAN SIX SIGMA—A GOOD MARRIAGE

Customers and shareholders are becoming increasingly demanding. As a result, companies must consistently deliver products and services that are of greater value. Many companies pursue either Lean or Six Sigma as means to meet these challenges. Individually, Lean and Six Sigma fill important needs. Both are based on improvement. However, using one or the other alone has limitations. Six Sigma reduces scrap rates and quality defects by focusing on measurement systems, as well as, capability or process quality variation; however, it doesn't optimize process flow. Lean doesn't dramatically improve process capabilities but it does target cycle times, wastes and other process costs. However, used together, these methods complement and reinforce each other.

If your company has excess inventory, lack of space or lead time issues, Lean tools are applied to attack these problems. If your company has reject, scrap, overall yield issues, or service errors, Six Sigma tools are used to define, measure, analyze, improve, and control (DMAIC) these issues. Then both methodologies, Lean and Six Sigma, are continually applied in tandem to sustain the realized improvements and allow for a continuous improvement program to take hold within your enterprise. Companies can expect to see greater speed, less process variation, and more bottom line impact by focusing the use of statistical tools and establishing baseline performance levels.

Lean Six Sigma combines the speed and power of both Lean and Six Sigma to achieve process optimization. Speed, quality and cost are the components that drive the success of any organization. Lean Six Sigma works on all three simultaneously because it blends Lean, with its primary focus on process speed, and Six Sigma, with its primary focus on process quality, within a proven organizational framework for superior execution. Both are necessary pillars of any continuous improvement process. Integrating Lean (working faster) and Six Sigma (working better) helps an organization move quickly with higher quality and lower cost. True need is to incorporate both concepts Lean and Six Sigma, by eliminating waste, we create "speed" and by eliminating variation, we create "quality."

3.13 TPS-LEAN SIX SIGMA—A PERFECT MARRIAGE

Total Performance Scorecard is about working smarter. By now, you should be starting to see for yourself why Total Performance Scorecard-Lean Six Sigma (TPS-Lean Six Sigma) is so powerful and is truly the perfect marriage, in order to working faster, better, and smarter. We are combining all the powerful tools and methodologies of Lean and Six Sigma with personal power optimization of the Total Performance Scorecard. The result is a breakthrough program that increases speed, reduces waste, motivates the workforce, satisfies customers, and drives up profit. TPS-Lean Six Sigma is a holistic approach to drive optimum business results. Let's take a look at what makes TPS-Lean Six Sigma unique and powerful.

In previous chapters, we reviewed the benefits of each element of Lean Manufacturing, Six Sigma, and the Total Performance Scorecard. While each element on its own is, in fact, a useful and intelligent tool, today's business is starving for a single initiative that addresses all their needs; TPS-Lean Six Sigma does this.

Consider this; only until recently have companies realized the need to improve human capital. Even some in the Lean world started adding an eighth form of waste, human capital. Companies were realizing that they could optimize their processes from now until eternity, but if their workforce is unhappy, unknowledgeable, or unwilling to push the envelope further, the organizational growth realized from these efforts would become stagnant. Total Performance Scorecard is a groundbreaking methodology that ties organizational goals to personal goals.

Now, let's step back a little, remember what we were saying before? Is there something better than Lean Six Sigma? The answer is TPS-Lean Six Sigma, the perfect marriage of Lean Six Sigma and the Total Performance Scorecard. With TPS-Lean Six Sigma, your business, your project, your customer, and your employee's personal goals are all realized in concert with each other. By integrating human capital into the Lean Six Sigma equation, organizations have the opportunity for exponential, quantum levels of improvement and success. Your customers will be happy, shareholders will be happy, Management will be happy, employees will be happy, processes will be optimized, waste will be eliminated, and profits will soar. It is quite possible that now, with TPS-Lean Six Sigma, we actually have reached nirvana. Chapter 4 will be devoted entirely to defining the TPS-Lean Six Sigma business improvement model. It will show how the Total Performance Scorecard works, and how the Personal, Organizational, and Project Balanced Scorecards are created and inter-related with each other, and how based on the new revolutionary TPS-Lean Six Sigma concept a strong foundation can be created for a real learning organization, effective talent management and successful implementation of TPS-Lean Six Sigma projects.

NOTES

1.   Kiichiro Toyoda (1894–1952) was a Japanese industrialist and the son of Toyoda Loom Works founder Sakichi Toyoda. He made the decision for

Toyoda Loom Works to branch into automobiles, considered a risky business at the time. Shortly before Sakichi Toyoda died, he encouraged his son to follow his dream and pursue automobile manufacturing—Kiichiro created what eventually became Toyota Motor Corporation.

2. Taiichi Ohno (1912–1990) is considered to be the father of the Toyota Production System, also known as Lean Manufacturing. He wrote several books about the system, the most popular of which is Toyota Production System: Beyond Large-Scale Production. He was an employee first of the Toyoda family's Toyoda Spinning, then moved to the motor company in 1939, and gradually rose through the ranks to become an Executive.

3. Shigeo Shingo (1909–1990) was a Japanese industrial engineer who distinguished himself as one of the world's leading experts on manufacturing practices and The Toyota Production System. Shingo is known far more in the West than in Japan, as a result of his meeting Norman Bodek, an American entrepreneur and founder of Productivity Inc. in the United States. In 1981, Bodek had traveled to Japan to learn about the Toyota Production System, and came across books by Shingo, who as an external consultant had been teaching industrial engineering courses at Toyota since 1955. Shingo had written his study of The Toyota Production System in Japanese and had it translated, very poorly, into English in 1980. Norman Bodek took as many copies of this book as he could to the United States and arranged to translate Shingo's other books into English, eventually having his original study retranslated. Bodek also brought Shingo to lecture in the United States and developed one of the first Western Lean manufacturing consultancy practices with Shingo's support.

4. Bill Smith (1929–1993) is the "Father of Six Sigma." Born in Brooklyn, New York, Smith graduated from the U.S. Naval Academy in 1952 and studied at the University of Minnesota–School of Management (now known as the Carlson School of Management). In 1987, after working for nearly 35 years in Engineering and Quality Assurance, he joined Motorola, serving as vice president and senior quality assurance manager for the Land Mobile Products Sector.

5. Mikel Harry is the cofounder and chief Executive of the Six Sigma Academy, Inc. He was one of the original architects of Six Sigma while working at Motorola in the 1980s. He later served as corporate vice president at Asea Brown Boveri Ltd. He received his BS and MA in electronic from Ball State University and PhD at Arizona State University. Harry lives in Scottsdale, Arizona.

CHAPTER 4

TPS-LEAN SIX SIGMA

What we need to do is learn to work in the system, by which I mean that everybody, every team, every platform, every division, every component is there not for individual competitive profit or recognition, but for contribution to the system as a whole on a win-win basis.

—W. Edwards Deming

The fundamental task of management is to make people capable of joint performance through common goals, common values, the right structure, and the training and development they need to perform and to respond to change.

—Peter Drucker

A new blueprint and road map for addressing the primary concerns of manufacturing and service in a more sustainable and humanized way is urgently needed, whereby personal and organizational performance, and learning mutually reinforce each other and create a stable basis for a high performance company. Traditional business management concepts are insufficiently committed to learning, and rarely take the specific personal ambitions of employees into account. In consequence, there are many superficial improvements, marked by temporary and cosmetic changes, which are coupled with failing projects that lack engaged personnel. This chapter emphasizes the introduction of this new blueprint, called TPS-Lean Six Sigma. This model entails the integration of Total Performance Scorecard (TPS) and Lean Six Sigma. TPS-Lean Six Sigma and the related new tools provide an excellent and innovative framework for

---

creating a high performance culture and a sustainable breakthrough in both the manufacturing and service industries.

4.1. THE TPS-LEAN SIX SIGMA CYCLE

The TPS-Lean Six Sigma Cycle will be helpful for successfully implementing of TPS-Six Sigma projects. It consists of the following four phases (see Figure 4.1):

1. **Formulating**—This phase involves the formulation of the Organizational, Project, and Personal Balanced Scorecard. Identification and selection of TPS-Lean Six Sigma projects are strongly related to the Organizational Balanced Scorecard. The Project Balanced Scorecard is one of the outcomes of the Organizational Balanced Scorecard (OBSC). The role of the Personal Balanced Scorecard (PBSC) here is to let employees/team members work smarter (by enhancing their effectiveness and improving themselves continuously based on their Personal Balanced Scorecard) and improve their engagement by aligning their personal ambition with their shared project and organizational ambition.

2. **Deploying**—Here all stakeholders participate in the business strategy by communicating and cascading the corporate scorecard to the scorecards of all the underlying business units and teams, and finally linking the team scorecard to the individual performance plan of the employees. This top-down and bottom-up process is implemented, step by step, by all successive organization levels in increasing detail. In this way, the overall strategy of the organization (OBSC) is systematically translated into more specific plans on each organization level. This is needed to shift the strategic vision into action. Every individual on all these organizational levels formulates his/her own PBSC and shares this with his/her colleagues. The concordance of personal ambition and the shared organizational ambition takes place at all levels of the organization. This deployment process should be followed as well when cascading and breaking down the overall TPS-Lean Six Sigma Project Balanced Scorecard to smaller Project Balanced Scorecards. The Project Balanced Scorecard is one of the outcomes of the OBSC, Department BSC, and Team BSC.

3. **Improving**—This means continuously improving yourself and your work. It concerns the implementation of the personal, organizational and TPS-Lean Six Sigma project improvement actions based on the PBSC, OBSC, and Project BSC respectively.

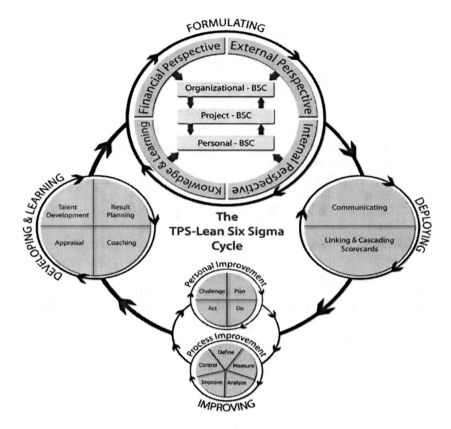

Figure 4.1. The TPS-Lean Six Sigma Cycle.

The focus here is on correcting mistakes, improving existing capabilities, doing right things right the first time, and acquiring new skills and capabilities through gradual improvement. The PBSC is implemented according to the Plan-Do-Act-Challenge cycle (Rampersad, 2006). This cycle consists of the following four phases (see Figure 4.20):

(a) **Plan:** Formulate or update your PBSC
(b) **Do:** Start with a simple objective and related improvement action from your PBSC, be determined in the realization of this, and ask for feedback
(c) **Act:** Check if the improvement is working and take action when it is not. Review the results according to your personal performance measures and targets, develop your skills and competencies to

achieve the objectives you have selected, implement the personal improvements, assess the personal results, document the lessons learned, and improve and monitor your actions and thinking continuously.

(d) **Challenge:** Accept bigger challenges by selecting a more difficult objective and the corresponding improvement action from your PBSC and act on it. Be conscientious in choosing a more challenging objective on part with your improved skills when the current improvement action starts becoming boring. Enjoy the experience and document what you have learned.

The OBSC and Project BSC are implemented according to the DMAIC cycle. This cycle consists of the following five phases (see Figure 3.6):

(a) **Define:** This involves formulating the Project BSC (clearly stating the project vision, mission, objectives, performance measures, and targets, improvement actions), forming the project team, and stating the scope in terms of customers' needs and identifying the key or core processes that are used to deliver these requirements. It is essential not only to identify the processes in terms of inputs, outputs, performance standards in terms of "Critical to Quality" criteria or "CTQs," controls, and resources required but also identify key stakeholders of the project. The project charter forms the input for the Project BSC.

(b) **Measure:** This phase involves planning how data on present performance a will be collected, defining the various variables (input, process and output), and implementing the Project BSC (related to the OBSC). This phase aids in not only determining the current process capability (based on the performance measures and targets included in the Project BSC) but also helps to locate and define them in a more focused way by clearly stating what is happening, when and where and the possible causes. This defined baseline performance can be used as a benchmark for comparing the effectiveness of improved processes envisaged.

(c) **Analyze:** This is the third stage in Six Sigma involves analyzing the data collected and the possible causes to determine the root causes of the poor performances identified in the measure stage. The idea is to prioritize problems for taking action in the next two stages.

(d) **Improve:** The objective of this stage is to develop alternatives, and select the best alternative, try it out, and implement the solution to improve the performance and prevent the problems from reoccurring (implementing the selected improvement actions included in the Project BSC). It also involves collecting data and depicting the improvement effected to bridge the gap between the desired and current performance, evaluating the effectiveness of the solutions and the way they were implemented.

(e) **Control:** This stage involves documenting the new methods and process to be used, communicating the results, of the last two stages, training all those concerned, especially new staff, and monitor the consistent use of the new method/processes to ensure that the improvement is maintained.

4. **Developing and learning**—Here, the emphasis is on job-related talent management and learning. To be able to manage and use the talents within the organization and project effectively, it is necessary that the personal, organizational and project balanced scorecards be embedded in the talent management process. This is done on the basis of the talent management cycle, which consists of the following phases (see Figure 2.4)—result planning, coaching, appraisal, and talent development. The learning process in this phase encompasses the review of the scorecards, the actualization of these scorecards by incorporating changing conditions, aligning the personal ambition with the shared organization and project ambition, the documentation of the lessons learned, and checking which things went well or wrong during the previous phases. Depending on these evaluation results, the implementation or the formulation of the scorecards may be adjusted. This phase deals with learning from gained experiences. It refers to internalizing acquired knowledge and actualizing it through experience in order to change both the individual and collective behavior of employees, thus enabling the organization and the TPS-Lean Six Sigma project to perform better.

As we can see from Figure 4.1, the TPS-Lean Six Sigma Cycle consists of a number of large and small wheels. These all need to be interrelated and to turn in the right direction in order to get the larger TPS-Lean Six Sigma wheel moving successfully. The model gives us insight into both the way this wheel can be mobilized and the coherence between its different aspects. After the last phase is complete, the cycle is again followed in order to align the scorecards with its surroundings on a continuous basis. Thus, your organization will come to know itself and its surroundings and so improve itself based on the OBSC. Naturally, the same applies to you, i.e. by reviewing your PBSC monthly with a trusted person and learning from your previous experiences; you will know both yourself and your surroundings better, which will allow you to improve yourself. The same applies to your Project BSC; reviewing your project BSC every week and having the ambition meeting regularly with the Champion/Master Black Belt/Black Belt/Green Belt/Project Manager based on this. By doing this, you will constantly improve your performance, and thus continuously satisfy yourself and others. Strategy formation, improvement, development of human potential, and learning are all part of a perpetual process. Progressing through the TPS-Lean Six Sigma Cycle will result in the continuous improvement of business results through the years. Through this approach the customer is satisfied, and the organization is able to come to know itself and its surroundings on an ongoing basis. The TPS-Lean Six Sigma Life Cycle Scan (see chapter 12) is a performance excellence model that will guide you in this process of total performance improvement. It's a measuring rod that is laid against the organization to define which development phase it is in, and the total score it has obtained.

The concepts embodied in the TPS-Lean Six Sigma Cycle provide solutions to preserving and utilizing individual rights and capabilities while adjusting the organizational/project culture and philosophy to this new environment. This has been done by expanding and integrating concepts such as the Personal Balanced Scorecard, Organizational Balanced Scorecard, Project Balanced Scorecard, Lean Six Sigma, and Talent Management into one overall holistic and organic framework (see Figures 4.2 and 4.3). This model will help organizations navigate through the above-mentioned problems, and the demanding and often frustrating road toward sustained employee engagement and improvement.

As we can see from Figure 4.3, the TPS-Lean Six Sigma concept consists of a number of large and small wheels. These all need to be interrelated and turning in the right direction in order to get the wheel of the larger TPS-Lean Six Sigma moving successfully toward a real learning and engaged organization. The implementation of TPS-Lean Six Sigma starts with the formulation of the Organizational BSC (organizational vision + mission + core values + critical success factors + objectives + performance measures + targets + improvement actions), which results in related Project BSCs (project vision + mission + values + critical success factors + objectives + performance measures + targets + improvement actions), and which should be aligned with the Personal BSC (personal vision + mission + key roles + critical success factors + objectives + performance measures + targets + improvement actions) in order to create employee engagement. The organizational improvement actions in the Organizational BSC are related to the Project BSC (business alignment), the desired organizational behaviors are related to the Personal BSC (cultural alignment), and the match between Personal BSC and Project BSC (project alignment) causes employee engagements within the project (see Figure 4.4).

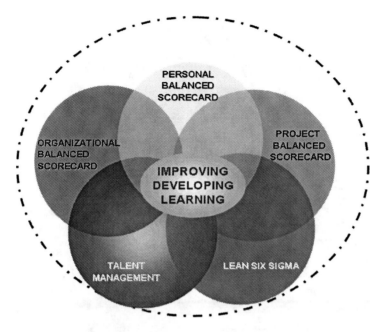

Figure 4.2.   The TPS-Lean Six Sigma Concept.

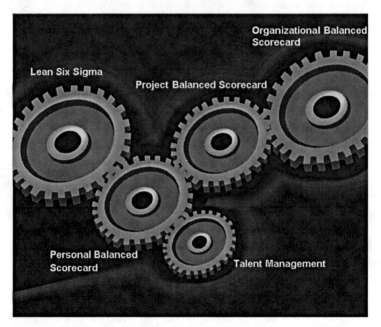

Figure 4.3.   Engaging TPS-Lean Six Sigma Gears lead to a High Performance Culture.

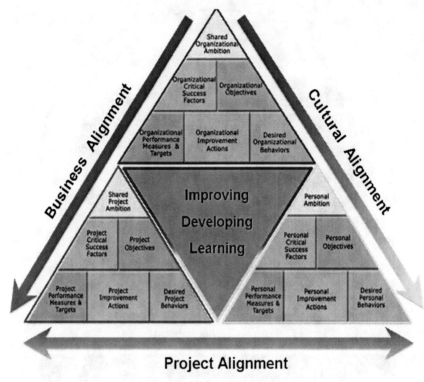

Figure 4.4.   TPS-Lean Six Sigma Shared Vision Flow Down.

In the following paragraphs, each of the three BSCs and each of the phases in the TPS-Lean Six Sigma Cycle will be discussed in depth. This concept differs in essential ways from traditional Lean Six Sigma and other quality management concepts, which insufficiently consider the important first step of formulating the personal ambition and aligning this with the shared ambition, needed to achieve enduring organizational and strategic development. Real change and organizational improvement are achieved only if people change and improve inwardly. Such personal involvement is an integral part of TPS-Lean Six Sigma. The aim is maximum commitment and devotion on the part of all involved, as well as, the encouragement of individual learning, team learning, and creativity. The thesis here is that if an employee is engaged, then he or she will work and think according to the shared ambition of the organization. This approach also inspires motivation, creativity, enjoyment, passion, and commitment. Through this, a more durable learning organization may be created.

4.2 FORMULATING

Formulation of the Organizational Balanced Scorecard, the related TPS-Lean Six Sigma Project Balanced Scorecards and the Personal Balanced Scorecard is the first phase in the TPS-Lean Six Sigma Cycle (see Figure 4.1). These Project Balanced Scorecards are one of the outcomes of the Organizational Balanced Scorecard. All these scorecards and the related alignments will be discussed in this section.

4.2.1 The Organizational Balanced Scorecard

The Organizational Balanced Scorecard (OBSC) is a top-down management instrument that is used for making an organization's strategic vision operational at all organizational levels. The PBSC, in contrast with Kaplan and Norton's Balanced Scorecard (2003), integrates people involvement and happiness into balanced scorecard and involves individual buy-in, in order to realize sustainable personal and organizational performance improvement. It would be too much to go into detail about the OBSC concept in the framework of this book. For more information about the OBSC, we refer you to Rampersad (2003). A brief overview is given in the box that follows. Figures 2.3 and 4.5 show the elements of the OBSC.

The Organizational Balanced Scorecard

Organizational Vision
The organizational vision contains the most ambitious dream of the organization, indicating how it envisions the future, what it long-term dream and intentions are, what it wants to achieve, where it goes from here, how it sees a desirable and achievable shared future situation, and so forth. It provides a shared vision of a desired and feasible future, as well as, the route needed to reach it. It indicates what the organization wants to achieve, what is essential for its success, and which critical success factors make it unique. It shows where and how the organization wants to distinguish itself from others. This implies that the organizational vision provides insight into *core competences*: the fields in which the organization excels the reasons why customers use its products and services, and the principles of the employees. Standards, values, and principles are also part of the organizational vision. The vision, in contrast to the mission, is tied to a timeline. An effectively formulated vision guides personal ambitions and creativity, establishes a climate that is fertile for change,

WHERE ARE WE GOING? (BECOMING)
How do we envision the future? What are our long-term dream and intentions? What do we want to achieve? Where do we go from here? How do we see a desirable and achievable shared future situation, and what are the change routes needed to reach it? What changes lie ahead in the business landscape? Who do we want to be?

WHO ARE WE AND WHAT DO WE STAND FOR? (BEING)
Why does our organization exist? What do we do? Where are we? What is our identity? What is the purpose of our existence? What is our primary function? What is our ultimate main objective? For whom do we exist? Who are our most important stakeholders? What fundamental need do we fulfill?

WHICH VALUES ARE PRECIOUS TO US?
What do we stand for? What connects us? What is important in our attitude? What do we believe in? How do we treat each other? How do we work together? How do we think of ourselves?

WHICH FACTORS MAKE US UNIQUE?
What is the most important factor of our organizational success? Which organizational factors are essential for our organizational viability? What are our core competencies?

WHAT RESULTS DO WE WANT?
Which short-term measurable results must we achieve?

HOW CAN WE MEASURE THE RESULTS?
What makes the organizational vision and objectives measurable? Which values must be obtained? What are the targets?

HOW DO WE WANT TO ACHIEVE THE RESULTS?
How can we realize the objectives? Which improvement actions are we going to implement? How do we create a platform for the developed strategies? How will we communicate this to the people? How do we see that we learn continuously?

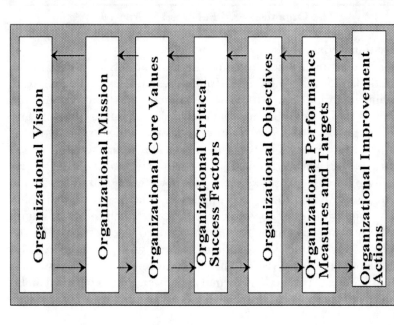

Organizational Vision

Organizational Mission

Organizational Core Values

Organizational Critical Success Factors

Organizational Objectives

Organizational Performance Measures and Targets

Organizational Improvement Actions

Figure 4.5.   OBSC Framework (Rampersad, 2003).

strengthens the organization's belief in the future, and therefore, releases energy in people.

Organizational Mission

The organizational mission consists of an organization's identity and indicates its reason for existing: Why, to what extent, and for who does it exist? What are the primary function and the ultimate objective? Which basic need does it fulfill, and who are its most important stakeholders? What it ultimate main objective is? For whom it exists? This *"genetic code"* of the organization is meant to help employees build a common understanding of the main objective, increase their devotion, and provide an explanation as to why their organization is different from the others. An effectively formulated and forcefully articulated mission creates unanimity in the behavior of employees, strengthens their single-mindedness, and improves the atmosphere of mutual communication within the organization.

Organizational Core Values

The organizational vision is also based on a set of shared values that are used to strengthen the like-mindedness, commitment, and devotion of employees and to influence their behavior positively. These core values determine how one must act in order to realize the organizational vision. They function as the guiding principles that support people's behavior at work. Core values hold people together if they act and think along the lines of these values. They articulate the way we treat each other and how we see customers, employees, shareholders, suppliers, and the community. If the principles, norms, and values of the employees match those of the organization, then their efforts and involvement would be optimal. Therefore, core values are strongly related to the personal ambition of the individual employees. After all, with an organizational mission and vision based on shared values, the personal objectives of individual employees will correspond closely to those of the organization. The core value must be ethical in order to pass the test of moral scrutiny. Everyone within the organization should act in accordance with these principles and moral standards.

The organizational vision and mission express the soul of the organization. Together with the core values they produce the shared ambition and have an important impact on the bonding of employees to the organization and to their performance. A successfully formulated shared ambition shows people how their activities can contribute to the whole, which allows them to work together with greater enthusiasm toward organizational objectives. Subsequently, they feel proud about making a useful contribution to something worthwhile. The shared ambition gives direction to an organization and function as a compass or road map. The convincing articulation of a decisive, inspiring, goal oriented, recognizable, challenging, and fascinating shared ambition through which people feel bonded and touched usually leads to more devotion, satisfaction, and commitment. After all, such a shared ambition inspires creativity and motivates and mobilizes people. It gives them energy and therefore leads to better performance. This process is a way to create the future of the organization together. Effectively formulated shared ambition statements comply with the following criteria:

- The emphasis is on unselfishness;
- The mission is short, concrete, simple and not focused explicitly on profitability or on any other financial element.
- The vision and mission appeal to the largest group of stakeholders and are formulated in positive terms.
- The vision and mission are organization specific; their emphasis is on those elements that distinguish it from other organizations. At the same time, the borders of the mission, specifically, are broadly defined to allow for the development of new initiatives.
- The vision and mission also include ethical starting points and cultural components, such as respect for the individual, contributions to society, helping people to develop their possibilities, and so on.
- The vision is ambitious and challenging; it inspires the employee, gives an attractive view of the final objective, gives guidance to initiatives and creativity, appeals directly to people, and joins forces within the organization.
- The vision gives direction; it determines today's actions in order to achieve an optimal future.
- The vision is linked to time, and the mission is timeless.

Organizational Critical Success Factors

Organizational Critical Success Factors are derived from the shared ambition. An organizational critical success factor is one in which the organization must excel in order to survive, or one that is of overriding importance to organizational success. Such strategic issues determine the competitive advantage of an organization. They are factors in which the organization wants to differ and make itself unique in the market, and as such are related to its core competencies. Critical success factors are also related to the four previously mentioned OBSC perspectives and thus form an integral part of the shared ambition. In this ambition you will always find a set of critical success factors, which is related to the four perspectives. The critical success factors form the link between the organizational vision, mission, and core values and the remaining OBSC elements.

Organizational Objectives

Organizational objectives are measurable results that must be achieved. They describe the expected results that should be achieved within a short time in order to realize the long-term shared ambition. These objectives are derived directly from the critical success factors and form realistic milestones. The objectives are formulated through a SWOT analysis. Chapter 12 describes the TPS-Lean Six Sigma Life Cycle Scan which can be used to carry out this analysis effectively. Quantifying objectives is avoided in the OBSC; it will take place at a later phase via performance measures and targets. The objectives form part of a cause-and-effect chain, resulting in the final organizational objective.

Organizational Performance Measures

An organizational performance measure is an indicator, related to a critical success factor and a strategic objective, and is used to judge the functioning of a specific process. These indicators are the standards by which the progress of the strategic objectives is measured. They are essential when putting strategic plans into action. When they are interconnected so that managers can deduce a certain course of action from them, they provide Management with timely signals of organizational guidance, based on the measurement of (process) changes and the comparison of the measured results to the norms. Therefore, performance measures make the organizational vision and objectives measurable. A whole list of performance measures according to each OBSC perspective can be found in Rampersad (2003).

Organizational Targets

An organizational target is the quantitative objective of a performance measure. It is a value that an organization aspires toward, the realization of which can be measured by means of a performance measure. In other words, targets indicate values to be obtained.

Organizational Improvement Actions

Organizational improvement actions are strategies undertaken to realize the organizational ambition. The how is central here: How can control our business processes more effectively? How can we generate more profit? How can we make our employees more engaged? Alternative strategies are formed on the basis of the before mentioned OBSC-steps, and from this, actions are chosen which result in the greatest contribution to the critical success factors. Selected TPS-Lean Six Sigma projects are part of these strategies.

The OBSC can be defined as the following formula:

OBSC = organizational vision + mission + core values + critical success factors + objectives + performance measures + targets + improvement actions (divided along the four perspectives: internal, external, knowledge & learning, and financial).

Shared Ambition = organizational vision + mission + core values (divided along the four perspectives: internal, external, knowledge & learning, and financial)

The OBSC should result into project prioritization and selection process, project review, reporting and tracking system, deployment of Champion (who is responsible for the deployment), Executive, Champion, Black Belt and Green Belt workshops. The workshops should clearly outline the role of Management, Champions, Master Black Belts, Black Belts and Green Belts. One of the results of the OBSC is the formulation of one or more TPS-Lean Six Sigma Project Balanced Scorecards, which will be discussed in the next section.

Business Jet's Organizational Balanced Scorecard

To illustrate what has been said about the OBSC, Business Jet's shared ambition is shown in the box below. Business Jet is an airliner for business people. Dave Jones is the CEO of this company. His PBSC will be described in the next section. Table 4.1 shows the related critical success factors of Business Jet that were derived from its shared ambition. The related OBSC is shown in Table 4.2.

Business Jet's Shared Ambition

Organizational Vision

In all aspects, we want to be a professional organization, one that is the customer's first choice for business travel in all the regions where we operate. We want to achieve this by:

Table 4.1. Business Jet's Critical Success Factors

Financial	*External*
• Good financial results and growing profitability	• Dominant share in the global market • First choice of customers for business travel • High quality services

Internal	*Knowledge and Learning*
• Safe and reliable • Timely departure and arrival of airplanes • Successful introduction of innovative products and services	• Continuous development of human potential • *Competitive advantage based on knowledge, skills, and capabilities of employees* • Open communication, integrity • Team spirit, enjoyment and passion • Motivated work force

1. Achieving excellent financial results through the successful introduction of innovative products and services;
2. Offering our customers high-quality services and, thanks to our image, having a dominant share in the global market of business travel;
3. Having airplanes depart and arrive on time, doing so more successfully than competitors;
4. Creating an inspiring work environment that provides an atmosphere of team spirit, open communication, and process thinking;
5. Continuously developing our human potential, and, based on our knowledge, skills, and capabilities, acquiring competitive advantage.

In order to be the safest and most reliable business travel company, everything within our organization will be focused on achieving top performance with a motivated work force that cares for the needs of the society we are part of.

Organizational Mission
We are a safe and reliable airline company for business people.

Organizational Core Values
We are being led by the following core values:

1. Integrity: Doing business with integrity. Integrity is never compromised.
2. Enjoyment and Passion: Working with devoted people who enjoy their work, are passionate, and are driven to achieve superior per-

Table 4.2. Business Jet's Organizational Balanced Scorecard

Organizational Critical Success Factors	Organizational Objectives	Organizational Performance Measures	Organizational Targets	Organizational Improvement Actions
Financial				
– Good financial results and growing profitability.	– Higher returns.	– Net profits at constant equity	– Increase of 15% in 3 years.	– Close down unprofitable business units such as rental car.
	– Higher returns.	– Gross margin growth.	– $15 million at the end of next year.	– Decrease cost price of airline tickets.
		– Costs reduction due to lower maintenance inventory.	– $3 million in the coming 3 years.	– Redefine minimal maintenance inventory.
		– % Decrease of operational costs.	– Each year an average of 10% lower than in 2006.	– Implement TPS-Lean Six Sigma. – Outsourcing of catering activities. – Execution cost failure study. – Introduction of departmental budgets.
External				
– Dominant share in the global market.	– Greater market share.	– Market share.	– 10% increase in 3 years.	– Expand our activities in North America through negotiation. – Develop program for goal-oriented marketing. – Develop plan for direct marketing. – Communicate with customers with e-business tools.

Objectives	Performance measures	Targets	Actions
– First choice of customers for business travel. – Improved customer satisfaction level regarding our products, services, and employees.	– Degree of customer satisfaction.	– At least 75% in 3 years.	– Set up customers' helpdesk – Develop guidelines for optimal customer satisfaction as part of a TPS-Lean Six Sigma implementation.
– High-quality services. – Greater degree of trust from our customers regarding the services we provide.	– Number of customer complaints. – Degree of customer loyalty.	– Decrease of at least 30% per year. – Increase of 30% in 4 years.	– Give extra rewards to customers-orient employees. – Formulate a customer complaints procedure and execute it routinely. – Measure the degree of customer loyalty. – Benchmarking with regard to customer loyalty.
Internal			
– Safe and reliable. – Optimal safety and reliability.	– % safety incidents.	– Reduction by at least 70% in 2 years.	– Improve safety awareness of employees through training and communication – Intensify safety controls on all operational levels.

Table continues on next page.

Table 4.2. Business Jet's Organizational Balanced Scorecard Continued

		Internal		
Organizational Critical Success Factors	*Organizational Objectives*	*Organizational Performance Measures*	*Organizational Targets*	*Organizational Improvement Actions*
– On-time departure and arrival of airplanes.	– Reduced departure and arrival delays.	– Check-in time.	– Shorten by 20% within 3 years.	– Development of a safety bulletin to be published quarterly – Stimulate alertness and passenger involvement regarding public safety. – Improve the efficiency of the Check-in process based on TPS-Lean Six Sigma – Develop work procedures.
		– Loading and unloading time of airplanes – Downtime of airplanes.	– Shorten by 15 % within 3 Years – Shorten by 25 % within 3 years.	– Introduce total preventive maintenance system and implement TPS-Lean Six Sigma.
– Successful introduction of innovative products and services.	– Newly developed products and services.	– % Sales from new products and services.	– Increase of 5 % per year.	– Offering Internet services on board of our jets (Internet and e-mail in the air).
		– Time needed to launch a new product and service in the market (time-to-market).	– Shorten by 15% in 3 years.	– Determine development criteria for new products and services.

Knowledge and Learning

Objective	Critical success factor	Performance measure	Target	Action/Initiative
Continuous development of human potential.	Higher labor productivity.	Labor productivity of personnel.	25% increase in 3 years.	Make career development plans for everyone. Conduct planning, coaching, and appraisal interviews with employees based on individual performance plans and competence profiles.
Competitive-advantage based on knowledge, skills and capabilities of employees.	Improved manager competencies.	Sales of each employee.	10% increase in 3 years.	Connect performance rewards to appraisal system.
		% of managers trained in TPS-Lean Six Sigma.	at least 50% in 1 year.	Provide training in TPS-Lean Six Sigma.
		Training costs of managers.	$1 million per year.	Determine training budget for managers.
Open communication, integrity.	Openness and honesty when exchanging information.	Experience level of employees regarding information exchange.	85% in 3 years.	Execute study of employee satisfaction regarding information exchange.
Team spirit, enjoyment and passion.	Managers act as coaches.	% of personnel who find that they are working under effective leadership.	25% increase per year.	Provide training in effective team coaching and leadership.
Motivated workforce.	Improved employee satisfaction degree.	% of personnel who find that they do challenging work.	85% in 3 years.	Execute employee satisfaction study.
		% of sick leave.	Less than 2% in 2 years.	Study improvement of working conditions.

formances in everything our company undertakes. Employee engagement is our way of life.

3. Customer Orientation: Listening continuously to our customers, discovering their expectations and providing them with the quality services they expect of us, and satisfying them constantly. They are the focus of everything we do.

4. Safe and Reliable: Being known as the safest and most reliable airline company.

Table 4.1 shows Business Jet's most important critical success factors which are related to Business Jet's shared ambition statement. These are factors which make Business Jet unique and in which it will further develop and distinguish itself. These factors have been identified in Business Jet's shared ambition statement and are in their OPBSC further developed below (see Table 4.2).

Because there are many possible improvement actions, it is recommended to make a selection through prioritizing. Rampersad introduced an integral method to give priority to these improvement actions in (Rampersad, 2003).

Business Jet's Strategic Map

The position of Business Jet's objectives, within the four perspectives, and their mutual relationships are made visible in Figure 4.6. In this cause effect chain, Business Jet's objectives are interrelated and affect one another. In this figure, all first-level organizational strategic objectives are formulated and illustrated; they all lead to a final objective, namely, higher return. The cause-and-effect chain is a handy tool for communicating the OBSC to lower organizational levels.

4.2.2 The Project Balanced Scorecard

The Project Balanced Scorecards are one of the outcomes of the OBSC. The Project Balanced Scorecard is a top-down Management instrument that is used for making the TPS-Lean Six Sigma project's ambition operational at all project levels. It is a participatory approach that provides a framework for the systematic and successful execution of a TPS-Lean Six Sigma project. The Project BSC is a balanced and holistic project charter.

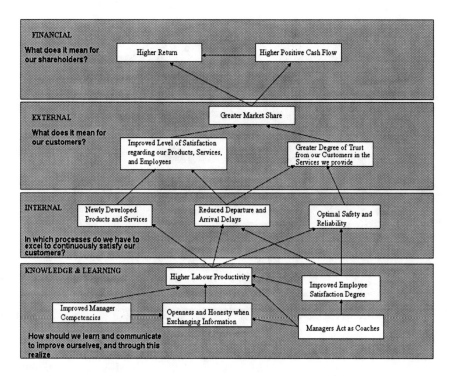

Figure 4.6.   Business Jet's Strategic Map.

It makes the project vision measurable and translates it systematically into project actions. The Project BSC entails project vision + mission + values + critical success factors + objectives + performance measures + targets + improvement actions. The elements of the Project BSC are divided along various perspectives. These perspectives are crucial categories of project results (see Figure 4.7):

1. *Financial*: What are the financial consequences of this project?
2. *External*: What does it mean for our customers?
3. *Internal*: How can we control the primary business processes in order to create value for our customers? In which processes, do we have to excel to continuously satisfy our customers?
4. *Knowledge and learning*: Skills and attitudes of the employees and the project/organizational learning ability. How should we learn and improve, and through this continuously realize our shared project ambition?

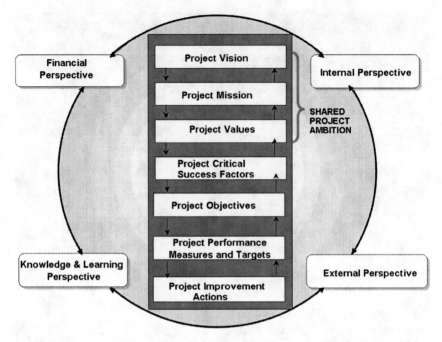

Figure 4.7.   The Four Perspectives in the Project BSC (Rampersad, 2007).

The elements of the Project BSC will be examined below (see Figures 4.8).

The Project Balanced Scorecard

Project Vision

The project vision contains the most ambitious dream of the project. It provides a desired and feasible future of the project, as well as, the route needed to reach this. It indicates what is essential for the success of the project, envisions the future after executing the project, the long-term project intentions, and which process changes lay ahead. An effectively formulated project vision guides personal ambitions and creativity of the project team members.

Project Mission

The project mission consists of a project's identity and indicates its reason for existing: Why, to what extent, and for who does it exist? What are the primary function and the ultimate objective of the

WHERE DO WE GO FROM HERE WITH THE PROJECT?
How do we envision the future after executing the project? What are the long-term project intentions? How do we see a desirable and achievable shared future situation, and what are the change routes needed to reach it? What process changes lie ahead?

WHY DOES THE PROJECT EXIST?
Why does the project exist? What is the project identity? What is the purpose of the project? What is the primary function of the project? What is the ultimate main project objective? Who are the most important stakeholders? What fundamental need does the project fulfill?

WHICH VALUES ARE PRECIOUS TO US?
What do we (team members) stand for? What connects us? What is important in our attitude? What do we believe in? How do we treat each other? How do we work together? How do we think of ourselves?

WHICH FACTORS MAKE THE PROJECT UNIQUE?
What is the most important factor for the success of the project? Which factors are essential for the project viability? What are our project core competencies?

WHAT PROJECT RESULTS DO WE WANT?
Which short-term measurable results must we achieve with this project? What ethical goals will be supported?

HOW CAN WE MEASURE THE PROJECT RESULTS?
What makes the project vision and objectives measurable? Which values must be obtained? What are the project targets?

HOW DO WE WANT TO ACHIEVE THE PROJECT RESULTS?
How can we realize the project objectives? Which improvement actions are we going to implement? How do we create a platform for the developed project strategies? How will we communicate this to the people? How do we see that we learn continuously? What additional projects will be enabled by this project?

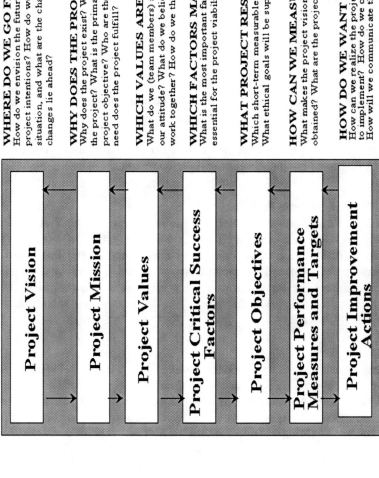

- Project Vision
- Project Mission
- Project Values
- Project Critical Success Factors
- Project Objectives
- Project Performance Measures and Targets
- Project Improvement Actions

Figure 4.8. Elements of the Project BSC (Rampersad, 2007).

project? Which basic need does it fulfill, and who are its most important stakeholders? An effectively formulated mission creates a sense of unity in the behavior of project members, strengthens their like-mindedness, and improves both communication and the atmosphere within the project team.

The project vision and mission express the soul of the project. Together with the project values, they form its shared project ambition. Creating a shared project ambition statement helps the project team present a clear understanding of the goals and objectives for the project deployment. A successfully formulated project ambition shows team members how their activities contribute to the larger TPS-Lean Six Sigma project. In a TPS-Lean Six Sigma project without a clear project vision and mission, project members are exposed to ad hoc decisions and short-term plans. A clear project shared ambition is the key to project success. It also includes the project scope, a clear problem statement and the project charter.

Project Values

The project vision is also based on a set of shared values that are used to strengthen the like-mindedness, commitment, and devotion of project members and to influence their behavior positively. These values determine how one must act in order to realize the project vision. They function as the guiding principles that support team member's behavior during execution of the TPS-Lean Six Sigma project. The project values hold people together if they act and think along the lines of these values.

Project Critical Success Factors

Project Critical Success Factors are derived from the project ambition. A project critical success factor is one in that is of overriding importance to the project's success. They are related to the four previously mentioned project BSC perspectives and thus, form an integral part of the shared project ambition. The critical success factors form the link between project, mission, vision, and core values and the remaining project BSC elements.

Project Objectives

Project objectives are measurable results that must be achieved. They describe the expected TPS-Lean Six Sigma project results that should be achieved within a short time in order to realize the long-term shared project ambition. These objectives are derived directly from the project critical success factors and form realistic milestones. The objectives form part of a cause-and-effect chain, resulting in the final project objective. A project SWOT-analysis and risk analysis can be executed to define the project objectives clearly.

Project Performance Measures

Project performance measures are the standards by which the progress of the TPS-Lean Six Sigma project objectives is measured. When they are interconnected so that team members can deduce a certain course of action from them, they provide team management with timely signals of project guidance, based on the measurement of process changes and the comparison of the measured results to the norms. Therefore, performance measures make the TPS-Lean Six Sigma project ambition and objectives measurable. A whole list of performance measures according to each BSC perspective can be found in Rampersad (2003, 2006).

Project Targets

A project target is the quantitative objective of a performance measure. It is a value that a TPS-Lean Six Sigma project aspires toward, the realization of which can be measured by means of a performance measure.

Project Improvement Actions

Project improvement actions are initiatives or strategies undertaken to realize the project ambition. *How* is central here: How can we improve the engagement of our project members? How do we create teamwork? How will we communicate the project results? How can we enhance the team performance?

The Project BSC can be defined as the following formula:

Project BSC = project vision + mission + values + critical success factors + objectives + performance measures + targets + improvement actions (divided along the four perspectives: internal, external, knowledge & learning, and financial).

Project Shared Ambition = project vision + mission + values (divided along the four perspectives: internal, external, knowledge & learning, and financial).

We have introduced the TPS-Lean Six Sigma Project BSCsoft in the Appendix, which is an interactive software system that will assist you with the successful formulation and implementation of your Project BSC.

Two Cases of a Project BSC

To illustrate what has been said about the TPS-Lean Six Sigma Project BSC, two practical real cases will be described in this section—Ravenwood Golf Club's TPS-Lean Six Sigma Project BSC and the Waterbury General Hospital's TPS-Lean Six Sigma Project BSC.

Ravenwood Golf Club's Project BSC

Ravenwood is a traditionally-styled course, located in Victor, New York. It includes several elevated tees, and the medium-sized greens (averaging 6,200 square feet) are for the most part flat and fast. Six holes involve water play. The course plays from 4,938 to 7,003-yards and there are five sets of tees to challenge all skill levels. Ravenwood was developed on open land whose owner wanted the land to be kept as open land rather than to have it covered with a housing development. The beautiful grounds at Ravenwood retain the natural beauty of this upstate New York Finger Lakes area. In addition to golf, Ravenwood also has facilities for special events, including golf outings, dinners, weddings, and associated parties and dinners.

Ravenwood Golf Club has organized its business practices into a series of procedures for marketing, selling, preparing for and conducting successful golf events and banquets and weddings. Prior to the TPS-Lean Six Sigma project, procedures required almost constant involvement by the food and beverage manager and the events coordinator to direct and monitor all seasonal staff involved in working at the Ravenwood Golf Club events. This reduced the time that these key personnel could spend on growing the business through client contact, proactive marketing, and sales. Ravenwood Golf Club's food and beverage manager initiated a Lean process improvement project to reduce, if not eliminate, the inherent waste associated with the many processes that keep the business running. To define, focus and control the scope of this project, the TPS-Lean Six Sigma Black Belt consultants worked with the food and beverage manager and the events coordinator to select two key processes for this project. Specifically, the food and beverage manager wanted to reduce the time associated with the contract proposal process, and to reduce the time required for event set-ups. The financial implications of the project were associated with the work content of the specified processes.

To execute this project, the following team members were selected:

- Black Belts: J. Nick Usher and Madeleine Anne Cuciti.
- Master Black Belt: Leslie Henckler.

- Project Champions: Tim Dunn and Jennifer Gossage.
- Project Team Members: Tim Dunn, Jennifer Gossage.

Project Schedule:

Define: Completed by June 1, 2006.

Measure: Complete for current processes by June 21, 2006. Complete for new processes by July 16, 2006.

Analysis: Complete Phase 1 by June 30, 2006, complete Phase 2 by August 1, 2006. Videotape current processes, use tapes for process analysis by team, and subsequent process improvement training.

Improve: Review with client during week of June 26, 2006. Create training process storyboards with photographs for table set ups. Define training with client. Observe new process.

Control: Complete by October 15, 2006.

For this project, the following Shared Project Ambition was formulated:

Ravenwood Golf Club's Shared Project Ambition

Project Vision
We will enhance the effectiveness of Ravenwood Golf Club by:

1. Achieving a yearly savings of $100,800.
2. Reducing time associated with the proposal process by 35%.
3. Reducing lead time associated with presenting contract to client.
4. Increasing managerial client facing time by 15%.
5. Letting key personnel spend more on growing the business through client contact, proactive marketing, and sales.
6. Reducing waste caused by nonvalue-added, labor-intensive steps required by the original current-state processes.
7. Increasing customer satisfaction, this in turn, will result in repeat business and referrals.
8. Empowering staff and developing human potential to work independently with minimum managerial supervision.

Project Mission
Our aim is to enhance the efficiency of the contract proposal and event set-up process within Ravenwood Golf Club.

Project Values
Our team members are being led by the following core values:

1. *Teamwork:* sharing knowledge, the work, the pressure, and the success with each other
2. *Commitment*: Working with devoted people who enjoy their work and are committed to process change and improvement.
3. Delivering exceptional customer service and value: Reducing event costs and operations overhead by reducing process time requirements, while providing standardized employee training procedures and tools which result in exceptional customer service.

Table 4.3 shows Ravenwood Golf Club's most important project critical success factors which are related to Ravenwood Golf Club's shared project ambition statement. These are factors which make Ravenwood Golf Club's TPS-Lean Six Sigma project unique. These factors have been identified in Ravenwood Golf Club's shared project ambition, and are in the Project BSC further developed below (see Table 4.4).

Table 4.3.   Ravenwood Golf Club's Project Critical Success Factors

Financial	*External*
• Achieving a yearly savings.	• Increasing customer satisfaction, which in turn, will result in repeat business and referrals.
	• Delivering exceptional customer service and value.

Internal	*Knowledge and Learning*
• Reducing time associated with the proposal process.	• Empowering staff and developing human potential to work independently with minimum managerial supervision.
• Reducing lead time associated with presenting contract to client.	
• Increasing managerial client facing time.	
• Letting key personnel spend more on growing the business through client contact, proactive marketing, and sales.	
• Reducing waste caused by nonvalue-added, labor-intensive steps required by the original current-state processes.	

Table 4.4. Ravenwood Golf Club's Project Balanced Scorecard

		Financial		
Project Critical Success Factors	*Project Objectives*	*Project Performance Measures*	*Project Targets*	*Project Improvement Actions*
Achieving yearly savings	Increased savings in labor; event set up and break down time, and employee training.	Savings	$100,800 within 1 year	Develop test plan to measure resource savings achieved by new processes.
	Reduced costs	Training costs	Decrease of at least 10% within 1 year	Videotape current processes and then measure required steps, material movements, resources and time involved to complete process. Standardizing training tools and process documentation
	Increased number of wedding events	Number of wedding events	Increase of at least 10% within 1 year	Using Visio room layout charts and process spaghetti charts. Measuring process distances required for material movement, placement of materials storage areas, resources, and required times.
	Increased number of dining events	Number of dining events	Increase of at least 10% within 1 year	
	Increased number of golf events	Number of golf events	Increase of at least 10% within 1 year	

Table continues on next page.

Table 4.4. Ravenwood Golf Club's Project Balanced Scorecard Continued

Financial

Project Critical Success Factors	Project Objectives	Project Performance Measures	Project Targets	Project Improvement Actions
			50% decrease in labor costs related to kitchen, set up and staff.	Calculate cost of resources (via burden rate) to complete processes, as well as, number of resources. Construct SIPOC process charts to lay out suppliers, inputs, process steps, outputs, and customers for each updated process. Review golf event procedures and wedding event procedures and determine: – processes that include several processes in one, – identify those overlapping processes and reformat them into individual processes that can be applied to both golf and wedding events; – Identify processes that are unique to either golf or wedding events and redesign them so that they are separate from basic processes that can be used for both golf and wedding events. Hire a dedicated resource who set up all required supplies, dishes, flatware, linen, etc., in event-specific kits the day before each event. Use separate mobile supply carts for each half of the room.

				Time-test current and future state processes. Introduce linked spreadsheets and contract templates and use of laptop computer rather than desk top computer to eliminate paper and pen-based proposals which then had to be typed into Excel spreadsheets. Computerize entire event contract preparation time.
External				
Increasing customer satisfaction, which in turn, will result in repeat business and referrals.	Increased degree of customer satisfaction.	Degree of customer satisfaction.	At least, 85 % in 1 Year.	– Routinely conduct surveys among customers – Give extra rewards to customer-oriented employees – Enable staff to work more independently of event manager.
Delivering exceptional customer service and value.	Reduced number of customer complaints.	Number of customer complaints.	Decrease by at least 30% per year.	– Formulate a customer complaints procedure and execute it routinely – Increase face time that event manager is able to spend with clients on day before and day of their events.

Table continues on next page.

Table 4.4. Ravenwood Golf Club's Project Balanced Scorecard Continued

Project Critical Success Factors	Project Objectives	Project Performance Measures	Project Targets	Project Improvement Actions
External				
Increasing managerial client facing time .	Increased managerial client facing time.	Managerial client facing time.	20% increase within 6 months.	Let staff work more independently.
Letting key personnel spend more on growing the business through client contact, proactive marketing, and sales.	Higer business growth.	Time spend by personnel on growing the business through client contact, proactive marketing, and sales.	15% increase within 1 year.	Formulate procedures for proposal preparation and presentation.
Internal				
Reducing time associated with the proposal process.	Reduced time associated with the proposal process.	Proposal process time.	Decrease of at least 35% within 1 year.	Use of linked spreadsheets to eliminate rework and duplication of data entry.
Reducing lead time associated with presenting contract to client.	Reduced lead time associated with presenting contract to client.	Lead time associated with presenting contract to client.	Decrease of at least 35% within 6 months.	Use of laptop during event planning meetings. Ability to enter event service and menu options, calculate costs and make changes with client present. Able to generate cost and complete contract and event planning more quickly.

Table continues on next page.

Reducing waste caused by nonvalue-added, labor-intensive steps required by the original current-state processes.	Reduced waste.	Waste caused by nonvalue-added and labor-intensive steps.	Decrease of at least 20% within 1 year.	Develop new procedures to streamline processes, reduce/eliminate waste, and standardize procedures across events to eliminate duplication of effort and facilitate employee. Develop measurements of process times, resource usage (i.e. time in minutes/hours or steps), food and beverages used, wastage.
Establishing standard processes and process training to reduce training time, and training costs.	Efficient training process.	Efficiency training process.	Increase of at least 10% within 1 year.	Develop procedures to streamline training process and standardize procedures. Add preevent set-up person to collect all related supplies the day before the event to decrease set up time. Introduce supply carts to enable staff to move from table to table set without having to walk back and forth between each table and fixed supply tables.
Knowledge and Learning				
Empowering staff and developing human potential to work independently with minimum managerial supervision.	Staff work independently with minimum managerial supervision.	Number of employees which work independently with minimum managerial supervision.	Minimum of 90% of all employees, within one year, will be able to work independently with only the basic training.	Initial start-of-season training and storyboards for reference during set up process.

Table continues on next page.

Table 4.4. Ravenwood Golf Club's Project Balanced Scorecard

	Knowledge and Learning			
Project Critical Success Factors	*Project Objectives*	*Project Performance Measures*	*Project Targets*	*Project Improvement Actions*
Teamwork and commitment.	Happy workforce.	Percent of personnel who feel they have challenging work.	At least 85 % in 1 year.	– Introduce the ambition meeting. – Provide training in effective leadership—limited to key employees. – Measure degree of satisfaction regarding internal customers. – Offer a prize for the *"Best Improvement Suggestion of the Month."* – Reward employees with gift cards for superior performance.

Ravenwood Golf Club's Project Strategic Map

The position of Ravenwood Golf Club's project objectives, within the four perspectives, and their mutual relationships are made visible in Figure 4.9. In this cause effect chain, Ravenwood Golf Club's project objectives are interrelated and affect one another. In this figure, all project objectives are formulated and illustrated; they all lead to a final project objective, namely, *increased savings*. The cause-and-effect chain has been used as a tool for communicating the Project BSC within the project team, with the customer and with the management. Through the efforts of this project we were able to reduce the costs associated with the suspect process by 82%. These savings are expected to increase as the business grows. Labour hours were reduced by 50% from the start of the 2006 season to the completion of the season. The client facing time was increased by 20%.

Waterbury General Hospital's Project BSC

Waterbury General Hospital is a part of the Holden Healthcare network in the state of Connecticut. The Holden Healthcare network is comprised

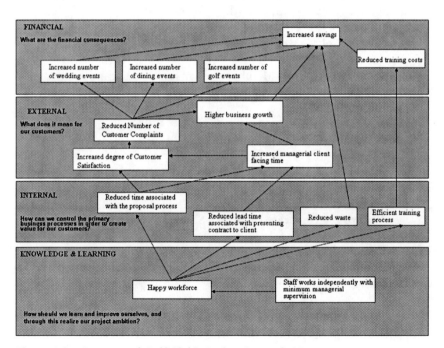

Figure 4.9.   Ravenwood Golf Club's Project Strategic Map.

of two primary hospitals, four after hour's medical centers, and one cancer research center. Waterbury General Hospital was built in 1959 and is the oldest of the hospitals in the network. At the time the structure was built, the community population was approximately 80,000 residents. Since then, the population has swollen to over 120,000 residents. Waterbury General has been struggling to keep up with not only technology, but also patient flow. The president of the hospital has embraced TPS-Lean Six Sigma and is using this model as a boilerplate for other departments down the road. There is strong support for the TPS-Lean Six Sigma initiative throughout upper management, and the workforce has been briefed on the value of the TPS-Lean Six Sigma initiative.

This project was executed in the Waterbury General Hospital Pediatrics Department. The pediatrics department is responsible for the care of all young patients at the hospital including infants to early age teenagers. The department consists of eight full-time pediatricians, five patient service representatives (PSR), and an assortment of nurses, medical assistants, and administrative positions.

The TPS-Lean Six Sigma project team consists of the following members:

Sponsor:	Eric Lawrence – President and CEO
Champion:	Adam Schafer – Pediatrics General Manager
Master Black Belt:	Chuck Hardy.
Black Belt:	Deborah Crowley – PSR
Green Belt:	Meg Foranzo – RN

Additional Project Team Members:
Jeavanna Fuino – Admin
Steven Kang – PSR
Shirley McMillin – RN
Sandra Willard – Medical Assistant

The Shared Project Ambition of Waterbury General Hospital is shown in the box below.

Waterbury General Hospital's Shared Project Ambition

Project Vision
We will enhance the efficiency of Waterbury General Hospital Pediatrics Department by:

1.   Reduce admittance cycle time by 20%.
2.   Reduce discharge cycle time by 20%.
3.   Reduce material costs by 35%.

4. Reduce patient complaints by 50%.

5. Achieve annual savings of $350,000.

6. Empowering and developing the staff within the pediatrics department

Project Mission

Our aim is to improve department throughout by eliminating waste and improving patient flow and patient satisfaction within Waterbury General Hospital Pediatrics Department.

Project Values

Our team members are being led by the following core values:

Compassionate Care: We treat every child, every family, and our visitors, with the respect, kindness, and hope. We project a family-centered spirit at every opportunity. We recognize the importance of each situation. We look for ways to ease suffering and provide comfort.
Integrity: We are ethical and honest in our work and in the way we interact with others. We keep our promises and admit our mistakes. We are responsible for all our actions.
Excellence: We rely on exceptional people to provide exceptional quality health care and services. We set high standards and we support each other. We value each patient and recognize there may be cultural differences that make us strong. We are proud of our achievements and results.

Table 4.5 shows Waterbury General Hospital's most important project critical success factors which are related to Waterbury General Hospital's shared project ambition statement. These are factors, which make the

**Table 4.5. Waterbury General Hospital's
Project Critical Success Factors**

Financial	*External*
Annual savings of $350,000	Reducing patient complaints by 50%
Reduce material costs by 35%	Compassionate care, excellence, and integrity

Internal	*Knowledge and Learning*
Reduce admittance cycle time by 20%	Empowering and developing the staff within
Reduce discharge cycle time by 20%	the Pediatrics Department

Waterbury General Hospital's TPS-Lean Six Sigma project unique. These factors have been identified in Waterbury General Hospital's shared project ambition and are in their Project BSC further developed in Table 4.6.

Waterbury General Hospital's Project Strategic Map

The position of Waterbury General Hospital's project objectives, within the four perspectives, and their mutual relationships are made visible in Figure 4.10. In this cause effect chain, Waterbury General Hospital's project objectives are interrelated and affect one another. In Figure 4.10, all project objectives are formulated and illustrated; they all lead to a final project objective, namely, annual savings of $350,000. This cause-and-effect chain has been used as a tool for communicating the Project BSC within the project team, with the customer and with management.

The Waterbury General Hospital TPS-Lean Six Sigma project completed 2 weeks after the planned completion date. All project goals were realized. The project team worked relentlessly on mapping the

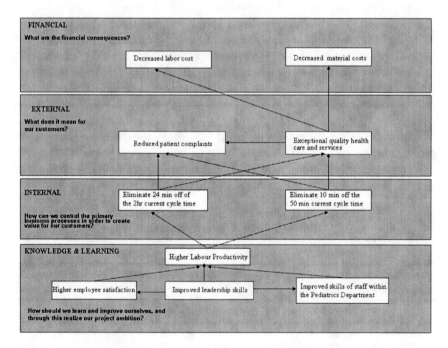

Figure 4.10.   Waterbury General Hospital's Project Strategic Map.

Table 4.6. Waterbury General Hospital's Project Balanced Scorecard

		Financial		
Project Critical Success Factors	Project Objectives	Project Performance Measures	Project Targets	Project Improvement Actions
Annual savings of $350,000.	Decreased labor cost from reductions in head-count.	Number eliminated positions in Department Headcount.	2 positions in 2007.	– Value stream map the entire admittance and discharge pro-cesses. Note all process steps and include all associated paperwork or clerical PC enter-ing.
	Decreased labor cost from admittance cycle time reduction.	Annual savings.	$350,000 in 2007.	
	Decreased labor cost from discharge cycle time reduction.	Cycle time x labor rate.	Reduce by 20% in 2007.	– Eliminate nonvalue added activities in the process.
Reduce material costs by 35%.	Decreased material costs from reduction of redun-dant paperwork, forms, and other materials.	Cycle time x labor rate.	Reduce by 20% in 2007.	– Eliminate all duplicated infor-mation including paper forms, unnecessary documents, etc.
		Material budget.	Reduce by 35% in 2007.	– Put in place a new departmen-tal database program that will track all patients and log all forms and information.

Table continues on next page.

Table 4.6. Waterbury General Hospital's Project Balanced Scorecard Continued

Project Critical Success Factors	Project Objectives	Project Performance Measures	Project Targets	Project Improvement Actions
Financial				
				– Streamlining the entire process flow of the department including reducing cycle time, eliminating redundant work, and eliminating material costs will allow the department to reduce two full-time positions; it will also result in measurable budget savings.
External				
Reducing patient complaints by 50%.	Reduced patient complaints.	Number of patient complaints.	Reduce average by 50% per month; Current rate is 6/100 (6%).	– Institute patient satisfaction surveys. – Solicit patients and families for improvement suggestions.
Compassionate care, excellence, and integrity.	Exceptional quality health care and services.	Patient satisfaction.	At least 90% within 1 year.	– Taking a proactive approach to patient satisfaction.
Internal				
Reduce admittance cycle time by 20%.	Eliminate 24 min. off of the 2 hour current cycle time.	Total time from patient entry (login) to seating.	Reduce total time by 20% in 2007.	– Value stream the process and remove nonvalue added tasks and activities.

Reduce discharge cycle time by 20%.	Eliminate 10 min. off the 50 min. current cycle time.	Total time from start of signing discharge form to patient exit.	Reduce total time by 20% in 2007.	– Review all clerical processing and eliminate redundant work. – Eliminating redundant processes and paperwork, and migrating to a new database system will reduce the cycle times of both admissions and discharge.

Knowledge and Learning

Empowering and developing the staff within the Pediatrics Department.	Improved skills of staff within the Pediatrics Department.	Amount of staff that receive training.	At least 50% of the current staff receive additional training within 1 year.	– Hold department meeting discussing the importance of continuing education. – Provide dollar incentive for employees wishing to seek continuing education. – Post suggested workshops on message board. Providing a higher degree of training and adding incentive to the employee for seeking training will improve the knowledge of the workforce and increase innovation.
	Higher employee satisfaction.	Employee satisfaction	Minimum 80%, within 1 year.	Support staff in formulating their PBSC and introduce ambition meeting within Pediatrics Department.
	Higher labor productivity.	Labor productivity.	Increase with at least 10% within 6 months.	Standardize roles and responsibilities within Pediatrics Department.
	Improved leadership skills.	Percent of personnel who find they are working under effective leadership.	Minimum 90% within 1 year.	Develop coaching skills of PD-manager.

process and detailing all value added and nonvalue added tasks. The project team then started to attack the processes with the most waste. They successfully eliminated and consolidated 12 patient forms and rolled out a new database that has shown to be very successful. All of the forms are completed on a pc terminal and if there is an incomplete entry, there is instant notification and help provided on-screen. As a result, there have been virtually zero form errors and all forms have been processed instantly. This has reduced the overall average admittance time from 2 hours to 34 minutes, and the discharge time from 50 minutes to 15 minutes. Both of these results far exceeded the 20% reduction the team was looking for. In addition, the team identified and was able to eliminate or reduce the cost of consumable materials by over 42% of the planned budget. There were 2 full-time positions eliminated due to the reduction in needed paperwork. The only target that was not exceeded was the amount of training received by the staff. While 12 members of the staff received training, that was 50% of the staff and this target was realized but not exceeded. Overall, as a result of the project, the monthly budget savings was $32,000 and is expected to reach $384,000 for the year, exceeding the planned savings of $350,000 by $34,000.

The president was excited about the results of the project and threw a "celebration" party (picnic) for the whole hospital workforce. There was an article written in the hospital newsletter and members of the team were photographed and told stories about the project. There are currently two other project teams forming for new projects in other hospital departments including the emergency room and the neurology department.

4.2.3 The Personal Balanced Scorecard

The Personal Balanced Scorecard (PBSC) encompasses your personal vision, mission, key roles, critical success factors, objectives, performance measures, targets, and improvement actions. These are divided into four perspectives: the internal, the external, the knowledge and learning, and the financial perspectives. Your personal vision can be thought of as a synonym for your dream. Your dream is related to a higher calling. Everyone has a higher calling, a so called inner assignment. We should be aware of this higher calling and must have the courage to follow this in order to be successful in life. Bill Gates's dream about 30 years ago was— *A PC on each desk in each house.* Recently he said, "When I was 19, I saw the future and based my career on what I saw. I have been right." Oprah Winfrey's dream was/is—*Using television as a service to God.* Walt Disney's dream was—*Making life more enjoyable, and fun.* Albert Einstein's dream was— *Understanding the universe.* Henry Ford's dream was— *I will build a motor car for the great multitude ... constructed of the best materials, by the best men to be hired, after the simplest designs that modern engineering can devise ... so low in price that no man making a good salary will be unable to own one—and enjoy with his family the blessing of hours of pleasure in God's great open spaces.* They all identified and leveraged their authentic dream, responded to their dream with love and passion, succeeded by living according to their dream and doing related work they love(d), had/have faith in themselves, and had/have the courage to pursue their dream. We admire them because of their genius, achievements and added value to others. Anyone can increase their ability and deliver peak performances, because all of us have the genius within us to do so. You must have a dream in life if you expect exceptional success. You will surely have it, since people who give their peak performance attract success. This is strongly related to the Law of Attraction. The Law of Attraction has it roots in Quantum Physics. According to this law, thoughts have an energy that attracts like energy. Once you are aware of this law and how it works, you can start to use it to deliberately attract what you want into your life. The Law of Attraction simply says that you attract into your life whatever you think about. Remember what Buddha said: "What you have become is the result of what you have thought." Your dominant thoughts will find a way to manifest. Whatever you focus on the most is what will be most attracted to your life. Some definitions of the Law of Attraction:

- Like attracts like, energy attracts like energy, you are a living magnet.
- You get what you think about, whether wanted or unwanted, you get what you put your energy and focus on.

The discussed role models have proven that if someone has a clear authentic dream, responses to it with love and passion, has the courage to pursue this dream, has faith in himself, and lives according to his dream, this dream will guide that person's life and will result in purposeful and resolute actions. They took the responsibility to identify their authentic dream and to respond to it with love. Stop complaining and do not blame others for your failures. Take the initiative and the responsibility to develop and implement an authentic dream as well, and keep it at the forefront of your mind each day. You also have the ability to deliver peak performances, because you have the genius within you to do so and you have a higher calling as well. The only thing you need is to do is to discover this and to respond to it with love, faith, and courage. It's your ethical duty to do so. Your dream is an integral part of your personal ambition (comprised of personal vision, mission and key roles). Your personal ambition or Personal Brand is your personal lighthouse keeping you steadily on the course of your dream.

Your personal ambition entails the first part of your PBSC, which allows you to express your wishes, desires, intentions, identity, ideals, values, and driving force, as well as, to gain more insight about yourself. Self-knowledge or self-image includes self-awareness *and self-regulation*. Self-awareness is the ability to recognize and understand your strengths, weaknesses, needs, values, ambition, moods, emotions, and drives, as well as, their effect on others. Self-regulation is the ability to control or redirect disruptive impulses, feelings, and moods. Self- awareness and self-regulation have an impact on self-confidence, trustworthiness, integrity, and openness to learn. It is an inner and spiritual learning process, which is related to both emotional and spiritual intelligence. This inner process starts with self-knowledge, or *knowing*. By routine application of the PBSC method, self-knowledge will lead to *wisdom*. Between knowing and wisdom lies an enormous distance which can be reduced by the PBSC system.

The PBSC strikes a personal note in terms of self-examination. The changes in the thinking process and mindset which forms its foundation are meant to prepare you for action and to stimulate your resolution, passion and energy so as to create inner involvement for work. By formulating and implementing your PBSC, you raise a mirror to yourself. On the basis of insights acquired through PBSC, you become more proactive and self-assured. Application of the PBSC method involves working smarter instead of harder through learning and knowledge of the self. We become more creative as we grow more conscious of ourselves—our real character, inner processes and driving forces. To fathom your life, or to get a better self-image and greater self-knowledge, together with challenges, your learning ability gets greater. This leads to inner harmony. Through PBSC, you will be able to change your behaviour, to unlearn bad habits and to let go of things. Change in behaviour at the individual level results in collective behavioural change, which we call organizational change. The more innovative that an organization wants to be, the more its employees and managers should develop self-knowledge. The connections between employee behavior and organizational performance can be illustrated as follows: A study among 800 Sears stores in the United States found that a 5% increase in employee attitude scores resulted in a 1.3% increase in customer satisfaction scores as well as a 0.5% increase in revenues (Rucci et al., 1998).

Working smarter is also related to the effective use of and the balance between the left and right side of your brain. This is one of the results of applying the PBSC method along with the breathing and silence exercise and the Plan-Do-Act-Challenge cycle (both will be discussed later). With the left half of your brain having mainly an analytical, logical and quantitative function, the right half of your brain has an intuitive and holistic function. Many people do not have a proper balance between the left and right sides of their brain. Most people only use the left side of their brain; because of this, they miss opportunities that allow them to become more adept at using the right hemisphere of the brain and to deal with complex problems in an integrated way. The personal vision, mission, and key roles relate specifically to the right side of the brain, while the personal objectives, performance measures, targets, and improvement actions within the PBSC have to do with the left side of the brain. Based on your PBSC, you will start acting intuitively thus making more effective use of the right side of your brain. Research has shown that top managers who believe in their intuition and make decisions intuitively are usually the most successful. You will enhance the quality and the performance of your TPS-Lean Six Sigma project if you formulate your PBSC, improve yourself continuously based on this, and align your PBSC with the related Project BSC. This process will be discussed later in this chapter.

In recent years, we have applied the PBSC system in large companies in many countries, and have observed that this system has also a very positive affect on the self-awareness and individual's self-regulation. People, who have a high degree of self-awareness, recognize how their feelings affect them, others, and their performance. This leads to a more astute understanding of their clients, due to the fact that they are more honest, proactive, innovative, and goal oriented, speak openly, have self-confidence, and willing to take calculated risks. People who have a high degree of self-regulation are able to create an environment of trust and fairness, can master their emotions, and are action oriented, trustworthy, and very effective in leading change. We have also noticed that the PBSC system offers and excellent framework for successful personal branding. We refer here to Rampersad's (2007) new book *Personal Brand Management; The Way to Powerful and Sustainable Personal Branding*.

The PBSC allows you to formulate your own ambition, objectives, principles, standards, and values and makes these available to you and to those you care for, to the benefit of the ideas you hold. Peter Senge said that when an organization uses the personal ambition of its employees as a starting point, it becomes an instrument of self-realization, rather than a machine, which enslaves them. He points out that managers usually assume that encouraging employees to develop and express their personal ambition will only lead to organizational anarchy and confusion. However, it has been seen that these assumptions are unfounded, and that most employees are more than willing to align their personal ambition with their organization's ambition. Stephen Covey argues for an "inside out" approach. He explains that your starting point must be the core of your identity. In order to improve your relations with others, you must begin with having a better relationship with yourself. In other words, you must succeed in your personal life before you can achieve something in the world, and that you must be loyal to your self before you make promises to others. He has described it as a natural learning process, which through awareness of independence will lead to awareness of reciprocal dependence.

Figures 2.2 and 4.11 show the framework of the PBSC. Every element in this framework will be explained in detail, see below boxed text.

Personal Balanced Scorecard

Personal Vision

Your personal vision statement is a description of the way in which you want to realize your dream on long term, indicating where you are going, which values and principles guide you on your way, what you want to achieve, what your long-term intentions are, what talents, skills and experience you need to add value to others, where you would want to be at the end of your life, what you hope to become, where would you like your life to be headed, the ideal characteristics you want to possess, your ideal job situation, and what you want to be. Your personal vision takes care of inner guidance and determines today's actions in order to reach the most desired future. It functions as an ethical compass, which gives meaning to your life. It is a concrete translation of your inner longings, and keeps in mind the four aforementioned perspectives. Your inner voice and convictions as to how life should play an important role in this. Your personal vision must result in purposeful long term actions and efforts to realize your dreams. It gives direction to your efforts. An example of a personal vision statement:

Always act and serve out of love. I want to realize this in the following manner:

1. Inspire others and earn their respect.
2. Continuously pay attention to optimize my spiritual development, my emotional balance and physical health.
3. Control my learning process purposefully, and, on this basis, be intuitive and creative.
4. Develop my moral character and personal integrity.
5. Keep my financial independence.

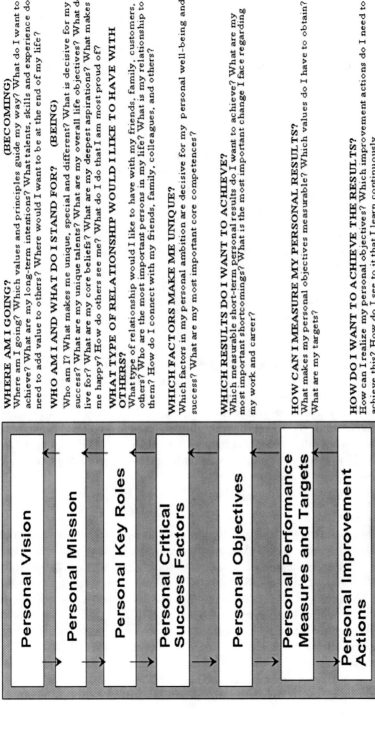

WHERE AM I GOING? (BECOMING)
Where am I going? Which values and principles guide my way? What do I want to achieve? What are my long-term intentions? What talents, skills and experience do I need to add value to others? Where would I want to be at the end of my life?

WHO AM I AND WHAT DO I STAND FOR? (BEING)
Who am I? What makes me unique, special and different? What is decisive for my success? What are my unique talents? What are my overall life objectives? What do I live for? What are my core beliefs? What are my deepest aspirations? What makes me happy? How do others see me? What do I do that I am most proud of?

WHAT TYPE OF RELATIONSHIP WOULD I LIKE TO HAVE WITH OTHERS?
What type of relationship would I like to have with my friends, family, customers, and others? Who are the most important persons in my life? What is my relationship to them? How do I connect with my friends, family, colleagues, and others?

WHICH FACTORS MAKE ME UNIQUE?
Which factors in my personal ambition are decisive for my personal well-being and success? What are my most important core competences?

WHICH RESULTS DO I WANT TO ACHIEVE?
Which measurable short-term personal results do I want to achieve? What are my most important shortcomings? What is the most important change I face regarding my work and career?

HOW CAN I MEASURE MY PERSONAL RESULTS?
What makes my personal objectives measurable? Which values do I have to obtain? What are my targets?

HOW DO I WANT TO ACHIEVE THE RESULTS?
How can I realize my personal objectives? Which improvement actions do I need to achieve this? How do I see to it that I learn continuously

Personal Vision

Personal Mission

Personal Key Roles

Personal Critical Success Factors

Personal Objectives

Personal Performance Measures and Targets

Personal Improvement Actions

Figure 4.11. PBSC Framework (Rampersad, 2006, 2007).

The four basic perspectives—*internal, external, knowledge & learning, and financial*—are clearly recognizable in this example. These perspectives must be an integral part of personal ambition in order to be able to formulate the PBSC completely.

Personal Mission

Your personal mission statement encompasses your philosophy of life and your overall objectives, indicating who you are, what do you stand for, what makes you unique, special and different, what is decisive for your success, what are your unique talents, what are your overall life objectives, what do you live for, what are your core beliefs, what are your deepest aspirations, what makes you happy, how do others see you, what do I do that you are most proud of. These are seemingly easy questions, which are difficult to answer and nevertheless central to your sense of self. Imagine stepping outside of your physical body, taking a look at the real you, and ask yourself some of these questions. Listen carefully to the answers of your inner voice. "Who am I?" is an identity question. It initiates self-examination of your *personal identity* (the unique position you find yourself in) and a voyage of discovery.

An example of a personal mission statement: *To be authentic and gracious, creating joy and deeper meaning in others' lives based on my uniqueness.*

Personal mission is aimed at the *being,* and personal vision at *becoming*. Your personal mission and vision have to do with your inner need and motives, as well as your self-awareness, imagination, and conscience. Through your conscience you realize what your principles are, which can be effectively rendered through your talents. Thus, you will be able to give direction to your life through your mission and vision. They need to be formulated in such a way that you will be stimulated to reflect on your life and on everything you undertake.

Personal Key Roles

Your key roles relate to the way you wish to fulfil the many essential roles in your life and thus realize your personal mission and vision. They indicate what type of relationship you would like to have with your friends, family, customers, and others, who the most important persons in your life are, what your relationship to them is, how you connect with your life companion, friends, family, colleagues, and others, and for whom you exist. The formulation of your key roles will also result in work life balance and a better self-image, which in turn, improves your learning ability. Key roles have to do primarily with the external perspective in the PBSC. Elements from the key roles should also be identified as critical success factors and then be translated in the PBSC to personal objectives, performance measures, targets and improvement actions. This will create work-life balance. Some examples of personal key roles:

- *Spouse: To build a future together, in which, I give and receive love, show respect and give trust.*
- *Mother: A support for my children on which they can fall back, and to be there while they strive toward a happy life.*
- *Friend: My friends can always count on me, I will never disappoint them.*
- *Manager: To help make the organization for which I work successful and through this, serve the community.*

The personal ambition statement entails your Personal Brand. You must have a personal ambition statement in life if you expect exceptional success. You will surely have it, since people who give their peak performance attract success. Keep the personal ambition you desire to achieve at the forefront of your mind each day. Personal ambition is simply a set of guiding principles which clearly state who you are, where you are going, where you want to be, which roles are you fulfilling in your life, and so forth. and which embodies your values. It is your personal lighthouse keeping you steadily on the course of your dreams. Personal ambition statements are most effective when they comply with the following criteria:

- The four perspectives—financial, external, internal, and knowledge and learning—are a part of it.
- The emphasis is on unselfishness *and* authenticity.
- Is specific to each person and includes ethical starting points, with an emphasis on your dream, uniqueness, genius, skills, principles, and values.
- Personal mission is short, clear, simple, and formulated in the present tense; it is concrete and may be used as a guideline.
- Is unique for each person and are recognizable as such to others.
- Is formulated positively, in an arresting manner, and are durable. The mission is not time-bound, while the vision is (approximately 10 years).
- Personal vision is ambitious and inspiring; it should give direction to personal initiative and creativity, and combines personal power and energy.
- Personal mission indicates how a person wants to distinguish him or herself in society.

- Is based on self-image, self-knowledge, self-acceptance, and self-development; it requires a positive image of ourselves and of others.

Personal Critical Success Factors

The personal Critical Success Factors (CSFs) are derived from the personal ambition. They are related to the four perspectives, internal, external, knowledge and learning, and financial. A personal ambition without these four perspectives results in an incomplete PBSC. The personal CSFs form the bridge between the personal ambition (long term) and on the other side the personal objectives, performance measures, targets, and improvement actions (short term). This link is made by identifying your personal core competencies in your personal ambition related to the four perspectives. These personal CSFs will then be translated into concrete personal objectives. They are factors, which make you unique and in which you can further develop yourself and make a difference.

Personal Objectives

The central question here is—Which measurable short-term personal results do I want to achieve? Personal objectives describe a result that you want to achieve in order to realize your personal ambition. Your personal ambition is aimed at the long-term future and your personal objectives at the short-term. The personal CSFs form the bridge between these. Your personal objectives are derived from your personal CSFs and from an analysis of your strengths and weaknesses. Each personal CSF has one or more personal objectives that are related to one of the four scorecard perspectives. Make a list of all your strengths and weaknesses. You have to acknowledge things, which you are not good at. Weaknesses also include habits that restrict you, have an unfavorable influence on your life and deliver poor results. It is also important to focus on things in which you are accomplished, so as to make your performance even better. When analyzing your strengths, ask yourself the following questions—what are some of the strengths that have contributed to my success up to the present? How might these create problems for me in the future? Which problems would I like to solve first? While analyzing your shortcomings, you should think about the following questions—what do you think are your biggest shortcomings? Has anyone ever mentioned any of these shortcomings to you? Can you describe a situation where any of these shortcomings would be a serious handicap? You could also ask yourself this question—what is the most important challenge I face regarding my work and career? Factors that may be related to these questions are, for example, aptitude, talent, ability, intelligence, goal-orientation, perseverance, self-control, health, integrity, creativity, tolerance, enthusiasm, the home and work environments, responsibility, job prestige, status, power, freedom, having more free time, and so on. Some examples of personal objectives could be—appreciation from customers, improved leadership skills, inner peace, and greater knowledge. Your objectives could be to develop a dynamic, charismatic personality and to become a highly competent, strong, disciplined, calm and a decent individual.

Personal Performance Measures

Personal performance measures are standards to measure the progress of your personal objectives. With it, you can assess your functioning in relation to your personal critical success factors and objectives. Without performance measures and targets, it is difficult to coach yourself with feedback. Performance measures urge you to action if they are related to your objectives, giving you a certain direction. They measure the changes, and compare this with the norm, and thus, in time, give you information about steering yourself. This section of the PBSC deals with the following questions—how can I measure my personal results? What makes my personal objectives measurable? Some examples of personal performance measures: *body weight, number of innovative ideas, ratio earnings and expenses, number of hours of quality time with my family.* A whole list of personal performance measures according to each PBSC perspective can be found in Rampersad (2006).

Personal Targets

A personal target is a quantitative objective of a personal performance measure. It is a value that is pursued and then assessed through a personal performance measure. Targets indicate values that you want to achieve, and depend on your level of ambition. Some examples of personal targets could be—*increase of 15% over 2007, minimum 85% in 2 years, and maximum of 92 kg before December 31, 2007.*

Personal Improvement Actions

Personal improvement actions are strategies used to realize your personal ambition. They are utilized to develop your skills, improve your behavior, master yourself, and improve your performance. *How* is central here: How do I want to achieve my personal results? How can I realize my personal objectives? How can I improve my behavior?

We have introduced the TPS-Lean Six Sigma Personal BSCsoft in the Appendix, which is an interactive software system that will assist you with the formulation and implementation of your PBSC. The PBSC can be defined as the following formula—

PBSC = personal vision + mission + key roles + critical success factors + objectives + performance measures + targets + improvement actions (divided along the four perspectives: internal, external, knowledge & learning, and financial).

Personal Ambition = personal vision + mission + key roles (divided along the four perspectives: internal, external, knowledge & learning, and financial).

Dave Jones's Personal Balanced Scorecard

To illustrate the foregoing, Dave Jones's personal ambition is shown in the box given here, which he formulated with the help of the breathing and silence exercise (described in the next section). This is his Personal Brand, which is related to his dream. His related PBSC is included in the Tables 4.1 and 4.2. Dave Jones is the CEO of Business Jet, an airliner for business people. The complete OBSC of this company is described in the previous section.

Dave Jones's Personal Ambition

Personal Vision

To be authentic and gracious, creating joy and deeper meaning in others' lives based on my uniqueness. I want to realize this in the following way:

- Strive for physical and mental health.
- Build strong, viable organizations and guide people to healthful and joyful living.
- Experience enjoyment by sharing knowledge, taking initiatives, accepting challenges, and improving myself continuously.
- Retain financial stability.

Personal Mission

Live with integrity and do things that make a difference in the lives of others

Personal Key Roles

In order to achieve my vision, the following key roles have top priority:

- *Spouse*: Build a future with my wife together, in which I give and receive love, show respect and give trust.
- *Father*: Promote the capabilities and creativity of my children continuously and to help them reach a happy existence.
- *Manager*: Help the organization where I work become successful and by doing this serve society.
- *Scholar*: Keep developing my knowledge and strive for perfection.

Table 4.7 shows Dave Jones's most important critical success factors which are related to his personal ambition statement. These are factors which make him unique and in which he will further develop and distinguish himself. These factors have been identified in his personal ambition statement and are in his PBSC further developed (see Table 4.8). Work and spare time are explicitly included.

Because there are many possible improvement actions, it is recommended to make a selection through prioritizing. Rampersad (2006) introduced an integral method to give priority to these improvement actions in.

Table 4.7. Dave Jones's Personal Critical Success Factors

Internal	External
• To be authentic and gracious. • Strive for physical and mental health. • Experience enjoyment.	• Creating joy and deeper meaning in others' lives. • Build strong, viable organizations and guide people to healthful and joyful living. • Live with integrity and do things that make a difference in the lives of others. • Build a future with my wife together, in which I give and receive love, show respect and give trust. • Promote the capabilities and creativity of my children continuously and to help them reach a happy existence. • Help the organization where I work become successful and by doing this serve society.
Knowledge and Learning	Financial
• Sharing knowledge, taking initiatives, accepting challenges, and improving myself continuously. • Keep developing my knowledge and strive for perfection.	• Retain financial stability.

Table 4.8. Dave Jones's Personal Balanced Scorecard

		Internal		
Personal Critical Success Factors	*Personal Objectives*	*Personal Performance Measures*	*Personal Targets*	*Personal Improvement Actions*
To be authentic and gracious.	Be happy.	Level of feeling happy.	> 80% of the time.	Starting the day with a breathing and silence exercise, accept new challenges continuously, update my PBSC frequently and ask for feedback.
Strive for physical and mental health.	Emotionally strong.	Number of hours of sleep.	7 hours per day.	Not endlessly continue activities butdefine a deadline and stick to it. Pay attention to the quality of sleep, not the quantity.
	Be physically strong and fit.	Weight.	By June 1, 2007, weight loss of at least 15 lbs.	Continue current diet. Less candy. Red wine instead of beer. Healthy food (fruit/vegetables).
		Body fat.	By May 1, 2007, decrease of 47.4 % to 29.1%	Initiate a training roster. At least 2 times a month a 20 mile bicycle trip. Golf once a week.
		Fit score.	By May 1, 2007, fit score of 27.	Three times a week, exercise at home. Rejoin tennis club.

Experience enjoyment.	No stress.	Level of stress.	Decrease of at least 75% within 6 months.	Learn to do yoga effectively. Balance the times of stress with times of pure relaxation and leisure.
Creating joy and deeper meaning in others' lives. Live with integrity and do things that make a difference in the lives of others.	Satisfaction.	Degree of satisfaction of others with regard to my actions.	Satisfaction score of at least 80% within half a year.	Act more helpful without trying to gain profits from it. Provide positive recognitions and say "I'm sorry" and "thank you" more often.
Build strong, viable organizations and guide people to healthful and joyful living.	Be of additional value to organizations.	Satisfaction score of my customers.	Minimum 90% within one year.	Ask feedback from customers and document this. Be more involved in the customer's situation. Demonstrate effective emotional responses in a variety of situations. Get my TPS-Lean Six Sigma Master Black Belt.
Build a future with my wife together, in which I give and receive love, show respect and give trust.	Caring and loving relationship with my wife.	Number of loving and appreciating feedback received from her.	Minimum of once per day.	Make loving remarks myself. Be open for her real needs. Go on vacation three times a year with her.

Table continues on next page.

Table 4.8. Dave Jones's Personal Balanced Scorecard Continued

Personal Critical Success Factors	Personal Objectives	Personal Performance Measures	Personal Targets	Personal Improvement Actions
		Internal		
Promote the capabilities and creativity of my children continuously and to help them reach a happy existence.	Be a good father.	Number of times that my children involve me in their decisions.	Whenever needed.	Show more patience, listen more carefully to them. Take an interested position, not a correcting one. Periodically inform, coach, advice and facilitate. Help them build their confidence and to deeply understand their own strengths and weaknesses.
Help the organization where I work become successful and by doing this serve society.	Greater trust of my employer in fulfilment of my job.	Level of satisfaction of employer.	At least 90% within 1 year.	Improve my leadership skills. Act as a role model. Encourage creativity and innovation in my employees. Act more pro-actively by being attentive of trends and developments. Implement TPS-Lean Six Sigma.
		Knowledge and Learning		
Sharing knowledge and taking initiatives.	Enjoyment	Level of enjoyment	Increase by at least 30% in 2008	Invest more in learning about future trends. Effectively translate creative ideas into business results. Share more.

Accepting challenges and improving myself continuously.	Being innovative.	Number of new successful initiatives.	At least 4 per month.	Develop my self-trust and self-confidence. Get trained in TPS-Lean Six Sigma.
Keep developing my knowledge and strive for perfection.	Improved listening skills.	Number of times positive feedback received from others regarding my listening skills.	At least 1 per week.	Genuinely listen to others with more respect. Invest in ongoing personal development. Listen to people more patiently.
Financial				
Retain financial stability.	Improved asset management.	ROI stock portfolio.	At least 8 % per year.	Pursue proven investment strategies.
Retain financial stability.	Reliable future earnings.	Pension.	13% of gross salary.	Effectively anticipate in future opportunities
		Disability Insurance.	5% of gross salary.	Get disability insurance.
	Manage expenditures.	Income and expense ratio.	Increase of minimum 10% per year.	Be more costs conscious.

Dave Jones's Personal Strategic Map

The position of Dave Jones's objectives, within the four perspectives, and their mutual relationships are made visible in Figure 4.12. In this cause effect chain, his personal objectives are interrelated and affect one another. An objective is used to achieve another objective, which will result in a final objective. His final objective is *being happy*. All his goals result in this final overall objective, which is related to his personal ambition. He has included only the objectives that lead to this final objective. On the basis of this diagram, he is able to gain more insight into himself. It is also a handy tool in communicating his PBSC to a trusted person. A trusted person is somebody who you trust, who respects you, who will guide you, who gives you honest feedback, who has consideration for you, is a mentor with your best interests in mind and offers you good guidance based on your PBSC.

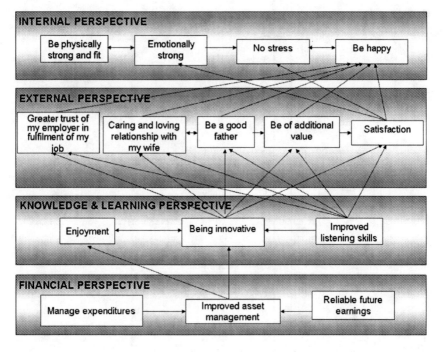

Figure 4.12.   Cause-and-Effect Chain Regarding Dave Jones's Personal Objectives.

4.2.4 An Integrated Breathing and Silence Exercise

By paying attention to your own thoughts by way of a breathing and silence exercise, you can discover your identity and you will be able to distance yourself from your mindset. Through this exercise, you learn to look at life with new eyes, and you can perceive what goes on within you. Because of this, you will know where you stand in life. Formulating your personal ambition can serve as a crowbar to pry off your rusty prejudices which block your creativity. You will be better equipped to create your future and discover a destination for yourself. After all, only if you know yourself will you be able to discover your talents and develop your personal goals. Then, you can put them to the service for yourself and others. Breathing and silence exercises will assist you in turning your attention inward and in gaining control over your awareness. They help in bringing the left and the right side of your brain in balance. Breathing and thinking ability arise from the same center. Once breathing control is achieved, thought control follows and vice versa. There are several forms of breathing and silence exercises. In the following boxed text,

Hubert Rampersad introduced a simple integrated breathing and silence exercise, which has proven to be very effective.

An Integrated Breathing and Silence Exercise (Rampersad, 2006, 2007)

Step 1: Breathing Exercise

1. Look for a quiet spot with fresh air and make sure that you will not be disturbed.
2. Sit in a comfortable chair with an upright back, and keep your back straight, and your shoulders and neck relaxed.
3. Gently rest your hands on your knees, with your palms upward and shut your eyes.
4. Breathe deeply through your nose according to the following rhythm: inhale deeply during a count to four (your stomach fills like a balloon), hold your breath during four counts, and exhale fully during a count of six (your stomach flattens again) and stop for a count. Focus on the rhythm of breathing in and out.
5. Focus your attention entirely on your breathing during this process and observe how your life energy flows through your body. During the breathing, you will become more relaxed. Concentrate on the feeling of relaxation in your whole body (face, shoulders, hands, feet, etc.).

6.   Repeat this process for 10 minutes.

Step 2: Silence Exercise

1.   After finishing the breathing exercise, remain in your sitting position with your back straight, relax your arms, keep your eyes closed, and breathe normally through your nose.
2.   Focus entirely on your thoughts; do not concentrate on anything else. If thoughts do enter, do not force them out but simply let them pass like clouds making way for the beautiful blue sky.
3.   Allow your thoughts to come and go, including the thoughts related to the personal ambition questions.
4.   Be open to all images that come up in your mind. Imagine that you are in a garden and that a wise man approaches you who, after introducing himself, he asks you some of the personal ambition questions mentioned below. Listen carefully to the answers of your inner voice.
5.   Open your eyes after 10 minutes slowly and write the answers of your inner voice in your personal ambition statement and an ambition diary. The purpose of this diary is to be able to use this information to update your personal ambition and Personal Balanced Scorecard and keep record of your experiences and progress in each session.

Personal Ambition Questions

- Where am I going? Where would I like my life to be headed?
- What do I want to be? What do I hope to become? What do I want to achieve with my life?
- What future would I like to have? Where would I want to be at the end of my life? What is my main purpose in life?
- Who am I? What is my identity? Why am I on this earth? Why am I here?
- What do I stand for? What do I live for?
- What makes me unique, special and different?
- What is decisive for my success? What are my unique talents?
- What talents, skills, and experience do I need to add value to others?
- What gives me satisfaction? What am I passionate about?
- What makes me happy or sad?
- When I was happy, what made me so happy?

- What do I enjoy the most? Will I enjoy this in the future as well?
- What is my self-image? How do I see myself?
- What kind of person am I? What do I believe in?
- Which values and principles are closest to my heart, are sacred to me, and are rooted most deeply in my life?
- Which of these values clash with each other and with my strong sides
- How do I create meaning in my life and see to it that everything is not about earning money?
- To what extent is material wealth important to me?
- How do I want to know myself and be known to others?
- What would I like to have engraved on my tombstone?
- Which memories would I like to leave behind after my death?
- What do I want to be remembered for?
- If I die, what legacy would I like to leave behind, and what would I like to have meant to others?
- What difference will it have made that I existed?
- What constraints stand in the way of realizing that future? What weaknesses do I have to deal with those constraints?
- What prevents me from being who I want to be and what I want to be?
- Who will find me and my unique strengths valuable in the market-place?
- What do others say about me? What do I think about others?
- How much do I know about my audience?
- What are my ambitions and deepest aspirations about the community in which I want to live? What do I want to help realize?
- What is good and what is bad?
- What do I most want to learn? Which habits would I like to unlearn? What do I very much like to do? What do I think is very important? What do I find nice and attractive? What am I willing to sacrifice to realize my objectives? What do I really want?
- What do I want to invest in life and what do I want to gain from it?
- How would I prefer my daily life to be?
- In which kind of environment do I prefer to be?
- How is my health?
- What are the five best qualities of individuals who I admire?
- To what extent are spiritual values important to me? What do I think of religion?

- Who are the most important persons in my life? What is my relationship to them?
- How do I connect with my life companion, friends, family, colleagues, and others?
- What type of relationship would I like to have with my friends, family, customers, and others?
- Why do I do what I do? What is the importance of what I do?
- What am I good at and what not? In what did I fail? What are my biggest failures?
- What are my problems? What are the effects of my problems on my relationships with others? What effects have the problems on my physical health?
- Why did I go to work for my present employer?
- How am I at work?
- What have I done up till now, and what have I achieved?
- What is difficult for me to give up in my private, social, and business life?
- Which social questions intrigue me? Which social contributions would I like to make?
- What do I want to be in my organization? What am I trying to achieve? What is keeping me back?
- How can I serve mankind?
- Which contribution am I trying to make to the realization of my organizational ambition?
- What are the most important motivators in my job?
- To which job do I aspire? What are my wishes? What do I strive for? What are my concerns?
- What is happening to my profession, material possessions, family, life companion, friends, and others?
- Why am I active in a certain club?
- Will the things mentioned above still be important to me in 10 years from now?

If you involve a trusted person as a personal coach, allow this person to help you with the breathing and silence exercise by:

1. Counting softly
2. Reminding you to allow your thoughts to come and go

3. Asking you several of the personal ambition questions, and pausing between the questions to allow time for thought.

4. Helping you with the selection of these questions

5. Helping you to keep record of your experiences and progress during the exercise

All the seemingly simple personal ambition questions are difficult to answer, when people are not open, who do not want to make an effort to find out what they want from their life and are blind to it. The breathing and silence exercise is meant to create an atmosphere of silence and inner peace, so that you will be able to answer these questions. By doing these exercises for 10–20 minutes (later to be expanded to 30–40 minutes), you will be able to achieve a lot of things on your own. This exercise allows you to think deeply about yourself and makes you aware of yourself and your core beliefs. By questioning yourself and listening intently to your inner voice, which systematically answers the above questions for you, you will be able to discover and change your obstructive beliefs. By doing this, you will gain more insight into the workings of your mind and the influence this has on your personal behavior, thoughts, and learning ability. Through this you can also accomplish the following—

- To enable you to come into contact with your self, and to clarify your personal ambition, and the human values within you.
- To reach a mental state wherein you can forget about yourself and feel happy.
- Increase your personal effectiveness and deliver mind-expanding performances.
- Discover your subconscious motives and through this get more out of yourself and coach yourself effectively.
- Understand your thoughts better and thus control your inner conflicts (between feelings and reason) better, and come in contact with your inner truth.
- Deal with your environment with greater inner peace, harmony, self-confidence, and involvement.
- Create positive energy and utilize this effectively for the sake of yourself and others.
- Make optimum use of your personal abilities and capabilities, and eliminate annoying behaviour.
- Think and act more proactively, deal with your attitude in a more conscious way, and create a positive atmosphere.
- Deal better with emotions, stress, and burnout.

- Divide your attention more satisfactorily between work, hobbies, and family.
- To improve your personal learning style, as well as, your self-aware-ness, self-discipline and consciousness and about self-responsibility.
- Formulate and implement your personal ambition and PBSC effec-tively.

4.2.5 Developing Personal Integrity Based on the Personal Balanced Scorecard

Formulating your PBSC and finding the proper balance between your personal ambition and your behavior, results in inner peace and personal integrity. People with this perspective on life matter to one another and create a stable basis for their own credibility. The balancing process is about the interaction between your aspirations, intentions, purpose, principles, ethical standards, and values—in other words, your personal ambition—and how others interpret you (your ethical behavior). There is always a potential difference (which is often difficult to accept) between how you see yourself (who you want to be), and how others see and judge you. To become the person envisioned in your personal ambition, you also have to know how others see you and what they think of you. When you know this, your self-knowledge increases and you are able to improve the effectiveness of your actions. Therefore, this process of developing self-knowledge involves the establishment of a balance between your personal ambition (which envisions a higher level of consciousness) and your personal behavior (which refers to your present behavior) (see Figure 4.13). In order to achieve real personal improvement and growth, it is necessary first to find a balance between your personal behavior and your personal ambition. The central questions in this contemplative process are:

- Do I act in accordance with my conscience?
- Have I followed my conscience?
- Have I done what was right?
- Is there consistency between what I am thinking and what I am doing?
- How do my ideals, ambitions, intentions, needs, and deepest desires fit my present actions?
- Are my thoughts and my practices the same?
- Do I act in accordance with my personal ambition?

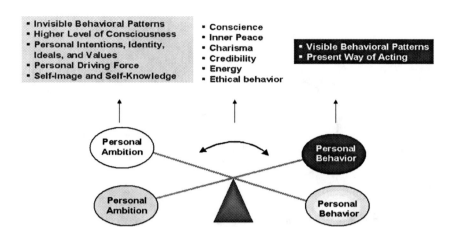

Figure 4.13.   Aligning Personal Ambition with Personal Behavior.

- Does my personal ambition reflect my desire to act ethically?
- Are there contradictions in my personal ambition?
- In what way, does my behavior influence my views, and vice versa?

Your personal ambition and your practices must be the same. When people find harmony between their personal ambition and their personal behavior, they will not come into conflict with their conscience.

Then, you can work authentically and purposefully at continuous personal improvement and development without wasting energy. Harmony between personal ambition and personal behavior ensures that your deeds are in accordance with your conscience. This also has to do with attentiveness, namely, to continuously perceive what you do and be aware of the influence of your behavior on human beings, animals, plants, and the environment. As this attentiveness develops, your ethical behavior will increase.

4.2.6 Aligning Personal Ambition With Shared Organization and Project Ambition

Matching of the personal ambition with the shared organization and project ambition has to do with reaching a higher degree of compatibility between personal and organizational/project objectives and mutual value addition (as shown in Figures 4.14, and 4.15). A study, by CO2 Partners

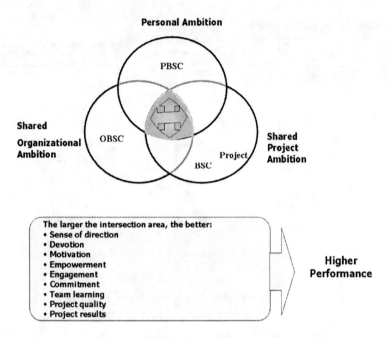

Figure 4.14.   Match Between the Three Ambitions.

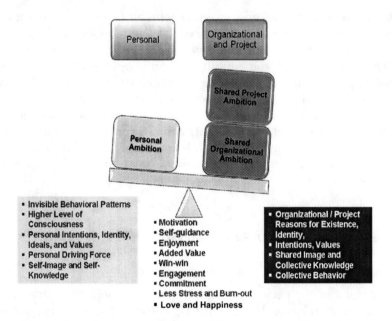

Figure 4.15.   Aligning Personal Ambition with Shared Organization/ Project Ambition.

(2007), found that 30% of U.S. workers values mismatch with the company:

- One in three U.S. workers said their employer's core values are not consistent with their own.
- Fourty-four percent said their values were consistent.
- Eleven percent said they were uncertain about their own core values but never uncomfortable working for their employer.
- Ten percent said they didn't feel their core values had much connection to the work they do.

Another study, by Towers Perrin (2005), found that while many people are keen to contribute more at work, the behavior of their managers and culture of their organizations is actively discouraging them from doing so. The study, the largest of its kind, was carried out among more than 85,000 people working for large and midsize companies in 16 countries on four continents. It shows that there is a vast reserve of untapped "employee performance potential" that could drive better financial results if only companies could tap into this reserve. Instead of matching the right employee to the right position for long-term success, most companies and H/R departments put the emphasis on simply filling the position as quickly as possible. As a result, American businesses are losing money as fast as they're losing employees. Another study, by America Online and Salary.com, found that the average U.S. worker wastes more than 2 hours a day, and that's not including lunch. This means companies spend as much as U.S.$759 billion on salaries annually for which they receive no apparent benefit. Americans who feel bored and underpaid do work hard—at surfing the Internet and catching up on gossip, according to a recent survey of Salary.com (2007). This survey found U.S. workers waste about 20% of their working day. The online survey of 2,057 employees by the online compensation company found about 6 in every 10 workers admit to wasting time at work with the average employee wasting 1.7 hours of a typical 8.5 hour working day. "While a certain amount of wasted time is built into company salary structures, our research indicates that companies with a challenged and engaged workforce can expect more productivity in return," said Bill Coleman, chief compensation officer at Salary.com.

People do not work with devotion or expend energy on something they do not believe in or agree with. Clarity and uniformity of personal and organizational values and principles are therefore essential for the active involvement of people. Research has shown that when an individual has some input regarding the shared ambition that affects his or her work/

project, they will be more supportive, motivated, and receptive toward organizational change. The experience of applying the PBSC in the past 2 years has shown that most employees want to be content and happy at their workplace. They really enjoy going to work and that they strive for a balance between work and life.

Experience tells us that workers are often willing to work together toward the goals of the organization/project with dedication when there is a match between their personal ambition and the shared ambition of their organization/project. It is, therefore, recommended to encourage Executives/TPS-Lean Six Sigma Champions/Master Black Belts/Black Belts/Green Belts/Project Managers and employees/project team members to formulate their PBSC and to let them reflect regarding the balance between their own personal ambition and the shared organization/ project ambition. We recommend that Executives/TPS-Lean Six Sigma Champions/Master Black Belts/Black Belts/Green Belts/Project Managers introduce an *ambition meeting* within the organization/project between the line-Manager and his/her employees and also between the Champions/ Master Black Belts/Black Belts/Green Belts/Project Managers and their project team members. *The ambition meeting is a periodical, informal, voluntary and confidential meeting of a maximum duration of one hour between the manager and his/her employees/project members, with the employee's/project team member's PBSC and the shared organization/project ambition as topics for discussion.*

It is recommended that the ambition meeting is held structurally at least once every month, preferably more often when using this in TPS-Lean Six Sigma projects. The outcome of these *informal* meetings should be highly confidential and should be kept out of the personnel file and not be used against the employee. The Executive/Champion/Master Black Belt/Black Belt/Green Belt/Project Manager should act as a trusted person and informal coach. To be able to talk about the employee's/project team member's PBSC, one needs a confidential, informal and friendly atmosphere, an atmosphere of trust and open communication. This is essential as human values will be discussed. Experience has shown that this intimate atmosphere can be reached if the Executive/Champion/Master Black Belt/Black Belt/Green Belt/Project Manager formulates his/her own PBSC beforehand and shares it with his/her employee. The implementation of the employee's/project team member's PBSC comes up for discussion, and includes private matters, as well as, work-related aspects. At least those private matters that have an impact on job/project performance will be discussed confidentially.

The Executive/Champion/Master Black Belt/Black Belt/Green Belt/ Project Manager can make a selection of the following ambition questions, which he/she can use during in the ambition meeting (Rampersad, 2006):

- Does your personal ambition correspond with the shared organizational/project ambition?
- Can you identify yourself with the shared organization/project ambition? In doing this, do you feel personally involved and addressed by the shared ambition? Are your personal vision, mission, and key roles to be found in the shared ambition? If not, do they have to be expanded or adjusted? Are they acceptable? How can they flourish within the organization/project?
- Is it possible that your personal ambition level or that of the organization/project should be lowered?
- Do your personal values and principles match the shared vision and values? If they conflict, is leaving the best answer? Are your most important personal values done justice to here? Which points in your personal ambition are strengthening and which conflict with the shared ambition? Which ones are neglected?
- Is there a win-win situation between your own interests and the ones of your organization/project?
- Which skills do you need to be a pillar of the organization/project and thus realize the shared ambition? What do you want to gain through this?
- Are your developmental expectations in tune with those of the organization/project?
- Do your job/project requirements match your capabilities and needs?
- How is the implementation of your PBSC and project going? Did you reach your target? Could it be better? Where did it go wrong? What have you learned? What did you unlearn?
- What motivates you? What causes you not to be motivated? What makes you happy or sad? What do you enjoy the most? Where do you stand and where do you want to go? What prevents me from being who you want to be and what you want to be? What do you most want to learn? What do you very much like to do? What do you really want? What gives you satisfaction? In which kind of environment do you prefer to be? What do you want to be in this organization or in the project team? Which contribution are you trying to make to the realization of our shared ambition? To which job, do you aspire? What are your wishes? What do you strive for? What are your concerns?

- Do you have ethical problems on the job/project?
- Have you considered a job change?

Experience has shown that deeper involvement and harmonious working relationships created among employees through the PBSC method and the ambition meeting also reduces organizational stress and burnout. Stress and burnout have also a major negative impact on productivity. According to the experts at the Centers for Disease Control and National Institute for Occupational Safety and Health (Genco, 2007), job burnout is experienced by 25% to 40% of U.S. workers; $300 billion, or $7,500.00 per employee, is spent annually in the U.S. on stress related compensation claims, reduced productivity, absenteeism, health insurance claims, and direct medical expenses (nearly 50% higher for workers who report stress symptoms). Some people decide to look for another job/project after they have discovered themselves and have tried to align their personal ambition with the shared ambition. Sometimes, this can be the best option for both yourself and the organization/project. During the alignment process, the Executive/Champion/Master Black Belt/Black Belt/Green Belt/Project Manager should provide social support to the employees/project team members by being a good listener, providing help, and being someone the employee/team member can rely on.

The alignment of the personal ambition of the project members with the project ambition should be done in the following way: The Executive Management should have an ambition meeting with the Champions, the Champions have an ambition meeting with the Master Black Belts, Master Black Belts should have an ambition meeting with the Black Belts, the Black Belts should have an ambition meeting with the Green Belts, and the team leader should have an ambition meeting with the remaining team members.

In the Waterbury General Hospital's project (see previous section), Chuck Hardy (Master Black Belt) had a ambition meeting with Eric Lawrence (President and CEO). Eric Lawrence had the ambition meeting with Adam Schafer (Champion: Pediatrics General Manager), Adam had the ambition meeting with Deborah Crowley (Black Belt), Deborah had the ambition meeting with Meg Foranzo (Green Belt), and Meg had the ambition meeting with the additional Project Team Members (Jeavanna Fuino, Steven Kang, Shirley McMillin, and Sandra Willard).

Aligning personal ambition with shared organization and project ambition deals with the mutual concordance of the Personal Balanced Scorecard, Organizational Balanced Scorecard and Project Balanced Scorecard (see Figure 4.11). This has an impact on the bonding of the employees/project team members. It gives them the proud feeling that they count (that they are being paid attention to), that they are appreciated as human beings and that they make a useful and valuable contribution to the organization/TPS-Lean Six Sigma project. Employees are stimulated in this way to commitment, dedication and to focus on those activities which create value for clients. This will create a foundation of peace and stability upon which creativity and growth can flourish. The alignment of the personal ambition with the shared ambition has to do with reaching a high degree of compatibility between the PBSC, the OBSC and Project BSC, as shown in Figure 4.16. So there are three alignments: (1) alignment of PBSC with OBSC (2) alignment of PBSC with Project BSC and (3) alignment of the OBSC with Project BSC. Figure 4.17 shows the results of the alignments of these three BSCs, which forms the basis for Organizational Learning, Team Learning and Self-Learning.

4.3 DEPLOYING

Deployment of the Organizational BSC (OBSC) and Project BSC is the second phase in the TPS-Lean Six Sigma Cycle (see Figure 4.1). Here all stakeholders participate in the business strategy by communicating and cascading the corporate scorecard to the scorecards of all the underlying business units and teams, and finally linking the team scorecard to the individual performance plan of the employees. The project deployment planning is described in detail in paragraph 6.2.

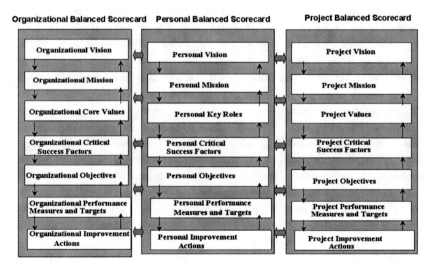

Figure 4.16.   Aligning PBSC with OBSC and Project BSC.

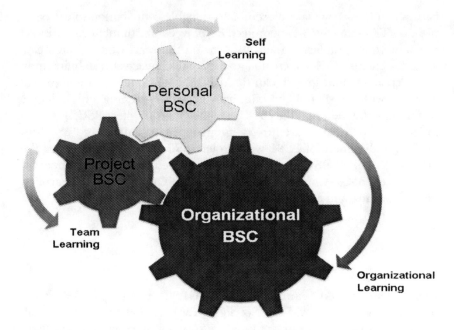

Figure 4.17.   Organizational Learning, Team Learning, and Self-Learning based on the alignment of the three BSCs (Rampersad, 2007).

4.3.1 Communicating the Balanced Scorecards

Communicating the formulated OBSC and the related Project BSCs to all stakeholders in clear, exciting terms is necessary in order to create organizational buy-in for it and to arouse organization-wide commitment. This can only be achieved if all stakeholders understand the BSCs and know which behaviour is necessary to realize the shared ambition. The BSCs should be communicated to employees and project members in a manner that is timely, honest, clear, correct, complete, structured, consequential, frequent, and preferably face-to-face. It is important that this communication does not happen too early, or the message may be forgotten by the time the goals of the message have been actualized. The BSC should also not be communicated too late, or it may lead to mistrust. The amount of the information communicated at any time should also be balanced: there should not be so much information that employees do not have time to absorb it, but there should be enough information that they get the impression that something important is happening.

The OBSC should be communicated internally, as well as, externally. This process should be coherent, continuously informative, and handled in a systematic and structured way. The communicative objectives, core message, and medium for each stakeholder should be clearly defined beforehand. Use a communication matrix indicating all stakeholders: shareholders, CEO, middle management, team leaders, employees, customers, and suppliers. The communication process should include many means of communication, such as brochures, posters, monthly newsletters, monthly reports, e-mail, memos, video, electronic bulletin boards, and publication boards, as well as, business meetings, conferences, office parties, staff meetings, shareholders meetings, and other gatherings. The frequency of communication should be indicated in the communication plan. Communicate the scorecard orally, as well as, in writing, top-down, as well as, bottom-up, vertically, as well as, horizontally (two-sided communication between sender and receiver) throughout the organization.

The core message should deal with the formulated OBSC and the related Project BSCs. Also use the cause-and-effect diagrams in this communication process. Articulate the corporate scorecard with conviction, and create clarity about tasks, responsibilities, and authorities. Indicate what is open for discussion and what is not, such as the formulated scorecard perspectives. The people within the organization must be convinced of the necessity for improvement, development, and learning. This may be accomplished by comparing the organization to its more successful competitors, by bringing into the open the dissatisfaction of customers, and by constantly emphasizing declining performance measures that are related to these factors. In extreme cases, make it clear that the long-term survival of the organization is at stake. By doing this last point, the sceptics may be convinced of the necessity to change. Employees should also be informed about the advantages of the improvement actions and how the gap between the actual and prospective situation can be closed. These suggestions for improvement should be structured well and clearly argued, whereby a concrete, improved result is promised to the employees. Communicate not only the scorecard but also the complete TPS-Lean Six Sigma concept to colleagues, employees, and others. Everyone within the organization has to know about the content of the scorecards, why it is important that the organization works in this way now, of which methods and techniques the TPS-Lean Six Sigma concept consists, and how these can be applied successfully.

Communicate this information to your customers and suppliers as well, explaining to them why you are working this way and how it will affect them. The routine adaptation of the TPS-Lean Six Sigma concept can be encouraged by developing and distributing a pocketsize TPS-Lean Six Sigma booklet, customized for the company (developing customized pocketsize TPS-Lean Six Sigma booklets for companies is one of the services of TPS-Lean Six Sigma $_{LLC}$). As part of your continuous self-improvement, it is advisable to communicate your personal ambition (Personal Brand) to others as well. As you learn from their feedback, you will improve your self-image and gain greater knowledge about yourself, which, in turn, is essential to learn, be creative, and improve your behaviour. After all, your self-knowledge and self-image are not only determined by your inner voice but also by the image others have of you. That is why feedback is so very important.

4.3.2 Cascading the Balanced Scorecards

Communicating and linking of the OBSC and Project BSCs are critical to the success of TPS-Six Sigma project implementations. To be able to convert the strategic vision of an organization into action, it is necessary to link the corporate scorecard (OBSC) to the BSC of departments and teams, as well as, the individual performance plan of managers and employees at lower levels of the organization. Each business unit or department sets up its own specific scorecard (which is attuned to the OBSC), as a team under the guidance of the department manager. Each team develops a team scorecard based on the scorecard of its business unit. Then, with the help of the team leader, each team member translates the team scorecard into his or her own individual performance plan, which concentrates on the individual's job and their unique contribution to the team goals.

The organizational mission, formulated in the OBSC, applies to all organizational levels. The organizational vision and linked critical success factors, objectives, targets, and improvement actions are then adjusted and fine-tuned to the related business units and teams. Here, the OBSC is used as a frame of reference. Members of each lower level should also reflect upon the alignment between their personal ambition and the shared organizational, business unit, and team ambition. The organizational objectives in the OBSC form the point of departure when linking the OBSC to the scorecards at lower organizational levels. For each objective, it is determined whether the respective business unit influences this objective significantly, and if improvement actions can be formulated to directly influence the accomplishment of this objective. If so, the objective will be incorporated into the scorecard of the respective business unit. To finalize the business unit's scorecard, the remaining objectives and scorecard elements are formulated, based on the strategy of the respective business unit. This top-down and bottom-up process is executed iteratively in increasing detail at all successive organizational levels. In this manner, the overall organizational strategy is systematically translated into more specific plans at each organizational level.

The level of detail in which the translation takes place depends on the organizational typology and the business size. Each department selects those objectives and performance measures from the OBSC that it influences, and then translates them into their own situation. When the objectives are linked in this way, local efforts are aligned with the overall organizational strategy. Brainstorming with employees in several workshops allows them to gain better insight into the organizational course to be followed. This formulation process is identical for the strategic, tactical, and operational levels within the organization.

Every participant in this process formulates his/her own PBSC as well. The ambition meeting between line-manager and employees takes place at every organizational level. One needs to reflect about the match between one's own personal ambition and the shared ambition. The above described cascading process applies for the Project BSC as well. The ambition meeting between Champion/Master Black Belt/Black Belt/Green Belt/Project Manager and project team members takes place in all TPS-Lean Six Sigma Projects as well.

Figure 4.18 illustrates the different cascading layers of this top-down process regarding the PBSC and OBSC. The linked scorecard framework consists of the following four organizational levels (see also Rampersad, 2006, and paragraph 6.2)

1. **Strategic**—As a team, the corporate BSC (OBSC) and related Project BSCs are formulated. Subsequently, all senior management team members first formulate their own PBSCs and share these with their colleagues, in order to promote team learning and mutual trust and respect. The chairperson or CEO acts in this process as a trusted person of the other board members. An external senior consultant functions as facilitator and trusted person of the chairperson or the CEO. Based on this, the chairperson or the CEO holds a periodical, informal, voluntary, and confidential ambition meeting with his/her board members, in order to align their personal ambition (personal BSC) with the shared corporate ambition. Initially, top Management is not ready to develop a proper deployment plan without more detailed understanding of TPS-Lean Six Sigma, for this reason, it is highly recommended that the leadership team attend an Executive and Champion workshops to obtain the knowledge needed for a successful deployment.

2. **Tactical**—Then, as a team, the business unit manager and his or her team leaders formulate the vision, critical success factors, objectives, performance measures, targets, and improvement actions of his/her business unit (business unit BSC) and related

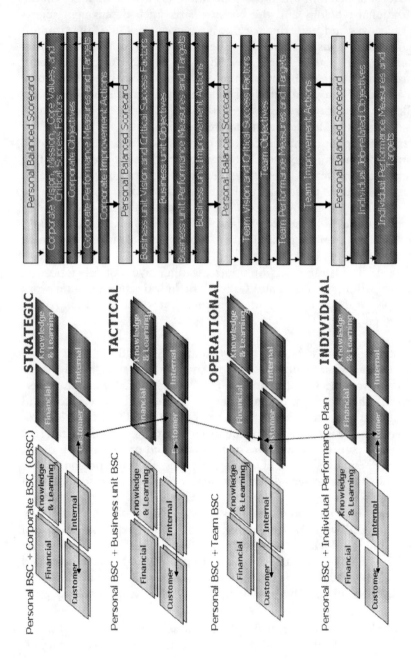

Figure 4.18.   Cascading the OBSC to the Business Units, Scorecard, Team Scorecard, and Individual Performance Plan.

Project BSCs. Subsequently, the business unit manager (middle manager) shares his or her PBSC with the team leaders, functions as their trusted person for the formulation of their PBSCs and stimulates them to share their PBSCs with each other. This in turn, gives rise to team learning and mutual trust and respect within his/her business unit. Following this, the business unit manager holds a periodical, informal, voluntary, and confidential ambition meeting with his/her team leaders in order to align their personal ambition (personal BSC) with the shared business unit ambition (business unit BSC). Every business unit does the same.

3. **Operational**—After this, as a team, the team leader and his/her team members formulate their vision, critical success factors, objectives, and performance measures, targets and improvement actions of the team (team BSC) and related Project BSCs. Subsequently, the team leader shares his or her PBSC with his or her team members, functions as their trusted person in formulating their PBSCs and stimulates them to share their PBSCs with each other in order to enhance team learning and mutual trust and respect within his/her team. Then, the team leader holds a periodical, informal, voluntary and confidential ambition meeting with the team members in order to align their personal ambition (personal BSC) with the shared team ambition (team BSC). Every team within the business units does the same.

4. **Individual**—The team leader formulates with each of the team members their individual performance plan as part of the performance agreement. This plan consists of the job-oriented objectives, performance measures, and targets of each team member which agree with the team BSC and the Project BSC, and with which the team member can identify. To facilitate a good match between personal ambition and team ambition, it is recommended that some elements of his/her PBSC will be brought into the individual performance plan of the team member. This can only take place if the team member is receptive. This must be done in consultation with each other. Although the PBSC and individual performance plan are strongly interrelated, there are significant differences between them. With the PBSC the emphasis is on the personal life of people, their attitudes, skills, and behaviour in society (also in their private life). The individual performance plan, on the other hand, is formulated at the operational level and focuses on the job to be done by the employee within the organization (job-oriented competences) and the improvement of the daily job-related performances. This plan is linked to the team scorecard and

could also contain ingredients of the PBSC and Project BSC. Figure 4.19 shows where the OBSC and the PBSC meet the Project BSC. This counts for employees only, associated with the organization (not for external project members).

As a result of this deployment process, it is logical to also link the individual performance plan explicitly to the reward system, without losing track of intrinsic incentive compensation. Several organizations have linked part of their incentive compensation to the financial objectives in the OBSC and the remainder to the objectives related to the perspectives of *customers, internal processes, and knowledge and*

++*learning*, depending on reaching or exceeding related targets. By appointing the different objectives, a "weight" (priority number), the delivery of unbalanced performances will be prevented.

The above described deployment process should be followed as well when cascading and breaking down the TPS-Lean Six Sigma project to lower detail projects. It is highly recommended that you first select a small scale pilot project to complete before a company wide implementation (see chapter 6). This way, you can identify early on, in the deployment phase, any cultural and operational issues and initiate a corrective action to resolve it.

4.4 IMPROVING

Improving yourself and the business processes is the third phase in the TPS-Lean Six Sigma Cycle (see Figure 4.1).

4.4.1 Continuous Personal Improvement

The next step in the personal development process is the implementation of your Personal Balanced Scorecard. Hubert Rampersad has introduce a new learning cycle to accomplish this, the Plan-Do-Act-Challenge cycle (PDAC cycle), which is followed continuously (see Figure 4.20). This new cycle focuses on human beings and Deming's Plan-Do-Check-Act (PDCA) cycle and the DMAIC cycle focus on processes (processes do not have challenges). To live in accordance with the PBSC through its implementation using the PDAC cycle results in cyclical learning and in a step-by-step process through which happiness, awareness, enjoyment, fun and creativity, at work, as well as, in your spare time, are increased. After all, when people are in control of their own actions and are free to face challenges, they tend to be happier. This

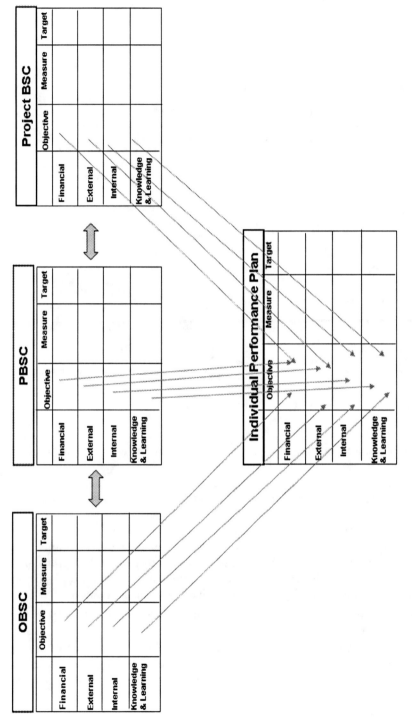

Figure 4.19. Where the OBSC and PBSC meet the Project BSC.

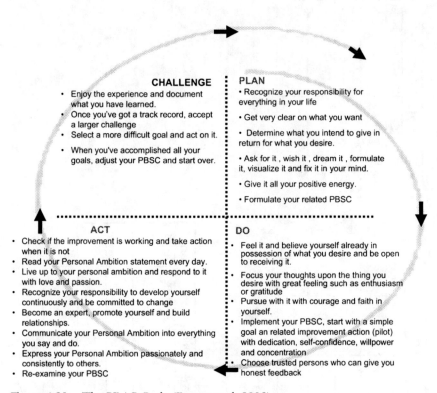

Figure 4.20.   The PDAC Cycle (Rampersad, 2006).

approach is related to six steps of the Law of Attraction for your life (see box text below.

How do you Create Your Desires Using the Law of Attraction

1. Get very clear on what you want; Ask for it, wish it, dream it, formulate it, and fix it in your mind. List in your personal ambition what you want to achieve. You must accept personal responsibility for everything in your life. Determine what you intend to give in return for what you desire. Give it all your positive energy

2. Visualize it; visualize the end results in your mind and on a vision board.

3. Formulate your PBSC for carrying out your desire. List what you must do to achieve your goals. Specify how you are going to measure success at each step along the way. Based on the PBSC you will be accountable for your results, which can help you become more aware of what you're doing to yourself.

4. Feel it; Focus your thoughts upon the thing you desire with great feeling such as enthusiasm or gratitude. Feel and behave as if the object of one's desire is on its way. Read your personal ambition statement every day. Feel yourself already in possession of what you desire. The feeling will create the power of attraction.
5. Allow It; Believe it and be open to receiving it.
6. Enjoy it and accept a larger challenge. Move on to a more complex goal. When you've accomplished all your goals, adjust your PBSC and start over. Reexamine your goals regularly.

The PDAC-cycle consists of the following four phases (Rampersad, 2006):

Plan—Get very clear on what you want, include this in your personal ambition statement, visualize it, and formulate your PBSC, which focuses on your work, as well, as on your free time.
Do—Feel it, believe it, and allow it. Start with a simple objective from your PBSC and the corresponding improvement action, keeping in mind the priorities that have been identified. Each morning when you rise, use the breathing and silence exercise, focus on a selected improvement action which you should then strive to implement during the day. Execute the improvement action with dedication, self-confidence, willpower and concentration. This must be in concordance with your present skills. Submit yourself with courage to the related objective, even when you run into resistance. Be determined in the realization of your personal objectives and don't give up. Share your good intentions with a trusted person (spouse, friend, colleague, or manager), who will ask questions, discuss with you, and give you honest feedback. Doing this entails acting with purpose and making efforts to realize your objective. Ask for feedback often from the trusted person. This gives you the opportunity to measure what progress you have made. Start with habits which restrict you, influence your life unfavorably, and deliver poor results.
Act—Review the results according to the personal performance measures and targets you have defined earlier, measure your progress, and check to what extent you have realized your personal objectives. Check if the improvement action is working, and take action if it is not. It becomes a habit to do things right the first time if you evaluate your PBSC each month with your trusted person, and learn from experience. Think of three people, who can act as your trusted person; who give you inspiration and motivation for the realization of your objectives and improvement actions. Plan to meet with each one of them

regularly. Listen enthusiastically to them, brainstorm with them, and take their counsel. Develop your skills and competencies to achieve the objectives you have selected. Recognize your responsibility to constantly develop yourself.

Challenge—Accept bigger challenges by selecting a more difficult objective and the corresponding improvement action from your PBSC and act on it. Be conscientious in choosing a more challenging objective on par with your improved skills when the current improvement action starts becoming boring. Enjoy the experience and document what you have learned and unlearned during the execution of the improvement action. Refine it and review your PBSC regularly.

Summary of Personal Improvement Activities

- Understand yourself.
- Recognize your responsibility and ethical duty to make personal improvement a routine and a continuous process.
- Assess relationships with your family, supervisor, peers, subordinates, customers, and others.
- Regularly evaluate your need/desire to improve and the necessity of personal growth.
- Formulate and examine your PBSC and apply this to your non-work life as well.
- Share this with a trusted person (family, supervisor, colleague, subordinate, and/or customer).
- Obtain your supervisor's agreement on the job-related PBSC elements before proceeding.
- Start off with the implementation of your PBSC according to the Plan-Do-Act-Challenge cycle.
- Improve and monitor your actions and thoughts continuously based on your PBSC.
- Ask for the trusted person's comments and perceptions.
- Also focus on the things that you are not good at, habits that limit you, and habits that have an unfavorable influence on your life and deliver poor results.
- Review the results according to the personal performance measures and targets earlier defined.
- Check to what extent you have realized your personal objectives and adjust your PBSC if needed.

- Achieve behavioral changes and constantly challenge your behavior.
- Make time in your schedule to improve and to help others improve.
- Attend to your continued education and see your job as a learning experience.
- Take advantage of learning opportunities and take initiative.
- Understand the capabilities and limitations of your processes, and your customers' needs and expectations.
- Pursue innovation and new ideas based on Plan-Do-Act-Challenge cycle.
- Be observant, a good listener, and remove the barriers you normally erect.
- Maintain a positive attitude toward life and never get carried away by anger.
- Perform the breathing and silence exercise regularly; in the morning and in the evening.
- Demonstrate commitment and leadership, set an example.
- Foster co-operation and communication.
- Avoid extreme behavior and remain calm.
- Trust others and be worthy of their trust.
- Find a balance between your personal ambition and your behavior.
- Have respect for others and speak honestly and well of others.
- Be the most honest person that you know; be trustworthy.
- Judge others fairly and correctly.
- Communicate effectively; the quality of your life is the quality of your communication with others and yourself.
- Cultivate and foster new friendships, especially with those who have shared many experiences and laughs with you; relationships are essential for maintaining a healthy and successful life.
- Show compassion and sincere consideration for all your friends and develop long-lasting friendships by being a good friend.
- Treat everyone who crosses your path as if he/she is the most important person in your world.
- Overlook the weaknesses of others and see the good that each inherently possesses. We can learn from everyone. Be open to this.
- Develop the habit of punctuality; it reflects discipline and a proper regard for others.
- Revive your habit of laughter.

- Learn to be still and enjoy the power of silence for at least ten minutes a day.
- Speak less; listen 60% of the time. You will learn much, as everyone we meet, every day has something to teach us. Listening is the beginning of all wisdom. Learning is listening effectively.
- Learn to always think positively; when a negative thought comes to your mind, immediately replace it with one that is positive.
- Dedicate yourself to leaving a powerful legacy to the world.
- Be truthful, patient, persevering, modest and generous; be someone with a warm heart and great character.
- See every opportunity as a chance to learn.
- Be an explorer; find pleasure in the things that others take for granted.
- Develop your ability to focus for extended periods of time and to build your concentration.
- Have courage and inspire others with your actions.
- Take anyone you think is highly effective and ethical as your role model. Visualize this person and do like her/him.
- Never feel that you have no time for new ideas, you are investing in yourself.
- Become an adventurer and revitalize your spirit and sense of playfulness. Take time out for the renewal of your mind, body, and spirit.
- Follow your conscience.
- Never do anything you wouldn't be proud to tell your mother.
- Know your best qualities and cultivate them.
- Never complain, be known as a positive, strong, energetic, and enthusiastic person.
- Fill your mind with thoughts of serenity, positivism, strength, courage, and compassion.
- Create an image of yourself as a highly competent, strong, disciplined, calm, and decent individual.
- Schedule relaxation time into your week; spend time in reflection, unwinding, and recharging your batteries.
- Make time for the things that matter most; choose what is important and filter out what is of no value. Focus on those objectives that are truly important; read only those materials that will be useful to you.
- Be disciplined in following the schedule of your PBSC.

- Seek out knowledge. Knowledge is power. The more you know, the less you fear. The more one knows the more one achieves.
- Read more, learn more, laugh more, and love more.
- Show your appreciation and respect for your loved ones.
- The essence of a person is his character; make yours unique, unblemished, and strong.
- Place greater importance on staying happy than amassing material possessions; be happy with what you have.
- Strive to be humble and live a simple, uncluttered, and productive existence.
- Be committed to what you are doing and to being a better parent, friend, and citizen.
- Be known as an idea person, willing to take on challenges, and tackle them with passion and enthusiasm.
- Spend at least half an hour every day alone—in peaceful introspection, reading or just relaxing.
- Cultivate the habit of optimism.
- Develop a focused state of mind. Pay attention to your spiritual development so as to gain greater self-confidence.
- Give attention to the development of spirit, health, and useful activities; you cannot do well unless you feel good. When you are serene, relaxed, and enthusiastic you are also more productive, creative, and dynamic.
- Dedicate yourself to higher knowledge and to the development of a higher level of consciousness.
- Always pursue your personal objectives.
- Be in control of yourself and live in harmony with your personal mission, vision, and key roles.
- Align your personal ambition with your personal behavior and match it with the organizational ambition.
- Assess the results and evaluate your improvement.
- Learn to measure and understand processes and to use data that support your decisions.
- Recognize the processes you use and understand how they are linked to others.
- Know your internal and external customers. You should know and understand your colleagues and clients, not only yourself.
- Document the lessons learned.
- Celebrate your success.

- Successively select a more difficult personal objective with the corresponding improvement action from your PBSC, and start working on it.

Source: Personal Brand Management; The Way to Powerful and Sustainable Personal Branding, Information Age Publishing Inc. (Rampersad, 2007).

4.4.2 Continuous Process Improvement

Continuous process improvement is implemented according to the *define, measure, analyze, improve,* and *control* model (DMAIC) (see Figures 3.6 and 4.21).

The Define Phase

First, management executes the TPS-Lean Six Sigma Life Cycle Scan (see chapter 12) to define the "pain," bottle necks and related objectives. Based on this, they formulate the OBSC and recognize business opportunities that significantly impact both the customer and business. Potential projects are identified, evaluated and selected. The Project BSCs are formulated for each of the selected projects by the Champion and the Master Black Belt. They then select the most appropriate team of personnel for the project. The selection of team members is based on their skills, experience, and the alignment of their own PBSC with the Project BSC. We therefore recommend stimulating the Champions/ Master Black Belts/Black Belts/Green Belts/Project Managers and all project team members to formulate their own PBSC and share this with each other in order to create team learning, trust and open-

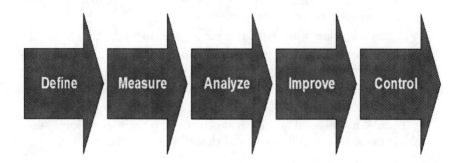

Figure 4.21.   DMAIC Model.

communication within the project team. The team assigns the necessary priority, and project progress is then monitored to ensure success.

The team's main objectives are to review the Project BSC, gather the voice of the customer (VOC), summarize and prioritize the customer's needs and to identify critical to quality characteristics (CTQ) to be measured, assessed, and improved. To achieve these objectives, the team will define the problem (opportunity) and set goals and benefits. The problem (opportunity) statement is summarized along with the project goals and objectives in the team charter (see Figure 4.22) and in the Project BSC. To assure on-going Management support, the charter needs to be approved by management.

Team charter includes:

1. Project information
2. Team members
3. Business case
4. Problem statement
5. Project objectives
6. Project scope

The above information will then be used to formulate the Project BSC. The Project BSC can be seen as an extended and balanced team or project charter. The charter forms the input for the Project BSC. It provides all the necessary information about the project including project name, company's name, department involved, and so forth. Team members list all the individuals who provide project support including attending meetings, data collection, data analysis, and so forth. The business case should state why this project is important to the customer and to the business. Management should make it a priority to review, revise and approve the business case to assure it aligns with business's strategic objectives before the team starts. The project objectives and goals are part of the Project BSC and should be specific and measurable. The team defines the improvement they need to accomplish based on the Project BSC. The focus of the goals should be on the results the team hopes to achieve. The project scope should specify the resources available and the process boundaries where the team should focus their improvement on. A well defined scope is critical to the success of the project. A broadly defined scope may lead to infective solutions or on the other hand, too narrow a scope can produce limited solutions and results. The team should set dates for project reviews with management. The reviews may cover resources allocated, the project scope, project

PROJECT INFORMATION		PROJECT TEAM	
		TITLE / ROLE	NAME
Project No.:		Project Champion	
Project Name:		Master Black Belt	
Business Unit:		Finance Champion	
Location / Dept:		Process Owner	
Start Date:		Black Belt	
Target Completion Date:			
Estimated Project Savings:			

BUSINESS CASE (list problem, opportunity, strategic alignment, and impact on the business)

OBJECTIVE / GOALS (list business and financial objectives, include all metrics to be used)

SCOPE (list what part of the process will be investigated, what will be excluded, and if there are any limitations)

GATES

	ESTIMATED COMPLETION DATE	COMMENTS
DEFINE		
MEASURE		
ANALYZE		
IMPROVE		
CONTROL		

APPROVALS

	SIGNATURE	DATE
Project Champion:		
Master Black Belt:		
Black Belt:		
Finance Champion:		

Figure 4.22.   Team or Project Charter.

effectiveness and progress, and alignment with company strategic objectives.

Remember: Critical to Quality Characteristics (CTQ's) are physical, measurable responses that are directly linked to customer requirements. They are design requirements that the product must satisfy. Criticality is related to fulfilling customer needs.

The Measure Phase

The primary objectives of the measure phase is to identify the types of measures needed to support (link to) customer requirements and to assess the measurement system for measurement errors, bias, and stability (see Appendix, TPS-Lean Six Sigma Tools. Measurement System Analysis, MSA). These measures and the related targets are included in the Project BSC. If the measurement system is adequate, the team then develops a data collection and a sampling plan in order to assess the capability of the process. Process capability evaluates the process ability to meet customer requirements and the specified project targets in the Project BSC. The process variation is compared to customer's specifications. Process capability study should answer two questions: (1) Does the process need to be improved? (2) How much improvement is needed? Process capability study is covered in more detail in the Appendix.

The Analyze Phase

The analyze phase involves the application of statistical tools with the purpose to better understand the potential causes of process poor performance. In the analyze phase, the project team analyzes past and current process performance data, in order to check if the performance has met the targets included in the Project BSC. Hypotheses on possible cause-effect relationships are developed and tested. Appropriate statistical and graphical tools and techniques are used such as process flow maps, value stream map histograms, Pareto chart, Box Plots, scatter plot, correlation and regression analysis, hypothesis testing, and analysis of variance (ANOVA). All these tools will be explained in the Appendix, under the analyze tools.

The Improve Phase

In the improve phase, the team identifies, assesses and implement effective solutions to the problem. They usually conduct Design of Experiment (DOE) to determine the relationship between process input variables (X_i) and process outputs (Y_i) or CTQ's, customer requirements. Design of experiment helps the team develop a mathematical equation which describes the process. This equation is then used to predict, improve and optimize the process performance.

The Control Phase

The objective of the control phase is to sustain the improvement achieved in the previous phase. Only stable processes will assure the improvement is sustained. The team usually implements the necessary controls and quality plans to ensure that improvement gain is held after the changes to the process have been implemented. Statistical Process Control (SPC), standardized work, and mistake-proofing are some of the tools used. To learn about these tools, we refer our readers to the Appendix. By applying the TPS-Lean Six Sigma Life Cycle Scan (see chapter 12), it will be possible to steer the improvement actions systematically, always aiming for higher levels of personal and business excellence.

4.5 DEVELOPING AND LEARNING

Developing and Learning are forming the forth phase in the TPS-Lean Six Sigma Cycle (see Figure 4.1).

To be able to manage and utilize the talents within the organization and project effectively, it is necessary that the PBSC, the OBSC, the Project BSC, and the ambition meeting are embedded in the talent development process. Appendix D describes the TPS-Lean Six Sigma Knowledge Management Quick Scan to be used to increase the learning ability of organizations based on this approach. Figures 2.4 and 4.23 talent management models which are being introduced here. The left side of the model in Figure 4.23 includes the individual personal coaching route or individual learning, which consists of the formulation and implementation of the PBSC (aimed at personal effectiveness), including the first alignment step (aimed at integrity and ethical behavior). The right side of the model shows the OBSC and the Project BSC. The left and right side come together at the second balance step, which is aimed at employees' inner involvement, motivation, and happiness through the informal and voluntary ambition meeting between the Manager and his/her employees and between the Champion/Master Black Belt/Black Belt/Green Belt/ Project Manager and his/her project team members. Informal coaching is central here. By integrating the left side, you will humanize your organization/project. The integration of the left side is currently the missing link in management and in Lean Six Sigma. Further, the left and right side, as well as, the second balance step form the input for the formal talent development process.

The formal talent development process consists of:

1. Formulation of the individual performance plan; this entails a summary of the required results (objectives, performance indica-

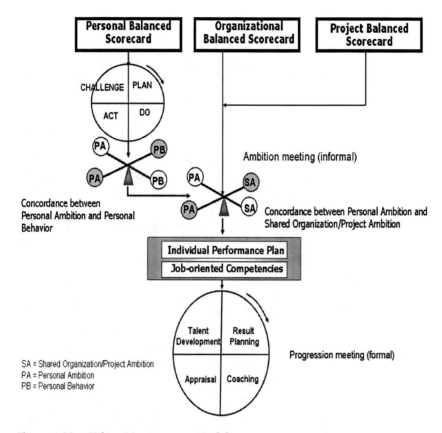

Figure 4.23. Talent Management Model.

tors and targets) pertaining to the employee's function about which periodical result agreements are made. This is related to the OBSC and the Project BSC (focused on internal employees involved in the TPS–Lean Six Sigma project).

2. Defining a set of job-oriented competencies (inclusive of successive gradations for each competency), which an individual worker must possess to enable him to realize the OBSC and the Project BSC.

3. Helping employees develop their job-oriented competencies and, as such, improve their functioning. This happens in accordance with the four phases of the introduced talent development cycle (see Figure 2.4):

- *Result Planning:* This phase deals with the creation of result agreements based on job-oriented performance objectives in the individual performance plan and the selection of a set of job-oriented competencies, which support these objectives. The individual performance plan is prepared in collaboration with the line-Manager. Based on this plan and the set of competencies, periodic result agreements are made between the line-manager and employee regarding the employee's performance and realization of development objectives. In this planning meeting, result agreements are made about the use of selected competencies also. It is recommended to include some job-related elements from the employee's PBSC and the Project BSC in the result agreement. This will aid the match between personal ambition and shared ambition, and increase the employee's motivation and commitment.

- *Coaching:* In this phase, the line-manager and employee get together at fixed intervals to discuss the employee's progress; individual guidance occurs, agreements are tested and adjusted, and feedback is given.

- *Appraisal:* The formal appraisal takes place after a certain period to confirm whether all agreements were met, if the agreed results were achieved, and if so, how this was done.

- *Talent Development:* This phase involves the talent development of employees through, for example, courses and on-the-job training, the creation of practice situations, accompanying experienced colleagues, customer feedback meetings, traineeship, development tips, and execution of talent development programs. These are all focused on or related to the employee's own work situation.

By systematically unfolding the above mentioned activities, the job-oriented talent development of the employees can be guided and managed. By way of this gradual development, the employee's self-efficacy increases, the quality of work improves and optimum use is made of his/her abilities, so that the required organizational and project performances can occur. For greater detail about this talent management approach, we refer you to Rampersad (2003, 2006).

Measures for Effective Talent Management

- Provide time to communicate authentically with your employees and project team members—not just about work, involve them in decision making whenever possible, show appreciation to each employee frequently and laugh more often.

- Make people happy by letting them control their own actions and lives and face challenges. They will be happiest if they are given freedom. This requires the opportunity to build self-respect, trust, feelings of responsibility, and involvement.

- Empower people; help them to be capable of what they really are capable of.

- Organizations and TPS-Lean Six Sigma Projects are living organisms, in which people are involved; treat them like human beings. If you have a sound business strategy that is based on caring for people and not harming anyone, then financial success will come automatically.

- Train and coach employees and project team members continuously to gain new skills that are within their capacity. Assist employees and project team members in developing their intuitive skills on the basis of the PBSC approach. To make decision on the basis of intuition is fast, accurate and effective. Choose new employees also on the basis of these skills.

- Stimulate management, employees, and project team members to formulate their PBSCs themselves, and to implement them in accordance with the Plan-Do-Act-Challenge cycle, and on this basis continuously enter into new challenges. The more innovative an organization needs to be, the more its members need to formulate and implement their PBSCs. Let managers, employees, and project team members define their specific and measurable personal development objectives on the basis of the PBSC and make them responsible to reach these goals. These must be attuned to their specific learning situation. The personal development objectives and activities must correspond with the Organizational BSC and their Project BSC

- Stimulate employees and project team members to gain more understanding for self-responsibility and let them understand that their development is their own responsibility. Let them understand that it is their ethical duty and responsibility to develop themselves and become more proactive, for the good of themselves, their loved ones, their work, their project, their organization, their country, and the world.

- Ensure a safe environment in which employees and project team members are willing to learn, try out new things, take on new challenges, and develop related skills in accordance with the PDAC cycle.

- Ensure a work-life balance and an enjoyable atmosphere.
- Trust your employees and project team members.
- Give employees and project team members self-confidence.
- Stimulate Champions/Master Black Belts/Black Belts/Green Belts/ Project Managers and all project team members to formulate their own PBSC and to share this with each other, in order to create team learning, mutual trust and open-communication within the project team.
- Stimulate management, Champions/Master Black Belts/Black Belts/Green Belts/Project Managers/employees/project team members to act ethically while balancing between their personal ambition and their personal behavior, so that inner peace and personal credibility can be developed. Without ethical action, there is no sustainable individual learning and improvement.
- Strive for the best fit between employee/project team member and organization project on the basis of the balance between personal and shared ambition and, through this, to stimulate commitment, engagement, and inner involvement.
- Perform the breathing and silence exercise each morning.
- Introduce the discussed periodic, informal, voluntary and confidential ambition meeting between the Executive/Champion/Master Black Belt/Black Belt/Green Belt/Project Manager and his/her employees/project team members. Help Managers, Champions, and Belts (via train-the-trainer sessions) to enable them to effectively fulfill the role of trusted person and informal coach.
- Help Executives/Champions/Master Black Belts/Black Belts/Green Belts/Project Managers and human resources officers understand that they need to fulfill the role of trusted facilitator. It is their tasks to improve the quality of life of employees/project team members on the basis of the PBSC method and the PDAC cycle, and have them enter into greater challenges and let them enjoy their work and make them happy. Quality of life of customers will also improve and they will be more contented and more satisfied.
- Help Executives/Champions/Master Black Belts/Black Belts/Green Belts/Project Managers and human resources officers to understand that a healthy home situation has an important influence at work and this should not be ignored. Their task is also to encourage their employees and project team members to systematically apply their PBSC within their family and to help improve the situation at home on the basis of the PDAC cycle.

- Make a real priority of talent development, and take it up as a challenge.
- Teach Executives/Champions/Master Black Belts/Black Belts/Green Belts/Project Managers and employees/project members how to learn.
- Stimulate informal contact between them.
- Make sure that role models exist.
- Chase away fear and distrust from the organization on the basis of the TPS-Lean Six Sigma concept. With no fear, less management intervention, and higher autonomy, work becomes more satisfying.
- Create conditions whereby people are prepared to bring their knowledge into action, to share this with each other and to learn how to learn.
- Promote simplicity of the organizational structure and simplicity of language used by Managers, Champions, Master Black Belts, and Black Belts.
- Let employees/project team members identify and solve common problems as a team.
- Give top priority to the interests of your staff, second priority to the interests of your customers, and third priority to the interests of your shareholders.
- Organize multidisciplinary brainstorming sessions, problem-solving meetings, in-company project valuation meetings, and speeches with external experts.
- Stimulate trust between Executives/Champions/Master Black Belts/ Black Belts/Green Belts/Project Managers and employees/project members by encouraging them to share their personal ambition with each other.

Summarizing this chapter we can conclude that TPS-Lean Six Sigma creates a paradigm shift in Quality Management. It creates new tasks for managers to continuously improve the quality of life of their staff, not only at the workplace, but also in their spare time on the basis of the methods and techniques presented here. Following such practices would encourage employees to continuously feel free and safe, and able to accept bigger challenges, and through this, provide enjoyment in work and experience well-being and happiness. The results of this are higher labour productivity, higher project performance, shorter throughout times of projects and higher project quality. This attitude will also have its effect on customers and shareholders, improving their quality of life and adding to their well-being and satisfaction. It is therefore critical that Managers/Champions/Master Black Belts/Black Belts/Green Belts/Project Managers realize that their employees' / team members' home situation (healthy or not) has an impact on their work performance. This can no longer be ignored. Leaders have to look beyond themselves, and understand that those who are not able to function well in their families cannot function well at work either. They need to rapidly unlearn the practice of ignoring the private circumstances of employees.

CHAPTER 5

DESIGN FOR
TPS-LEAN SIX SIGMA

and

TPS-Lean Six Sigma in Service

*Almost all quality improvement comes via simplification of design, manufacturing ...
layout, processes, and procedures.*

—Tom Peters

*Failure of management to plan for the future and to foresee problems has brought
about waste of manpower, of materials, of the machine-time, of all which raise the
manufacturer's cost and price that the purchaser must pay.*

—W. Edwards Deming

As we stated earlier in this book, speed to market is one of the top challenges for companies. We live in an ever changing world; new technologies are developed, improved, and shortly after become obsolete. It is
widely believed that any company who is the first to introduce a new product to market wins about 50% of that market. This principle is called

*TPS-Lean Six Sigma: Linking Human Capital to Lean Six Sigma: A New Blueprint for
Creating High Performance Companies*, pp. 151–176

"time to market." We have seen many companies spend hundreds of millions of dollars on developing a new product and are forced to introduce it before it was ready just because their competitions released theirs first. The consequences were disastrous. Many recalled their product, damaged their reputation and never fully recovered. This rush creates pressure on companies to develop new tools and techniques to help them speed up the product commercialization process and design, and develop new products with higher reliability, better quality and capability, more resource efficient, and reduced design and manufacturing cycle times. In this chapter, we introduce the process of designing new products/services and related business processes that meet TPS-Lean Six Sigma quality level in performance and reliability while shortening the product/service commercialization process. It's related to the continuous process improvement stage in the TPS-Lean Six Sigma model (see Figure 4.1). Some tools and techniques related to this chapter such as Quality Function Deployment (QFD), and Design of Experiment (DOE) will be discussed in detail. Other related tools are included in the Appendix.

5.1 WHAT IS DESIGN FOR TPS-LEAN SIX SIGMA?

Design for TPS-Lean Six Sigma is a structured, rigorous, and disciplined process for designing products or services that meet Six Sigma quality level in performance and reliability. It is a product development (PD) methodology with a "built-in" toolset to be used during the development of new or substantially new product, manufacturing processes or services. It begins when the need for a new product or service has been identified. It ends when the product has been transferred to the manufacture for steady state production or for routine delivery of a service. It is also used to optimize a process which has been improved using the DMAIC model and still not capable of meeting customer requirements. The main objective of design for TPS-Lean Six Sigma is to improve the design quality and to shorten the time of the development of the new product from concept to product launch (see Figure 5.1) by maximizing the creative impulse of your employees through the rigorous application of a proven toolset. The utilization of the TPS-Lean Six Sigma tools and methods will increase the successes of your new product or service development process; with products/services that are designed right the first time, and are better than existing and competing products. This is accomplished because of greater participation of the energized/engaged individuals on the cross functional and multi-disciplined development team and because of the result oriented and performance based approach.

Figure 5.2 shows the product commercialization process. It starts with the understanding of customer's needs, followed by the development of

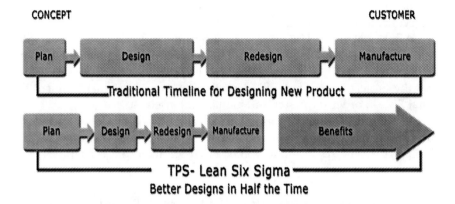

Figure 5.1. Benefit of the Application of TPS-Lean Six Sigma.

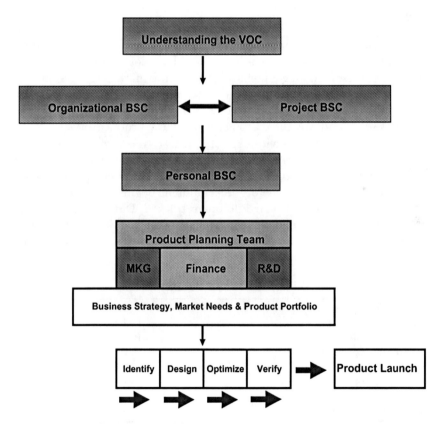

Figure 5.2. Product Commercialization Process.

the organizational balanced scorecard (BSC) and the initiation of the project balanced scorecard. This will evaluate shareholder values and targeted financial goals. The project identification and selection process will be discussed in detail in Chapter 7. The product planning team; will then assess market needs, and create the product portfolio based on the OBSC and the Project BSC. They will also formulate and implement their Personal BSC in order to master and manage themselves.

The Identify, Design, Optimize, and Verify (IDOV) model links design for TPS-Lean Six Sigma tools and metrics to your product commercialization process. The IDOV model will be discussed later in this chapter.

5.2 UNDERSTANDING THE VOICE OF THE CUSTOMER (VOC)

A survey conducted by the Standish Group in the mid-1990s indicated that incomplete customer's requirement is the main reason why most products fail (see Table 5.1).

Identifying and summarizing your customer's requirements is not an easy task, nor is translating those requirements into product or service specifications. It requires the cooperation of a cross-functional team, with all areas represented (e.g., including sales and marketing, design and development, manufacturing, quality, reliability, etc.). The main purpose of this team is to understand exactly what customers expect from the product/service and why the customer will buy the product/service.

As we discussed in a previous chapter, market research, surveys, focus groups, and interviews are some of the tools used to obtain the voice of the customer (VOC). Successful design and development projects have well defined requirements before development begins. All requirements must be documented and their fulfillment tracked. Distinction should be made between critical requirements and all other requirements. Quality Function Deployment is an excellent tool to summarize customer's

Table 5.1.   Why Products Fail

1. Incomplete requirements	13.10%
2. Lack of user involvement	12.40%
3. Lack of resources	10.60%
4. Unrealistic expectations	9.90%
5. Lack of executive support	9.30%
6. Changing requirements/specs	8.70%
7. Lack of planning	8.10%
8. Didn't need an longer	7.50%

Sources: Standish Group (1995, 1996) and *Scientific America* (1994, September).

requirements and translate them into solutions. We will discuss this tool in more detail later in this chapter. In addition to stated customer requirements, the development team should consider all other types of requirements such as internal business requirements and policies, regulatory requirements, environmental requirements, and legal requirements (see Figure 5.3).

Well defined requirements should have the following characteristics: correct, feasible, clear, consistent, complete, measurable, and finally design independent.

5.3 THE IDENTIFY, DESIGN, OPTIMIZE, AND VERIFY (IDOV) MODEL

All Design for TPS-Lean Six Sigma projects follows the Identify, Design, Optimize, and Verify (IDOV) model. Figure 5.4 list the steps and the tools necessary for each of the IDOV phases. In the Identify phase, the company seeks to identify the key customers and their needs, lists, and prioritizes product/service requirements/expectations. Quality function deployment (QFD) is the ideal tool to be used to define customer's requirement, prioritize them, and translate these requirements into engineering/technical metrics to help developers develop high quality products or services. This phase also involves the development of Personal and Organizational Balanced Scorecards, creating of a team

Figure 5.3.   List of product requirements.

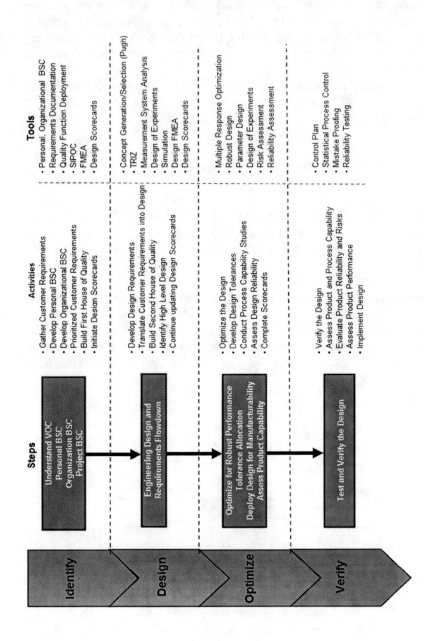

Steps

Understand VOC
Personal BSC
Organization BSC
Project BSC

Engineering Design and
Requirements Flowdown

Optimize for Robust Performance
Tolerance Allocation
Deploy Design for Manufacturability
Assess Product Capability

Test and Verify the Design

Identify

Design

Optimize

Verify

Activities

• Gather Customer Requirements
• Develop Personal BSC
• Develop Organizational BSC
• Prioritized Customer Requirements
• Build First House of Quality
• Initiate Design Scorecards

• Develop Design Requirements
• Translate Customer Requirements into Design
• Build Second House of Quality
• Identify High Level Design
• Continue updating Design Scorecards

• Optimize the Design
• Develop Design Tolerances
• Conduct Process Capability Studies
• Assess Design Reliability
• Complete Scorecards

• Verify the Design
• Assess Product and Process Capability
• Evaluate Product Reliability and Risks
• Assess Product Performance
• Implement Design

Tools

• Personal, Organizational BSC
• Requirements Documentation
• Quality Function Deployment
• SIPOC
• FMEA
• Design Scorecards

• Concept Generation/Selection (Pugh)
• TRIZ
• Measurement System Analysis
• Design of Experiments
• Simulation
• Design FMEA
• Design Scorecards

• Multiple Response Optimization
• Robust Design
• Parameter Design
• Design of Experiments
• Risk Assessment
• Reliability Assessment

• Control Plan
• Statistical Process Control
• Mistake Proofing
• Reliability Testing

Figure 5.4.   The TPS-Lean Six Sigma IDOV Model.

charter, specifying Critical to Quality Characteristics (CTQs), and the required performance based on competitive analysis.

The Design phase highlights the product's CTQs and also identifies functional requirements, develops/designs concepts, evaluates alternative concepts and selects the best-fit concept using Pugh process. The concept design is then formulated, and potential risks are identified and addressed using design Failure Mode and Effect Analysis (FMEA) tool. Tools such as theory of inventive problem solving (TRIZ), Measurement System Analysis (MSA), design scorecards, Failure Mode and Effect Analysis (FMEA), and Design of Experiments (DOE) are often used in this phase. These tools will be described in the Appendix of this book.

The Optimize phase requires the use of process capability studies, statistical tolerances, and reliability assessment. Also, activities such as developing detailed design essentials, optimizing the design, and predicting performance take place in this phase. Robust design, Multiple Response Optimization (MRO), parameter design, reliability testing are among the tools used in this phase and also will be outlined in the Appendix.

The Verify phase is critical to the success of the project. The transition from the Optimize phase to the Verify phase indicates the end of the product development process and the beginning of the effort to commercialize the new product or service. The Verify phase consists of testing and verifying the design. The capability of the critical to function responses (CFRs) should be measured to quantify the product's robustness to stressful noise. As increased testing occurs to verify the design, a feedback system should be implemented and the results communicated to the proper developer so that improvements can be initiated. An effective corrective action system should be in place. Reliability testing, control plans, Measurement System Analysis (MSA), and Statistical Process Control (SPC), and surveys are among the tool used in the validate phase covered in the Appendix.

Another important part in the Verify phase involves the transition of product ownership to the process owner. It is important to include a transition plan in the project deliverables. A good transition plan should include how and when the process owner will take control of the product and its associated process from the project team. It is important that the organization accepting ownership has the authority to say when all issues are resolved to their satisfaction. This is to assure that a production or service delivery process is put in place that is achievable on a routine basis. A control plan is a key document used during transfer, which outlines the products critical to functions (CTF) specifications, appropriate measurement systems, and process controls. This will assure ongoing success of the program and prevent problems in the future.

5.4 QUALITY FUNCTION DEPLOYMENT (QFD)

Quality Function Deployment is used to systematically and structurally convert customer wishes into critical product and process aspects at an early stage. In this approach, which originated in Japan, customer wishes are addressed with the help of matrices that use detailed technical parameters and project objectives (see Figure 5.5). Due to the form of the matrix, it is called the "quality house" (Hauser & Clausing, 1988; Rampersad, 1994). Using three "sequel houses," the critical product specifications (technical parameters) are translated into the necessary process. This detailed translation allows the process to be executed in a controlled fashion for the purpose of achieving stable and acceptable product quality (see Figure 5.6). In the first house, customer wishes are linked to product specifications. In the second house, the relationship between these product specifications and the characteristics of the product parts is central. In the third house, product parts and process characteristics are linked. As a result, the performance measures of critical processes are established. Finally, in the fourth house, the process characteristics are translated into the manufacturing process operations that are to be executed in a controllable way—that is, manufacturing specifications. Among other things, this results in standard working procedures for each process step. For the pur-

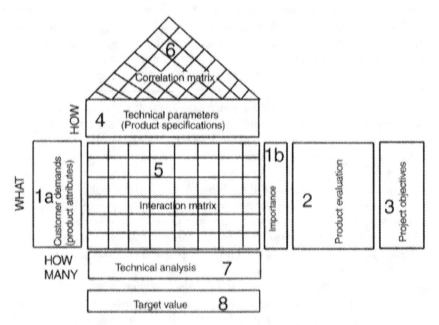

Figure 5.5.   Fundamental Building of QFD Scheme.

VOICE OF THE CUSTOMER

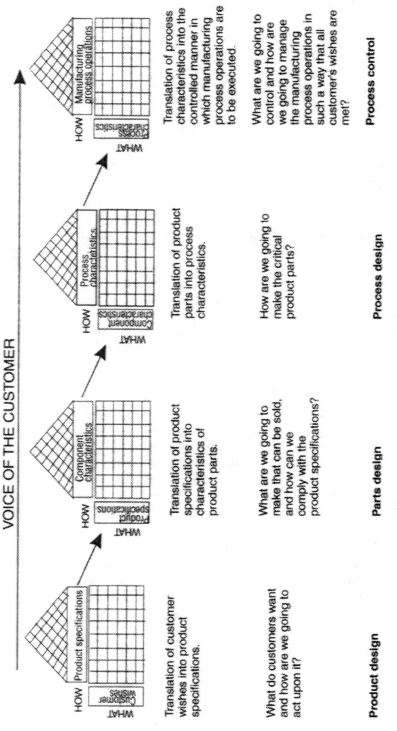

Translation of customer wishes into product specifications.

Translation of product specifications into characteristics of product parts.

Translation of product parts into process characteristics.

Translation of process characteristics into the controlled manner in which manufacturing process operations are to be executed.

What do customers want and how are we going to act upon it?

What are we going to make that can be sold, and how can we comply with the product specifications?

How are we going to make the critical product parts?

What are we going to control and how are we going to manage the manufacturing process operations in such a way that all customer's wishes are met?

Product design

Parts design

Process design

Process control

Figure 5.6. Steps within the QFD (Rampersad, 1994).

poses of this book, the emphasis is on the first quality house, which focuses on the relationship between customer wishes and product specifications.

QFD is used to improve your understanding of the customer and to develop products, services, and processes in a more customer-oriented way. The objective of QFD is to allow the "voice of the customer" to be heard more clearly in the development process of new products and their related processes, and also to comply with the "do it right the first time" principle.

A multidisciplinary expert team coached by a team leader and assisted by a QFD facilitator must be put together. When dealing with product development, the team leader should preferably be a *product manager* or a *product engineer*. The QFD facilitator is someone who is an expert in this area. He or she acts as the source of information and advises the team regarding the effective use of this method. In this preparatory phase, also formulate the objectives and *scope* of the QFD project. The central questions here are: Is top Management committed? Which important product are we going to improve? Which target markets do we focus on? Who are our customers? To which competing products are we comparing ours? How long will the project's execution take? Which milestones can we distinguish? What does the reporting structure look like? Steps to be used for constructing the first quality house, which is aimed at product development (Rampersad, 1994) (see Figure 5.5):

1. Define who the customer is, make an inventory of customer wishes, and measure the importance (priority) of these wishes with the help of weighing scores. We can make an inventory of customer wishes (product attributes) through interviews, inquiries, and other endeavours such as visiting trade shows, the experience of sales associates, customer registration, direct contact with customers, and contact with the competition. These are all important information sources for appraising and mapping customer wishes. *Benchmarking* can also be of use here.

2. Compare your product's performance to that of competitive products. Evaluate your product and note the strong and weak points according to the customer.

3. Identify and quantify the improvement objectives. Determine which customer wishes need to be improved in relation to the competitive product and indicate this in a score.

4. Translate customer wishes into quantifiable technical parameters, that is, product specifications. State *how* client wishes can be used to your advantage. Examples of technical parameters are: dimensions, weight, number of parts, energy use, capacity, and so on.

5. Investigate the relationship between customer wishes and technical parameters. Indicate in the matrix to what extent customer wishes are influenced by technical parameters, and indicate this relationship in a score.

6. Identify the interactions between the individual technical parameters. Make the relationships between these parameters explicit in the roof of the quality house (see Figure 5.5).

7. Record the unit of measurement for all technical parameters. Express these parameters in measurable data. For example, the dimensions of an object are 150 mm (l) x 320mm (w) x 550mm (h) and the weight is 15 kg (33 lbs).

8. Determine the target values of the new product design or indicate the proposed improvements of the technical parameters.

An Example of Quality Function Deployment (QFD)

This example entails the design improvement of an attaché case. Figure 5.7 shows the filled in quality house for the improved design of the attaché case based on the customer's wishes (Roozenburg & Eekels, 1995).

Step 1: Establishing the Customer's Wishes

The customer's wishes are established by means of brainstorming and are classified in the part named 1a of the quality house (see Figure 5.5). This step deals with what is important to the customer, such as: nice to wear, easy to open, easy to fill, and so forth. (see Figure 5.7). These demands are not all of equal importance. The importance of these demands is indicated with the help of weight factors (part 1b in Figure 5.5). A 5-point scale is used here, with: 5 = very important, 4 = important, 3 = less important (but nice to have), 2 = not so important and 1 = not important. Accordingly, the "easy *to carry*" demand has a value of 2 points because it is not so important, and "*durable*" has 5 points because it is very important (see Figure 5.7).

Step 2: Product Evaluation

In this step, our current product (attaché case) is compared to one or more important competitive products. In this way, insight is gained as to how our product performs compared to that of the competition. In

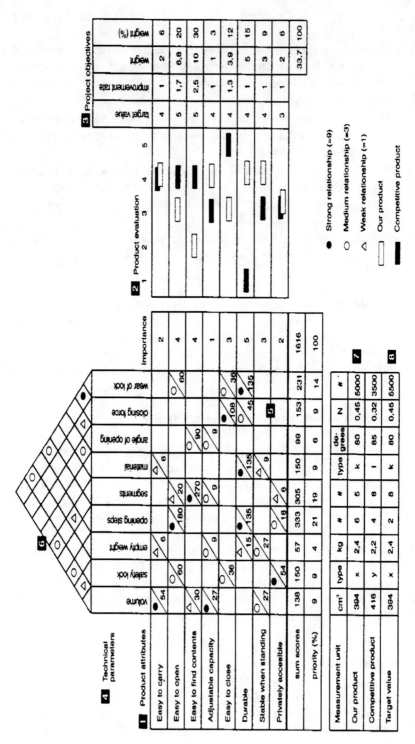

Figure 5.7. A Filled in Quality House.

this case, a five-point scale from excellent to poor is used: 5 = excellent, 4 = good, 3 = fairly good, 2 = not so good and 1 = poor. This is indicated in part 2 of the house (see Figure 5.6). Here, our product is shown as a white square and that of the competitor as a black square. Our attaché case was considered more durable and more stable in a standing position than that of the competition. On the other hand, the attaché case of the competition is easier to open and close, and the layout of the interior is more conveniently arranged. As a result, the contents are easier to find. This immediately shows the potential for improvement of our product.

Step 3: Project Objectives

In this step, the customer's wishes that we want to improve in relation to the competitor are indicated. In other words, the target value for each product attribute is indicated through a score (in Part 3 of the house). Once again, a 5-point scale is used. For the attributes that need no improvement, the target value is put on a par with the current score of the product evaluation. In the project team, it was decided that the product attributes "*easy to carry*," "*adjustable capacity*," "*durability*," "*stable when standing*," and "*privately accessible*," did not need improvement. They received a target value of 4, 4, 4, 4, and 3 respectively. The customer's wishes "*easy to open*" and "*easy to find contents*," which now have a score of respectively 3 and 2 (lower than that of the competition) will be improved to a score of 5 (better than the competition). The wish "*easy to close*" (score 3) will be improved to a score of 4 (small improvement). On the basis of the target value, the improvement grade can now be established.

The improvement rate = target value/evaluation score

From this part of the house, it can be concluded that the QFD-team has decided to improve the opening and closing of the suitcase, and to improve the ease of finding the contents; an improvement rate of 1.7, 1.3, and 2.5 respectively (see Figure 5.7). Next, the weight (importance) of each customer's wish or product attribute is established as a project objective.

The weight = improvement rate x the
relevant importance-weight factor

Accordingly, the weight of "easy to carry" = 1 x 2 = 2.
The weight of "easy to open" = 1.7 x 4 = 6.8.

The weight of "easy to close" = 1.3 x 3 = 3.9, an so forth.

All weights were then added to each other after which the total in the last column was used to calculate the weight in percentage of each attribute. For example, the weight of the attribute "easy to carry" has a percentage value of 6/33.7 x 100% = 6%. Durability has a weight percentage of 15/33.7 x 100% = 15%. The total of all weight percentages is 100 (see Figure 5.7, Part 3).

Step 4: Technical Parameters/Product Specifications

After the activities to visualize the importance of the customer's wishes were finished, it was decided on HOW to handle these wishes. Through brainstorming, it was decided which technical parameters or characteristics are influenced by the different customer wishes; that is, more specifically, the measure in which a "HOW" (specification) relates to a "WHAT" (customer's wish). In this example, nine technical parameters related to the customer's wishes are distinguished, namely: *volume, safety latch, weight when empty*, and so forth (see Part 4 in Figure 5.7). The product design is determined by these parameters.

Step 5: Interaction Matrix

In this step, the level in which the technical parameters influence the customer's wishes is studied. This is done in the interaction matrix (see Part 5 in Figure 5.7). In this matrix, the relationships between the customer's wishes or product attributes and technical parameters are being studied. This involves a coupling between WHAT and HOW. An empty row in the matrix means that there is no relationship between the technical product characteristics and the related customer's wish (the product does not satisfy this need). An empty column points to an unnecessary product characteristic, which is included; making the product too expensive. For each cell of the matrix, it is determined whether there is a relationship between the attributes and the parameters, and if so, how strong this relationship is. The following applies: *a black dot relates to a strong relationship (9), a blank point is a medium relationship (3), a triangle encompasses a weak relationship (1), and an empty cell means that there is no interaction between customer's wishes and product specifications.* Also the speed with which the contents of the suitcase can be found, strongly related to the number of segments or compartments, and to a lesser degree to the volume (weak relationship) and opening angle of the suitcase (medium relationship). *"Easy to carry"* has a strong relationship with the volume and a weak relationship with *"empty weight"* and *"material"* (see Figure 5.7, Part 5). Next, the project importance is indicated for each cell in a score.

Cell score = relationship's strength x the weight (%)

So, cell score "easy to carry volume" = 9x 6 = 54.

Cell score "easy to open wear of the lock" = 3 x 20 = 60, and so forth. The sum of the cell scores per column indicates the priority of the technical parameters for the project. Accordingly, the technical parameter "volume" has a total score of 138 points and material has a total score of 150 points. All these scores are then added up. In this example, it is 1,616 points. Next, the priority per technical parameter is indicated, that is, which product specifications deserve special attention in order to meet the demands of the customers? In this example, the parameters "number of opening steps," "number of segments," and "lock wear" have the highest priority of 21%, 19%, and 14% respectively. In the redesigning phase, these specifications received special attention.

Step 6: Interactions Between Product Specifications (Technical Parameters)

The interactions between the technical parameters are indicated in the roof of the House of Quality. The "number of segments" has a weak relationship with "empty weight" and a medium relationship with "volume." "Lock wear" has a strong relationship with "closing force" and a medium relationship with "number of opening steps" and "safety lock." All these relationships are made explicit in the roof of the House of Quality, which is important for improvement of product specifications.

Step 7: Technical Analysis

In this part of the House of Quality (Part 7 in Figure 5.7), the measure unit of all technical parameters is indicated (HOW MANY). For example, the measure unit of "volume" is cm^3, the measure unit of "closing force" is Newton (N) and the measure unit of "empty weight" is kg. After this, our product and the competitive product are technically judged on these parameters. Our case has six steps to open it, whereas the competitive product requires four. Our lock is also lasting till 5,000 acts of use, whereas the lock of the competitive product already starts showing defects after 3,500 acts of use.

Step 8: Target Value

Target values are determined based on the technical data and the priorities of the parameters. Target values regard the improvements of technical parameters which management pursues. Design teams executed these improvements. In this example, the emphases were mainly on reducing the number of steps to open the case, for which a target value of two is chosen. The solution to this problem was a central safety lock as the locking principle. With this, the durability has been improved even further. Furthermore, the number of segments has also been increased (from five to eight) to improve the clarity of the arrangement.

5.5 IDOV CASE STUDY—MEMORY CELL DESIGN OPTIMIZATION

In this case study, we will demonstrate the application of the IDOV model to optimize the design of a memory cell that will be installed in a medical device. The objective of this project was to identify, evaluate, and select the key product variables/inputs that will have the largest influence on the performance to optimize the outputs/responses of the memory cell. The main challenge of the project would be to select the vital few input variables that would contribute to the optimization of the performance of the output.

The Identify Phase

The purpose of the Identify phase was to develop a clear definition of the project and to define a detailed plan that would drive the overall implementation of the project. The company's first step was to formulate the Organizational Balanced Scorecard (OBSC) and the related Project BSC. They also stimulated their employees to formulate their Personal Balanced Scorecard (PBSC) in order to let them work better, to improve their effectiveness and to engage them based on the discussed alignment technique (ambition meeting between the project leader and his project team members (see chapter 4). As a result, the (based on the Project BSC) a project was established (based on the Project BSC) and the right people were selected to be members of this project team. The business case provided compelling reasons why the memory cell design optimization project is critical to the organization from a strategic perspective. Once the business case had been clearly established and management had signed off on it, the team moved forward with implementing the Project BSC. Also the team addressed expectations, scope, deliverables, preliminary schedule, and resources, all included in the Project BSC.

At the end of the Identify phase, the team prepared for the first tollgate review, presenting the work to date to senior management and key personnel to ensure that the project was on track.

Completion of the Identify phase of the IDOV model ensured the following:

- Business and market opportunities were well defined.
- Potential roadblocks had been addressed.
- External and internal risks had been identified.
- Critical milestones and tollgates had been recognized.

The following IDOV tools were used in this phase:

- Personal Balanced Scorecard.
- Organizational Balanced Scorecard.
- Project Balanced Scorecard.
- Customer interviews.
- Benchmarking.
- Quality Function Deployment (QFD).

The Design Phase

For this project, the purpose of the design phase was to facilitate the design of robust products through Design of Experiments (DOE) or simulation in order to determine the critical drivers of conformance. Starting with the concept, the team developed both the high-level and the detailed design. Once the key elements of the design had been identified, the team prioritized these elements and established requirements for the critical ones. Alternative designs were also developed to the required level of detail and then tested against the requirements. A final design was then selected for further development or implementation. This design was formally tested by modeling the relationships between the design requirements and the process variables that affect output performance. Statistical tolerance was used to ensure that the variation of the detailed design elements combined did not exceed the overall targets for variation. Finally, the team tested the design components and prepared for pilot and full-scale deployment.

Completion of the design phase of the IDOV model ensures the following:

- A list of detailed design requirements had been generated.
- Critical process control items had been identified.
- Process capability had been calculated.
- Critical part characteristics had been defined.
- A complete technical specification of the product had been developed.

After evaluating several concept designs, it was determined that Design of Experiments (DOE) method was the best tool to help us meet the project objective. DOE is a series of structured tests where deliberate, simultaneous changes are conducted on the process input variables such (i.e., temperature, pressure, etc.) to evaluate the effect of these changes on the process output variables or responses. These tests are analyzed as whole.

Based on previous experimentation, competitor benchmarking, customer input, and engineering judgment, the number of factors to be investigated were reduced to four input variables: A, B, C, and D. These input variables were tested at two levels, Low and High. The output measured was R (response). The objective of this experiment was to test the hypothesis that R was a function of A, B, C, and D variables. The main goal is to optimize R (the higher R value, the better).

The variables were summarized in Table 5.2 and test design matrix with eight tests:

The plus/minus notation illustrates the high/low level of the input variables. When a run is performed, the factors are set to the noted + and – levels and a response value is then recorded for the test. The following steps were followed to conduct the analysis of the Design of Experiment:

1. Objective was stated
2. Factors and level of interest were selected
3. The appropriate sample size was selected and experimental runs were randomized.
4. Experiment was run
5. Main effects of these inputs were estimated

Table 5.2. The Variables Summarized and Test Design Matrix With Eight Tests

Inputs Variables	(+) Value	(–) Value
A	Low	High
B	Low	High
C	Low	High
D	Low	High

		Input	Variables			Response
Run Order	Run #	A	B	C	D	R
6	1	–	–	–	–	
2	2	+	–	–	+	
7	3	–	+	–	+	
8	4	+	+	-	–	
1	5	–	–	+	+	
4	6	+	–	+	–	
5	7	–	+	+	–	
3	8	+	+	+	+	

The following preliminary results for the response/output were obtained using the above steps. Minitab was used to analyze the experiment. Minitab is statistical analysis software; we will cover an overview of Minitab in the Appendix.

- Looking at (Figure 5.8), the Pareto chart of the effects in Minitab showed that variables A and C were the most influential factors on the response R.
- The main effects plot (Figure 5.9) shows similar result that A, C were the most influential variables.

The Optimize Phase

The next step was the Optimize phase. The objective of this phase was to optimize the design and improve its capability. The team applied Response Surface Method (RSM) to optimize the response/output R using only A and C variables and ignore variables B and D since they have little influence on the output. Response surface methodology is a set of techniques used to determine the Optimum relationship among several input variables and the response variable. The optimization helped us select the best setting of variables A and C which resulted in the optimum value of the response R.

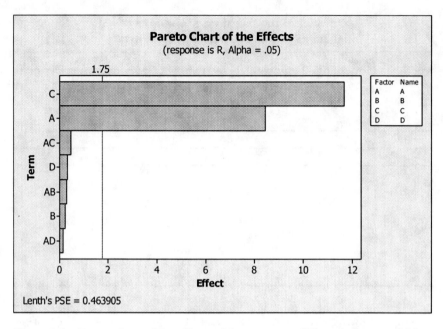

Figure 5.8.   Pareto chart of the effects of the memory cell battery input variables.

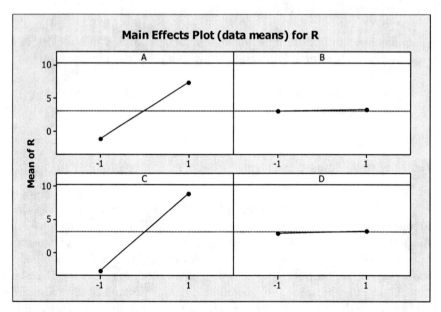

Figure 5.9.   Main effect plot of the effects of the memory cell battery input variables.

The following IDOV tools were used in this phase:

Design of Experiment (DOE)
Monte Carlo Simulation
Robust Design
Parameter Design

The Verify Phase

The goal of the verify phase was to test the proposed design and to prepare for implementation. The deliverables of this phase included a working prototype and plans for full implementation that also reveal how the process will be controlled to ensure process capability. The team used a pilot to verify that the product is capable of meeting customer requirements. Once the pilot had been conducted and reviewed, the team developed an implementation plan that identified how the design would be rolled out. Once responsibilities for implementation had been transitioned, the team conducted a formal closure process to capture lessons learned.

The final tollgate review was intended to ensure that the organization is prepared to assume responsibility for the ongoing monitoring of the design. Completion of the verify phase ensured the following:

- A pilot had been completed and pilot test results had been evaluated.
- Full-scale implementation plans had been produced.
- The project had been handed off to an implementation team.

Tools used during the verify phase included the following:

- Reliability Testing.
- Control Plan.
- Statistical Process Control.
- Project documentation.

As a result of this project, the company was awarded a 400 million dollar manufacturing contract from one of their major customers.

5.5 TPS-LEAN SIX SIGMA IN SERVICE

Service industry and functions are often overlooked in traditional quality efforts. This is amazing when one considers how many people are actually employed in a service role. A recent analysis reported by the department of Statistics presentation at the University of Idaho, a recent analysis by shows that 79% of the U.S. workforce is employed in commercial businesses. Ninety percent of those employed in manufacturing industries are actually doing service work such as finance, marketing, sales, distribution and purchasing. This is an additional 19% of the workforce. This leads to 98% of the U.S. workforce is involved in "service" work.

79% commercial business + 19% service employees at manufacturers = 98%

Think about this in your everyday life. The last time you had a complaint about an interaction with a business, was your complaint about a product or about the service and delivery of that product? Most of the complaints we have had in my personal interactions are with the delivery of the service. During our years in a professional role in working with suppliers of product, most of the complaints we have had are related to the service aspects of the company and its people, not the quality of the product. Some of the factors contributing to these service problems are that deadlines are not met, the wrong information is given, there is a failure to communicate needs internally, refusal to acknowledge the need to improve quality and stonewalling, just to mention a few.

In the business world, early quality efforts focused on manufactured goods. Due to the fact that early successes were in manufacturing, there is a misconception that these methodologies do not apply to service or transactional type industries or processes. It is important to remember the long history of quality methods being applied in manufacturing. Early breakthroughs came through in the manufacturing world, from Deming Cycle (Plan-Do-Check-Act), statistical evaluations such as SPC, and flow charting. Manufacturers were also the early adopters of Lean and Six Sigma, building on the history of previous programs and successes. These methods do apply, and with creative thought on the part of employees, and patience of management to bring employees along the learning curve, it is proven out. In fact, we believe that the more dependent on human input/creativity a process is perceived to be, the more it will potentially benefit from reevaluation using Lean Six Sigma thinking. As TPS-Lean Six Sigma is more directly linked to how people work and their experience, education, and desires, it is more intuitive how TPS-Lean Six Sigma will apply to these services and transactional processes.

First, let's discuss today's office environment. Much of the work is done on computers and communicated electronically—either through e-mails or updates in systems such as enterprise resource planning, ERPs, or data. Add the effects of globalization, and these e-mails and updates occur 24 hours a day, 7 days a week in many offices around the world. How can a company "walk the flow" or pull together a Kaizen to streamline? How can team work on reducing defects without a common language as to what constitutes a defect? Each person probably has his or her own definition of quality and perception as to what the process is or should be.

These common concerns with applying TPS-Lean Six Sigma to nonmanufacturing processes are precisely the reasons why TPS-Lean Six Sigma will provide the greatest benefits in service environments. In production settings, over time, people have commonly walked along the production processes, understood how raw materials were transformed to the final product, and had ideas on how to improve this. For the service industry, how can we overcome this barrier and apply TPS-Lean Six Sigma to a process that we can't see? First, to steal the title from a popular Lean book titled *Learning to See*. Where is a value stream map more valuable then when it is the first time an invisible process has been laid out in black and white? How wonderful the revelation when a group of people that input data/pull data from that behind the scenes agree on the process, yes, that's how it works or yes, this is how it would work in an ideal world. It can be a truly revolutionary moment.

Here is an example where we witnessed this moment when folks in service functions successfully applied TPS-Lean Six Sigma to their process, and discovered how these "manufacturing" tools applied to their field.

Case Study—Advertising

Several years ago, one of the authors was working with a commodity manager (CM) responsible for advertising from a supplier. Advertising is successful due to creativity and the ability to pull together data, information, and goals in a unique way that supports a company's brand. It is also the critical intersection of several service functions for any company: marketing, research, purchasing, "production," and advertising.

The problems the commodity manager was seeing, as she worked on building the relationship between all these functions and across company lines, were many. The main issue was there was a problem with the cycle time. It took too long for advertising programs to be launched, for the newest market research to be pulled into new campaigns, for approvals of purchase orders to go through. Adding to this, there was the pressure to get more value for less money, and the attitude that Advertising is a creative process and—you can't apply Lean Six Sigma to a creative process. The net result was that the ultimate item being procured—the ad agency's employees' time for creativity—was being squeezed. Most of the time available was being spent on communications, miscommunications and approvals.

The commodity manager needed to get all the players on the same page fast. She had to shrink the time from initial request to delivery of approved campaigns/ads while freeing up time for the creative aspects of the project. Bottom line, she saw a lot of wasted time and she didn't like being in charge of a process that was broken and seeing the company throwing away money on a process that wasted more time then any she had ever seen.

We agreed that mapping the process was important to understand the process through both companies. This could only occur with openness and teamwork by an empowered team.

The team met in one location for 4 days. This included training sessions followed by application of Value Stream Mapping and DMAIC methodology. The team went through the following steps:

1. Agree on WHAT it was that we as a customer wanted—what we were willing to pay for (creative ideas quickly, not high salaried execs chasing down approvals)

2. Create Process Flow/Value Stream of current process, including how data (ideas) are transferred and stored. (For many service processes, the main process is the flow of information) Since cycle time was a concern, the team included times on flow chart—whether approval time, "inventory" time (e.g., sitting in e-mail folder), waiting for updated research data to be analyzed, and so forth. Also identify any key linkages (Item E cannot happen until B and H are approved).

3. Define an ideal state as to how it should work (Future State Map). This is where the team challenged their "we've always done it that way" thinking by considering "is the customer willing to pay for this activity?"

4. Brainstorm a list of things that could take them from current state to ideal state.

5. Implement as many of the quick fixes identified as possible immediately after the meeting. This was only possible due to empowered team members.

6. Prioritize longer lead items. Assign a point person for each. Agree to the next "update" meeting to review the progress of the longer lead items.

The team walked out of this meeting with a common understanding of the process. They decided what the ideal process would need to look like and what would work, and that involved a large reduction in cycle time, reduction in the number of approvals, and a higher confidence in the approval process. Due to the immediate success of the "quick fixes" people had time to work on the longer lead items.

Case Study—Successfully Avoiding Medical Errors in Rotterdam Eye Hospital and The Hague Medical Centre in the Netherlands Based on the TPS-Lean Six Sigma Risk Management Model

Administering the wrong medicine, amputating the wrong leg, operating on the wrong eye.... With an effective risk analysis process, these errors could have been prevented, and considerable cost, as well as, a lot of suffering would have been avoided. By including preventive actions in the process execution in a routine way and making this a way of life in the organization, the number of medical errors can be drastically decreased. In the Appendix, we describe the successful application of the TPS-Lean Six Sigma Risk Management Model (Process FMEA) at two large hospitals in the Netherlands; Rotterdam Eye Hospital (*Oogziekenhuis Rotterdam*) and The Hague Medical Centre (*Medical Centre Haaglanden*–MCH). We did apply the TPS-Lean Six Sigma Risk Management model successfully in order to reduce the risk of medical errors. This Appendix describes the results of these very successfully executed risk management analyses in both hospitals. The results were very positive; using a team approach over three sessions of 1 hour, more than 30 improvement points were generated. Using this process, a stable basis was created for an efficient and manageable process. Cost control and implementation time are positively influenced through this process.

CREATIVITY

One of the biggest barriers that are faced in applying programs such as TPS-Lean Six Sigma to service processes is that these are the processes that are viewed as creative enterprises. We have worked with computer programmers, research scientists, purchasing, accountants, lawyers, advertising executives, market research, food service, insurance companies and mechanics that have all had the same concern with applying rigor to their profession. Professions they view as more of an art than a science. However, the greatest singers are able to improvise because they have studied the basic techniques of scales, notes, harmony, theory, and so forth. Then when that singer works with other musicians, they have a common framework in which to communicate and define how the song will go. They are then able to apply that knowledge in a systematic and creative manner to generate wonderful music. The rigor and practice of a basic process brought out the best they had to offer when they worked together. The same holds true in service functions. Development of basic "rules" or "processes" (i.e., "scales") allows improvisation within that framework.

This concept is important as one of the greatest wastes that we have seen in working with companies is that of human ability. So many organizations drive a culture of do as you are told, we don't want your ideas. This attitude isn't a conscious one in most cases, but it is there. And as companies expect people to do more with less, it becomes even more apparent. This reality of wasting human ability is why many Lean Sensei's now talk of the "8th Waste" in addition to the traditional 7 Wastes. The eight form of waste, they say, is human capital. While it is acknowledged, how to eliminate this waste—that is, creating a happy and energized workforce—we have not until now seen a solid approach to how to remove the encumbrances on people. TPS-Lean Six Sigma has been recognized as a revolutionary concept because it takes into consideration human capital, in harmony with its deployment of Lean Six Sigma. In the next chapter, we will discuss the implementation of this concept in detail.

CHAPTER 6

IMPLEMENTING
TPS-LEAN SIX SIGMA

To find out how to improve productivity, quality and performance—
ask the people who do the work.

—Harvard Business Review

Change is the law of life. And those who look only to the past or present are certain to
miss the future.

— John F. Kennedy

In this chapter, we will focus on the successful implementation of TPS-Lean Six Sigma. It's related to the continuous improvement and knowledge and learning stages in the TPS-Lean Six Sigma model (see Figure 4.1). Some companies underestimate the importance of a well planned and defined TPS-Lean Six Sigma implementation strategy. The one question that is often asked is "Is there a right way to implement TPS-Lean Six Sigma?" In actuality, there is no one right way to implement TPS-Lean Six Sigma. It very much depends on the culture and the knowledge of the organization. A successful implementation is a function of many elements such as establishing leadership buy-in, employee buy-in, having a well defined deployment plan, creating an effective organizational infrastructure, utilizing the right resources, having the proper training and knowledge, and selecting the right projects. We will discuss the importance of

TPS-Lean Six Sigma: Linking Human Capital to Lean Six Sigma: A New Blueprint for
Creating High Performance Companies, pp. 177–217
Copyright © 2007 by Information Age Publishing
All rights of reproduction in any form reserved.

each of these elements in more detail in this chapter. These elements are the key to obtaining the expected return on investment (ROI), and organizational growth. It is recommended that an organization benchmark and provide success stories and examples of successful TPS-Lean Six Sigma deployments from other organizations.

Implementation Success Equation:

Implementation Success = f (leadership and employee buy-in, deployment plan, infrastructure development, right resources, proper training, and project selection)

6.1 LEADERSHIP AND EMPLOYEE BUY-IN

The toughest part of deploying TPS-Lean Six Sigma is getting top management's and employee's/project team member's interest and commitment prior to a full scale deployment. Active involvement of all relevant stakeholders and alignment of the company's leadership are extremely critical to the success of the deployment. Any company, who does not achieve this commitment, is doomed to failure. To achieve this commitment, it is recommended that top management and employees be trained to realize the value and the benefit of TPS-Lean Six Sigma and understand their roles to support the initiative. A very effective way to create commitment throughout the whole organization is to coach (project) leaders and employees/project members in how to formulate their Personal Balanced Scorecard (PBSC) and align this with the shared ambition of the organization and the TPS-Lean Six Sigma project (see chapter 4). If there is an effective balance between their interests (their personal ambitions) and those of the organization and the project (shared ambitions), they will work with greater commitment toward the deployment of the TPS-Lean Six Sigma project. The emphasis here lies on intrinsic motivation.

Intrinsic motivation is inherently pleasurable and it arises from within. People do something because they enjoy doing it.

Development of the personal and organizational/project ambition takes place simultaneously. When we answer the question of what we want for the organization/project and where we want to go together, we also ask what we want for ourselves, and which situation accommodates both sets of interest's best, so it's a win-win. Champions/Master Black Belts/Black Belts/Green Belts/project leaders and project team members will work with dedication for something they believe in, which is interesting, exciting, and ultimately a learning experience. A foundation is hereby created for a true learning organization. For the sake of leadership development, commitment, employee engagement, and buy-in, we have introduced the TPS-Lean Six Sigma Coaching framework in chapter 10, which is part our Academy for TPS-Lean Six Sigma Certification program.

Implementation of TPS-Lean Six Sigma is related to change. As we have stressed earlier, before there can be effective organizational change *you* should change first. You must learn new things and unlearn others, before you can change yourself based on the Personal Balanced Scorecard. This individual learning must then be converted into collective learning.

Learning is a behavioral change; individual behavioral change has to be converted into collective behavioral change, which leads ultimately to organizational change.

Despite the necessity for change, many people despise it. They are afraid of change and by nature resist it because it may affect their established ideas and opinions. Disappointments from previous experiences, fear of the unknown, distrust, lack of information, and insufficient affiliation with the current culture are the most important factors that account for this resistance. In an organization, therefore, we can distinguish two kinds of people:

1. People who think they will be victims of change and who therefore resist, become angry, and get depressed; and
2. People who completely support, design, and plan the change.

Especially in the initial phase of the implementation, resistance to change seems very high because certain people in the organization, due to their own uncertainties and insecurities, see the proposed change as a threat. Conflicts then emerge in which the old trusted situation is frequently referred to. Examples of expressions of people resistant to change related to the implementation of TPS-Lean Six Sigma includes:

- Let's just stay with both feet on the ground.
- I do not see why we have to change—everything is going so well as it is.
- It is going well with our lean Six Sigma project—why should we do it differently?
- We are already the best in the market.
- Organizationally, this is absolutely impossible.
- This is ridiculous.

- We have always done the Lean Six Sigma way, without any problems.
- It has always been like this, and we have always done it like this.
- At the moment, we are too busy to do this.
- This will be costly; do we have the money for it?
- Is this necessary? We have already tried new quality concepts numerous times before and it hasn't worked.
- Do those Managers know how busy we are?
- Stop it; it will never work.
- It is against our principles.
- We are too small for this.
- There is something else behind this.
- I know it is not going to work.
- Think about it if you must, but I like the way things are going now and will continue on this path.

Examples of expressions of people who accept the change include:

- When are we going to start with TPS-Lean Six Sigma?
- How can we learn more about this new concept?
- We can use the TPS-Lean Six Sigma software as well.
- How can we measure the results?
- Let me see if there are any alternatives.

According to James O'Toole (1996), there are many reasons for people to resist change. These are described in the following boxed text.

James O'Toole's Thirty-Three Hypotheses on Why People Resist Change

1. Homeostasis—Change is not a natural condition.
2. Stare decisis—Presumption is given to the status quo; the burden of proof is on change.
3. Inertia—It takes considerable power to change course.
4. Satisfaction—Most people like things the way they are.
5. Lack of ripeness—The preconditions for change have not been met; the time isn't right.
6. Fear—People fear the unknown.
7. Self-interest—The change may be good for others but not for us.

8. Lack of self-confidence—We are not up to the new challenges.

9. Future shock—Overwhelmed by change, we hunker down and resist it.

10. Futility—We view all change as superficial, cosmetic, and illusory, so why bother?

11. Lack of knowledge—We do not know how to change or what to change to.

12. Human nature—Humans are competitive, aggressive, greedy, self-ish, and lack the altruism necessary to change.

13. Cynicism—We suspect the motives of the change agent.

14. Perversity—Change sounds good, but we fear that the unintended consequences will be bad.

15. Individual genius versus group mediocrity—Those of us with mediocre minds cannot see the wisdom of the change.

16. Ego—The powerful refuse to admit that they have been wrong.

17. Short-term thinking—People cannot defer gratification.

18. Myopia—We cannot see that the change is in the broader self-interest.

19. Sleepwalking—Most of us lead unexamined lives.

20. Snow blindness—Groupthink, or social conformity.

21. Collective fantasy—We do not learn from experience, and we view everything in the light of preconceived notions.

22. Chauvinistic conditioning—We are right; they who want us to change are wrong.

23. Fallacy of the exception—The change might work elsewhere, but we are different.

24. Ideology—We have different worldviews and inherently conflicting values.

25. Institutionalism—Individuals may change but groups do not.

26. *Natura no facit saltum*—"Nature does not proceed by leaps."

27. The rectitude of the powerful—Who are we to question the leaders who set us on the current course?

28. "Change has no constituency"—The minority has a greater stake in preserving the status quo than the majority has in changing.

29. Determinism—There is nothing anyone can do to bring about a purposeful change.

30. Scientism—The lessons of history are scientific, and therefore there is nothing to learn from them.

31. Habit.

32. The despotism of custom—The ideas of change agents are seen as a reproach to society.
33. Human mindlessness.

Source: Used with permission from Joseph Boyett and Jimmy Boyett. *The Guru Guide.* New York: John Wiley & Sons, 1998, p. 51.

These reactions of resistance can frustrate the change process completely if there is no adequate response. Resistance to change, and expressions of negative reaction to it, often occurs in the following six phases:

1. *Passivity:* People are informed about the new plans and react reserved and with uncertainty.
2. *Denial:* People are skeptical and deny the appropriateness of the suggested improvement plans. This is often expressed in comments such as: "What a backward idea; who thought this up? This is certainly not going to work here."
3. *Anger:* If the plans continue, people react angrily and withdraw.
4. *Negotiation:* They try to reach a compromise (through negotiation) by minimizing proposals and partially accepting the plans.
5. *Depression*: Because the complete plan proposal must be implemented, without any unfinished work, people have to accept the change. This results in passive behavior, which eventually leads to depression.
6. *Acceptance:* Changes are now part of the work process. Now what is often heard is: "Yes, it works! We should have started this earlier."

These different phases must be acknowledged in time to take the proper measures. During the passivity phase and depression phase, management should adopt an understanding attitude and be open to hearing negative reactions. During the phases of denial, anger, and negotiation, a firmer attitude on the part of management is required. The different phases in the responses of employees must be recognized early and should be moved through to the phase of acceptance as soon as possible. That is why those who completely accept the changes should be involved in change projects. The force field analysis (see Appendix) can be used to systematically identify areas of resistance. It involves creating a force field of driving forces, which aid the change or make it more likely to occur, and restraining forces, which are points of resistance or things getting in the way of change.

John Kotter (1996) explains that before most people can understand and accept a proposed change they seek answers to a lot of questions, such as:

- What will this mean to me?
- What will it mean to my friends?
- What will it mean to the organization?
- What other alternatives are there?
- Are there better options?
- If I'm going to operate differently, can I do it?
- How will I learn the new skills I need?
- Will I have to make sacrifices? What will they be? How do I feel about having to make them?
- Do I really believe this change is necessary?
- Do I really believe what I'm hearing about the direction for the future?
- Is this the right direction for us to take?
- Are others playing some game, perhaps to improve their position at my expense?

"Not understanding" is, according to McCall (1998), one of the most common reasons why people do not change. Table 6.1 presents McCall's summary of the answers he received from managers in his workshops whom he had asked the following question: Why didn't you change what you knew needed to change? This summary shows how an inadequate or inaccurate flow of information severely hampers the learning process. According to McCall, many of these obstacles have to do with the person in question, who does not want to listen, is defensive, or refuses to accept feedback. As explained earlier, a very effective way to tackle this is to coach leaders and employees to formulate their Personal Balanced Scorecard (PBSC) and align this with the shared ambition(s) of their organization and project.

There are important methods to handle resistance to change in a positive way, however. These included the following, among others:

- Create inner involvement, self-confidence and commitment in your leaders and employees, and change their mindsets by empowering them to formulate their own Personal Ambition and align this with their shared organizational and project ambition (see chapter 4).
- Top management must communicate with employees face-to-face and supply them with information about the context of the TPS-

Table 6.1.   Reasons why People do not Change (McCall, 1998)

• Mutilated feedback	• Rewarded to remain the same	• The context has not been changed
• Confused announcements	• The cost in time and energy	• too busy
• No feedback	• The benefits do not out-weigh the costs	• busy with other things
• Do not understand	• The benefits are unclear	• Other people do not change
• Do not listen	• Imposed upon from the outside	• Other people do not see the changes
• Do not believe	• No personal involvement with change	• Other people do not allow the change
• Do not accept	• Does not know what is really important	• Painful, demeaning
• Make me have to admit mistakes or shortcomings	• Not clear what should change	• Afraid of manipulation
• Does not fit in the self image	• Not clear what the result of change will be	• Fear for the unknown
• Pertinent do not hear it	• Does not know what is really important	• Arrogance
• Take it personal	• Requires giving up something worthwhile	• Afraid to make mistakes
• Are inclined to overreact	• Does not know how to change	• Vulnerable during change efforts
• Do not take criticism	• No possibility to practice	• Fear of failure
• Distrust the motives of others	• No role models	• Fear that I won't be good enough
• Untrustworth source	• I function well the way now I am	• Earlier failed effort to change
• Others do not know the real me	• I feel fine now	• Too lazy
• The fear that unpleasant facts may be true	• Do not want to change	• Afraid to take up a vulnerable position.
• Distrust people who give feedback	• Cannot change	• Convinced of own right
• It hurts to hear negative things	• It would be ridiculous	• Has the need to be thought of as nice by others
• Negative feedback angers me	• Feeling of incompetence	• Undermines self-trust
• I have the feeling it is not correct	• No support	• Threatens self-image
• Gives me the feeling of being put in a corner like a child	• No stimulation to change	• Deforms self-image
• Too much pride	• Intimidated by others	

Lean Sigma project and related organizational changes; in addition, be honest about the actual situation. State clearly how long the change will last and what the consequences will be. Provide timely information to personnel. Silence creates doubt and usually causes rumors to spread, which undermines trust in Management. Do not provide too much information at once, because employees need time to absorb the information.

- Support the TPS-Lean Six Sigma project proposals with clear arguments.
- Inform project members and employees about the advantages of change and how the gap between present and future situations will be closed.
- Have meetings with those people who resist change and give a detailed reaction to all their objections.
- Involve project members and employees in the development and implementation of the scorecards and create transparency in responsibilities and authorities.
- Involve key-persons in the decision-making process; when stakeholders are included in a decision, acceptance will greatly increase, and therefore also the effect of the implementation.
- Put the project on hold if there is too much resistance and you are not able to count on the support of the majority.
- Drive out organizational fear and distrust. These inhibit the ability to learn. According to Pfeffer and Sutton (2002), fear and distrust can be driven out by:

  - *Predictability:* As much as possible, give people information on what will happen to them and when.
  - *Understanding:* Explain in detail why certain actions were taken, especially those that alarm and hurt.
  - *Control:* As much as possible, give people influence over what is happening, when it happens, and how it happens; allow them to decide their own future.
  - *Compassion:* Show sympathy and concern about the disruption, emotional needs, and financial burdens confronting employees.

There are also other methods to motivate and stimulate the TPS-Lean Six Sigma related change, such as the following (Rampersad, 2003):

1. Probe continuously to determine whether or not people are ready for change.

2. Discuss the TPS-Lean Six Sigma project and related new ways of working with employees in a series of meetings; articulate this actively. Inform employees directly, honestly, clearly, and consistently (i.e. uniformly throughout the entire organization). Clearly indicate what can be discussed and what cannot. Communicate these both internally and externally and orally, as well as, in writing. Use brochures, newsletters, and other documents. Keep your communications simple, and use analogies and case studies. Williams Pasmore (1994) states that much of your communication effort may involve educating your employees about the business and competitive environment, such as the points listed in the following boxed text.

What Employees Need to Know About Their Company

- Employees need to know what managers know, including how to read an income statement and a balance sheet, what makes the number on each get larger or smaller, what the numbers really mean, and where the company stands today as compared to where it was before, and how it stands versus the competition.
- Employees need to know the threats to the organization and the plans about how to deal with them, including the rationale for these plans and what alternatives were considered before deciding on this course of action.
- Employees need to understand decision-making processes and criteria and how much risk is acceptable.
- Employees need to understand the consequences of poor decision making and what to do when the unexpected happens.
- Employees need to understand customers' expectations and how to better meet them.
- Employees need to be introduced to global economics.
- Employees need to know about health-care costs and workers'
- Compensation, about the costs of carrying inventory and liability insurance.
- Employees need to understand the technical system used to produce goods or services, how it functions, and why it was designed the way it was designed.
- Employees need to understand what technical alternatives are possible and what will be involved in applying them.
- Employees need to develop the social skills that allow them to take part in participative activities, including speaking in front of

others, confronting differences, understanding how to reach a consensus, facilitating the participation of others, and listening.

Source: Used with permission from Joseph Boyett and Jimmy Boyett. *The Guru Guide.* New York: John Wiley & Sons, 1998, p. 64.

---

3. Indicate why there is a need for change; the organization must be convinced of the need for this change. A popular way to do this is to compare the organization to more successful competitors. Another way is to map customer dissatisfaction and use it to illustrate decreasing performance. Under extreme conditions, make it clear that the long-term survival of the organization is at stake. In such cases, the present situation must be perceived as negative. Making people acknowledge how poorly the organization is doing creates dissatisfaction with the present situation. This helps to convince even skeptics of the need to change.

4. Base the TPS-Lean Six Sigma proposals on solid facts and promise employees concrete improvements; a distinct solution must be presented.

5. Illustrate clearly how the TPS-Lean Six Sigma change will be realized, based on a solid implementation plan, in which the steps to be taken are explained. During the implementation of the change, inform employees regularly with trustworthy information.

6. Introduce new training to develop new skills such as interpersonal skills, customer orientation, teamwork, leadership, coaching, and others. Involve employees in the planning and introduction of the TPS-Lean Six Sigma project; acceptance by and involvement of the employees is essential for implementing change successfully. Without the continuous involvement of people, every TPS-Lean Six Sigma project is doomed to fail. After all, the effectiveness of a strategy is not only dependent on its quality but on the acceptance of it by the employees and project members as well.

7. Reward those who produce results; intrinsic rewards (such as acknowledgment and recognition) are preferred over extrinsic rewards (such as money).

8. Provide the TPS-Lean Six Sigma project with a strong identity; give it an ambitious name so that employees can feel they have a real objective to accomplish and a dream to realize.

9. Start cautiously with a pilot project and practice with it. Start with the easiest part of the TPS-Lean Six Sigma project, one that can produce quick results.

10. Top management must take the lead in the introduction of TPS-Lean Six Sigma concept to achieve change. Place this subject on the agenda of monthly management team meetings. In this context, keep in mind the following statements (Senge, 1990):

   • Substantial change is hardly possible, if it is only directed from top Management.

   • Cynicism is mainly cultivated when there are elaborate announcements from the CEO and programs rolled out by headquarters that distract everyone from the actual change activities.

   • Support of top management does not measure up to the real commitment and learning capacities at all levels of the organization. When Management authority is used unwisely, it diminishes the chances that commitment and learning capacity will develop.

11. Start the process of continuous improvement, learning, and development at the top management level, and use a layered implementation approach to reach lower levels (see cascading/deployment process in chapter 4).

12. Eliminate those elements that have a negative effect on people's morale and motivation within the organization. In practice, opponents of change seem to slow down, boycott, and sabotage things; use old rules and hidden agendas; supply wrong information; evade new tasks; and play the victim. Those who block and oppose change must be guided to improve their attitude based on the PBSC. If this does not succeed, they will have to be put on a sidetrack elsewhere in the organization or even removed, if possible. Dare to take these measures, because my experience has shown that "rotten apples" in the organization can completely disrupt and frustrate the TPS-Lean Six Sigma project. Therefore, do not hold off taking the appropriate measures!

13. Give project leaders and team's authority and "ownership" over the processes for which they are responsible.

14. Make employees shareholders, so that they will behave as owners.

Before you implement the TPS-Lean Six Sigma project, verify if the circumstances for implementation are favorable. Insight into the problems that may occur during execution will be needed. In Table 6.2, we introduced a checklist that can be used to create insight into the introductory circumstances of the TPS-Lean Six Sigma project (based on Rampersad, 2003). To this end, complete the survey in Table 6.2 by marking the number that best reflects the accuracy of the assertions in

Table 6.2. TPS-Lean Six Sigma Implementation Quick Scan

Circle the correct number: 1 = no, 2 = somewhat, 3 = yes

Areas of Attention	Yes	Somewhat	No
1. Is there commitment in top management to implement the TPS-Lean Six Sigma project?	3	2	1
2. Do those involved consider the related change crucial to the company's survival, and do they realize the usefulness of it?	3	2	1
3. Has attention been paid to the involvement of all key-persons at the decision-making process?	3	2	1
4. Has a competent TPS-Lean Six Sigma manager been appointed to coach and facilitate the TPS-Lean Six Sigma process?	3	2	1
5. Can managers handle the change?	3	2	1
6. Has special attention been given to developing the new skills the employees will need?	3	2	1
7. Has a cultural diagnosis been conducted and the results communicated to the employees?	3	2	1
8. Can the idea behind the change be made understandable to all involved?	3	2	1
9. Can adequate and clear information be given about the what, why, how, and consequences of the TPS-Lean Six Sigma project?	3	2	1
10. Is there sufficient necessity for the introduction of the TPS-Lean Six Sigma project?	3	2	1
11. Is the necessity for and advantage of the TPS-Lean Six Sigma project been clearly communicated to all those involved?	3	2	1
12. Have the advantages of the TPS-Lean Six Sigma project been carefully weighed against the disadvantages?	3	2	1
13. Do the employees know what has to be changed?	3	2	1
14. Does a TPS-Lean Six Sigma plan exist in which the steps of the change to be implemented are clearly defined?	3	2	1
15. Has special attention been given to those who feel they will become victims of the change?	3	2	1
16. Have you listened effectively to the people who resist the implementation of the TPS-Lean Six Sigma project, and have you studied their situation?	3	2	1
17. Have the problems that accompanied previous changes been solved?	3	2	1
18. Has there been benchmarking regarding the change?	3	2	1
19. Have you driven out fear and distrust among the employees regarding the implementation of the TPS-Lean Six Sigma project?	3	2	1
20. Will enough people change?	3	2	1
Total Score		points	

your organization. Use the scoring key (1 to 3) at the end of the Table 6.2; 1 = no, 2 = somewhat, 3 = yes. Add these scores vertically. The closer your total score gets to 60, the better the circumstances of implementing TPS-Lean Six Sigma is. The closer your total score is to 20, the lower the chance to implement TPS-Lean Six Sigma effectively. The implementation of the change project will be unfavorable if there are too many questions answered with "no." Such questions should receive extra attention beforehand. Discuss your scores in your TPS-Lean Six Sigma project team and in your organization and indicate what could have been done better.

6.2 DEPLOYMENT PLANNING

The planning stage is critical to the success of TPS-Lean Six Sigma implementation, see chapter 4. When most companies decide that TPS-Lean Six Sigma is the right business initiative, they want to launch it as soon as possible. Traditionally, management may send a few people for Black Belt training and expect them to solve the company's chronic problems. Our experience has been that most companies who take this approach fail. Initially, Management is not ready to develop a proper deployment plan without more detailed understanding of TPS-Lean Six Sigma, for this reason, it is strongly recommended that the leadership team attend Executive and Champion workshops to obtain the knowledge needed for a successful deployment.

The deployment plan should focus on the resources and the activities which contribute the most to the project BSC, OBSC and PBSC. The organizational improvement actions in the Organizational BSC are related to the Project BSC (business alignment), the desired organizational behaviors are related to the Personal BSC (cultural alignment), and the match between Personal BSC and Project BSC (project alignment) causes employee engagements within the project (see Figure 6.1). The elements of this model have been described in chapter 4.

Deployment Planning will outline the scale and the timing of the initiative, and will take into account any concerns about resources, training cost, company policies, guidelines, rules, and goals. The deployment plan should be continually evaluated and updated throughout the deployment phases. The deployment plan should cover the following key elements:

- Is passionate and has courage, self-responsibility, self-confidence, and self-knowledge (to be developed by the PBSC).
- Project BSC related to the Organizational BSC.

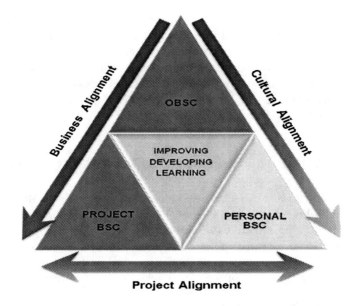

Figure 6.1.   TPS-Lean Six Sigma Shared Vision Flow Down.

- Project and operational metrics (how success is measured, part of the Project BSC).
- Project prioritization and selection process.
- Project review, reporting and tracking system.
- Using the TPS-Lean Six Sigma Project BSCsoft; an interactive software system that will assist you with the successful formulation and implementation of the Project BSC.
- Deployment Champion (who is responsible for the deployment).
- Executive, Champion, Black Belt, and Green Belt workshops. These TPS-Lean Six Sigma workshops should clearly outline the role of Management, Champions, Master Black Belts, Black Belts, and Green Belts.
- Personal BSC of Executive, Champion, Black Belt, Green Belt, and project team members; Stimulate them to formulate their Personal Balanced Scorecard in order to let them work better, to improve their effectiveness and to engage them based on the discussed alignment technique (ambition meeting between Executive/Leader/ all the Belts and his/her project team members, see chapter 4).
- Communication plan.
- Reward and recognition plan.

It is highly recommended that an organization, first select a small scale pilot project to complete before a company wide implementation. This way, they can identify early on in the deployment phase any cultural and operational issues and initiate a corrective action to resolve them. Figure 6.2 shows the TPS-Lean Six Sigma business improvement process that will help organizations in the early stages of the planning process (see also Figure 4.13).

6.3 BUILDING THE TPS-LEAN SIX SIGMA INFRASTRUCTURE

Most experts agree to the fact that building an effective infrastructure to support TPS-Lean Six Sigma program is also a key to a successful implementation. An effective infrastructure is needed before selecting the right projects and identifying the right people to lead projects should be done before any improvement activities are initiated. It lays the foundation to support all players to achieve their objectives. Black Belts

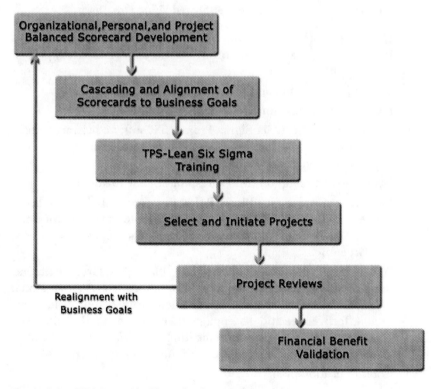

Figure 6.2.   TPS-Lean Six Sigma business improvements.

without a successful infrastructure to support their work are doomed to failure. It is important to have the business strategic goals (OBSC) defined and the resources needed before creating the company's infrastructure.

An organizational infrastructure must be comprised of two levels of players, see Figure 6.3. The first level includes the Executive leadership, the Champions, and the finance department. These are usually called the "*Sponsors*" and should be first trained in the TPS-Lean Six Sigma concepts and philosophies. The second level includes Master Black Belts, Black Belts, Green Belts and project team members. These are usually called the "*Doers.*" The roles and the responsibilities of each of the players are outlined below.

6.3.1 The Right Resources—Selecting the Right People

Since TPS-Lean Six Sigma is a project-based methodology, selecting the right people is another important component for its success. Leadership is one of the key characteristics to keep in mind when selecting people to lead projects. The most challenging process is selecting the best of the best within the organization. These people will become the Black Belts or Green Belts. The ideal Black Belts are the kind of employees who are considered to be agents of change. They should demonstrate a well-balanced set of leadership, analytical and project management skills. They should be experts in the TPS-Lean Six Sigma tools and have good communication, coaching, mentoring, and facilitation skills. They should be able to overcome all operational and cultural barriers to achieve their goals. Some Black and Green Belt characteristics are:

- Influences change.
- Provides leadership.
- Facilitates teamwork.
- Consults with management
- Discovers new opportunities.
- Continuously improves TPS-Lean Six Sigma skills.

But this traditional approach of selecting the right people is not enough and is not always leading to successful selection of the right people. The PBSC is namely a better way and an excellent method to select the right Black Belts or Green Belts for the TPS-Lean Six Sigma project. The PBSC method can ensure the necessary job fit by matching the abilities, attitude and motivation (personal ambition) of the candidates with not just the project requirements but also with the shared project ambition (Project BSC). The personal ambition of a candidate tells a better story than his/her resume. It is possible that a candidate seems suitable for a specific project on the basis of his/her CV, skills and experience, but if there is no match between his/her personal ambition and the project ambition, this would not aid his/her performance nor the quality and throughput time of the project (because of their engagement and devotion). A good match between the Project BSC and the PBSC of the candidate therefore results in a successful project execution. TPS-Lean Six Sigma Personal BSCsoft can guide you in this process (see Appendix). The importance of this can be appreciated from the following observation of Akio Morita in his book titled *Made in Japan* (1994), "In the long run, your business and its future are in the hands of the people you hire. To put it a bit more dramatically, the fate of your business is actually in the hands of the youngest recruit on the staff."

Their main responsibilities of Black and Green Belts include (see also Table 6.3):

- Advising, assisting, facilitating, and stimulating the steering group and the improvement teams, and stimulating recognition.
- Providing a link between senior Management and improvement teams, by giving progress reports and ensuring senior management continue to provide support.
- Liaising with workers' groups (unions, etc.) through regular meetings to explain the TPS-Lean Six Sigma program, give reports, and discuss issues raised by workers.
- Monitoring the TPS-Lean Six Sigma program by providing reports and feedback to all groups on their successful projects.
- Coordinating all activities of the improvement teams to ensure improvements actions undertaken do not overlap, repeat or conflict.
- Ensuring resources are channeled to improvement teams when they are needed.
- Ensuring management is taking the program seriously and is responding to all proposals made by improvement teams.
- Making logistical arrangements for meetings and presentations.
- Formulate and implement their Personal BSC and align this with the Project BSC.
- Coach project team members effectively and provide support and guidance in formulating and implementing their Personal BSC.

- Actively involved in the formulation and implementation of the project BSC.
- Organizing internal quality assessment, customer satisfaction surveys, benchmarking, and quality events.
- Helping the improvement team to identify potential problems.
- Advising the team in using a proper problem-solving methodology and ensuring the methodology is followed. This may involve training.
- Ensuring adequate interpersonal communications at all levels and among all team members.
- Resolving or avoiding conflicts among team members.
- Helping the team to allocate resources evenly and appropriately.
- Helping the team with implementation decisions, such as whose commitment is needed, how to communicate, and so forth.
- Observing how the team is working together and ensure that all members are participating effectively (function as a process keeper).
- Counseling team members about behavior and leadership skills.
- Motivating the team, as commitment and enthusiasm tend to fluctuate.

6.3.2 The Role of the Executive Management Team

Since TPS-Lean Six Sigma is a top down initiative, the role of the Executive Management/Leadership team is vital. Again, without their active support and involvement, the whole process will lack the commitment and support needed and TPS-Lean Six Sigma might become another "program of the month." Their role depends on the size of the company. In large companies, there should be a leadership team at the corporate level, as well as, a leadership team for each of the business units. The Executive Management/Leadership team roles include:

- Create the OBSC; provide related strategy/direction and set clear objectives.
- Have an ambition meeting regularly with the Champions (see chapter 4 on how this should be done).
- Help TPS-Lean Six Sigma Champions understand that they need to fulfill the role of trusted facilitator/informal coach and how to create mutual trust and stimulate passion in their team, based on the techniques discussed in chapter 4.

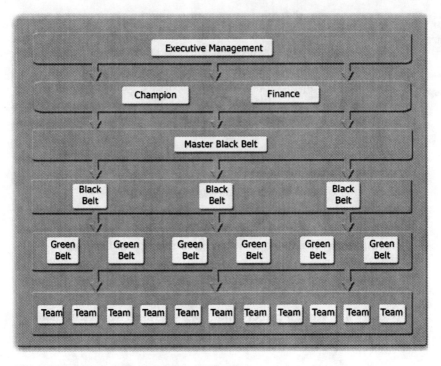

Figure 6.3.   Typical Organizational Infrastructure.

- Communicate effectively according to the TPS-Lean Six Sigma interpersonal communicative guidelines included in the Appendix.
- Show real commitment and act as a role model.
- Create trust.
- Formulate and implement their Personal BSC and align this with the Organizational BSC.
- Enable and provide resources.
- Conduct implementation reviews.
- Provide visible leadership support for TPS-Lean Six Sigma initiatives.
- Demand solid measure of results.
- Communicate purpose, progress, and results.
- Act according to the guidelines included in Table 6.3.

Table 6.3 shows a list of tasks, skills and attitudes of effective Executives, Champions, Master Black Belts, Black Belts, and Green Belts.

**Table 6.3.   Skills, Tasks, and Attitudes of
Effective Executives, Champions, Master Black Belts,
Black Belts, and Green Belts (Rampersad, 2003)**

Skill and Tasks	*Attitudes*
• Considers his/her employees as human beings more than as employees	• Has a high degree of self- awareness, self-regulation and empathy.
• Stimulates a fundamental learning attitude and working better instead of harder	• Is open, honest, trustworthy, and consistent, without a hidden agenda
• Pays attention to own and employee's spiritual development	• Is unselfish and a servant
• Relies on his/her intuitions	• Has no ego
• Knows and understands employee's personal ambition, life circumstances, strengths, habits, weaknesses, problems, feelings towards the work, likes and dislikes	• Has self-knowledge based on his/her PBSC
• Teaches the employee how to learn and encourages him/her to share knowledge with colleagues	• Has intuitive abilities
• Does not hide or try to get around problems	• Is patient, decisive, positive, enthusiastic, proactive, result-oriented and open to change
• Gives the employee the recognition due and shows appreciation for contributions	• Has perseverance and power of persuasion
• Listens actively to the employee and respects him/her	• Has the ability to bring out the hidden possibilities of the employee
• Lets the employee keep self-esteem and respect, and support his/her skills	• Thinks conceptually without losing contact with reality
• Helps the employee take on responsibilities and encourages employee independence	• Knows how to get the best out of the employee
• Is a sounding board and continuously focused on developing and mobilizing knowledge	• Listens well
• Lays down the boundaries where the employee can make independent decisions	• Can place him/herself in the position of the employee
• Keeps appointments and shows the drive to obtain results	• Is serviceable and modest
• Supplies the employee with a feeling of safety	• Can carry out norms and values so that a "we feeling" develops
• Builds trust and respect, and cherishes them	• Can convince the employee that the agreed upon way is the right one
• Shows vision and propagates this decisively	• Can build a confidential relationship
• Shows involvement, gives the employee space but is visible	• Can handle constructive confrontation

Table continues on next page.

**Table 6.3.   Skills, Tasks and Attitudes of
Effective Executives, Champions, Master Black Belts,
Black Belts, and Green Belts (Rampersad, 2003) Continued**

Skill and Tasks	Attitudes
• Stimulates teamwork, based on mutual respect, openness, and mutual trust	• Can distinguish the important from the less important and can balance short- and long-term priorities well
• Creates a climate of enjoyment, passion, devotion, and enthusiasm	• Can communicate clearly, openly, and at the right time
• Allows arguments to influence his/her decision making	• Can solve problems systematically and structurally
• Is accessible to the employee, inspires him/her and gives constructive feedback	• Has the talent to identify notable trends
• Shows the employee how his/her activities contribute to the greater whole	
• Inspires the employee to set concrete, practical, and measurable goals, and to accomplish them	

6.3.3 The Role of Champions

The success of TPS-Lean Six Sigma initiatives lies in the hand of the Champions. They have the toughest and most important responsibilities. They are often referred to as overall deployment leaders. They are typically business unit managers and have the responsibility for the successful completion of the projects. Champion roles include:

- Formulate the Project BSC (based on the OBSC).
- Formulate and implement his/her Personal BSC and align this with the Project BSC.
- Help and coach the Master Black Belts to formulate and implement their Personal BSC effectively and to align this with the Project BSC.
- Set rational and goals
- Nominate and select Green and Black Belts.
- Identify, screen, prioritize, and select projects.
- Set rationale and goal.
- Have an ambition meeting regularly with the Master Black Belts (see chapter 4).
- Help Master Black Belts understand that they need to fulfill the role of trusted facilitator/informal coach and how to create mutual

trust and stimulate passion in their team, based on the techniques discussed in chapter 4.

- Communicate effectively according to the TPS-Lean Six Sigma interpersonal communicative guidelines included in the Appendix.
- Act according to the guidelines included in Table 6.3.
- Use the TPS-Lean Six Sigma Project BSCsoft and TPS-Lean Six Sigma Personal BSCsoft (see Appendix) to manage and execute the project.
- Allocate resources.
- Assign teams to projects.
- Review projects.
- Tackle critical projects.
- Remove barriers.
- Help quantify the impact of TPS-Lean Six Sigma efforts.

6.3.4 The Role of Finance

A well-understood financial system is needed to track, report, and validate the benefits from TPS-Lean Six Sigma initiatives. The finance department is a key participant in the improvement effort. They are actively involved in the financial evaluation of the project and its impact to the company prior to approval. The finance roles include:

- Help define the Project BSC (especially aspects related to the financial perspective).
- Help establish and validate estimated and actual project savings.
- Incorporate actual project savings into revised budgets/standard costs.
- Quantify the overall return on investment (ROI) from TPS-Lean Six Sigma initiatives.

6.3.5 The Role of Master Black Belts

Master Black Belts are individuals who are respected in the organization and embody strong leadership and technical skills. A Master Black Belt has more extensive training than that of the Black Belt and has typically completed several Black Belt projects. The Master Black Belt provides training, coaching and mentoring for Black Belts and Green Belts. Master Black Belt roles include:

- Formulate the Project BSC (based on the OBSC).
- Trainer of TPS-Lean Six Sigma tools and techniques.
- Provide technical support & mentoring to Black Belts.
- Formulate and implement his/her Personal BSC and align this with his/her Project BSC.
- Help and coach the Black Belts to formulate and implement their Personal BSC effectively and to align this with their Project BSC.
- Have an ambition meeting regularly with the Black Belts (see chapter 4).
- Help Black Belts understand that they need to fulfill the role of trusted facilitator/informal coach and how to create mutual trust and stimulate passion in their team, based on the techniques discussed in chapter 4.
- Communicate effectively according to the TPS-Lean Six Sigma interpersonal communicative guidelines included in the Appendix.
- Act according to the guidelines included in Table 6.3.
- Use the TPS-Lean Six Sigma Project BSCsoft and TPS-Lean Six Sigma Personal BSCsoft (see Appendix) to manage and execute the project.
- Review and approve TPS-Lean Six Sigma projects.
- Facilitate multiple projects led by Black Belts.
- Provide consulting assistance to Champions and Executive Management.
- Devote 100% of time to TPS-Lean Six Sigma initiative.
- Act as an internal consultant, trainer, and expert.

6.3.6 The Role of Black Belts

Black Belts are, most often referred to as, change agents. They are knowledgeable and highly skilled in the use of TPS-Lean Six Sigma tools such as team facilitation, change management, and statistical techniques. They lead improvement projects to completion. Black Belt roles include:

- Help define and formulate the Project BSC.
- Lead TPS-Lean Six Sigma projects (Min. 4 projects per year).

- Provide training in TPS-Lean Six Sigma tools and concepts.
- Formulate and implement his/her Personal BSC and align this with his/her Project BSC.
- Help and coach the Green Belts to formulate and implement their Personal BSC effectively and to align this with their Project BSC.
- Have an ambition meeting regularly with the Green Belts (see chapter 4).
- Help TPS-Lean Six Sigma Green Belts understand that they need to fulfill the role of trusted facilitator/informal coach and how to create mutual trust and stimulate passion in their team, based on the techniques discussed in chapter 4.
- Communicate effectively according to the TPS-Lean Six Sigma interpersonal communicative guidelines included in the Appendix
- Act according to the guidelines included in Table 6.3.
- Use the TPS-Lean Six Sigma Project BSCsoft and TPS-Lean Six Sigma Personal BSCsoft (see Appendix) to manage and execute the project.
- Review and approve TPS- Lean Six Sigma team charters.

6.3.7 The Role of Green Belts

Green Belts make up the largest population of trained belts in the workforce. Green Belts are the "worker bees." They take their direction from the Black Belts. Green Belts are the ones who are hands-on, taking measurements, collecting data, and doing whatever else is necessary for the project. Green Belt roles include:

- Formulate and implement his/her Personal BSC and align this with his/her Project BSC.
- Part time lead projects (Min. 2 projects/year).
- Utilize Statistical and Quality Techniques.
- Support TPS-Lean Six Sigma project teams.
- Assist in the Implementation of TPS-Lean Six Sigma philosophy in their daily jobs.
- Train others in basic TPS-Lean Six Sigma tools.
- Communicate effectively according to the TPS-Lean Six Sigma interpersonal communicative guidelines included in the Appendix
- Act according to the guidelines included in Table 6.3.

- Use the TPS-Lean Six Sigma Project BSCsoft and TPS-Lean Six Sigma Personal BSCsoft (see Appendix) to manage and execute the project.
- Identify project opportunities.
- Be actively involved in the formulation and implementation of the Project BSC.
- Assist project team members to formulate and implement their Personal BSC effectively and to align this with their Project BSC.

6.3.8 The Role of Project Team Members

Project teams' members are a cross-functional mix of the organization put together for the specific purpose of executing the TPS-Lean Six Sigma project. While the team is comprised of a variety of 'belts' including Black and Green Belts, there may also be other significant personnel needed to support the project. As a minimum, all team members will have TPS-Lean Six Sigma overview training. The project team member's roles include:

- Formulate and implement his/her Personal BSC and align this with his/her Project BSC.
- Complete assignments between meetings.
- Actively participate and contribute expertise.
- Communicate effectively according to the TPS-Lean Six Sigma interpersonal communicative guidelines included in the Appendix.
- Use TPS-Lean Six Sigma tools to solve problems.
- Assure the project ambition remains aligned with personal ambition (PBSC).
- Be actively involved in the implementation of the Project BSC.
- Have an ambition meeting regularly with the team leader (Black Belt).
- Attend project meetings according to below guidelines (see boxed text below).

Project team meetings are held regularly when following the TPS-Lean Six Sigma model. In practice, meetings often tend to be unstructured, chaotic, and too amiable; this usually means that they're a waste of time, money, and creative ideas—which does not fit into the TPS-Lean Six Sigma concept. It is advisable to do away with the traditional way of conducting project meetings. Holding a TPS-Lean Six Sigma project meeting is a learning process, as well as, a means of communication for the benefit of sharing, receiving, and exchanging knowledge, as well as, solving problems and taking initiatives. A meeting consists of a group of people who discuss a previously scheduled item, under the supervision of a chairperson. For a meeting to be most effective, the following guidelines should be met:

- The objectives of the meeting are clear.
- There is open discussion.
- The right people attend the meeting; invite only those who are indispensable.
- The meeting is evaluated based on improvement possibilities.
- A chairperson is appointed to lead the meeting, a minute taker to record the minutes, a timekeeper to check the time, and a process keeper to guard the meeting process. This person sees to it that people listen to each other, do not speak out of turn, and brainstorm in the correct way (see Appendix).
- There is a time frame for every item on the agenda.
- The minutes are available within a week.
- The meeting starts on time.
- The meeting is closed as soon as the objective of the meeting is reached.
- A clear agenda is formulated and its items divided into announcements, information items, and discussion items. These items should be separated during the meeting.
- The agenda is put together beforehand and circulated, so that everyone can prepare for the meeting.
- The agenda is followed.
- Consensus is not necessary; the eagerness to reach a consensus often leads to vague and slow decision making, stifles personal initiatives, and confuses where responsibilities lie.
- Learning themes should be discussed in every meeting.

Answering a few technical questions is central to preparing and conducting successful meetings. These include:

- What subjects are going to be discussed?
- Who should attend and who should not?
- When and where will the meeting be held?
- What are the requirements for the meeting room?
- Should guest speakers be invited?

- Is the agenda made, and has it been sent to all participants ahead of time?
- Who is the timekeeper?
- Who is the process keeper?
- Who is the minute taker?

The boxed text below provides an overview of the most important activities, tasks, and roles for conducting effective meetings in the context of the TPS-Lean Six Sigma concept.

Overview of Activities, Tasks, and Roles for Conducting Effective TPS-Lean Six Sigma Meetings

Chairperson

Prior to the meeting

1. Provide the right team composition.
2. Read the minutes of the previous meeting and formulate the agenda and objectives of this meeting.
3. Send invitations, agenda, and additional information to the participants on time and provide an adequate meeting room.
4. Prepare yourself.

During the meeting

1. Begin on time.
2. Ask if everyone has received the information and can be present during the entire meeting.
3. Discuss reporting (who will take the minutes), the objectives of the meeting, and the expected contribution of the participants.
4. Delegate supporting tasks to a time and process keeper.
5. Go through the agenda in order.
6. Guard the meeting process by: asking questions, summarizing opinions, asking silent persons for their opinions, clarifying opinions, stimulating listening, expressing appreciation, accentuating conclusions.
7. Give a summary of the most important points and encourage discussions focused on the realization of team goals.

8. Ask questions such as: Who has a suggestion? Who agrees and who disagrees? Who wants to comment on this? Who can complete or clarify this? Who has counterarguments? Who can summarize this?

9. What mistakes were made? How can we learn from them?

10. Establish relationships between different ideas and stimulate open communication.

11. Ask for facts, suggestions, and information, and focus on what must be realized.

12. Do not tolerate latecomers, private discussions, and abandoning of the meeting.

13. Do not permit moving away from the subject; determine clearly who will do what.

14. Take stimulating actions to keep the meeting going if it threatens to deadlock.

15. See to it that all available information is accessible to all participants.

16. Stay neutral with respect to the subject and participants; treat everyone equally.

17. Do not discuss more than one agenda item at a time.

18. Maintain a relaxed, informal, and disciplined atmosphere.

19. Increase enjoyment and lessen tensions.

20. Encourage people to be open and take risks.

21. Consensus is not always necessary; strive for single-mindedness to achieve a particular goal.

22. Allow quiet time (for thinking).

23. Try to find a link between different ideas.

24. Make sure that decisions and actions are understood and written down.

25. Act as a coach; don't dominate or display an authoritarian attitude.

26. Interrupt small talk.

27. During the last ten minutes, give a short summary and note points of action.

28. End the discussion as soon as the subject has been treated exhaustively.

29. Evaluate the team effectiveness.

30. Document the lessons learned in this meeting.

31. Make an appointment for the next meeting.

Participants

Prior to the meeting

1. Read the minutes of the previous meeting, study the agenda, and prepare yourself.
2. Figure out what the objective of the meeting is, focus on it, and stick to it.
3. Be on time.

During the meeting

1. Make sure that your items are on the agenda and stick to the ones being discussed.
2. If you do not understand certain statements, ask for clarification.
3. Participate actively by listening well, summarizing opinions, asking for clarification, building on the ideas of others, making constructive arguments, not moving away form the subject.
4. Speak up if you have something to say, and be silent if you have nothing to say.
5. Avoid remarks that will divide the team and jot down the agreements.
6. Accept the chairperson.
7. Contribute to the solution and do not create more problems.
8. Don't be noisy; don't hinder progress or participate with a hidden agenda.
9. Don't be guided by emotions; remain objective. Keep personal feelings to yourself.

After the meeting

1. Do what was agreed upon, do not complain about the decisions taken, and do not try to reverse decisions outside the meeting; discuss disagreements in the following meeting.
2. Do not broadcast what was said during the meeting.
3. Evaluate the meeting.

Timekeeper

During the meeting, the timekeeper should:

1. Monitor how much time the team takes to execute its tasks.
2. Give directions on how to spend time.
3. Discuss the planned duration of each agenda item at the beginning of the meeting.
4. Regularly announce the progress of time so that the team knows how far along they are.
5. Interrupt the team when it exceeds the allotted time.
6. Give suggestions about possible adjustments to the agenda.
7. Continuously guard the pace at which the different phases of the meetings are reviewed.
8. The meeting should not take more than 1½ hours.

Minute Taker

During the meeting, the minute taker should:

1. Listen well
2. Write fluently
3. Summarize the discussion quickly
4. Keep important questions in mind, such as:

- Which questions were discussed?
- Which answers were given?
- Which arguments and considerations were important?
- Which problems were identified?
- Which mistakes were made, and what has been learned from them?
- Which decisions were made?
- Which actions will be undertaken?
- Which conclusions were drawn?
- Which agreements were made (who will do what and when)?
- Attendance registration.
- Date for the next meeting.

Process Keeper

The process keeper is responsible for an efficient meeting. During the meeting, the process keeper should:

1. Evaluative comments are not allowed during brainstorming sessions.
2. All participants must actively participate in the discussions.
3. All activities should be followed through in phases and according to the tools described in the Appendix (problem-solving cycle, risk analysis, etc.)
4. Do participants respect the opinions and suggestions of others?
5. Stop small talk or digressions to subjects that are beside the point.
6. The TPS-Lean Six Sigma interpersonal communication guidelines in the Appendix should be followed.

Source: Rampersad, 2003

There are also some other roles project team members, Champions, and all the Belts should play, see boxed text below.

What Project Team Members, Champions, and all the Belts Should Do

Project team members, Champions, and Belts should:

- Share their Personal Ambition with each other (to create trust).
- Formulate their own Personal Balanced Scorecard and balance it with their behavior (to develop personal integrity, see chapter 4) and the shared project ambition.
- Know their team role and those of other team members, whom they should accept, value, and respect.
- Devote themselves to the Project BSC.
- Consider themselves to be equal and responsible.
- Be interested and motivated.
- Give high priority to continuous improvement, development, and learning.
- Participate actively in the activities of the project team.
- Know, trust, understand, complement, and help each other.
- Know their internal and external clients.
- Communicate openly and maintain an open mind regarding expectations about their surroundings.
- Use each other's information freely.
- Channel the experiences from the team back to their own working environment.
- Abide by the team's decisions.

- Be responsible for their own contribution, as well as, for team results.
- See problems as an opportunity for improvement.
- Be aware of their responsibility for improvement.
- Make personal improvement, development, and learning based on their PBSC a way of life.

6.4 TRAINING THE ORGANIZATION FOR TPS- LEAN SIX SIGMA

Acquiring the right knowledge is at the heart of TPS-Lean Six Sigma. All levels of the organization are required to be trained in TPS-Lean Six Sigma's concept and philosophy. Each employee has his/her own role and responsibility in the initiative to implement TPS-Lean Six Sigma. Some organizations will try to cut costs by minimizing the training effort required for successful implementation of TPS-Lean Six Sigma. This is proved to be unwise decision by many organizations who selected this path to follow. By training only key members of the team, and not the rest of the employee population, or by only training members of the implementation team and not Management are recipes for failure. It can not be overstressed the importance of training of the entire workforce for success. Here is an example:

Company A decides to implement a Lean Six Sigma program. Upper Management arbitrarily selects three Managers and sends them to Lean Six Sigma training. The Managers come back from the training and are asked to start running some programs to cut costs. The managers try to run the projects on their own but quickly run into problems. They meet resistance from the workforce and can not find the right resources to be successful. The projects ultimately fail and upper management decides the initiative is not worth while. The reason this strategy failed is because of many reasons. For one, there was a serious misunderstanding about Lean Six Sigma and its deployment. Lean Six Sigma will fail if the entire organization is not involved. A second reason is because there was no alignment of the program to the organization and personal goals. This is one reason why we created the TPS-Lean Six Sigma approach. When TPS-Lean Six Sigma is implemented, our experts assure there will be success *before* a deployment is executed.

While it is true that the entire organization needs to be trained, this may seem daunting to upper management. "How much will this cost? How will we ever recover the lost time for training? Is all this training really needed?" These are typical responses we receive when reviewing TPS-Lean Six Sigma programs to upper management for the first time.

The answer is that there is a fairly significant cost to TPS-Lean Six Sigma, however training is targeted. What we mean by targeted is that everyone in the organization does receive training, but for some employee's it is just the overall awareness training (Yellow Belt), and others are selected for Green, and Black Belt training. Some parts of management will receive only White Belt training, while others will go to Executive and Champion training. As you can see, TPS-Lean Six Sigma provides very specific training targeted to serve the purpose of successful deployment. At this point, the concerned members of upper management start to feel a little more at ease. Next, we answer their questions about costs. We explain that while the costs of TPS-Lean Six Sigma is a significant investment, the return on investment (ROI), that we can virtually guarantee, will be a minimum of two fold. Now, at this point, we have their ears perking up and they all want to hear more.

What we have described in this example above is actually the first phase of training. What was accomplished is that we just trained upper management in company A on the benefits of TPS-Lean Six Sigma. This is a very important step of the process. By gaining upper management support, TPS-Lean Six Sigma can now be successfully deployed.

If your organization is considering sending more than 10 people through Green or Black Belt training, it is recommended that you consider a customized on-site deployment to maximize your return on your training investment. There are different levels of training:

6.4.1 Executive Workshop

This workshop needs to be conducted first and should be attended by the CEO, the president and C-level managers and it is typically 2 days in length and should cover the following topics:

- TPS-Lean Six Sigma concepts and philosophy.
- Personal, Organizational, and Project Balanced Scorecard.
- Use of the TPS-Lean Six Sigma Project BSCsoft and TPS-Lean Six Sigma Personal BSCsoft to manage and execute the project effectively.
- How to coach Champions effectively.
- Personal leadership development based on the PBSC.
- How to create an atmosphere of trust, commitment, teamwork, creativity, and learning within project teams, based on TPS-Lean Six Sigma.
- Personal effectiveness and employee engagement.

- Working smarter and result oriented.
- Employee performance and effective talent management.
- Personal responsibility and personal integrity.
- Enjoyment and inner involvement (commitment) at work.
- Defined roles and responsibilities of the leadership team.
- TPS-Lean Six Sigma metrics.
- TPS-Lean Six Sigma deployment.
- TPS-Lean Six Sigma tools and techniques.
- TPS-Lean Six Sigma certification programs.

6.4.2 Champion Workshop

TPS-Lean Six Sigma Champions have the most important role. They lead change throughout the organization and are responsible for the success of the implementation. The Champion acquires the skills and tools to select projects, implement improvements and remove roadblocks to success. The workshop is typically 2 days in length and should cover the following topics:

- TPS-Lean Six Sigma concepts and philosophy.
- Personal, Organizational, and Project Balanced Scorecard.
- Use of the TPS-Lean Six Sigma Project BSCsoft and TPS-Lean Six Sigma Personal BSCsoft to manage and execute the project effectively.
- How to coach Master Black Belts effectively.
- How to create an atmosphere of trust, commitment, teamwork, creativity, and learning within project teams, based on TPS-Lean Six Sigma.
- Personal leadership development based on the PBSC.
- Personal effectiveness and employee engagement.
- Working smarter and result oriented.
- Champion roles and responsibilities.
- Process for identifying potential TPS-Lean Six Sigma projects.
- Guidelines for managing TPS-Lean Six Sigma projects.
- Measures for evaluating project success.
- Selection and retention of Black Belt and Green Belt candidates.
- TPS-Lean Six Sigma certification programs.

6.4.3 Green Belt Workshop

TPS-Lean Six Sigma Green Belt candidates are selected because of their process knowledge and experience. After training, they will typically spend about 15%–25% of their time on TPS-Lean Six Sigma projects. Their main responsibility when functioning as a Green Belt is to support Black Belts on their projects by collecting and conducting simple data analyses and prepare reports. Some more experienced Green Belts may also lead small focused projects within their departments. The workshop is typically 80 hours (2 weeks) in length and should cover the following topics:

- TPS-Lean Six Sigma concepts and philosophy.
- Personal, Organizational, and Project Balanced Scorecard.
- Use of the TPS-Lean Six Sigma Project BSCsoft and TPS-Lean Six Sigma Personal BSCsoft to manage and execute the project effectively.
- How to create an atmosphere of trust, commitment, teamwork, creativity, and learning within project teams, based on TPS-Lean Six Sigma.
- Personal leadership development based on the PBSC.
- Personal effectiveness and employee engagement.
- How to coach project team members effectively.
- Working smarter and result oriented.
- Project charter preparation and team facilitation and management.
- Understanding the Voice Of The Customer (VOC).
- Cost of Poor Quality (COPQ).
- Value Stream Mapping/Process Mapping.
- Kaizen Techniques.
- 5 S.
- Introduction to Statistics.
- DMAIC process.
- Measurement Systems Analysis (MSA).
- Analysis of Variance (ANOVA).
- Process capability studies.
- TPS-Lean and Six Sigma metrics.
- Process Failure Mode and Effect Analysis (FMEA).
- Design of Experiment planning.
- Overview of Design of Experiments (DOE).

- Statistical process control
- Mistake Proof/Fail Safe
- TPS-Lean Six Sigma certification programs

6.4.4 Black Belt Workshop

TPS-Lean Six Sigma Black Belts are change agents and technical leaders who have developed a high proficiency in TPS-Lean and Six Sigma philosophies, concepts and tools and understand how these two powerful methodologies augment each other. They are the "doers" in implementing TPS-Lean Six Sigma strategies who lead and manage all aspects of the improvement projects. The workshop is typically 160 hours (4 weeks) in length and should cover the following topics:

- TPS-Lean Six Sigma concepts and philosophy.
- Personal, Organizational, And Project Balanced Scorecard.
- Use of the TPS-Lean Six Sigma Project BSCsoft and TPS-Lean Six Sigma Personal BSCsoft to manage and execute the project effectively.
- How to create an atmosphere of trust, commitment, teamwork, creativity, and learning within project teams, based on TPS-Lean Six Sigma.
- Personal leadership development based on the PBSC.
- How to coach Green Belts effectively.
- Personal effectiveness and employee engagement.
- Working smarter and result oriented.
- Project chartering and management.
- Team facilitation and management.
- Understanding Voice of the Customer (VOC).
- Benchmarking.
- Quality Function Deployment (QFD).
- Cost of Poor Quality (CPQ).
- Value Stream Mapping/Process Mapping.
- Kaizen Techniques.
- Kanban and WIP Management.
- 5 S.
- Introduction to Statistics.
- DMAIC process.

- Measurement Systems Analysis (MSA).
- Analysis of Variance (ANOVA).
- Process capability studies.
- TPS-Lean and Six Sigma metrics.
- Design and Process FMEA.
- Design and Analysis of Experiments (DOE.)
- Regression analysis.
- Statistical process control.
- Mistake Proof/Fail Safe.
- TPS-Lean Six Sigma certification programs.

6.4.5 Overview Workshop

This workshop is indented for the rest of the company's employees to get them to understand why this is important to the company and what their role is to support management in this program. The workshop is typically 4 hours in length typically and covers an overview of TPS-Lean Six Sigma concepts.

6.5 SELECTING THE RIGHT PROJECTS

Selecting the right projects is probably the most important step of deployment. By selecting the right project related to the Organizational BSC, there will be an immediate success story and support from management and the employee's will be solidified. On the contrary, if the right project is not selected and there are problems and failure, management, and employee support will rapidly deteriorate. That is one reason, we spend a good amount of time educating and training our clients for TPS-Lean Six Sigma project selection.

Projects should mostly be selected for their financial impact on the bottom line; however, other good reasons include projects that remedy a customer complaint, or specification that is not currently being met. Regardless of the target for the project, the first TPS-Lean Six Sigma project should be one that is certain to be successful in a short amount of time. As we have discussed in previous chapters, and as we will continue to stress throughout this book, is the importance of management and employee support for these initiatives. This is why; we encourage our clients to select a 'quick-win' for the first project. Getting your TPS-Lean Six Sigma program off on a good foot will ensure continued involvement and support from the organization and it will make continuing deployment much easier to implement.

For these reasons, we have developed a TPS-Lean Six Sigma Project Selection Template and dedicated an entire chapter to helping you identify, prioritize, and select the right projects. See chapter 7 for more information.

6.6 SUSTAINING THE TPS-LEAN SIX SIGMA PROGRAM

All our TPS-Lean Six Sigma Certification programs (see chapters 9 until 12) are offered through our Academy for TPS-Lean Six Sigma Certification. When we launched this academy, one of our overall goals included finding a way to improve business bottom line results, while at the same time, improve personal well-being. Benchmarking found many success stories with Lean Six Sigma as a primary driver for improved business, and the Personal Balanced Scorecard (PBSC) as a primary driver for improved personal wellbeing. TPS-Lean Six Sigma is an integration of Lean Six Sigma and the Personal Balanced Scorecard. With our unique program, business and personal goals are met concurrently. What this means is the workforce is highly motivated and dedicated to the cause and with this culture, business will continue to foster improvement and success.

That is why we say, TPS-Lean Six Sigma is an ongoing process. Once TPS-Lean Six Sigma has been successfully implemented, a "snowball" effect follows. After the first projects are completed and the results are communicated, other departments, divisions, managers, and units all want to get involved. Remember previously that the first project selected should be a "quick sure win," this is why, and it is to get everyone excited and onboard.

As the company continues to grow, more people are trained, more Belts are added to the population and consequently, more projects are running concurrently. This entire activity means there is a greater return on investment, and as the company prospers financially, the wealth is shared across the organization and employee satisfaction and personal growth continues. After 6 months to a year of sustaining TPS-Lean Six Sigma deployment and growth the principles and philosophies are embedded and become the culture of the company. There is really no limit to growth that can be realized, this is the power of TPS-Lean Six Sigma.

Sustaining the TPS-Lean Six Sigma program is as important as launching it. TPS-Lean Six Sigma is not a one shot deal; rather, it is an ongoing process. Sustaining TPS-Lean Six Sigma implementation requires regular audits and reviews of all the elements covered in the chapter including deployment process, strategy, and infrastructure of the TPS-Lean Six Sigma program. There are three key components to sustaining the implementation: Leadership support, utilizing the right resources, and defining business objectives to measure success.

A Summary of Critical Success Factors for Successful TPS-Lean Six Sigma Implementation:

- Active commitment and involvement from Senior Executives.
- Improvement goals integrated into the OBSC, Project BSC, and Personal BSC.
- Deployment of the communications plan.
- Project selection, prioritization, tracking and reviewing process.
- Extensive education and training.
- An atmosphere of trust, commitment, teamwork, creativity, and learning within project teams.
- Sustainable project results.
- Technical support and training (Master Black Belts).
- Full-time versus part-time resources.
- Human resource management and human capital embedded in the project.
- Alignment of personal ambition of project members and project ambition (Project BSC).
- Alignment of personal ambition of employees and shared organizational ambition (OBSC).
- Project BSC is related to the OBSC
- Incentives, recognition, reward, and celebration.
- Supplier involvement.
- Management accountability for quality improvement.

The boxed text below provides an overview of the 15 TPS-Lean Six Sigma implementation steps.

TPS-Lean Six Sigma Implementation Steps

1. Assessment of the organization based on the TPS-Lean Six Sigma Life Cycle Scan—understand gaps and to determine "areas of opportunities."
2. Developing/fine tuning the Organizational Balanced Scorecard on strategic level.

3.   Cascading/deploying the company BSC to lower levels in the organization.
4.   Identifying TPS-Lean Six Sigma projects based on the company BSC.
5.   Establishing the project organization for each selected project.
6.   Coaching Executives, Champions, and Master Black Belts to build their Personal Balanced Scorecard and to implement this successfully based on the PDAC cycle.
7.   Blending of their personal ambition with the shared company and project ambition to create commitment and engagement.
8.   Providing tailor made TPS-Lean Six Sigma training and certification programs to the project members: Executive "Platinum Belt", Champion, Master Black Belt, Black Belt, and Green Belt Certification Programs.
9.   Coaching project team members to build their Personal Balanced Scorecard and to implement this successfully based on the PDAC cycle.
10.   Blending of their personal ambition with the shared company and project ambition to create commitment and engagement.
11.   Training Executives, Champions, Master Black Belts, Black Belts, and Green Belts to coach their employees/project team members based on the TPS-LSS Coaching framework.
12.   Formulating and executing the Project Balanced Scorecard of each identified TPS-LSS project.
13.   Monitoring the project execution continuously with the help of the TPS-LSS project BSC software.
14.   Linking the Company BSCs, Project BSCs and Personal BSCs to effective Talent Management (appraisal system); Integrate this in the current HR system.
15.   Technical project support.

In chapters 9-12, we will discuss our TPS-Lean Six Sigma Certification program, TPS-Lean Six Sigma Coaching Certification program, how to become a Certified TPS-Lean Six Sigma Consultant, and our TPS-Lean Six Sigma Company Certification program. These are all available through our Academy for TPS-Lean Six Sigma Certification (a separate business unit of TPS-Lean Six Sigma Inc.).

CHAPTER 7

SELECTING WINNING TPS-LEAN SIX SIGMA PROJECTS

*Six Phases of a Project: (a) Enthusiasm (b) Disillusionment (c) Panic
(d) Search for the guilty (e) Punishment of the innocent (f) Praise and
honor for the non-participants*

—Karla Jennings

*There is only one valid definition of a business purpose: to create a satisfied customer.
It is the customer who determines what the business is.*

—Peter F. Drucker

The success or failure of any business improvement initiative depends on selecting the right project. In the previous chapter, we emphasized the importance of selecting the right project. This chapter will address the process of identifying, evaluating, and selecting the right TPS-Lean Six Sigma projects. This is related to the continuous process improvement stage in the TPS-Lean Six Sigma model (see Figure 4.1). Before we outline this process, let's define a project. A project is a concerted effort to create a specific result. It should also bring about a change in the organization. A project should:

*TPS-Lean Six Sigma: Linking Human Capital to Lean Six Sigma: A New Blueprint for
Creating High Performance Companies*, pp. 219–244
Copyright © 2007 by Information Age Publishing
All rights of reproduction in any form reserved.

- Have a defined beginning and end.
- Target a specific deficiency and not be global in nature.
- Progress in a calculated, organized manner.
- Result in an expected outcome.
- Be the follow up (implementation) of the OBSC.
- Have a Project Balanced Scorecard (is a holistic and balanced project charter).
- Take the project member's PBSC into account.

Project ideas are usually identified by Upper Management, Champions, Master Black Belts, or Black Belt. The right projects will then be determined by evaluating the completed Organizational Balanced Scorecard and selecting ones with the greatest impact on the company for the least effort. After the desired projects are identified (based on the OBSC), a Project Balanced Scorecard will be created that identifies the personnel who make the best fit based on their PBSC.

Selecting the right project is not a simple task; rather it is a complex decision-making process. Experts agree that the project selection process is the most difficult element of TPS-Lean Six Sigma deployment. If it is done properly, it's a win-win situation, and processes will become more efficient, employees will feel satisfied, and management will achieve the desired financial benefits. If not done properly, the project team will encounter roadblocks, resistance, be unsuccessful in achieving its goal, and ultimately loose management support and fail.

Since TPS-Lean Six Sigma is a business and personal improvement initiative, Project BSCs must be clearly linked to OBSC and PBSC. The project team should consider two types of strategies when selecting a project; (1) a growth strategy, which addresses customer satisfaction, market share, and revenue; or (2) a productivity strategy, which addresses cost savings, capacity, and cycle time. This strategy is part of the Project BSC (see chapter 4). Figure 7.1 shows the process of identifying, prioritizing, and selecting winning projects. The project prioritization and selection guidelines are covered in detail during the Executive and Champion workshops. We will discuss some of these steps in this chapter.

7.1 UNDERSTAND THE VOICE OF THE CUSTOMER

One main objective of TPS-Lean Six Sigma is customer satisfaction. Understanding customers' needs and desires will drive improvements in

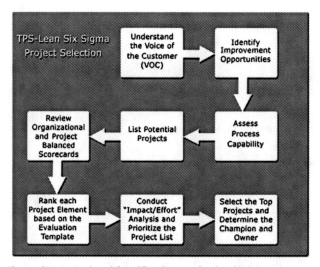

Figure 7.1.   Project identification and selection process.

the organization. Market research, surveys, focus group interviews, and customer complaints are some of the methods available to gather Voice of the Customer (VOC) data. Salespersons and Technicians can also be important sources of information. Customer value must always be part of the criteria used in prioritizing and selecting projects. To understand VOC, we first need to define their requirements and then assess the capability of the company's processes in meeting these requirements. The central questions at this point are:

- Which products and services do we deliver, and what do we have to offer?
- Who are our customers, and how do they get what we have to offer?
- What do they want, and what do they expect of us?

By answering these questions on an ongoing basis, we will understand the customer better, and the product or service will better match market demands. These questions were already addressed in part during the formulation of the strategic objectives.

Which Products and Services Do We Deliver, and What Do We Have to Offer?

It is important to define the product or service as concretely as possible. This definition indicates your actual function as a supplier. The more specific the definition, the better your customers' needs can be met.

What the company thinks its customer wants
is not necessarily the same as
What the company thinks it has to offer
is not necessarily the same as
What the company actually offers
is not necessarily the same as
How the customer experiences this
is not necessarily the same as
What the customer really wants

Source: Philips Electronics, 1994.

Who Are Our Customers, and How Do They Get What We Have to Offer?

In the framework of the TPS-Lean Six Sigma philosophy, it is important to understand the entire customer chain; this means intimately knowing all your customers. The needs of each customer must be examined separately, and not only external but also internal customers should be considered. In fact, if the company does not satisfy the needs of its internal customers, how can the organization comply with the needs of its external customers? All employees determine the degree of customer satisfaction. Employees of different sections and within different business units must be considered as customers of and suppliers for each other. The customer is the next link in the chain of production activities. By bringing individual employees together as customers and suppliers, the traditional barriers between business units will be broken. Each employee delivers something to a colleague, whereby one functions as the internal supplier and the other as the internal customer. Strengthening this relationship results in an internal network of customer-supplier relationships, which is beneficial to the quality of services provided to the external customer. Everyone in the organization must learn to think in terms of: *Who are my internal customers, and how can I satisfy their needs?*

To illustrate this approach, the internal customer checklist of Hewlett-Packard is shown in the boxed text. Here it is expected that each section of the organization asks itself seven questions, which are regarded as fundamental to the operation.

Hewlett Packard's Internal Customer Checklist

1. 1.Who are my customers?
2. What do they need?
3. What is my product or service?
4. What are my customers' expectations and measures?
5. Does my product or service meet their expectations?
6. What is the process for providing my product or service?
7. What action is required to improve the process?

Problem-Solving Methodology

1. Select the quality issue.
2. Write an issue statement.
3. Identify the process.
4. Draw a flow chart.
5. Select a process performance measure.
6. Conduct a cause and effect analysis.
7. Collect and analyze the data.
8. Identify the major causes of the quality.
9. Plan for improvements.
10. Take the corrective action.
11. Collect and analyze the data again.
12. Are the objectives met?
13. If yes, document and standardize the change.

What Do They Want, and What Do They Expect of Us?

As a supplier, you should try to determine what the customer needs and wants. Here communication is very important. Talk to your customers: ask them what they think of your product or services; try to figure out how they use it; try to find out what they really want— which gains they are looking for in your product, which needs your product satisfies, and what motivates them to keep buying your product and stay loyal to you. Ask these questions: Which needs or expectations do your customers have? Which ones are you aware of? To what extent, do you comply with the needs and expectations of your customers? If you do not satisfy their needs, what are the reasons according to your customers? Listen attentively to what they have to say and indicate which customer-supplier relationships needs improvement. Quality Function Deployment (QFD) is an excellent tool to listen effectively to them and to gather and prioritize their requirements (see chapter 5). Another tool, which we are introducing here, is the TPS-Lean Six Sigma Customer Orientation Quick Scan.

TPS-Lean Six Sigma Customer Orientation Quick Scan

Table 7.1 shows the TPS-Lean Six Sigma Customer Orientation Quick Scan, consisting of 70 painful questions regarding your customer orientation (Rampersad, 2003). The questions are divided into the following five dimensions: (1) *general*, (2) *management style*, (3) *strategic vision*, (4) *internal processes*, and (5) *human resources*. Judge the customer orientation of your organization based on this checklist, and, as a team, check why this is characteristic for your organization. To this end, complete the survey in Table 7.1 by marking the number that best reflects the accuracy of the assertions in your organization. Use the scoring key (1 to 3) at the end of the table; 1 = no, 2 = somewhat, 3 = yes. Add these scores vertically. The closer your total score gets to 200, the more customer friendly your company is. The closer your total score is to 70, the lower the customer orientation. Discuss your scores in your team and indicate what could have been done better in your organization.

Business Jet completed this quick scan to determine the organization's customer orientation and to finalize their OBSC (external perspective) based on this (see chapter 4). The shared evaluation results are marked in Table 7.1. The total score was 123 points; this implies that the customer orientation of Business Jet leaves much to be desired on several points. Statements with a score of 1 and 2 in the Table 7.1 suggest areas where objectives and improvement actions in the OBSC may be formulated (the quick scan functions as a SWOT analysis tool). Many of the recommendations related to this customer orientation checklist also apply to your relationships with external suppliers. According to the TPS-Lean Six Sigma philosophy, you should treat your suppliers as if they are an integral part of your organization. Listen to their ideas on how you can work closely and productively together; create joint improvement teams; invite suggestions; assist them in improving their own processes; build mutual trust and respect; reward them if they achieve improvements; let them participate in the celebration of success; involve them in the development of new products and processes; and become a better customer yourself. Expanding your culture of continuous improvement and learning to all

Table 7.1. TPS-Lean Six Sigma Customer Orientation Quick Scan, Used on Business Jet (Rampersad, 2003)

Circle the correct number: 1 = no, 2 = somewhat, 3 = yes

I General

	Yes	Some-what	No
1. Do you know who your customers are and how many there are?	3	2 x	1
2. Do you listen effectively to all your customers and do you familiarize yourself with their situation?	3 x	2	1
3. Do you routinely conduct surveys among your customers about your products and services?	3	2	1 x
4. Do all your employees know about the results of these surveys?	3	2	1 x
5. Did you segment your customers based on their needs?	3	2	1 x
6. Are more than 75% of your customers satisfied?	3	2	1 x
7. Do you anticipate customer needs?	3	2 x	1
8. Do you consider each customer a unique partner?	3	2	1 x
9. Are complaints addressed within two business days and resolved within one week?	3	2	1 x
10. Do you encourage dissatisfied customers to notify you of their complaints?	3 x	2	1
11. Do you undertake unsolicited additional actions and do you provide additional unsolicited services to satisfy your customers?	3	2	1 x
12. Do you have a customer helpdesk or a call center?	3	2	1 x
13. Do you know the percentage of customers who terminate their relationship with your organization due to dissatisfaction?	3	2	1 x
14. Are complaints systematically registered and analyzed in your organization?	3	2	1 x
15. Have you established procedures for handling complaints and are these routinely used in your organization?	3	2	1 x
16. Do you measure the degree of customer loyalty?	3	2	1 x
17. Do you regularly advice customers about your products/services that best fit their needs?	3	2 x	1
18. Do you know what the costs are when you lose a customer?	3	2	1 x
19. Do you know what the costs are to gain a new customer?	3	2	1 x
20. Do you know how much you lose in sales due to dissatisfied customers?	3	2 x	1
21. Do you maintain relations with your customers and do you expand these relationships?	3 x	2	1
22. Do you regularly organize meetings with customer groups to learn about their needs, wants, ideas, and complaints?	3	2	1 x

Table continues on next page.

Table 7.1. TPS-Lean Six Sigma Customer Orientation Quick Scan, Used on Business Jet (Rampersad, 2003)

Circle the correct number: 1 = no, 2 = somewhat, 3 = yes

	Yes	Somewhat	No
II Leadership Style			
23. Is there commitment to customer orientation at top management?	3 x	2	1
24. As a manager, do you know how many complaints are received yearly?	3	2 x	1
25. Is management convinced of the importance of satisfied customers and do they act accordingly?	3 x	2	1
26. Have you integrated customer satisfaction into your organization's vision?	3 x	2	1
27. Has this vision been clearly communicated to all your employees and customers?	3	2 x	1
28. Does management recognize notable trends, and do they anticipate these in a timely manner?	3	2 x	1
29. Does management set a good example regarding customer-friendly behavior?	3 x	2	1
30. Is management open to suggestions and ideas from customers?	3 x	2	1
31. Does management personally reward those employees who deliver a valuable contribution to increased customer satisfaction?	3	2 x	1
32. Are relationships of management with customers supported and warmly encouraged?	3	2 x	1
33. Is management at all times available to customers?	3	2	1 x
34. Do all managers have regular personal contact with customers?	3	2	1 x
35. Does customer satisfaction also belong to the evaluation criteria of management?	3	2 x	1
36. Are the customer wishes continuously taken into consideration when taking decisions?	3	2 x	1
37. Does top management also personally handle complaints of customers?	3	2	1 x
III Strategic Vision			
38. Are there at least five customer orientation objectives and related performance measures formulated in the corporate scorecard or strategic business plan?	3 x	2	1
39. Have you developed E-business strategies for the coming years to increase customer satisfaction?	3	2 x	1
40. Is the strategy regarding customer orientation continuously communicated to all employees?	3	2 x	1
41. Do you have a partnership relation with all your customers based on mutual respect and trust?	3	2	1 x
42. Do you guarantee your customers a minimal service level and/or complete satisfaction?	3 x	2	1
43. Do you continuously benchmark with regard to customer satisfaction?	3	2	1 x
44. Do you involve your customers with the execution of improvement processes?	3	2	1 x

Question	3	2	1
45. Are all of your employees involved with the improvement of customer orientation?	3	2	1 x
46. Do you have guidelines regarding the optimal satisfaction of customers?	3	2	1 x
47. Do you consider customer information a strategic asset?	3 x	2	1
48. Do you have an up-to-date databank in which all customer characteristics are registered?	3	2	1 x

IV Internal Processes

Question	3	2	1
49. Have you appointed process owners for controlling business processes?	3	2 x	1
50. Are products/services delivered within the period expected by the customer?	3	2 x	1
51. Does your phone, fax, Internet, and other E-business tools match the way your customers prefer to communicate?	3	2 x	1
52. Is the phone in your organization answered within 3 rings in more than 80 % of the cases?	3 x	2	1
53. Is every process in your organization arranged in such a way as to optimally comply with customer expectations?	3	2 x	1
54. Do these expectations form the basis for performance measures?	3	2 x	1
55. Have you implemented a customer relationship management (CRM) system within your organization?	3	2	1 x
56. Do you use measured customer satisfaction as an indicator for process improvement?	3 x	2	1
57. Do you involve your customers in the development of new products/services?	3	2	1 x
58. Do you also measure the satisfaction of your internal customers?	3	2	1 x
59. Are employees personally responsible for solving customer problems?	3	2 x	1
60. Do you translate customer needs into product and process improvements and the development of new products and services?	3	2 x	1
61. Do supporting departments within your organization guarantee the quality of the work they deliver?	3	2	1 x
62. Are your marketing employees free to spend what is necessary to correct a mistake made with a customer?	3	2	1 x

V Human Resources

Question	3	2	1
63. Do you give extra rewards to employees who continuously perform in a customer-oriented manner?	3 x	2	1
64. Do you regularly organize trips to your important customers for your employees?	3	2 x	1
65. Are your customer service employees free in taking decisions in order to satisfy customers?	3	2	1 x
66. Are your employees' interests and the interests of your customers related?	3	2 x	1
67. Do you encourage your employees to generate ideas regarding the increase of customer satisfaction?	3 x	2	1
68. Do you have an introductory program in which new employees are also educated concerning the importance of satisfied customers?	3	2	1 x
69. Are customer orientation and continuous work towards improvement criteria for promotion?	3	2 x	1
70. Do your marketing employees receive training of at least two weeks each year in customer orientation?	3	2	1 x
Total Score			**123 points**

your suppliers will ensure that the quality of your inputs is sufficient to meet your own improvement objectives. If possible, minimize the number of your suppliers; go with the few best, improvement-oriented suppliers who have a demonstrated TPS-Lean Six Sigma culture and effective leadership by top management, and collaborate with them based on a long-term partnership contract.

The Kano model is also a useful tool that can be used to understand and define important customer requirements. This will be discussed in the next section.

7.2 THE KANO MODEL

Noriaki Kano (1996) developed a model of customer satisfaction nearly 20 years ago, based on Herzberg's motivation theory. This model has been used in manufacturing, as well as, service industries to identify the basic (or must-be), expected, and attractive or unexpressed needs of customers or clients. Whether these needs are fulfilled or not will determine whether the customers are satisfied, dissatisfied, neutral, or delighted with an organization's offering as illustrated in Figure 7.2. The classification of customer needs into different categories helps prioritize the need for action, as resources are usually limited. These categories include:

1. Spoken and stated requirements (*satisfiers*) are easily identified and expected to be met. These features are typically performance related.
2. Innovative or attractive features (*exciters*) that would excite and delight a customer but could quickly become expected features, as customers get used to the idea and their expectations are raised.
3. Expected but unspoken requirements (*dissatisfiers*) are ones that, when not satisfied, result in a dissatisfied customer. These unspoken (must-be) requirements are the most difficult to define but prove very expensive, if ignored (Besterfield, 1995).

7.3 IDENTIFY IMPROVEMENT OPPORTUNITIES

Most organizations are able to identify improvement opportunities, but they have some difficulties selecting the right ones. Not all opportunities are candidates for a TPS-Lean Six Sigma project, nor should they

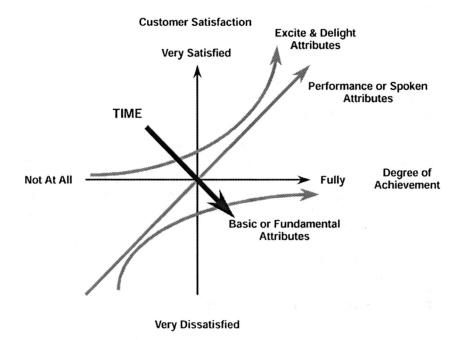

Source: Kano et al. (1984).

Figure 7.2.   Kano Model.

be. Projects that are not connected to the OBSC should not be considered. The steps that need to be taken in selecting a project vary as per your line of business and the scale of the operation. Two of the main points that need to be considered when selecting projects include are customer satisfaction and return on investment. Other criteria which also should be taken into consideration are:

- Time needed for the implementation of the TPS-Lean Six Sigma project and the realization of the related organization and personal objectives.
- Costs related to the project execution.
- The costs-benefits ratio.
- The chances of the related improvement action being successful (both manageable and realizable).
- Employee engagement.

There should be project identification criteria to help companies focus on the opportunities that have the most impact on the business. Knowing where to look will help companies identify potential improvement opportunities. Some criteria to consider are:

Customer Satisfaction

Customer satisfaction must be the first consideration when selecting projects. We therefore advise you to execute the TPS-Lean Six Sigma Customer Orientation Quick Scan in the initial stage of each project (see Table 7.1). TPS-Lean Six Sigma projects are tied to improving critical to quality characteristics (CTQs). CTQs are physical, measurable responses that are directly linked to customer requirements. They are design requirements that the product must satisfy. After understanding customer's requirements, the organization needs to assess if their processes are capable of meeting these requirements. Process capability is accomplished by comparing process variability to customer's specifications. Processes that create a high value-addition and have poor capability receive the most attention and are eligible and are excellent candidates for improvements. A process capability analysis study is covered in the TPS-Lean Six Sigma tools, see Appendix, under the Measure Phase. Customer complaints can also provide clues to problems that should be addressed. Companies can look through customer complaint logs and can ask the customers what are the greatest quality concerns.

Process Yield

Process yield is a measure that tells you what fraction of total units produced in your process that is defective. Poor yield means higher defects and this is translated into more scrap and reworks resulting in poor cost of quality and higher production cost. Critical processes are directly linked to customer's requirements and any critical process with poor yield is also a good candidate for improvement.

Cycle Time Reduction

Cycle time is defined as the total time it takes for a unit to be processed from the beginning to the end of the process, in another words, the cycle time is the total elapsed time to move a unit throughout the process. Any process that produces less than expected results, or requires a lot of overtime, is associated with higher costs, and is a good candidate for improvement. Cycle time reduction results in a more efficient process and less waste.

The TPS-Lean Six Sigma Way to Determine Which Processes are Relevant for Improvement

The above mentioned ways are traditional approaches to identify improvement opportunities. Another and more effective way (TPS-Lean Six Sigma Way) to determine which processes are relevant for improvement is by making a detailed division in subprocesses and process sections for each business process up to the action level and determine which of these processes are relevant from the Critical Success Factor (CSF) standpoint (Rampersad, 2003). Start with the key processes. For example, the production process of Jet Interior (supplier of the airline industry) is divided into the subprocesses of manufacturing, assembling, spray painting, testing, and packaging. The subprocess manufacturing is then subdivided into supplying, sorting, sawing, drilling, bending, sanding, and so forth. Supplying can again be subdivided into the activities of picking up, moving, putting down, fastening, and other procedures. With the aid of a matrix, we can now determine which operational processes are relevant from the CSF standpoint (related to the OBSC and Project BSC). If a process is essential, it is indicated in the matrix. Nonessential processes (those with few marks in the matrix) can better be outsourced. Table 7.2 shows an example of this exercise with respect to Jet Interior. Outlining business processes in this manner provides an impression of the most important business processes that add value for the customer. Processes that create a high value-addition receive the most attention and are eligible for continuous improvement. From Table 7.2, it can be seen that order processing, distribution, and administration in this company are nonessential processes that hardly add any value; they are thus eligible for outsourcing.

For each process-CSF combination, Performance Measures (PMs) related to the Project BSC can be defined. These measure the activities that have crucial organizational importance and, as such, deliver a valuable contribution to the controllability of business processes. They give Management timely signals regarding efficient organizational guidance based on measuring (process) changes and comparisons of the measurement results with the norms. For example, the following PMs belong to a customer-oriented organization: number of customer complaints; how fast complaints are handled; repair time; percentage of completed on-

Table 7.2.   CSF Matrix Versus Business Processes of Jet Interior

	Critical Success Factors (CSF)			
Business Processes	Motivated Employees	Customer Orientation	Product Quality	Cost Control
1. Selling				
1.1 Order Acquisition	X	X	X	X
1.2 Order Processing		X		
2. Purchasing				
2.1 Selecting Suppliers	X	X	X	X
2.2 Closing Purchase Contract	X		X	X
2.3 Placing Purchase Order			X	X
2.4 Receiving Goods	X		X	X
2.5 Paying Purchase Invoices	X			X
3. Manufacturing	X	X	X	X
4. Distributing			X	
5. Administrating	X			

time deliveries handled according to specifications; and order handling time. The PMs linked to high product quality include: number of customer complaints; percentage of rejects; percentage of damaged returns; number of process interruptions; and quality grade. The following PMs correspond to motivated employees: percentage of sick leave; percentage of tardiness; labour productivity; turnover; and so forth. Table 7.3 shows an example of the Jet Interior Company where one or more possible PMs are presented for each process-CSF combination.

7.4 EVALUATION OF POTENTIAL PROJECTS

Some specific priorities should be defined when evaluating potential projects. Financial benefits, strategic alignment, and personnel alignment (i.e., human capital) are too few to be considered. It is important to look for a project that is certain to produce a successful outcome. Using the TPS-Lean Six Sigma Project Prioritization Template (or PET) in Figure 7.3 with weighting the criteria, one can rank the relative strength of each potential project with regards to the following nine important elements:

- Expected savings.
- Adaptability.
- Meets strategic goals.
- Customer value.

Table 7.3. Business Process/CSF and Performance Measures Matrix of Jet Interior

Business Processes	Critical Success Factors (CSFs)			
	Motivated Employees	Customer Orientation	Product Quality	Cost Control
1. Selling				
1.1 Order Acquisition	–% of Sales per—salesperson –% of Sick Leave	–% of customers lost –Number of "non-sales" –Accessibility of sales department –% of available marketing competences –Number of customer complaints –Market share –Market growth -Degree of customer loyalty	–Number of customer complaints regarding product quality	–% of Sales returns from new products –Marketing costs –% of Decrease in marketing costs
1.2 Order Processing	–Labor productivity –% of Personnel turnover –Process speed	–Completing rush orders –Throughput time of orders	–Number of processing mistakes –% of mistakes in customers' information	–Efficiency –Turnover of the marketing business unit
2. Purchasing	–Level of satisfaction of purchasing personnel –Training costs purchasing personnel –% of Personnel who find they are working under effective leadership	–Delivery speed (time between ordering and delivering) –Time needed for the supplier to make a firm invoice –% of orders delivered too late –% of orders where too much or too little was delivered	–% of Approved materials –% of Returns –Delivery reliability of suppliers	–Purchase vs. market price –Purchase share as opposed to sales –Number of suppliers –Number of suppliers supplying one article –Average order size per supplier

Table continues on next page

Table 7.3. Business Process/CSF and Performance Measures Matrix of Jet Interior Continued

	Critical Success Factors (CSFs)			
Business Processes	Motivated Employees	Customer Orientation	Product Quality	Cost Control
3. Manufacturing	–% of Sick Leave for manu-facturing personnel –Labor productivity Value-added per personnel costs –% Of Personnel turnover	–Number of customer complaints –Throughput time during manufacturing	–% of Manufacturing waste –% of Rejects during production –Effectiveness –ISO norms in manufacturing process –Value-added –Quality grade	–Availability machines –Quality costs –% of Manufacturing waste –Efficiency –Integral productivity –Capital productivity –Material productivity –Value-added per sales
4. Distributing	–% of sick leave at distribution business unit -Labor productivity	–% of completed, on-time deliveries, according to specifications –Delivery speed	–% of Damaged goods returned –Effectiveness	–Warehouse utilization –Stock levels –Circulation speed –Availability of transportation resources –Capital productivity
5. Administrating	–Labor productivity –% of personnel who feel they have challenging work	–Time needed to fix a complaint	–Effectiveness –Number of administrative mistakes	–Billing speed –Age accounts receivable –Efficiency

		IMPACT						EFFORT		
		Financial Benefits		Strategic Alignment		Human Capital		Effort & Risk		
Project Number	List of Possible Projects	Expected Savings	Adaptability	Meets Goals	Customer Value	Employee Engagement	Resources	Complexity	Time Needed	Relative Strength
Weight =		5	1	3	4	4	1	2	2	
1										0%
2										0%
3										0%
4										0%
5										0%
6										0%
7										0%
8										0%
9										0%
10										0%
11										0%
		Estimated dollar savings	Likelihood the project can be duplicated in other areas across the company	Project addresses key business objective	Value to the customer	Likelihood employees will be engaged to the project	The ease or difficulty in obtaining resources needed (human, financial, space, machines, etc)	Overall perceived complexity of the project	Estimated time to complete project	
		1 = 0-100K 2 = 200-500K 3 = 600K-1M 4 = >1M	1 = not likely 2 = at least one 3 = more than one 4 = company wide	1 = not at all 2 = partially 3 = a high percentage 4 = fully	1 = no value 2 = maintains business 3 = grows business 4 = resolves concern	1 = not likely 2 = partially 3 = a high percentage 4 = fully	1 = a lot of effort 2 = some hurdles 3 = relative ease 4 = no-brainer	1 = very complex 2 = somewhat difficult 3 = doo-able 4 = easy	1 = >1yr 2 = >6mo 3 = 4-6 mo 4 = <4mo	

Figure 7.3   TPS-Lean Six Sigma Project Evaluation Template (PET).

- Employee engagement.
- Resources.
- Risks.
- Complexity.
- Time needed to complete.

After ranking each element, one can then determine the impact and effort required to complete each project. Once all the projects are identified and ranked, you can study the effort impact analysis graph to determine which projects to select. The projects with high impact and low effort are the ideal selection. After selecting top projects, the project teams are identified by fitting the shared ambition of the members to the project. Through this process, the Champion, Black Belt, and team members are selected and placed in the project charter. Let's take a moment to look at each element of the TPS-Lean Six Sigma Project Evaluation Template.

7.5 TPS-LEAN SIX SIGMA PROJECT EVALUATION TEMPLATE

The Project Evaluation Template (PET) (see Figure 7.3) is divided in to two main sections, Impact and effort. As we discussed previously, the right project is one that provides the greatest impact for the least effort. When reviewing the impact on the company, we consider the estimated expected savings the project would achieve, the adaptability of the project to similar areas of concern across the company, the ability of the project to positively affect personal and key business objectives, and the value of the project to the customer. When reviewing the effort required executing the project, we will consider the likelihood that employee will be engaged, the ease or difficulty in obtaining resources (human, financial, space machines, etc.), the overall perceived complexity, and estimated time needed to complete the project.

Weights

Although each of these elements is important to project selection, there are obvious benefits to certain elements. For example, a project that has small financial benefit, yet is highly adaptable is not as appealing as a project that may not be adaptable, but achieves a superior financial benefit. Hence, the expected financial savings of the project is much more significant than the adaptability of the project. For this reason, we added "weights" to each of the elements of the PET.

Ranks

Another facet of the PET is the "ranking" of each element. Each element has a numerical rank of one to four (1-4) that is assigned. The rank system used is similar to that of a survey instrument, whereas the number four (4) is assigned to the most desired state and one (1) is assigned to the undesired state.

Relative Strength and the Impact-Effort Graph

The relative strength on the right-most column of the PET is used as the final grade for the project. In other words, a strength (or grade) of 100% is the best possible. A strength of 100% means that there is maximum impact (100%) and minimum effort (0%) for the project. As you complete the PET, you will notice data points are plotted on the Impact-Effort Analysis graph (Figure 7.4). The Impact-Effort graph is a visual display of each of the projects. Any project plotted in the upper left quadrant is a good candidate for a TPS-Lean Six Sigma project.

Expected Savings

Expected savings is the expected savings the project will yield at completion. This is the most important element of the project. The power of TPS-Lean Six Sigma implementation is the impact it has on the bottom line. This is an important statement that should be reiterated. Every so-called quality initiative in the past has failed because of the fact they were not tied to bottom line results. The power and uniqueness of TPS-Lean Six Sigma is that it increases profitability for the organization. TPS-Lean Six Sigma is not a quality initiative, it is a business initiative.

Adaptability

Adaptability is the ability of the project to be applied to other processes, departments, divisions, or products in the company. A project that

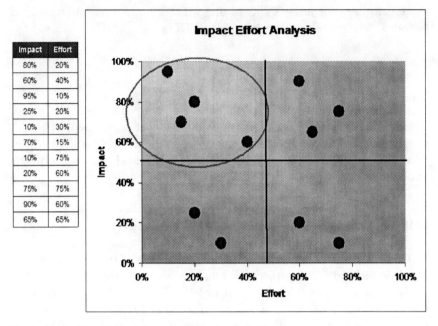

Impact	Effort
80%	20%
60%	40%
95%	10%
25%	20%
10%	30%
70%	15%
10%	75%
20%	60%
75%	75%
90%	60%
65%	65%

Figure 7.4.   Example of Impact Effort Analysis Graph.

can be adapted will be more desirable to management as the savings can be multiplied easily.

Meets Strategic Goals

This is how well the project result (the Project BSC) will align with key business objectives/goals (the OBSC). If a project is not improving a business objective, it probably is not a worthwhile project to pursue.

Customer Value

Customer value is the value of the project to the customer. As we discussed earlier, a key attribute of a TPS-Lean Six Sigma project is customer satisfaction. Without customers, there is no business and catastrophic failure. Customer value can be a financial benefit, or it could also be something like added features or quicker delivery time. In some cases, a project is selected because it will resolve an outstanding or perceived customer concern.

Employee Engagement

For a project to be successful, you will need the right people to be involved. To find the people that will be most engaged, we must focus on the best fit between personal ambition and project ambition (PBSC and project BSC). The discussed PBSC method can ensure the necessary fit by matching the abilities, aptitude and motivation of the candidates with not just the job requirements but also with the shared project ambition (see chapter 4). The personal ambition of a candidate tells a better story than a resume. It is possible that a candidate seems suitable for a specific project on the basis of his/her CV, but if there is no match between his/her personal ambition and the ambition of the TPS-Lean Six Sigma project, this would not aid his/her performance. A good match between the project BSC and the PBSC of the candidate therefore results in higher customer satisfaction, higher personal performance, higher project quality and a shorter project execution time. When employees are satisfied, they will work with greater motivation and not loose interest. The optimum project is one that not only satisfies the customer and the company, but it also satisfies the personal needs of the project members. Employee engagement is the key to the success of the project.

Resources

Resources can come in many types including, but not limited to; material availability, space, equipment, sufficient funding, and lets not forget, human resources, to name a few. The proper way to rank this element is to consider the all the resources needed, and make a determination on how difficult it will be to obtain them.

Complexity

Complexity is determined by the business or organization. What is complex for one company may not be, for whatever reason, for another company. You will need to review and understand all elements of the project to provide the right ranking. For example, if your project involves making a change to a preestablished software package, but no one in your company is capable of making such a change, this will be very complex. You will need to find someone capable, contract or hire them to perform the work, and so forth. The main concept to remember when ranking this element is to consider the probability for success. Is this project going to be difficult or simple to complete?

Time Needed

This is an estimate of the time needed to complete the project. For obvious reasons, projects extending greater than a year will be less desirable than projects that can be completed in a few months. The optimum time frame for a TPS-Lean Six Sigma project is 4 to 6 months.

7.6 COMPLETING THE TPS-LEAN SIX SIGMA PROJECT EVALUATION TEMPLATE

Once all the projects have been identified, they will be listed on the PET. Completing the PET is not a difficult process as you have already gathered the required information. Again, the purpose of the PET is to visualize all the prospective TPS-Lean Six Sigma projects and make valued decisions on which projects fit with the OBSC and PBSCs. On the right side of the PET template is the overall ranking. This is based on the weighting levels shown on the chart. You will assign the rankings for each element and make your decision on which project(s) to select using the Impact-Effort graph as a guide. The Impact-Effort diagram (see Figure 7.4) is a valuable tool to show which projects will have the greatest impact with the least effort. Overall, the PET and the Impact-Effort Diagram provide a unique visual tool for your team to select the right TPS-Lean Six Sigma project. You will have confidence that the project you selected will be supported by Management and you are ready to proceed with TPS-Lean Six Sigma implementation.

7.7 PROJECT SCOPE AND SCALE

As we stated in previous chapter, defining project scope is one of the hardest tasks for the Black Belt and Champion. Many projects fail as a result of "scope creep," a term used for a project that continues to grow out of control in scope (Figure 7.5). Projects with a narrow scope may not deliver the ROI needed for the company to embrace; on the other hand, projects with wide scope tend to cause the team to loose focus and interest. Therefore, it is of utmost importance to properly define a project's scope. Some issues leading to scope creep and project failure are:

Scope and Scale

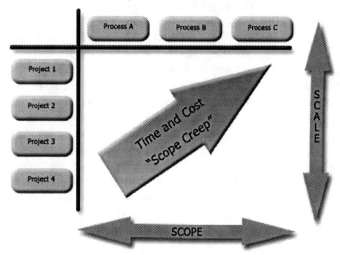

Figure 7.5.   Project scope and scale relationship.

- Project is too large.
- Project is too small.
- No Project BSC formulated.
- Trying to achieve perfection.
- Overzealous "experts" or "guru's."
- Inadequate resources.
- Wrong or missing people on the team.
- Misunderstanding of the complexity of the project.

Since Black Belt training length is about 4 months, it is recommended to select a project that will be completed within 4 to 6 months. Below are some key questions which will help defining the project scope:

- What areas in the process the team needs to focus on (process A, B, or C)?
- What are the process boundaries?
- What are the project vision, mission, and values (project ambition)?
- Is the project scope is achievable in 4-6 months?
- What is off-limits or out-of-bounds for the team?
- What are the constraints the team needs to work under?

The scope is usually addressed during the project evaluation process. Projects are analyzed with respect to their impact (realization of the Project BSC) and their effort. The impact is linked to the company's strategic business objectives (OBSC) and the effort is related to the resources and time needed to complete the project. Projects with low effort and high impact are preferred. Sometimes, the process that needs to be improved is located at many locations (wide scale). In theses situation, the Champion may limit the improvement to only one location and after successful completion, the same solution can be adapted at the other locations.

Let's take a look at a couple of examples. We remember one of the first TPS-Lean Six Sigma deployments at a financial investing company in Stuttgart, Germany. Although, their CEO was sold on the benefits of TPS-Lean Six Sigma, their president was not so convinced. We knew going in that it was going to be critical to have the first few projects be successful to keep the commitment from the president. After the first round of training, we had all potential team members complete personal BSCs. We then formulated the OBSC and selected a few potential TPS-Lean Six Sigma projects that would achieve quick results. We selected two projects that could be completed in less than 2 months and each yielded about 100K in savings. So, while they weren't projects with major scope, they were effective, because we were able to complete them quickly and hold onto the support of the president. After the success of the first two projects, it was funny that the president himself started to get more involved in the process, and he actually helped us identify the next series of projects. That is what we mean when we say how important it is to have some quick success for your first projects. Not only does this provide an immediate impact to the company, it paves the way for future projects and secures commitment from management.

Another example is from a TPS-Lean Six Sigma project we ran at an auto parts warehouse in Atlanta, Georgia. This was a smaller company of about 30 full-time employees. One of the nice things is that almost everyone in the organization was trained in TPS-Lean Six Sigma and was eager to get involved with projects. We started out with what seemed like a fairly simple project. Our project mission was to incorporate a new method for identifying and storing parts. We first formulated the TPS-Lean Six Sigma project BSC which was related to the OBSC. At first the project team was keeping on track. They were able to develop a new part number coding system that would allow them to quickly identify the part, quantity available, and its storage location. But what started to happen is new actions were slipping into the project causing the project scope to grow and grow. Where the team started out developing a new identification and storage system, they were now getting involved with making changes to the physical layout of the storage area. At this point, we got involved.

While the team had good intentions and the re-arranging of the storage area was a viable project on its own, the rearranging of the storage room was outside of the scope of the current project. What we just described is called "scope creep," this is a term used for a project that keeps growing and growing. The problem with scope creep is that the project will never end. The resources that were originally committed will be exhausted, and we have even seen where team's totally collapse as a result of frustration. Remember at the beginning of this chapter, we defined for you what the definition of a project is which included a defined beginning and end. When the scope to your project keeps growing, there is no end. Just to finish the story about the auto parts warehouse, they got back on track and successfully completed their project on the identification system and later went on to start another project that dealt with rearranging the storage area. When both projects were completed, the company realized savings in excess of $200,000 over a one year period by improving order processing time. Not only that, but their customer satisfaction rating went from 72% to 97%, a change of 25%.

In conclusion, good projects breed success. As seen from the last two examples, when you select the right projects, you are personally successful, the company is successful, and your customers are delighted.

7.8 PROJECT REVIEWS

The status of the each project needs to be reviewed on a regular basis to assure desired outcomes. Another reason for this review is to confirm alignment of the PBSC to the OBSC and to the Project's BSC is still strong. An informal project review is conducted at all stages by the Champion or by the project Sponsor, once every week and it covers resources allocated, project scope, project progress, effectiveness, and alignment with both personal and company goals. The Black Belts who are leading the projects should make reviews at least every two weeks and cover project deliverables and progress, and TPS-Lean Six Sigma tools and their application. The Black Belt may consult with the Master Black Belt at this time to gain an objective perspective. Finally, a formal review by upper management should be held every month until project completion. During the reviews, if there are discrepancies or concerns found, these concerns need to be recorded and the project team gathered for an action review. The results of actions taken during projects can be valuable to future projects and team members and should be listed in the final project review's "lessons learned" section. There are many commercial project tracking software packages available to companies to monitor project status and progress.

SUMMARY

In order to obtain the desired TPS-Lean Six Sigma benefits, organizations should formulate their OBSC, formulate related Project BSCs, and implement an effective and efficient project identification, evaluation, and selection process. Companies should also establish their values and define critical metrics to measure success, which are included in the OBSC (see chapter 4). There are many types of projects and all have their place. By selecting the right TPS-Lean Six Sigma project, both personal *and* company goals will be realized in concert with each other and success will breed success. As your organization continues to breed success, a snowball effect occurs; customer satisfaction, employee satisfaction, and company profits will all exponentially increase. This is the power of TPS-Lean Six Sigma. Finally; before you implement the TPS-Lean Six Sigma project, verify if the circumstances for implementation are favorable. Insight into the problems that may occur during execution will be needed. In Table 6.2, we have introduced a checklist that can be used to create insight into the introductory circumstances of the TPS-Lean Six Sigma project. Maybe your company is not ready for TPS-Lean Six Sigma yet. By filling in the quick scan, you will find this out. In the next chapter, we will focus on managing and tracking TPS-Lean Six Sigma projects.

CHAPTER 8

MANAGING AND TRACKING TPS-LEAN SIX SIGMA PROJECTS

Real learning gets to the heart of what it means to be human. Through learning, we re-create ourselves. Through learning, we become able to do something we never were able to do. Through learning, we perceive the world and our relationship to it. Through learning, we extend our capacity to create, to be part of the generative process of life. There is within each of us a deep hunger for this type of learning.

—Peter M. Senge

To improve is to change; to be perfect is to change often.

—Sir Winston Churchill

In the deploying phase of the TPS-Lean Six Sigma cycle (Figure 4.1), we are managing and tracking projects. This critical phase involves primarily the project Champions, Leaders, and Black Belts. The basic objective is to make sure the projects stay on track, supported, and continue to be linked with the PBSC, OBSC, and Project BSC's.

TPS-Lean Six Sigma can be a daunting process to manage, if you do not use the right tools. In most midsized organizations, there can be 3, 10, or even over 20 projects running all at once. While there may only be one Champion for all projects, Black Belts typically run 3 to 4 projects concurrently. While these projects are running in parallel with each other,

TPS-Lean Six Sigma: Linking Human Capital to Lean Six Sigma: A New Blueprint for Creating High Performance Companies, pp. 245–253

they are never all at the same gate or phase. So who is keeping track of all these projects? Moreover, how do we know if they are being completed on time? Most importantly, how do we know or not, if the project was successful?

As we discussed in previous chapters, without success there is failure, and with failure comes a loss of support from management, and unfortunately, the initiative will fail. This is one reason why we spend a lot of time and effort selecting the right TPS-Lean Six Sigma projects. Now that we have the right projects selected, what a pity it would be to loose support because we were not able to execute the project successfully, or articulate the results effectively. This is why it is so important to have a good management and tracking system in place for all these projects. In this chapter, we will discuss the fundamentals and elements of a good tracking system that will help you manage your projects to yield the greatest benefit. We will look at *What* needs to be tracked and *Why*, as well as, giving you some guidance on making a decision to design your own, or invest in a commercially available software package for this need.

8.1 MANAGING YOUR PROJECT

Given that, you have selected the right TPS-Lean Six Sigma project (based on the OBSC), formulated the Project BSC, and picked out all the right people (based on the alignment of the PBSC with the Project BSC). The next step is to put the plan in to action. You will need an effective tool that can track and coordinate projects, and yet be agile enough to respond to changing requirements. We have seen companies spend thousands of dollars and hundreds of hours developing software they 'thought' was going to work, only to find out it didn't suit all their needs. On the other hand, they developed software so restrictive, it was impossible to make changes. When developing your own tool, or when selecting one of the many commercially available packages, you want to pay attention to what your needs are, as well as, making sure whatever was developed or purchased can be modified easily. In addition to selecting your tool of choice to track and manage your projects, you will also need to confirm alignment of the PBSC with the OBSC and the Project BSC, and you will need team members to be able to access the project's data and status in real-time. Team members will need to know what actions are on their plate, and most importantly, you will need to assure upper management's confidence in your projects financial numbers. Finally, you will need to share your success and "lessons learned" throughout the organization.

TPS-Lean Six Sigma Project BSCsoft

We are launching the TPS-Lean Six Sigma Project BSCsoft together with this book (see the Appendix) in order to help you manage your TPS-Lean Six Sigma project successfully. TPS-Lean Six Sigma Project BSCsoft is an interactive software system that will assist you with the successful formulation and implementation of your Project Balanced Scorecard (Project BSC). It offers Champions/Master Black Belts/Black Belts/Green Belts the possibility to execute their project effectively. This software system consists of the following functions:

1. Formulating the Project BSC.
2. Implementing and tracking the project; to confirm the project is progressing through each of its defined tollgates and to assure the project and team members are staying on course.
3. Aligning the Project BSC with project member's Personal BSC (PBSC) and with the Organizational BSC (OBSC).
4. Monitoring the performance of the project continuously.
5. Effectively communicating the project results to Upper Management, Executives, and Champions, and to keep the TPS-Lean Six Sigma initiatives visible to them.

A Dashboard is part of the TPS-Lean Six Sigma Project BSCsoft. This is a visual status of all open and closed projects and is strongly related to the Project BSC. Dashboards are a common tool used by today's managers to provide quick reference to key objective data. Figure 8-1 is an example of a TPS-Lean Six Sigma Dashboard.

TPS-Lean Six Sigma Personal BSCsoft

We are also launching the TPS-Lean Six Sigma Personal BSCsoft together with this book (see Appendix) in order to help you coach yourself and your project team members successfully. BSCsoft is an interactive software system that will assist individuals with the formulation and implementation of their Personal Balanced Scorecard (PBSC). It offers individuals to coach themselves, TPS-Lean Six Sigma coaches to coach others, Champions/Master Black Belts/Black Belts/Green Belts/Project Managers to coach their project members and Executives/HR to effectively steer their organization on performance, happiness, joy, and motivation. This software system consists of the following parts:

TPS-Lean Six Sigma Project Dashboard

Project #	Business Unit	Project Name	Approval Status	D	M	A	I	C	Projected Savings	Actual Savings	Percent Achieved
				DMAIC Tollgate Status					Finacial Impact		
1	SLS01	Increase share by 20%	Approved						$250,000	$111,000	44%
2	MKT01	Develop tri-fold	Approved						$1,000,000	$0	0%
3	MFG11	Reduce cycle time shift 2	Pending						$200,000	$0	0%
4	PRO10	Shorten MG12 antenna by 2 ft	Pending						$1,500,000	$1,650,000	110%
5	SLS01	Increase net margin 3%	Pending						$500,000	$0	0%
6	MKT01	Reduce database pct by 30	Approved						$550,000	$0	0%
7	FIN03	Open sub-dept	Approved						$1,380,000	$1,250,000	91%
8	FIN03	Eliminate 10% waste control	Draft						$3,400,000	$0	0%
9	SHP04	Increase throughput mech #4	Closed						$1,675,000	$1,675,000	100%
10	TST15	Double prober speed	Approved						$1,200,000	$1,325,000	110%
11	CUS20	Resolve CTQ 5 on PN 09-SBT	Closed						$850,000	$950,000	112%
Totals	11								$12,505,000	$6,961,000	

Figure 8.1.   TPS-Lean Six Sigma Dashboard.

1. Formulating the PBSC.
2. Implementing the PBSC based on the Plan-Do-Act-Challenge cycle.
3. Aligning the PBSC with the OBSC and Project BSC.
4. Effectively managing of talents within the project and the organization.

ALIGNMENT OF THE PBSC, OBSC, AND TPS- LEAN SIX SIGMA PROJECT BSC

Chapter 4 provides detail on the creation of the Personal Balanced Scorecard (PBSC), Organizational Balanced Scorecard (OBSC), and the Project Balanced Scorecard. Additionally, chapter 4 provides methods for aligning each of the balanced scorecards with each other. During the process of managing and tracking progress on the TPS-Lean Six Sigma project, there needs to be continual review of these alignments. If one of these alignments, or links, is broken, the project could be in jeopardy of failure. For example, team members are selected based on alignment of their personal ambitions to the projects goals. If a team member changes roles in the organization or if a team member has a life-changing event occur such as marriage, newborn baby, divorce, major accident or surgery, cancer, and so forth. This could have an impact on the project and these types of dynamics need to be carefully analyzed by the project Black Belt via the ambition meeting between the Black Belt and the team member. The topics in this meeting are the match between the team member's PBSC and the Project BSC. The Black Belt should act as a trusted person during this meeting (see chapter 4). If the Black Belt decides that there is a problem with the scorecard alignment, changes will need to be made. These changes could involve dismissing, or replacing a team member. As discussed in chapter 4, the alignment of the personal ambition of the project members with the project ambition should be done in the following way: The Executive Management should have an ambition meeting with the Champions, the Champions should have an ambition meeting with the Master Black Belts, Master Black Belts should have an ambition meeting with the Black Belts, the Black Belts should have an ambition meeting with the Green Belts, and the Green Belts should have an ambition meeting with the remaining project team members.

8.3 WHAT NEEDS TO BE TRACKED?

Projects follow the TPS-Lean Six Sigma cycle shown in Figure 4.1. While some of the components of the model are utilized in the development of the workforce, and to formulate the overall organizational and Project BSC, the tactical needs of the individually selected project is what we are concentrating on in this chapter.

There are many valid reasons for effectively tracking the projects with the help of TPS-Lean Six Sigma Project BSCsoft; to confirm the project is progressing through each of its defined tollgates and project objectives/measures/targets (Project BSC), to assure the project and team members are staying on course, and to keep the TPS-Lean Six Sigma initiatives visible to upper Management and throughout the organization are only a few. Typically, there are several projects running concurrently, it is important to have a method for how you will track and manage your TPS-Lean Six Sigma projects. Let us look at what specific items need to be tracked.

From a project team standpoint, you will want to have the project charter information. This is valuable to show who all the players are and to be able to review and reassess the scope and objectives of the project from time to time. Another item, you will want to track is the status of each project phase or tollgate. These will be the DMAIC steps of the project. For each of these phases, you will want to show the actions, who is responsible for the actions, a status of the phase, the status of the deliverables (see chapter 9 for tollgate deliverables), and tollgate approvals. From a management standpoint, it is important to track and show measurable financial impact. Management is only concerned with one thing and one thing only, "money." They will want to see each project's projected and actual financial impact, as well as, a cumulative savings from all the projects. By showing management these numbers (affirmed by the finance department), their support for the TPS-Lean Six Sigma initiative will remain solid. Other items of interest of management will be ROI, and how any strategic goals are being met.

To summarize, this is a list of minimum items to be tracked:

- Project charter and Project BSC (including team members, scope and Project ambition statement).
- Description of Project.
- Each DMAIC phase (Define-Measure-Analyze-Improve-Control) and its status.
- Project objectives, measures and targets (Project BSC).
- Tollgate Approvals.
- Tollgate Deliverables.
- Action items (including actionee and due dates).
- Type of Impact (hard or soft).
- Project Costs.
- ROI (Return on Investment).
- Overall Project Status.

8.4 TYPES OF BENEFIT

There are two basic types of benefit for a project, hard or soft savings. Hard savings are measurable, quantifiable dollar savings, such as being able to do more work with less people (reduction in labor) and reducing the overall material cost of a product (reduction in material cost). As the finance department is an integral part of the project and project team (refer to chapter 6), they will be responsible to track, and be able to provide reliable financial data to the project. Soft savings, on the other hand, are a little more difficult to visualize. Soft savings can be related to human capital improvement, such as employee engagement, motivation, happiness, and morale. Soft savings can also be related to transactional, service, and manufacturing related, such as reducing cycle times, cost avoidance, or enhanced company image. As discussed in chapter 4 (talent management), the role of human resources and the line managers in evaluating, coaching, and developing the employee's is a key feature of the TPS-Lean Six Sigma infrastructure.

For example, if your project's objective is to reduce the cycle time from start to finish for making a submarine. The financial impact on the company is *soft*, this is because the cost of the submarine is still the same, but because the company is producing them faster, and it will be able to sell more of them per year. If your project goal is to reduce the cost it takes to make a camera, and you succeed, this is a hard impact because your profit margin has increased.

Some examples of hard and soft savings (benefit) are listed below:

Hard Savings

- Reduction in labor rate.
- Reduction in overhead.
- Reduction in workforce.
- Reduction in material cost.
- Reduction in waste.
- Reduction in transportation cost.
- Increased throughput.
- Decrease in spending.

Soft Savings

- Shortened cycle time.
- Improved yields.
- Improved employee morale, engagement, and motivation.
- Improved employee satisfaction.
- Cost avoidance.
- Enhanced company image and brand.
- Increased customer satisfaction.
- Increased safety.
- Reduction in cash flow.

8.5 FINANCIAL IMPACT VALIDATION

Financial impact validations are shown typically as a dollar savings (financial result). As we have stressed throughout this book, it is important to have a member from finance on the team. Realistically, we live in a world of snake salespersons and smoke-n-mirrors. It was not too long ago that the promise of higher profits through quality initiatives failed. Who can remember the promise of TQM? Well unfortunately, management does, and they still have a sour taste in their mouth from it. That is why, with TPS-Lean Six Sigma, they want to see *proven* results, and this means results that can be validated from the finance department. The finance department must be integrally involved in the planning and tracking of the project's numbers. This assures management that the financial results shown for the project have integrity. While it is perfectly okay to have Black Belts estimate financial results, a recognized financial officer of the organization must validate the numbers.

8.6 COMMUNICATE RESULTS

Everyone in the organization needs to hear about the success stories achieved with TPS-Lean Six Sigma projects. This is one of the most enjoyable, but necessary, parts of TPS-Lean Six Sigma deployment. Enjoyable, because its fun to celebrate success, and necessary because you have the opportunity to answer skeptics, and quiet cynics in the organization. Skeptics and cynics are always a part of any large organization and do nothing but put roadblocks up during deployment. It is important to disseminate positive results to the organization as quickly as possible to quiet these pessimists and hopefully, win them on your side. The Sponsor or Champion usually handles communicating the results. This is their time to shine and bask in the glory of the success of the project, and their opportunity to acknowledge publicly, the TPS-Lean Six Sigma team members, thus providing the necessary positive reenforcement for the initiative to continue to grow and prosper. This communication also helps to educate the newcomers to the value of TPS-Lean Six Sigma.

When communicating results, the Project BSC should be mentioned. How the project met its goals, what roadblocks were overcome, and describe the alignment of the project goal to the strategic objective. There will be projects finishing at various times, and the constant string of success stories being communicated to the workforce, will only continue to foster support for the TPS-Lean Six Sigma initiative. In addition to communicating the success message verbally, the success should also be reported in any available publications and to the media. This could be the company flyer, the company Web site, the local newspaper, posted on bulletin boards, and so on. The farther out, you can send the message, the better (see also paragraph 4.3.1).

8.7 LESSONS LEARNED

While all TPS-Lean Six Sigma projects share success stories, there will always be lessons that can be learned from the process. Whether it is a way to get around an obstacle, or how to implement a measurement method, all of the trials and tribulations of your project can provide a valuable benefit to others preparing to run new projects of their own by helping them avoid problems, or steering them in the right direction. Some organizations will collect all the lessons learned and put them into a knowledge base on a central computer for everyone to access. The important step is to sit down with the team postmortem and review where things went right, and where they went wrong. Then, to record this information in the final report for the project so the information will be available for future reference. By communicating the lessons learned, you help your organization motivate and "sell" the TPS-Lean Six Sigma initiative to others.

Another benefit to documenting lessons learned is for the fact there may be other projects, processes, or products in the organization that your project could be applied or adapted to. This is a great way to multiply TPS-Lean Six Sigma success to another application for a minimal cost to the organization. For example, we ran a TPS-Lean Six Sigma project at a local bank branch. The bank was receiving complaints from its customers for the time it took to process loan approvals. We found there were several disjointed processes in the bank causing the delays. There were redundant forms to be filled out, and the forms often sat idle waiting for the next department to pick them up. We were able to streamline the process by incorporating electronic review and signatures, and integrated it with the companies existing network. The processing time was reduced from three days to eight hours and the customers were delighted. The real benefit came to the organization because this same transactional process was not only applicable to the one local branch we did our initial project in, but also it was applied to the over twelve-hundred branches worldwide. This one simple TPS-Lean Six Sigma project yielded multi-million dollars in soft savings.

In the next chapter, we will discuss the TPS-Lean Six Sigma Certification program.

CHAPTER 9

TPS-LEAN SIX SIGMA BELT CERTIFICATION PROGRAMS

The most vital quality a soldier can possess is self-confidence
—George S. Patton

Giving people self-confidence is by far the most important thing that I can do. Because then they will act.
—Jack Welch

TPS-Lean Six Sigma $_{LLC}$ offers certification programs at both of its two unique academies; (1) Academy for TPS-Lean Six Sigma certification and (2) Academy for TPS-Lean Six Sigma Coaching, Consulting and Training. The first academy offers five types of certification "Belt" programs (Executive Platinum Belt, Champion, Master Black Belt, Black Belt, and Green Belt) and Coaching, Consulting, and Company certification programs. Each of the belts and certification programs has their own advantages and targeted participants. The second Academy offers coaching, consulting (implementation), and training. In this chapter, we will be discussing the 'Belt' certifications. In chapters 10-12, we will discuss the Coaching, Consulting, and Company certification programs in detail. The Belt certification programs to be discussed in this chapter include:

TPS-Lean Six Sigma: Linking Human Capital to Lean Six Sigma: A New Blueprint for Creating High Performance Companies, pp. 255–266
Copyright © 2007 by Information Age Publishing

- Executive "Platinum Belt" Certification Program
- Champion Certification Program
- Master Black Belt Certification Program
- Black Belt Certification Program
- Green Belt Certification Program

Also, in this chapter, we will focus primarily on the Green and Black belt programs for ease of understanding, and because these are the most common types of belts offered. Before we get into detail on some of the main components of the Green and Black Belt programs, below is a brief summary of what each of the programs consist of and what the target participants are. Detailed information for all of our belted programs can be found on our Web site at www.TPS-LeanSixSigma.com or by contacting the nearest TPS-Lean Six Sigma office in your area.

9.1 EXECUTIVE PLATINUM BELT CERTIFICATION PROGRAM

This certification program is for top-level Executives that typically include; CEOs, Presidents, CFOs, Owners, General Managers, and the like. These belts are usually called the "Sponsors" in the TPS-Lean Six Sigma Project Charter defined in chapter 6. The program is designed to provide the Executive with a complete high-level understanding of TPS-Lean Six Sigma program deployment and infrastructure. The Executives will gain an understanding of what all the roles are in the TPS-Lean Six Sigma infrastructure and will allow them to make important decisions concerning deployment. The program will also get into detail on how the program goals are articulated and measured. The participants will leave the program with the knowledge and understanding of their role in supporting the TPS-Lean Six Sigma deployment.

9.2 CHAMPION CERTIFICATION PROGRAM

This certification program is designed for what are called the Champions. Champions are typically process owners, Department, or business line Managers. The Champions are responsible for breaking down barriers and have the authority to remove obstacles that may be in the way of TPS-Lean Six Sigma Project executions. Champions are fully abreast of all project activities and participate in project reviews to assure alignment of the Project BSC to the Organization's BSC. The certification program provides the prospective Champions with a thorough understanding of

TPS-Lean Six Sigma program objectives and infrastructure. Additionally, the certification provides training in Project selection and how to manage and track projects. The Champions will learn how to coach the Black Belts effectively and how to conduct the ambition meeting with them in order to align their personal ambition with the project ambition. They will also need to understand the TPS-Lean Six Sigma Code of Ethics and Total TPS-Lean Six Sigma Standards (see chapter 11). Successful participants will leave the program with the knowledge and understanding to support TPS-Lean Six Sigma deployment and execution, they will be prepared to work with Black Belts and project teams.

9.3 MASTER BLACK BELT CERTIFICATION PROGRAM

Master Black Belt certification is our most extensive training. Master Black Belts are TPS-Lean Six Sigma technical experts who are responsible for the assistance of strategic planning and deployment, the development and the execution of TPS-Lean Six Sigma training company wide, the coaching and the mentoring of Black Belts, and the participation in project tollgate. The Master Black Belts will learn how to coach the Black Belts effectively and how to conduct the ambition meeting with them in order to align their personal ambition with the project ambition. They will also learn how to execute projects according to the TPS-Lean Six Sigma Code of Ethics and Total TPS-Lean Six Sigma Standards. The Master Black Belt devotes 100% of his/her time to TPS-Lean Six Sigma initiative. The Master Black Belt is qualified to teach TPS-Lean Six Sigma philosophy, concepts, and tools to all levels of the company. It is not uncommon for a company not to have any Master Black Belts on staff. Many companies hire the Master Black Belt as a Consultant during TPS-Lean Six Sigma implementation. TPS-Lean Six Sigma Master Black Belts is always available to our clients as needed.

9.4 BLACK BELT CERTIFICATION PROGRAM

Black Belts are required to lead TPS-Lean Six Sigma projects. This certification program is an intensive 4-week course that spreads out over several months. This program combines classroom time with concurrent in the field TPS-Lean Six Sigma project execution. TPS-Lean Six Sigma Black Belt candidates are change agents and technical leaders who have developed a high proficiency in TPS-Lean and Six Sigma philosophies, concepts and tools, and understand how these two powerful methodologies augment each other. They are the "doers" in implementing TPS-Lean Six

Sigma strategies who lead and manage all aspects of the improvement projects. The Black Belts will learn how to coach the Green Belts effectively and how to conduct the ambition meeting with them in order to align their personal ambition with the project ambition. They will also learn how to execute projects according to the TPS-Lean Six Sigma Code of Ethics and Total TPS-Lean Six Sigma Standards. Becoming a TPS-Lean Six Sigma Black Belt is an outstanding investment in your personal and professional development. Table 9.1 lists important roles the TPS-Lean Six Sigma Black Belt plays in the organization.

9.5 GREEN BELT CERTIFICATION PROGRAM

Green Belts are the most common belt category. Green belts take their direction from Black Belts. Typical candidates for Green Belt certification are technicians, operators, mechanics, and data specialists. The TPS-Green Belt Certification Program is a 2-week course that is actually the same as the first 2 weeks of the TPS-Lean Six Sigma Black Belt class. After the 2-week program is completed, some participants graduate with their Green Belts, while others continue onto the Black Belt curriculum. TPS-Lean Six Sigma Green Belt candidates are selected because of their process knowledge and experience. They will also learn how to execute projects according to the TPS-Lean Six Sigma Code of Ethics and Total TPS-Lean Six Sigma Standards. After their training, they will typically spend about 15%–25% of their time on TPS-Lean Six Sigma projects. Their main responsibility, when functioning as a Green Belt, is to support Black Belts on their projects by collecting and conducting simple data analyses and in the preparation of reports. Some more experienced Green Belt may also lead small, focused projects within their departments.

If you are not able to determine which program is best for you, please consult with a TPS-Lean Six Sigma training professional for the program or Belt that will best suite your specific needs.

9.6 BENEFITS OF TPS-LEAN SIX SIGMA BELT CERTIFICATION

TPS-Lean Six Sigma is an innovative approach that builds on the traditional Lean Six Sigma programs. While traditional Lean, Six Sigma and Lean Six Sigma programs have gained a world wide acceptance in the business community as the premier business improvement tool, our program boasts of a very important distinction. TPS-Lean Six Sigma is the only program that aligns itself with not only business objectives, but

Table 9.1. TPS-Lean Six Sigma Black Belt Function and Role

Influence Change	Provide Leadership	Facilitate Teams	Consult With Management	Discover New Opportunities	Continuously Improve Self Skills
Develop and implement strategies for driving change in the company, based on the OBSC and Project BSC.	Lead Black Belt projects. Master yourself based on your Personal BSC.	Facilitate improvement teams. Coach team members to formulate and implement their Personal BSC effectively.	Develop strategies for improvement and formulate Project BSCs.	Identify improvement opportunities and include these in the Project BSCs.	Constantly acquire new skills and knowledge based on your Personal BSC.
Interact with the team and management.	Plan improvement studies, collect, analyze, and date and results.	Select and manage team members.	Be active in project planning.	Integrate improvement company wide.	Work to achieve personal goals.
Lead project improvement teams.	Utilize appropriate TPS-Lean Six Sigma tools.	Communicate progress with improvement teams.	Define and monitor key improvement metrics.	Share valuable best practices and lessons learned.	Benchmark his/her own knowledge.
Identify and remove barriers to succeed in the project.	Promote TPS-Lean Six Sigma tools in the organization.	Schedule meeting.	Mentor Black Belts and Green Belts based on their Personal BSC and the Project BSC.	Network with other TPS-Lean Six Sigma professionals internally and externally.	Pursue perfection and refine your Personal BSC from time to time. Live according to the plan-do-act-challenge cycle.

personal objectives as well. The human element is what was missing from these predecessors to TPS-Lean Six Sigma. Attaining certification in TPS-Lean Six Sigma identifies you as a pioneer and leader in this movement.

Certification is a confirmation of an individual's understanding of the TPS-Lean Six Sigma body of knowledge, both from a principles standpoint and an application standpoint. Persons certified under the TPS-Lean Six Sigma program have not only demonstrated their proficiency to our trainers and instructors, but they have shown objective evidence of the application of their knowledge to their peers.

Applicants are required to demonstrate specific competencies including demonstrated knowledge of TPS-Lean Six Sigma methodologies, communication skills, inter-personal skills and leadership skills to name a few. Both the Green Belt and Black Belt programs require the selection and completion of a project. Classroom time is separated to allow for work on the project. A typical Black Belt program will average 4 weeks of classroom time that is spread out over 4 to 6 months in order to complete the project.

9.7 TPS-LEAN SIX SIGMA GREEN AND BLACK BELT CURRICULUM

Table 9.2 is an example of the TPS-Lean Six Sigma Green and Black Belt Curriculum. As we mentioned previously, the Green Belt program is identical to the Black Belt program in the first two weeks. Looking at Table 9.2, the Green Belt program will be weeks 1-2, and the Black Belt program is all weeks 1-4.

9.8 TPS-LEAN SIX SIGMA BLACK BELT PROJECT

The TPS-Lean Six Sigma Black Belt Project is an important element of the program. Completion of the project is one of the required components for graduation. Projects require approval of your TPS-Lean Six Sigma program administrator and your company sponsor. The project reflects the ability of the candidate to attain business results through the successful application of TPS-Lean Six Sigma tools and methodologies, while demonstrating team and leadership skills.

The project selected should return significant value to the company. While there are not any minimum or maximum limits to the monetary value, the project needs to have the ability to meet a business objective. These could be key metrics, goals, or other strategic objectives. It is

Table 9.2. TPS-Lean Six Sigma Green and Black Belt Curriculums

	Week	Monday	Tuesday	Wednesday	Thursday	Friday
Define Measure	Week 1	Welcome and introductions	Organizational BSC	Project management	Introduction to statistics	Measurement system analysis (MSA)
		TPS-Lean Six Sigma Overview	Personal BSC	Understand voice of the customer (VOC)	Graphical analysis	Understanding process capability
		Hoshin planning	Project BSC	Basics of Lean	TPS-Lean Six Sigma Life Cycle Scan	Lean and Six Sigma Metrics
Analyze	Week 2	Project reviews	Value stream map	Project management	Confidence interval and hypothesis testing	Correlation and regression analysis
		Management by fact (MBF)	Kaizen event	Understand voice of the customer (VOC)	Hypothesis testing	Regression analysis
		Basic quality tools	Project BSC	Personal SWOT Analysis	ANOVA comparing more than two means	Process Failure Mode and Effect Analysis
Improve	Week 3	Project reviews	Factorial designs	Two-level factorial designs	Response surface methodology (RSM)	Material replenishment systems: Kanban
		Sample size determination	Two-level factorial designs	Creating factorial designs in Minitab	Optimization designs	Facility layout
		Introduction to design of experiments (DOE)		Screening designs	Continuous personal improvement	Leadership Development
Control	Week 4	Project reviews	Introduction to design for Six Sigma (DFSS)	Robust design Taguchi approach to design of experiments	Standardized work	TPS-Lean Six Sigma Program Management
		Statistical process control (SPC)	TRIZ theory of inventive problem solving	Introduction to reliability engineering	5 S	Project portfolio management
		Effective talent management	Design failure mode and effect analysis	Reliability testing	TPS-Lean Six Sigma Coaching	Project closeout

understood that all projects are not created equal, each will deliver different benefits.

TPS-Lean Six Sigma success is achieved through process improvement projects that yield higher quality, efficiency, and customer satisfaction. Personal review and coaching on individual TPS-Lean Six Sigma project will be arranged during the course. In addition, the project incorporates hands-on experience with Minitab (statistical software) to support statistical calculations and analysis.

A Black Belt TPS-Lean Six Sigma project should:

- Provide a significant return to their organization.
- Be completed within the time frame of the program.
- Be within the candidate's authority to conduct.
- Have one or more of these objectives:

  o Improve customer satisfaction.
  o Optimize the supply chain.
  o Reduce defects.
  o Reduce cycle time.
  o Improve first-pass yield.
  o Shorten lead time.
  o Reduce variability.
  o Optimize product performance.
  o Optimize process performance.
  o Cut costs.
  o Reduce the cost of quality.
  o Improve delivery performance.
  o Enhance employee engagement, motivation, employee satisfaction, and labor productivity.
  o Enhanced labor productivity.
  o Project execution according to the TPS-Lean Six Sigma Code of Ethics and Total TPS-Lean Six Sigma Standards (see chapter 11).

It is expected that the Black Belt candidate will come to the program with a project in mind. They will work with the program instructors to formalize the content and the anticipated deliverables. This will be done early on in the classroom environment.

TPS-LEAN SIX SIGMA BLACK BELT PROJECT TOLLGATE REVIEWS

Tollgate reviews are time based checks of the Black Belt or Green Belt candidate's progress towards certification. Candidates should also use the reviews to request any assistance in removing barriers or constraints that may delay the project's progress. A tollgate can be moved sooner in the timeline, but cannot be postponed without the signed agreement of the Champion and the Instructor.

The Black Belt or Green Belt candidates shall conduct tollgate reviews at all project stages with the project Sponsor or Champion, the Instructor, and other applicable persons as defined in the project charter. All tollgates have required sign-offs. The signature of the responsible party indicates there was objective evidence of successful completion of the project through that phase. It is the responsibility of the candidate to provide documentation to the project Sponsor or Champion and the Instructor prior to the tollgate review.

Tollgate reviews may include:

- Completion of deliverables.
- Resources allocated.
- Obstacles encountered.
- Project effectiveness to-date.
- Overall progress.
- Application TPS-Lean Six Sigma tools.
- Alignment with OBSC, Project BSC, and PBSC being met?
- Action items.

Tollgate Examples:

Define Tollgate

Check	Deliverables	Comments
	1. Define the business opportunity. Project is linked to business objectives and TPS-Lean Six Sigma Life Cycle Scan has been executed.	
	2. Customer's requirements are defined.	
	3. OBSC and PBSC completed.	
	4. Project Balanced Scorecard completed.	
	5. Process maps completed (value stream map, SIPOC).	
	6. The cost of poor quality analysis is conducted and the project financial benefit is estimated and validated by the finance department.	

Table continues on next page.

Define Tollgate

Check	Deliverables	Comments
	7. Critical to quality (CTQ) metrics have been identified, and current baseline measures are calculated, and goal(s) are set.	
	8. Tentative action plan is developed.	
	9. Estimated date for define tollgate provided.	

Measure Tollgate

Check	Deliverables	Comments
	1. Measurement System Analysis assessment.	
	2. Data collection plan.	
	3. Process capability studies.	
	4. Sigma level calculation.	
	5. Estimated date for analyze tollgate provided.	

Analyze Tollgate

Check	Deliverables	Comments
	1. Root cause(s) identified and validated.	
	2. Statistical Analysis.	
	3. Validate Proposed Business Impact.	
	4. Nonvalue added analysis.	
	5. Estimated date for improve tollgate provided.	

Improve Tollgate

Check	Deliverables	Comments
	1. Critical or vital few inputs identified.	
	2. Solution(s) identified and implemented. Impact on root cause(s) validated.	
	3. Future state process map completed.	
	4. Improvement seen in key result metric(s) relative to goal(s).	
	5. Validate goal attainment.	
	6. Estimated date for improve tollgate.	

Control Tollgate

Check	Deliverables	Comments
	1. Control plan implemented.	
	2. Process Capability established.	
	3. Monitoring system in place.	
	4. New operating procedures developed.	

Control Tollgate

Check	Deliverables	Comments
	5. Transition and Training Plan.	
	6. Final report prepared.	
	7. Improvement benefits evaluated and summarized.	
	8. Key learning documented.	

Check	Color	Define Phase Evaluation	Recommendations
⬤	Green	1. All requirements are met.	Candidate can proceed with the training and continue working on the project.
⬤	Red	2. One or more of the requirements are not met.	Based on the evaluation, the instructor/sponsor will propose an action plan.

Name	Gatekeeper	Signature	Date
	Champion/Sponsor		
	Instructor		
	Finance Department		

TPS-LEAN SIX SIGMA BLACK BELT PROJECT FINAL REPORT

Upon completion of all requirements, the candidate must submit the TPS-Lean Six Sigma final project report for review. It includes the tollgate reviews and all associated documents such as a statistical data analyses. The report should also include a summary of the project charter, the challenges encountered, the process and tools used to solve the problem, the solution, the results and the benefits, and key learning from the entire experience.

9.9 GREEN BELT AND BLACK BELT CERTIFICATION EVALUATION

The candidate evaluation and certification review shall consist of the Candidate, Sponsor (or Champion) and the Instructor(s).The demonstrated knowledge and skill of the candidate will be evaluated to determine if he or she will be considered for certification. The candidate will first perform a self-evaluation and then be evaluated by the Sponsor/

Table 9.3.   Candidate Evaluation Sheet

Knowledge/Skills	Candidate	Sponsor/Champion	Instructor
TPS-Lean Six Sigma tools	X		X
Leadership skills	X	X	X
Project results/Tollgates	X	X	X
Class participation	X		X

Champion and Instructors with regard to the four categories shown in Table 9.3.

TPS-Lean Six Sigma Tools–Did the candidate utilize the necessary tools in their project? Did the candidate demonstrate knowledge of the tools in the classroom?

Leadership Skills–Did the candidate demonstrate ability to influence others, drive change in the organization, coach and mentor others, transfer knowledge and communicate results?

Project Results and Tollgates–Did the candidate's project meet its stated objective? Did the project achieve the predicted ROI? Were all the tollgates completed according to the project plan?

Class participation–Did the candidate meet the requirements of attendance? Did the candidate actively participate in the classroom?

CHAPTER 10

BECOME A CERTIFIED TPS-LEAN SIX SIGMA COACH

We are what we repeatedly do. Excellence, therefore, is not an act but a habit.

—Aristotle

Believe in yourself! Have faith in your abilities! Without a humble but reasonable confidence in your own powers you cannot be successful or happy.

—Norman Vincent Peale

Based on the PBSC system, we introduce here the TPS-Lean Six Sigma coaching process, which is based on a 10-Phase PBSC coaching framework (see Rampersad, 2006). The first 7 steps in this framework are related to life and career coaching, which focuses on personal effectiveness and growth in life. The emphasis here is on excelling in everything you do, making the right choices in developing your future, having a happier and more fulfilling life and facing new life challenges. The complete framework focuses on Executives, Champions, Master Black Belts, Black Belts, and Green Belts, Six Sigma Consultants, and Quality Management Consultants who would like to develop their personal leadership skills; improve employee performance; enhance employee engagement; empower their employees and team members; create trust and a real learning organization; increase

TPS-Lean Six Sigma: Linking Human Capital to Lean Six Sigma: A New Blueprint for Creating High Performance Companies, pp. 267–276
Copyright © 2007 by Information Age Publishing
All rights of reproduction in any form reserved.

employee's self-responsibility and work enjoyment; and ultimately, enhance sustainable organizational project effectiveness. The TPS-Lean Six Sigma coaching process involves 10 phases, with comprehensive exercises, tools, and activities associated with each phase to be used by the TPS-Lean Six Sigma Coach to coach others.

TPS-Lean Six Sigma Coaching Framework:
Ten Steps in the TPS-Lean Six Sigma Coaching Process

1. Look for a quiet spot and perform the PBSC breathing and silence exercise with your client (Executive, Champion, Master Black Belt, Black Belt, Green Belt) to help him/her reflect on the personal ambition question.

2. Act as a trusted TPS-Lean Six Sigma coach and ask/discuss the ambition questions with your client leading to his/her personal ambition statement.

3. Coach your client to draft his/her personal ambition statement (personal vision, mission, and key roles) based on the answers to these questions. Make sure that all four PBSC perspectives (internal, external, knowledge/learning, and financial) are included. Private life and business life should be taken into account.

4. Guide your client through the process of identifying and selecting the critical success factors within his/her personal ambition statement and help her/him to translate these into personal objectives with corresponding measures, targets, and improvement actions. This should be done for each of the four PBSC perspectives: internal, external, knowledge/learning, and financial.

5. Guide your client in the process of continuous personal improvement by implementing the PBSC according to the introduced Plan-Do-Act-Challenge cycle. Help him/her to get going with the improvement actions with dedication and resolution based on this PDAC cycle.

6. Meet with your client regularly, listen to him/her, and give feedback. Assist your client to reflect and update his/her PBSC based on the feedback from time to time. The PBSC is a *living document*.

7. Coach your client to develop inner peace and personal integrity by guiding him/her to align his/her personal ambition with his/her behavior. This self-awareness process is based on integrity questions from the TPS-Lean Six Sigma book.

8. Coach your client in aligning her/his personal ambition with the shared organization and project ambition, through the *ambition meeting*. The ambition meeting is a periodic, informal, voluntary and confidential meeting between your client and his/her manager, with the PBSC as the topic.

9. Work with your client in helping him/her to conduct successful ambition meetings. Help him/her to understand how to coach his/her project team members based on their PBSC and to create an atmosphere of trust within his/her team.

10. Encourage your client to share his/her PBSC with his/her colleagues and Manager, so that they get to know and understand each other better. This forms a stable basis for greater mutual respect, trust, and team learning.

Executive/Green Belt/Black Belt Coaching

Life and Career Coaching

LEARNING AREAS

Here's what you'll focus on during the intensive 2-day TPS-Lean Six Sigma Coaching workshop:

Introduction to TPS-Lean Six Sigma

PBSC and TPS-Lean Six Sigma Code of Ethics

Relationship Between PBSC and ICF Core Competencies

The TPS-Lean Six Sigma Coaching Framework

This portion of the workshop introduces attendees to the PBSC, what it is and how it can be used to facilitate clients' personal growth, as well as, in tandem with the TPS-Lean Six Sigma to align personal ambitions with organizational and project goals.

How to Formulate the PBSC

How to Use the PBSC to Create Work-Life Balance and Develop Personal Leadership Based on the PBSC

This section will discuss in more detail the various components necessary to formulate the PBSC including assisting clients in:

• Planning and goal setting through the development of:

– A personal vision, mission and key roles

– Personal critical success factors as they relate to four basic perspectives: Internal, External, Knowledge & Learning, and Financial

– Personal objectives, performance measures, targets, and improvement actions

• Utilizing the Plan-Do-Act-Challenge cycle to continue to refine and update client's PBSC for continuous personal improvement

• Examining the relations between the objectives developed for each of the four basic perspectives—Internal, External, Knowledge and Learning, and Financial— priorities can be developed for each area to help clients

•Understand the different, interrelated factors that affect them and their behaviors

• Help clients (Executives, Champions, Master Black Belts, Black Belts, and Green Belts) focus on and systematically explore specific concerns and opportunities in order to develop priorities.

• Assist clients in creating plans that feature objectives that are attainable, measurable, specific, and targeted and that balance personal and organizational objectives to achieve work-life balance

---

How to Perform the Silence and Breathing Exercise For Self-Awareness

This section of the workshop instructs attendees on the use of the silence and breathing exercises to develop self awareness. These exercises are intended to help clients achieve the proper mental state to explore powerful ambition questions intended to invoke discovery and insight. These questions help clients distinguish between trivial and significant issues and detecting the difference between what is being stated and what is being done.

How to Implement the PBSC According to the Plan, Do, Act, Challenge (PDAC) Cycle

An integral part of the PBSC' successful implementation is the PDAC cycle. This section of the workshop will explore this cycle as it relates to helping clients develop, achieve, and update personal objectives by:

Table continues on next page

Table continued from previous page

Planning–Formulating and updating PBSC and using it to achieve balance between work and free time.

Doing–Selecting a simple objective and its corresponding improvement action. Committing to the execution of your improvement action and seeking feedback to stay on track.

Acting–Evaluating if improvement plan is working and taking action. Developing competencies to achieve the selected objective.

Challenging–Accepting larger challenges by selecting a more difficult improvement objective or action in line with your improved competencies.

Coaching You in Formulating & Implementing Your PBSC

Attendees will work at developing their own PBSC with oversight by the instructor.

Effectively coaching Executives, Green Belts, and Black Belts Based on the PBSC

One of the benefits of the PBSC is how it can be easily integrated into the Organizational Scorecard and the TPS-Lean Six Sigma project. This segment examines how coaches can use this process to assist TPS-Lean Six Sigma project teams to align personal objectives with team objectives. This information can be used to assist executives and managers better align their goals with those of their company and it can be used within a company as part of a larger planning and review process for continual growth and improvement.

How to Stimulate Personal Integrity Based on the PBSC: Aligning Personal Ambition and Behavior

The PBSC is geared to helping individuals align their goals and actions to achieve personal integrity. This is achieved by helping clients discover new thoughts, beliefs, perceptions, and so forth, as well as, disparities between thoughts and action and then by helping them develop a plan to align their personal ambitions with their actions.

Facilitated Group Role-Playing of Coaching Scenarios, One-on-One Coaching

Attendees will practice coaching one another using the PBSC process

---

How to Improve Employee Engagement Based on the PBSC: Aligning Personal Ambition, Organizational Ambition, and Project Ambition Based on the Ambition Meeting.

Using the understanding of the PBSC developed in earlier parts of the workshop, the remaining sections explore in further detail the different ways to use the PBSC to increase employee engagement and commitment by aligning personal and organizational objectives.

Initially, this involves comparing personal ambition, organizational ambition and project ambition to identify and build on areas of overlap. "Ambition Meetings" can then be scheduled. These are periodic, informal, voluntary and confidential meetings less than one hour in duration between a manager (who acts in this case as an informal and trusted coach) and her/his employee/team member to review the employee's PBSC within the context of the organizational and project ambition. During this meeting, the manager and employee/team member discuss ways to facilitate the employee's growth and continual improvement. During these meetings, employee/team member progress is discussed, guidance and feedback is given, and agreements are formed or adjusted.

Table continues on next page

Table continued from previous page

Initially, this involves comparing personal ambition, organizational ambition and project ambition to identify and build on areas of overlap. "Ambition Meetings" can then be scheduled. These are periodic, informal, voluntary and confidential meetings less than one hour in duration between a manager (who acts in this case as an informal and trusted coach) and her/his employee/team member to review the employee's PBSC within the context of the organizational and project ambition. During this meeting, the manager and employee/team member discuss ways to facilitate the employee's growth and continual improvement. During these meetings, employee/team member progress is discussed, guidance and feedback is given, and agreements are formed or adjusted.

How to Embed the PBSC in the HR System for Effective Talent Management and Coaching You to Perform the Ambition Meeting Successfully

This segment describes a process for embedding the PBSC within the TPS-Lean Six Sigma project and organization as a formal tool for talent management. This involves a formal process of appraisal that provides for "result planning" focusing on work performance objectives and agreements, as well as, for periodic formal reviews of employee performance and the need for adjustment including training or other methods of talent development.

Coaching You to Share Your PBSC With Others

In this segment, attendees will share their own PBSC, developed earlier, with the other members of the workshop to understand how this stimulates trust. and open communication with others

How to use TPS-Lean Six Sigma Personal BSCsoft

Learn how to use the interactive TPS-Lean Six Sigma Personal BSC software that will assist them with the formulation and implementation of their PBSC. It offers individuals to coach themselves, TPS-Lean Six Sigma coaches to coach others (Champions, Master Black Belts, Black Belts, Green Belts) to coach their project team members and Executives/HR to effectively steer their organization on performance, happiness, joy and motivation.

How to Become Certified as a TPS-Lean Six Sigma Coach

In closing, the opportunities and benefits for building attendees credentials and practices by becoming a TPS-Lean Six Sigma certified coach are discussed.

PROGRAM BENEFITS

The TPS-Lean Six Sigma Coaching Certification will make you far more effective as a coach and facilitator in this new and growing field, and gives you the prestige and credibility of a TPS-Lean Six Sigma Academy endorsed certification. The TPS-Lean Six Sigma Academy recognizes practitioners who have demonstrated proficiency in using the PBSC system in ways that are in keeping with the PBSC and TPS-Lean Six Sigma Code of Ethics. The TPS-Lean Six Sigma Coach designation is an indication that you have met the Standards of Personal Balanced Scorecard and TPS-Lean Six Sigma as evidenced by your past work, knowledge, and TPS-Lean Six Sigma coaching skills. It shows that you have demonstrated proficiency in the PBSC and TPS-Lean Six Sigma profession. Participants who receive the TPS-Lean Six Sigma Coach designation must be re-certified every year to maintain the credential. Once you achieve the TPS-Lean Six Sigma Coach certification, your name will be listed on a registry that is available to potential clients and employers, you will be listed on the Academy for TPS-Lean Six Sigma Certification Web site (www.TPS-LeanSixSigma.com), and you may display the TPS-Lean Six Sigma Coach designation on your business cards, stationary, and marketing materials. You will also get the ability to set up a successful TPS-Lean Six Sigma coaching practice, networking opportunities with TPS-Lean Six Sigma coaches from all over the world and the ability to conduct TPS-Lean Six Sigma coaching business in an international environment.

You will learn how to:

- Coach and facilitate improved behavior in others in a holistic way.
- Enhance your effectiveness as a coach, manager or consultant, and the effectiveness of your clients.
- Evaluate and attain your full potential and the potential of your clients.
- Develop personal responsibility.
- Create awareness for personal integrity.
- Coach your clients to utilize their talents effectively.
- Develop employee engagement.
- Create work-life balance.
- Create conditions for a real learning organization/TPS-Lean Six Sigma project.
- Bring about the best fit between employee's and organization's/TPS-Lean Six Sigma project objectives and create lasting conditions for self-guidance, inner involvement, commitment and enjoyment.

What are the Requirements for TPS-Lean Six Sigma Coaching Certification?

The eligibility requirements to apply through the regular certification process include:

- at least 2 years experience as Executive/Manager/Champion/Green Belt/black Belt/Senior Quality Management Consultant.

- completion of an initial 2-day TPS-Lean Six Sigma Coaching workshop.
- ten hours individual coaching to help you finalize and implement your PBSC, after completion of the initial workshop. Participants will also talk with their instructors by phone as the coaching experience unfolds.
- a detailed description of TPS-Lean Six Sigma coaching with at least two clients for a total of 12 hours, performed in a manner that demonstrates the use of the TPS-Lean Six Sigma coaching framework with attestations from clients.

The TPS-Lean Six Sigma certification program entails 12 hours direct contact (classes) + 5 hours indirect contact (self-study) + 12 hours coaching of clients and 10 hours of being coached = 39 total program hours.

How Will Proficiency Be Assessed?

An applicant's proficiency will be assessed through a combination of a description of education, experience, testimonials by clients or employers, and a review of documents by qualified reviewers. Reviewers will be professionals from the Academy for TPS-Lean Six Sigma Certification who have received training and guidelines for doing the review. The TPS-Lean Six Sigma Coaching certification has a validity of 1 calendar year and can be extended based on the results of an annual audit conducted by the local Academy for TPS-Lean Six Sigma Certification which acts as a certifying institution.

Personal Balanced Scorecard Code of Ethics

The PBSC Code of Ethics is intended to promote ethical practice in the profession of PBSC technology. The objective is to provide coaches with the skills, knowledge, abilities, and attitude necessary to create opportunities for achieving desired and required individual, organizational, and societal results.

The PBSC Code of Ethics is based on the following six principles:

1. Add Value.
2. Validated Practice.
3. Collaboration.

4. Continuous Improvement.
5. Integrity.
6. Uphold Confidentiality.

1. Add Value

Conduct yourself, and manage your coaching practice, in ways that add value for your clients, their customers, and the global environment.

Guidelines

- Achieve useful results that can be aligned with personal ambition, organization's ambition and positive contributions to society.
- Recognize clients' training needs and address them.
- Set clear expectations about the systematic PBSC process you will follow and about the expected outcomes.
- Add value by serving your clients with integrity, competence, and objectivity as you apply the PBSC system.
- Respect and contribute to the legitimate and ethical objectives of the customer.
- Help the customer move to where it needs to be in the future.

2. Validated Practice

Make use of validated practices in PBSC strategies and standards.

Guidelines

- Deliver PBSC methods and procedures that have positive value and worth.
- Promote good PBSC practices by utilizing positive reinforcement.
- Clarify personal and organizational goals and desired accomplishments.
- Detect and analyze opportunities to improve human and organizational performance.
- Objectively evaluate the impact of interventions.

3. Collaboration

Work collaboratively with clients, functioning as a trustworthy strategic partner.

Guidelines

- Listen to the client's ideas, work closely and productively together, and build mutual trust and respect.
- Get information from your clients without making that person feel as if he or she is being interrogated.
- Integrate the client's needs, constraints, and concerns when coaching and facilitating them.
- Meet the interests of all parties involved in the PBSC coaching engagement, so there is a win-win outcome.
- Anticipate the client's issues; demonstrate empathy for their concerns and issues.

4. Continuous Improvement

Continually improve your proficiency in the field of PBSC.

Guidelines

- Improve and monitor your actions and thinking continuously, make personal improvement a routine and your way of life based on the Plan-Do-Act-Challenge Cycle.
- Make time in your schedule to improve yourself and recognize your responsibility to improve continuously.
- Evaluate your skills and knowledge of PBSC on a regular basis.
- Investigate new coaching methods, concepts, tools, strategies, and technologies that may be beneficial to your client.
- Ask your clients how you can improve the effectiveness of your coaching services.

5. Integrity

Be honest and truthful in presentations to your client, colleagues, and others with whom you may come in contact with while practicing PBSC. You have the moral duty to help and protect them.

Guidelines

- Acknowledge any factors that may compromise your objectivity.
- Accept only coaching engagements for which you are qualified by experience and competence.
- Exhibit the highest level of professional objectivity in gathering, evaluating, and communicating information or the results achieved.
- Let clients know when you believe they are going in the wrong direction.
- Give honest feedback to your clients.
- Do not use information for any personal gain that would be contrary to ethical objectives of the client.
- Take responsibility and/or credit only for the portion of results that are clearly linked to your efforts.

6. Uphold Confidentiality

Maintain client confidentiality, not allowing for any conflict of interest that would benefit yourself or others.

Guidelines

- Respect the intellectual property of clients, other consulting firms, and sole practitioners.
- Respect and value the ownership of information received.
- Do not disclose information without appropriate authority.

We have introduced the TPS-Lean Six Sigma Personal BSCsoft in the Appendix, which is an interactive software system that will assist you with the formulation and implementation of your Personal Balanced Scorecard. It offers individuals to coach themselves, TPS-Lean Six Sigma coaches to coach others, Champions/Master Black Belts/Black Belts/Green Belts/Project Managers to coach their project members and Executives/HR to effectively steer their organization on performance, happiness, joy, and motivation.

CHAPTER 11

BECOME A CERTIFIED TPS-LEAN SIX SIGMA CONSULTANT

Thinking is the hardest work there is, which is probably the reason why so few engage in it.

—Henry Ford

If a man advances confidently in the direction of his dreams to live the life he has imagined, he will meet with a success unexpected in common hours.

—Henry David Thoreau

TPS-Lean Six Sigma certification entails a program through which senior consultants can apply to receive the designation of Certified TPS-Lean Six Sigma Consultant. It is based on standards and criteria to distinguish practitioners who have proven they can produce results through the holistic TPS-Lean Six Sigma process. In this way, they can claim that they are professionals in the field of TPS-Lean Six Sigma.

TPS-Lean Six Sigma: Linking Human Capital to Lean Six Sigma: A New Blueprint for Creating High Performance Companies, pp. 277–298
Copyright © 2007 by Information Age Publishing
All rights of reproduction in any form reserved.

WHAT IS TPS-LEAN SIX SIGMA CERTIFICATION?

TPS-Lean Six Sigma Certification is a credential that is given to people who satisfy a set of requirements. The Academy for TPS-Lean Six Sigma Certification recognizes practitioners who have demonstrated proficiency in 9 Standards of TPS-Lean Six Sigma in ways that are in keeping with the TPS-Lean Six Sigma Code of Ethics. Individuals who receive the Certified TPS-Lean Six Sigma Consultant designation must be re-certified every year to maintain the credential.

HOW MIGHT TPS-LEAN SIX SIGMA CERTIFICATION BENEFIT YOU?

A TPS-Lean Six Sigma certification says you are a member of a profession. The Certified TPS-Lean Six Sigma Consultant designation shows that you have demonstrated proficiency in the TPS-Lean Six Sigma profession. The certification can set you apart from others who have not engaged in the same degree of examination by clients and peers. Once certified, your name will be listed on a registry that is available to potential clients and employers. You will also be listed on the Academy for TPS-Lean Six Sigma Certification Web site (www.TPS-LeanSixSigma.com). The Certified TPS-Lean Six Sigma Consultant designation is an indication that you have met the Standards of TPS-Lean Six Sigma as evidenced by your past work, knowledge, and skills in this field.

WHAT ARE THE REQUIREMENTS FOR
REGULAR TPS-LEAN SIX SIGMA CERTIFICATION?

The eligibility requirements to apply through the regular certification process include a Champion/ Master Back Belt/Black Belt/Green Belt/Six Sigma Consultant/Quality Manager and a detailed description of work performed in multiple Six Sigma related projects in a manner that demonstrates the use of each of the TPS-Lean Six Sigma Standards with attestations from internal/external clients or supervisors. A qualified TPS-Lean Six Sigma reviewer will review all the documentation received from a candidate and determine if all requirements have been met. All candidates for the certification must commit to the TPS-Lean Six Sigma Code of Ethics. Once certified, TPS-Lean Six Sigma professionals must apply for re-certification every year to maintain the Certified TPS-Lean Six Sigma

Consultant designation. The Academy for TPS-Lean Six Sigma Certification is the certifying body.

HOW WILL PROFICIENCY BE ASSESSED?

An applicant's proficiency will be assessed through a combination of a description of education, experience, attestations by clients or employers, and a review of documents by qualified reviewers. Reviewers will be TPS-Lean Six Sigma professionals who have received training and guidelines for doing the review. If the application is not accepted, the candidate will be notified as to which TPS-Lean Six Sigma standards have not been met. Candidates will have an opportunity to meet those specific standards within the next 6 months without additional charge beyond the balance of the original submission fee.

WHAT DO YOU GET ONCE YOU ARE
TPS-LEAN SIX SIGMA CERTIFIED?

Once you achieve the TPS-Lean Six Sigma certification:

- You receive a certificate of TPS-Lean Six Sigma Certification.
- Your name will be listed on a registry that is available to potential clients and employers.
- You may display the Certified TPS-Lean Six Sigma Consultant designation on your business cards, stationary, and marketing materials.
- You may use the credential to distinguish yourself in the marketplace.
- You will be listed on the Academy for TPS-Lean Six Sigma Certification Web site (www.TPS-LeanSixSigma.com).

TPS-LEAN SIX SIGMA CODE OF ETHICS AND
TOTAL TPS-LEAN SIX SIGMA STANDARDS

TPS-Lean Six Sigma certification entails a program through which management consultants can apply to receive the designation of Certified TPS-Lean Six Sigma Consultant. It's a credential that is given to people who satisfy a set of requirements. TPS-Lean Six Sigma Academy recognizes practitioners who have demonstrated proficiency in 9 TPS-Lean Six Sigma Standards in ways that are in keeping with the TPS-Lean Six Sigma Code of Ethics. These standards are intended to promote ethical practice in the profession of total performance technology. The TPS-Lean Six Sigma Code of Ethics and standards and are described in detail below, which are partly related to the ISPI Performance Standards.

A. TPS-LEAN SIX SIGMA CODE OF ETHICS

The TPS-Lean Six Sigma Code of Ethics and Standards are intended to promote ethical practice in the profession of total performance technology. The objective is to provide organizations and individuals with the skills, knowledge, abilities, and attitude necessary to create opportunities for achieving desired and required individual, organizational, and societal results.

The TPS-Lean Six Sigma Code of Ethics is based on the following six principles:

1. Add Value
2. Validated Practice
3. Collaboration
4. Continuous Improvement
5. Integrity
6. Uphold Confidentiality

1. Add Value

Conduct yourself, and manage your projects and their results, in ways that add value for your clients, their customers, and the global environment.

Guidelines

- Achieve useful results that can be aligned with the organization's mission, objective (OBSC), and positive contributions to society.
- Focus on results and consequences of the results. Measure performance based on results.

- Set clear expectations about the systematic process you will follow and about the expected outcomes.
- Add value by serving your clients with integrity, competence, and objectivity as you apply the TPS-Lean Six Sigma system.
- Respect and contribute to the legitimate and ethical objectives of the organization.
- Help the organization move to where it needs to be in the future.
- Prevent problems from occurring rather than solve problems that could have been predicted and avoided.

2. Validated Practice

Make use of validated practices in TPS-Lean Six Sigma strategies and standards.

Guidelines

- Deliver activities, methods, and procedures that have positive value and worth.
- Promote good TPS-Lean Six Sigma practices by utilizing positive reinforcement.
- Take decisions based on data.
- Clarify goals and desired accomplishments.
- Detect and analyze opportunities to improve human and organizational performance.
- Objectively evaluate the impact of interventions.

3. Collaboration

Work collaboratively with clients, functioning as a trustworthy strategic partner.

Guidelines

- Listen to the client's ideas, work closely and productively together, and build mutual trust and respect.

- Integrate the company's needs, constraints, and concerns when developing a solution.
- Meet the interests of all parties involved in the TPS-Lean Six Sigma project, so there is a win-win outcome.
- Anticipate the client's issues; demonstrate empathy for their concerns and issues.

4. Continuous Improvement

Continually improve your proficiency in the field of TPS-Lean Six Sigma.

Guidelines

- Improve and monitor your actions and thinking, continuously make personal improvement a routine and your way of life, based on your PBSC. Focus on the things that you are not good at, habits that limit you and which have an unfavorable influence on your life and your results.
- Make time in your schedule to improve yourself and recognize your responsibility to improve continuously.
- Evaluate your skills and knowledge of TPS-Lean Six Sigma on a regular basis;
- Investigate new methods, concepts, tools, strategies, and technologies that may be beneficial to your client.
- Ask your clients how you can improve the effectiveness of your services.

5. Integrity

Be honest and truthful in representations to your client, colleagues, and others with whom you may come in contact with while practicing TPS-Lean Six Sigma. You have the moral duty to help and protect them. Act according to your personal ambition (PBSC).

Guidelines

- Acknowledge any factors that may compromise your objectivity.

- Accept only engagements for which you are qualified by experience and competence.
- Exhibit the highest level of professional objectivity in gathering, evaluating, and communicating information about the process being examined, or the results achieved.
- Let clients know when you believe they are going in the wrong direction.
- Give credit for the work of others to whom it is due.
- Do not use information for any personal gain that would be contrary to ethical objectives of the client's organization.
- Take responsibility and/or credit only for the portion of results that are clearly linked to your efforts.

6. Uphold Confidentiality

Maintain client confidentiality, not allowing for any conflict of interest that would benefit yourself or others.

Guidelines

- Respect the intellectual property of clients, other consulting firms, and sole practitioners.
- Respect and value the ownership of information received.
- Do not disclose information without appropriate authority.

Examples of Ethical Behavior

- Let a client know that you receive a bonus if they choose a particular product that is included in your recommendations.
- Decline a job if you don't have the expertise the client is requesting.
- When possible recommend a colleague who does have the expertise.
- Don't promise results you can't deliver.
- Listen objectively to client concerns, constraints, issues, and so forth.
- Never knowingly mislead or lie to your client.

- Hesitate before recommending solutions you haven't been able to implement for yourself.
- Be responsible for the results of your work.
- Not to advertise the attainment of results that cannot be clearly linked to your work.
- Inform the client if, at any time, you are no longer qualified to complete a process or task, and help obtain a specialist, if appropriate.

B. TPS-LEAN SIX SIGMA STANDARDS

The 9 Standards of Total Performance Scorecard ensure that the certified TPS-Lean Six Sigma consultant has conducted his or her work in a manner that includes the following:

- Focus on results and help clients focus on results based on the TPS-Lean Six Sigma concept.
- Take a systems approach; taking into consideration the larger context including competing pressures, resource constraints, and anticipated cultural change.
- Add value in how you do the work and through the work itself.
- Work in partnerships with clients and other specialists.
- Analysis of the need based on the TPS-Lean Six Sigma concept.
- Analysis of the work and workplace to identify the cause or factors that limit individual and total performance.
- Design of the solution or specification of the requirements of the solution based on the TPS-Lean Six Sigma concept.
- Implementation of the solution based on the TPS-Lean Six Sigma concept.
- Evaluation of the process and the results based on the TPS-Lean Six Sigma concept.

1. Focusing on Results

As a TPS-Lean Six Sigma specialist, you measure the outcomes of an intervention and assess whether the performance has improved as a result of it.

Focus on Results		
Performances	**Criteria**	**Your Personal Balanced Scorecard**
You:	*So that you and the client can:*	*Note your personal objectives and improvement actions here:*
1. Determine the expected result of the assignment. You may help clients specify what they expect to change, or what benefit they expect to gain as a result of the assignment.	• Better evaluate if the effort was successful.	
2. Determine what will be measured or accepted as evidence that the business need was met.	• Communicate what the expected outcome is to stakeholders.	
3. Explain the importance of focusing on results and working according to the OBSC and Project Balanced Scorecard.	• Establish goals and performance measures with staff and key clients.	
	• Design your fact-finding efforts and recommend solutions that are more likely to accomplish the desired outcome.	
	• Celebrate and recognize those efforts that accomplished desired outcomes.	

For example, you:

- Confirm what the desired outcome is. This may include professional development, higher productivity, fewer errors, reduced costs, increased customer retention, and so forth.
- Determine what your client is trying to accomplish and what prevents them from accomplishing it, so you can identify what you have to provide in terms of training and total performance improvement.
- Identify what staff requires to be outcome focused. Direct and train staff to be outcome focused.

2. Take a Systems Approach

A systems approach is important, because organizations are very complex systems that affect the performance of leaders and employees. It is important to distinguish a systems approach from a process model. A process is a transformation of inputs into outputs. A process can be characterized by:

Internal/external customers; process definition begins by defining the internal and external customer.
Inputs; personnel, capital, materials, resources, information, opinions, or anything else a process uses in its transformation.
Process; a series of interconnected activities.
Outputs; products, services, and information.

A system implies an interconnected complex of functionally related components. The effectiveness of each unit depends on how it fits into the whole, and the effectiveness of the whole depends on the way each unit functions. A systems approach considers the larger environment that affects processes and other work. The environment includes inputs, pressures, expectations, constraints, and consequences.

For example, you:

- Orient and train staff to have a systems view.
- Model a systems view in your exchanges with functional managers in the organization.

3. Add Value

As a TPS-Lean Six Sigma specialist, you must set the stage for adding value by offering your clients a process that will help them fully understand the implications of their choices, set appropriate measures, identify barriers, and so forth.

	Add Value	
Performances	**Criteria**	**Your Personal Balanced Scorecard**
You:	*So that you and the client can:*	*Note your personal objectives and improvement actions here:*
1. Identify two or more possible solutions or courses of action.	• Establish what will be used as evidence of success and communicate that to all stakeholders.	
2. Identify the worth of the requested solution, by comparing factors such as:	• Determine if the argument for or against a course of action is documented and communicated.	
• Cost to develop, implement, and maintain each.	• State that what you do, adds value.	
• Likelihood of adoption by the target audience.		
• Probability of each solution achieving the desired goals.		
• Implication on employees, consumers, the community, and so forth.		
• Ability of the organization to support each solution (rewards the appropriate behaviors and results, provide the appropriate communication/information systems and equipment, maintain sponsorship, etc.).		
• Risks associated with the success or failure of each solution in terms of threats to safety, health, financial return, customer satisfaction, and so forth.		
3. Recommend solutions that add value, are feasible, and are more likely to accomplish the project goals.		

Table continues on next page.

	Add Value Continued	
Performances	**Criteria**	**Your Personal Balanced Scorecard**
You:	*So that you and the client can:*	*Note your personal objectives and improvement actions here:*
4. Describe the potential value added and how that value will be measured, such as: increased safety, customer satisfaction, number of customer complaints, reduced costs, time to market, cycle time, processing time, wait time, and so forth.		
5. Document the expected-value added, the costs (materials, resources, time, etc.), and a schedule of deliverables.		
6. Explain the importance of doing work that adds value and the importance of demonstrating the value gained.		

For example, you:

- Point out what interventions may be required to fully satisfy the need, such as a change in rewards, a change in the way to give feedback, the need to adopt new tools, and the consequences of not providing these.
- Help the client identify success factors, risks, and associated direct and indirect costs.
- Guide the client in choosing the solution with the best value added.
- Find out where the pain is or where the opportunities lie for the organization.
- Facilitate or participate in meetings on how to best relieve the pain.

4. Work in Partnership

Work in partnership with clients and other specialists. This means that you involve all stakeholders in the decision making around every phase of the TPS-Lean Six Sigma cycle. Partnerships are created from listening closely to your client and trusting and respecting each other's knowledge and expertise, so you both can make the best choices about accomplishments, priorities, and solutions. This requires teamwork. *Teamwork entails sharing knowledge, the work, the thoughts, the feelings, the excitement, the happiness, the pressure, the pleasure, the emotions, the doubts, and the success with each other.*

Work in Partnership		
Performances	**Criteria**	**Your Personal Balanced Scorecard**
You:	*So that you and the client can:*	*Note your personal objectives and improvement actions here:*
1. Collaborate with stakeholders, experts, and specialists, making use of their knowledge, capabilities, and influence.	• Trust and respect each other's roles, knowledge, and expertise.	
2. Take the initiative to define your expectations, relationships, roles, responsibilities, etc.	• Leverage expertise and influence of others to the client's benefit.	
3. Treat your partners as if they are an integral part of your organization. Listen to their ideas on how you can work closely and productively together; create joint improvement teams; invite suggestions; build mutual trust and respect; reward them if they achieve improvements; let them participate in the celebration of success; involve them in the development of new products and processes; and become a better partner yourself.	• Share responsibility for all decisions concerning goals, next steps to take in the process and implementation.	
	• Make the best choices about priorities and solutions because you understand your client's needs, challenges, and culture.	

Table continues on next page.

Work in Partnership Continued		
Performances	Criteria	Your Personal Balanced Scorecard
You:	*So that you and the client can:*	*Note your personal objectives and improvement actions here:*
	So that: All stakeholders are involved in the decision making around every phase of the TPS-Lean Six Sigma cycle and specialists are involved in their areas of expertise.	

For example, you:

- Recommend specialists to assist in the design of solutions or interventions outside of your expertise.
- Convene partners and facilitate meetings related to fact finding, uncovering resistance, setting priorities, weighing alternatives, and so forth.
- Identify your clients' issues and needs and help support them in their efforts.
- Recognize the contributions of the subject matter experts and specialists.

5. Needs Analysis

Needs analysis is about examining the current situation at any level (society, organizational, process, or work group) to identify the external and internal pressures affecting it. The types of analyses include the following:

- Job or Task Analysis—Identifies the required activities, information, processes, and outputs produced and then compares that to actual practice.
- Process Analysis—Identifies the cycle time, process time, waiting times, and so forth.
- Work Environment Analysis—Identifies and evaluates the effectiveness and efficiency of feedback, the reward and incentive system, communication, work and process designs, and work tools and equipment.

- Market Analysis—Identifies the market size, competition, market growth, and so forth. Use the TPS-Leans Six Sigma Life Cycle Scan and TPS-Leans Six Sigma Customer Orientation Quick Scan to do this.

Needs Analysis		
Performances	**Criteria**	**Your Personal Balanced Scorecard**
You:	*So that you and the client can:*	*Note your personal objectives and improvement actions here:*
1. Determine the type of analysis required.	• Develop recommendations on whether to act on the findings.	
2. Develop a plan for conducting the analysis.	• Use a survey format that complies with recommended practices.	
3. Develop tools or documents, such as interviews, surveys, or observation forms, required to capture the data.	• Identify the physical and technological opportunities and constraints in the work environment.	
4. Conduct the analysis.	• Identify the actual work processes used to	
5. Analyze the data.	• Identify the actual and expected outputs of the work.	
6. Interpret the results.	• Identify gaps between what is required and what actually occurs.	
7. Make recommendations based on the results.		

For example, you:

- Identify the objectives of the analysis, who to involve, what data you require, how best to get the data, how the data will be used and by whom, and when you want to begin and end.
- Determine which needs or opportunities lend themselves to further analysis.
- Develop hypotheses regarding why the current situation exists.

6. Cause Analysis

Cause analysis is about determining why a gap in performance or expectations exists. Some causes are obvious, such as new hires lack the required skills to do the expected task and, therefore, the solution must eliminate that gap. Use the TPS-Lean Six Sigma risk management model for systematically mapping the causes, effects, and possible actions regarding observed bottlenecks.

Cause Analysis		
Performances	**Criteria**	**Your Personal Balanced Scorecard**
You:	*So that you and the client can:*	*Note your personal objectives and improvement actions here:*
1. Make an inventory of most relevant process steps.	• Differentiate performance problems that are caused by lack of knowledge and skill from those that are due to environmental, job, or process design; inadequate feedback; insufficient tools; conflicting objectives; or inappropriate performance measures.	
2. Determine for each process step the possible failures.	• Facilitate the search for solutions of problems So *that*: Future design and development will cost effectively address the real need(s).	
3. Indicate what the cause of each failure is and what the effects of the failure are. Identify the causes, such as: • Lack of skills or knowledge • Insufficient environmental support • Inappropriate rewards or incentives or measures • Poorly designed jobs or processes.		

Table continues on next page.

4. Determine for each failure the actions (solutions) necessary to improve the weak points.
5. Implement the actions.
6. Report and review the results.

For example, point out:

- Those performance deficiencies due to a lack of knowledge and skill that lend themselves to instructional solutions, such as training.
- Why a performance deficiency exists, such as:
  o Product or process defects
  o Poor performance
  o Poor morale and employee satisfaction

7. Design

A design describes the features, attributes, and elements of a solution and the resources required to actualize it. Identify and describe one or more solutions in detail, what will be required to develop and implement them, which is preferred, and why. All Design for TPS-Lean Six Sigma projects follow the Identify, Design, Optimize, and Verify (IDOV) model.

Design		
Performances	**Criteria**	**Your Personal Balanced Scorecard**
You:	*So that:*	*Note your personal objectives and improvement actions here:*
1. Define the design requirements.	• The objectives, conditions, performances, and the criteria for judging are sufficiently detailed.	
2. Identify the objectives of the solution and all elements of the solution.	• The required terms, concepts, rules, principles, and procedures key to performance are present.	

Table continues on next page.

Design Continued		
Performances	**Criteria**	**Your Personal Balanced Scorecard**
		Note your personal objectives and improvement actions here:
You:	*So that:*	
3. Develop a plan for accomplishing the objectives and elements that includes strategy and tactics	• The method for evaluating the accomplishment of the objective and the effectiveness of the solution is feasible and sufficiently detailed.	
4. Identify key attributes of the proposed solution—such as learning strategy and tactics, feedback, and so forth.	• The client understands the investment in time and resources necessary to develop and implement the solution and can provide the resources to realize the design.	
5. Identify how the solution will be produced.		
6. Identify the resources required.		
7. Identify methods for delivering or deploying the solution.		
8. Identify how the solution will be maintained or reinforced.		
9. Identify methods for evaluating the effectiveness of the solution.		

For example, you develop a plan for:

- Accomplish the objectives.
- Develop, and maintain instructional materials.
- Redesign a process, job, or system.
- Change management practices.
- Evaluate the effectiveness of the solution.

8. Implementation

Implementation is about deploying the solution and managing the change. It's about helping clients adopt new behaviors or use new tools. You develop an implementation plan that includes how you or the client will track change, identify, and respond to problems, and communicate the results. Before the implementation, verify if the circumstances for implementation are favorable with the help of TPS-Lean Six Sigma Implementation Circumstances Quick Scan. This tool creates insight into the introductory circumstances of the change project. Use the TPS-Lean Six Sigma Project BSCsoft and TPS-Lean Six Sigma Personal BSCsoft to manage and implement the project successfully.

Implementation		
Performances	**Criteria**	**Your Personal Balanced Scorecard**
You:	*So that you and the client can:*	*Note your personal objectives and improvement actions here:*
1. Design a change strategy based. This includes the following:	• Send a uniform message about the why, what, when, and how of the change.	
• The change objectives, related performance measures, and targets.	• Determine what tools and procedures are needed to effectively support the implementation.	
• Communicating the change honestly, clearly, actively, and face-to-face in a timely way.	• Determine how best to track the speed of the deployment and any resistance.	
• Communicating the necessity and the advantages of the change to all involved. Base change proposals on clear arguments.	• Determine how to identify and best handle resistance against the change.	
• Paying attention also to those who delay, boycott, and sabotage the change.	*So that:*	
• What implementation materials and messages will be required and how they will be produced.	• The information serves as a guide for future work and provides information for ongoing evaluation.	
	• The change is implemented successfully.	
	• Change is sustained over time.	

Table continues on next page.

Implementation Continued		
Performances	**Criteria**	**Your Personal Balanced Scorecard**
You:	*So that you and the client can:*	*Note your personal objectives and improvement actions here:*
• Identify successive milestones, risk management activities, timelines, an so forth.		
• ?How the new behaviors and other evidence of adoption will be recognized and rewarded.		
• What to do in case of resistance.		
• Who will provide support and reinforcement during deployment?		
• Identify roles and responsibilities of management, change agent, employees, and other vested parties.		
2. Develop tools and procedures to help those involved in the implementation. For example, train the trainer sessions. Before implementing the change, verify if the circumstances for implementation are favorable. Use Table 6.3 in this TPS-Lean Six Sigma book to get insight into the introductory circumstances of the change project.		

For example, you:

- Participate on a team to design a change and the implementation strategy.
- Help develop and communicate the messages.

- Help train people who will deliver the training, or assist the target audience in adopting the new behaviors, executing the new process, or using the new tools.

9. Evaluation

Evaluation is about testing to what extent the formulated objectives having been realized. Depending on possible differences between objectives and results, the execution of the TPS-Lean Six Sigma project can be adjusted. This standard is about identifying and acting on opportunities throughout the systematic process to identify measures and capture data that will help identify needs, adoption, and results.

Evaluation		
Performances	**Criteria**	**Your Personal Balanced Scorecard**
You:	*So that you and the client can:*	*Note your personal objectives and improvement actions here:*
1. State outcomes of the evaluation effort in measurable terms.	• Determine whether the solution satisfied the need.	
2. Design a measurement plan based on the project's goals and outcomes. The plan includes the following:	• Determine whether data are valid and useful.	
• Develop tools or documents, such as interviews, surveys, or observation forms, required to capture the data.	• Determine if the measurement methods are valid and useful.	
• The program or project's key success indicators or goals in measurable terms	• Make timely decisions about the need to change and to better ensure the effectiveness of the solution.	
• How data will be collected and results validated		
• The goal against which results will be compared		
3. Develop the tools and guidelines for collecting and interpreting data.		
4. Measure the impact of the solution.		
5. Report your findings and recommendations.		

For example, you:

- Partner with clients to identify ways to capture and track performance data.
- Evaluate the results of the project

CHAPTER 12

BECOME A CERTIFIED TPS-LEAN SIX SIGMA COMPANY

Failure is simply the opportunity to begin again, this time more intelligently.

—Henry Ford

There is a kind of re-education needed to connect business management with normal life. There has always been an enormous gap between the way people treat colleagues at work and the way they treat friends and family. With regard to the latter, we do not see friendship, tolerance, etc. as sentimental and "soft" when we deal with friends and family, but rather as a lubricant for the relationship. Could we not extend this to the business community as well? The gap between these two views is currently decreasing; perhaps here rests the solution for tomorrow's problems.

—Roger Evans and Peter Russell (1991)

The TPS-Lean Six Sigma Life Cycle Scan is a performance excellence model aimed at continuous performance and process improvement. It is a holistic instrument for systematic self diagnosis that will help both public and private sector organizations to increase individual and organizational quality & performance in the direction of Total Performance. We present five development levels and eight dimensions (see Table 12.1) that follow the TPS-Lean Six Sigma concept. These levels and dimensions indicate the organization's level of performance maturity compared with that needed to excel in management. The five development levels are: *basic performance, improving performance, moderate performance, advanced*

TPS-Lean Six Sigma: Linking Human Capital to Lean Six Sigma: A New Blueprint for Creating High Performance Companies, pp. 299–336

performance. Each higher level, that is, toward total performance, can be considered as an increase in the organization's abilities to adapt and react to external and internal necessity for improved quality and performance. The TPS-Lean Six Sigma Life Cycle Scan is a measuring rod that can augment existing approaches being used by the organization. It helps to define in which development level it finds itself by its total TPS-Lean Six Sigma Life Cycle Scan score. By making performance management measurable in this way, it will be easier to manage related performance processes and to increase the score year by year. This makes it possible to steer improvement actions systematically, always aiming for higher levels of personal and business excellence.

TPS-Lean Six Sigma' Five Levels of Development

(Level 1) Basic performance: Hardly any attention is given to personal and organizational performance measurement, process mindedness, personal integrity, and knowledge and talent management. Inspection is the main method used to assure quality.

(Level 2) Improving performance: Sporadic and ad hoc manual attention is given to measuring personal and organizational performance. Any process mind set is only related to risk reduction, while performance implications of personal integrity are only related to regulatory compliance. Performance improvement depends on quarter to quarter extraordinary ad hoc actions, and tends to fall short of expectations. The company has implemented quality control and quality assurance functions, but has not applied these functions effectively.

(Level 3) Moderate performance: Measurement of personal and organizational performance is selective. An organizational balanced scorecard is produced. The company has implemented quality control and quality assurance functions, and has applied these functions effectively. ISO 9,000 quality system may be present in the organization. The performance of the organization is starting to improve selectively beyond previous expectations.

(Level 4) Advanced performance: Measurement of personal and organizational performance is structured and systematic. TQM, Six Sigma, and Lean Management/Manufacturing may be present in the organization. Every improvement project follows the define, measure, analyze, improve, and control (DMAIC) model. At this stage, some departments are piloting important TPS-Lean Six Sigma elements at the strategic level. Parts of the organization qualify for TPS-Lean Six Sigma distinction.

(Level 5) Total performance: TPS-Lean Six Sigma has become a natural and continuous learning process that runs smoothly and spontaneously. Personal and organizational performance measurement, a customer-ori-

ented process mind set, personal integrity, and the systematic management of knowledge and talent all have highest priority. All key elements of TPS-Lean Six Sigma have been implemented throughout the organization on strategic, tactical, operational, and individual levels. The performance of this organization is classified as *total* on the basis of these characteristics. The entire organization qualifies for the TPS-Lean Six Sigma certification on the basis of this result, and is considered to be practicing *Best Practices*.

HOW IS THE TPS-LEAN SIX SIGMA SELF-ASSESSMENT EXECUTED?

The TPS-Lean Six Sigma self-assessment system is a matrix in which the five development phases are indicated horizontally and the dimensions and subdimensions vertically. The subdimensions are derived from the TPS-Lean Six Sigma concept, with each subdimension having its own weighting factor. The matrix is graded from right to left; moving to the right side of the matrix means the higher one appraises the organization. At the intersection of a development phase and a dimension, statements are given that are characteristic for the organization in that specific phase. Table 12.1 shows the complete TPS-Lean Six Sigma matrix. The individual indicates a view of the organization's position in each subdimension by selecting the statement that corresponds most with the perceived situation in the organization/TPS-Lean Six Sigma project.

SCORING SYSTEM

Based on the Xs that have been inserted in the TPS-Lean Six Sigma Life Cycle tables, the position per subdimensions can be defined. Subsequently, this position is translated into a score per TPS-Lean Six Sigma subdimension and into a score per dimension. The total score defines the awarding of TPS-Lean Six Sigma recognition or a TPS-Lean Six Sigma Award. Each subdimension has a different weighing factor. The final subdimension score is defined by multiplying the subdimension score with a weighing factor. The dimension score is defined by adding all the subdimension scores. The total score can be visualized by a diagram, see Figure 12.1.

TPS-LEAN SIX SIGMA COMPANY CERTIFICATION PROCESS

TPS-Lean Six Sigma company certification entails a program through which companies can apply to receive the designation of Certified TPS-Lean Six Sigma Company. It is based on eight TPS-Lean Six Sigma stand-

Table 12.1. Eight TPS-Lean Six Sigma Dimensions

1. Personal management	*The way individuals are encouraged to increase their self-knowledge, awareness and consciousness and to increase their personal and professional effectiveness. This allows them to participate fully and authentically at work and home, reducing stress, and ensuring a creative, productive work environment which captures and values the intelligence of each employee.*
1.1 Personal ambition	I gain self-knowledge and develop my self-awareness and personal responsibility continuously, by formulating my personal ambition authentically; I continually strive to reach higher levels of accomplishment and mindset change. My personal ambition is formulated as a living document.
1.2 Personal strategy road mapping and life-career planning	I have formulated my personal balanced scorecard effectively. I made career and personal lifestyle choices, set goals for continuous improvement, track my accomplishments, and use the PBSC as a reminder of my priorities.
1.3 Continuous personal improvement	I recognize my responsibilities to improve myself continuously, based on my PBSC and the Plan-Do-Act-Challenge cycle; so I am constantly becoming more conscious, authentic, and creative and thus, increasing my personal effectiveness.
1.4 Personal work/life balance	I bring my whole self (physical, mental, emotional, and spiritual aspects) to work. I consciously and continuously seek to balance my work and personal life guided by my personal balanced scorecard and the Plan-Do-Act-Challenge cycle, and I use my time more effectively.
1.5 Personal leadership	I am absolutely clear on what motivates and drives me. I understand myself based on my personal ambition and there is harmony between my personal ambition and my behavior. I have balanced all aspects of my life based on my PBSC.
1.6 Serving leadership	As a leader, I continuously put myself at the service of my colleagues and employees in a trustful manner; I spontaneously inspire, stimulate, help, and encourage them, listen to them, and appreciate their contributions.
2. Strategic management	*The way the organization's vision, mission, and core values (shared ambition) are formulated by the stakeholders and translated into concrete organizational objectives, targets, performance indicators, and improvement actions aimed at achieving and sustaining competitive advantage.*
2.1 Shared ambition	The organization has a collective mission, vision, and core values reflecting the aspirations of the stakeholders. I identify with the shared ambition and it provides guidance and focus for me.

2.2 Business strategy road mapping	The organization has formulated organizational balanced scorecard (OBSC) effectively; with shared ambition translated strategically into organizational critical success factors, objectives, performance measures, targets, and creative strategies. Progress is tracked and the OBSC is constantly used as a reminder of organizational priorities.
2.3 Customer centric strategies	The needs to add value to customers are reflected in actionable business strategies set out in the OBSC. We are using Customer Relationship Management (CRM) techniques to understand customer's needs and desires and to continuously improve customer satisfaction.
2.4 Continuous organizational improvement	The corporate balanced scorecard is implemented systematically across the organization. Organizational improvement is a continuous learning process based on the OBSC and according to the DMAIC model, in order to achieve desired results.
2.5 Strategy communication	The corporate balanced scorecard is communicated timely, honestly, clearly, frequently and face-to-face with all stakeholders to renew ownership and commitment at all organizational levels. Two-way communication is encouraged.
2.6 Scorecard deployment	The organizational balanced scorecard is systematically cascaded through the whole organization using departmental scorecards (tactical level), team scorecards (operational level), and individual performance plans (individual level).
3. Business values management	*The way the organization concretely interprets and behaves according to high ethical norms, values and principles.*
3.1 Personal integrity	I take personal responsibility to act in accordance with my conscience creating a continuous balance between my personal ambition and my behavior. I strive to live authentically and it is a continuous learning process.
3.2 Business integrity	Trust is at the core of our company and it is easy to recognize. We act ethically towards all stakeholders and we treat others with professional respect and courtesy, regardless of differences, positions, titles, ages, or other types of distinctions. Ethical awareness and behavior are valued and encouraged and is integrated into our policies, practices, and decision making.
3.3 Corporate social responsibility	We continuously consider the economic, social, and environmental impacts of our activities and have formal structures in place to sustain the effort.
3.4 Transparency and accountability	We ensure that all information is available that can be used to measure the performance and to guard against any possible misuse of powers. We accept responsibility and are accountable for all our actions. Our business is a responsible community contributor.

Table continues on next page.

Table 12.1. Eight TPS-Lean Six Sigma Dimensions Continued

3.5 Regulatory compliance	We protect the privacy, integrity and accessibility of all critical information and comply with all local, state and federal regulations. This is reinforced through an effective corporate governance program.
3.6 Branding and trust	We take pride in having a brand name that is synonymous with trust in the eyes of our stakeholders. Our integrity is recognized by our competitors and all stakeholders.
4. Talent management	*The way talent in the organization is being effectively managed, succession is planned and developed across the enterprise, maximum self development of the employees is realized, talents are optimally deployed, and the employees rewarded and recognized.*
4.1 Individual competencies	The line-Manager regularly assesses the individual competencies to ensure that employees have the opportunity to identify both their areas of strength and opportunities for improvement. Individual competencies entail a combination of observable and measurable skill, knowledge, performance behavior, and personal attributes that contribute to enhanced employee performance and organizational success.
4.2 Individual capability and performance planning	Annually the manager and employee jointly formulate an Individual Performance Plan, in which is indicated which job-oriented performance objectives the employee is expected to fulfill. The emphasis of the individual performance plan focuses on the results to be obtained and the related performance measures, and targets. Continuous improvement choices are made on a desired path forward incorporating employee aspirations, organizational opportunity, growth path, and fit of employee capabilities with role and performance requirements.
4.3 Review and mentoring	Managers effectively guide employees continuously in optimizing their performance and competencies. Formal interim reviews of employee's progress take place, assessing employee's areas for further development.
4.4 Talent development	Training is a high priority for all employees to obtain new insights and acquire new skills. Guided "learning by doing" and "on the job" principles enable employees to work smarter and fulfill their role effectively.

4.5 Reward and recognition	The organization values every position regardless of level. Every position is value-linked with the organizational ambition. Fair and equitable treatment of employees in our code of conduct can only exist if we are successful in defining the importance of every position. Each position across the company and from top to bottom is founded on fair principles in compensation, recognition, and job-related rewards based on job responsibilities, capabilities, and experience.
4.6 Succession planning	There are highly qualified people in all positions within the organization. A map of role capability and experience relative to position is obvious to all. Leaders emerge naturally to move into these positions as the organization addresses changing conditions. The set of individuals suitable for the position is known and accepted by all.
5. Process management	*The way business processes are constantly being evaluated and modified or reframed and reformulated to continuously improve the satisfaction of Internal and external customers.*
5.1 Customer definition	Internal and external customers are defined according to the principles of TPS-Lean Six Sigma, reflecting the strategic focus of the organization. They are systematically reevaluated for fit and redefined or expanded according to changes in process and strategic focus.
5.2 Customer needs	Customer needs are surveyed, understood, and fed back into product and service improvement innovation for continuous process improvement.
5.3 Customer value and process definition	Every step in the process of engineering, producing, and delivering the product or services has been defined and designed to contribute to customer value. Key metrics monitor process performance and reflect the organization's commitment to delivering customer value.
5.4 Process evaluation and standardization	All critical business processes are described, communicated, understood, and standardized in order to continuously fulfill the customer's desires. The standard procedures are being used routinely and spontaneously to fulfill the customer's desires.
5.5 Process performance measurement	The effectiveness of all critical business processes is being measured and monitored continuously through key performance indicators in order to delight external customers.
5.6 Continuous process improvement	All critical business processes are continuously and pro-actively improved using a project approach and TPS-Lean Six Sigma techniques according to the DMAIC process, reflecting both internal and external customer needs.

Table continues on next page.

Table 12.1. Eight TPS-Lean Six Sigma Dimensions Continued

6. Knowledge management	*The way the organization's learning is increased and the knowledge stream managed, knowledge is developed, disseminated, transferred, and used to create a climate for sustainable innovation. All employees seek to continuously capture and transfer their learnings.*
6.1 Self-knowledge	Employees continuously strive to develop their self-knowledge and to get a better self-image, based on the formulation and implementation of their Personal Ambition and through thinking and doing.
6.2 Self-learning	Employees continuously reflect on their personal balanced scorecard according to the Plan-Do-Act-Challenge cycle. They have the freedom to challenge existing processes, take on new challenges, taking action, trying new things, making new informal contacts, gaining experience, and taking initiative, experimenting, and taking risks. Making mistakes is valued as learning.
6.3 Shared knowledge	Knowledge within our organization is managed in such a way that we spontaneously and intensively share knowledge with each other and the knowledge flow is being managed effectively. The continuous and intensive generation, cultivation, updating, mobilization, application, and sharing of relevant knowledge is a way of life in the organization.
6.4 Shared learning	We are learning together and from each other spontaneously, and knowing one another thoroughly. Our organization facilitates this process in all their divisions and based on this we continually transform ourselves.
6.5 Problem solving	Problem solving is a proactive part of each person's daily work and a structured approach to creativity. We solve common problems routinely and systematically in multidisciplinary teams, based on consistent application of problem-solving tools and techniques.
6.6 Knowledge infrastructure	We have an effective knowledge infrastructure of tools, systems, continuous training, brainstorm sessions, and review meetings that supports which facilitates all facets of the organizational learning process and which continuously stimulates creativity, systems thinking, self-confidence, innovations, and a conducive learning environment.
7. Team management	*The way individuals within the organization are committed to shared ambition and accept, acknowledge, trust, and respect each other - in order to achieve collective results—characterized by individuals within the company sharing knowledge, work, thoughts, feelings, excitement, satisfaction, pressure, pleasure, emotions, doubts, and successes with each other.*

7.1 Team balance	There is a balance between the team role and the job of individual team members and a balance of learning styles within and across all teams Team members know what their own roles, capacity, and capability are as well as those of other team members and accept these
7.2 Team development	My team is a mature group. Our team leader take serious notice of the team development phases—forming, storming, norming, and performing. He facilitates us by collaboratively setting goals challenging to all team members, looking for ways to enhance the team's ability to excel, developing an ongoing assessment of the team, recognizing individual contributions, and developing members' full potential through coaching and feedback.
7.3 Team learning	All team members share their PBSCs with each other spontaneously establishing the basis of team learning through trust and respect. We continuously seek out new learning opportunities through creative problem solving, vigorous and healthy conflict, taking risks, and forgiving and learning from mistakes.
7.4 Team diversity	Team members unconditionally acknowledge and accept each other's diversity. Respect and seeking to understand constantly govern our interactions. The team relies on diversity to be creative and continuously channels this into robust outcomes.
7.5 Team measurement and performance	The effectiveness of my team is constantly being measured and evaluated, in order to continuously improve team performance. The team results are a combined effort of all team members and are more important than individual results. All team members feel responsible for the team results and continuously understand progress towards goals.
7.6 Team communication	There is open communication among my team members. My team ensures adequate communication on the team's ambition and progress to all stakeholders. Feedback from stakeholders is constantly sought and acted upon to improve contribution and enrich learning.
8. Change management	*The attitude the organization has about change and what drives it; the manner in which change is supported and disseminated; and the way change is successfully adopted by all employees.*
8.1 Change infrastructure	Organizational changes are integrally and systematically being dealt with in a structured manner, based on a steering group, project group, sponsorship, and improvement teams, which are known to all affected employees.
8.2 Change circumstances	Employees are open to and embrace change. It is regarded as a challenge. They exhibit an attitude of mutual trust, commitment, dedication, willingness to learn, and inner involvement, realizing that change begins with them.

Table continues on next page.

Table 12.1. Eight TPS-Lean Six Sigma Dimensions Continued

8.3 Managing change	Resistance to change is recognized and openly discussed with all stakeholders and addressed by executives. The different phases in the responses of employees are recognized early and moved through to the phase of acceptance.
8.4 Change behavior	Fear and distrust are completely dispelled from the organization.
8.5 Implementing change	All key persons are involved as change leaders throughout the organization. Executives, managers, and all employees are committed to supporting change. The what, why, how, and the consequences of change are constantly, honestly, timely, consistently, decisively, and face-to-face being communicated by executives to all stakeholders.
8.6 Change sustainability	Employees accept personal responsibility for changing themselves first according to their PBSC and the PDAC-cycle. This forms the starting point for durable organizational change.

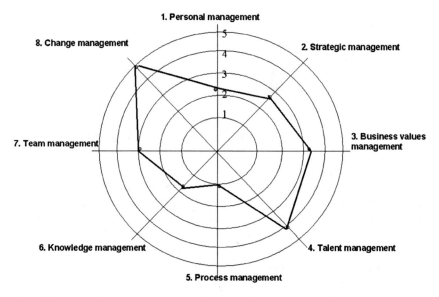

Figure 12.1.   TPS-Lean Six Sigma Life Cycle Diagram.

ards (dimensions) to distinguish companies who have proven they can produce results through the holistic TPS-Lean Six Sigma concept. The Academy for TPS-Lean Six Sigma Certification (separate business unit of TPS-Lean Six Sigma Inc.) is the certifying body.

WHAT IS TPS-LEAN SIX SIGMA COMPANY CERTIFICATION?

TPS-Lean Six Sigma Company Certification is a credential that is given to companies who satisfy a set of requirements. The Academy for TPS-Lean Six Sigma Certification recognizes companies who have demonstrated proficiency in 8 Standards of TPS-Lean Six Sigma in ways that are in keeping with the TPS-Lean Six Sigma system. Companies who receive the TPS-Lean Six Sigma Company Certification designation must be recertified every year to maintain the credential.

HOW MIGHT TPS CERTIFICATION BENEFIT YOU?

The TPS-Lean Six Sigma Company Certification designation shows that you have demonstrated proficiency according to the TPS-Lean Six Sigma system. The certification can set you apart from others who have not engaged in the same degree of examination by clients. Once certified, your name will be listed on a registry and on the Web site of the Academy for

TPS-Lean Six Sigma Certification (www.TPS-LeanSixSigma.com) that is available to clients. The TPS-Lean Six Sigma Company Certification designation is an indication that you have met the eight standards of TPS-Lean Six Sigma as evidenced by your work, knowledge, and skills. You may display the designation on your business cards, stationary, and marketing materials. In this way, you will distinguish yourself in the marketplace.

HOW WILL PROFICIENCY BE ASSESSED?

An applicant's proficiency will be assessed through a combination of attestations by clients and employees, and review by qualified reviewers, based on the TPS-Lean Six Sigma Life Cycle Scan. Reviewers will be TPS-Lean Six Sigma professionals who have received training and guidelines for doing the review. Organizations and/or business units that have achieved a certain total score and a balanced distribution over the eight dimensions (standards) are eligible for the TPS-Lean Six Sigma-recognition or the TPS-Lean Six Sigma Award. Organizations and/or business units that have obtained a TPS-Lean Six Sigma Award will be TPS-Lean Six Sigma certified.

TPS-LEAN SIX SIGMA RECOGNITION

To be eligible for the recognition, the following conditions have to be fulfilled:

1. The total score is at least 2,500 points
2. All eight dimensions have at least a level 4 score
3. The score is confirmed by an appointed local TPS-Lean Six Sigma Auditor.

TPS-LEAN SIX SIGMA AWARD

To achieve the TPS-Lean Six Sigma Award, the following conditions must be fulfilled:

1. The total score is at least 2,800 points
2. All eight dimensions have at least a level 5 score
3. The score is confirmed by an appointed local TPS-Lean Six Sigma Auditor.

Table 12.2. TPS-Lean Six Sigma Life Cycle Scan Matrix

TPS-Lean Six Sigma Cycle	Basic Performance	Improving Performance	Moderate Performance	Advanced Performance	Total Performance
1. Personal management					
1.1 Personal ambition.	Formulating	[ ] I do not have any mechanism to gain insight into myself, to reach higher levels of accomplishment.	[ ] I reflect on my motivations and consequent actions on an ad hoc basis to reach higher levels of accomplishment.	[ ] I regularly reflect on my motivations and consequent actions to reach higher levels of accomplishment.	[ ] I gain self-knowledge based on my formulated personal ambition. I reflect on this to reach higher levels of accomplishment and mindset change.	[ ] I gain self-knowledge and develop my self-awareness and personal responsibility continuously, by formulating my personal ambition authentically; I continually strive to reach higher levels of accomplishment and mindset change. My personal ambition is formulated as a living document that I have throughout my life.

Table continues on next page.

Table 12.2. TPS-Lean Six Sigma Life Cycle Scan Matrix Continued

TPS-Lean Six Sigma Cycle	Basic Performance	Improving Performance	Moderate Performance	Advanced Performance	Total Performance
1.2 Personal strategy road mapping and life-career planning.	Formulating	[ ] I do not have a mechanism to formulate personal career and lifestyle objectives.	[ ] I have informally formulated some personal career and lifestyle objectives.	[ ] I have formulated some personal career and lifestyle objectives. I have applied some personal improvement actions and occasionally reflect on my progress.	[ ] I have formulated my personal balanced scorecard, career and personal lifestyle choices. I have defined targets, measurements and improvement actions for some objectives and occasionally update my progress.	[ ] I have formulated my personal balanced scorecard effectively. I made career and personal lifestyle choices, set goals for continuous improvement, track my accomplishments and use the PBSC as a reminder of my priorities.
1.3 Continuous personal improvement.	Improving (Plan-Do-Act-Challenge)	[ ] I do not seek to improve myself on any organized basis.	[ ] I seek to improve myself in some ways but have no formal way of documenting my improvements.	[ ] I seek to improve myself based on my formulated personal objectives but on an ad hoc basis and have no formal way of documenting my personal improvements.	[ ] I improve myself at work and in private life based on my personal balanced scorecard and according to the Plan-Do-Act-Challenge cycle. I am not rigorous in improving my personal effectiveness.	[ ] I recognize my responsibilities to improve myself continuously, based on my PBSC and the Plan-Do-Act-Challenge cycle; so I am constantly becoming more conscious, authentic, and creative and thus, increasing my personal effectiveness.

		[ ]	[ ]	[ ]	[ ]	[ ]
1.4 Personal work/life balance.	Improving (Plan-Do-Act-Challenge)	I do not try to balance my work and personal life. I seldom think about it.	I try to keep a balance between work and personal life, but I have no process.	I have taken the time to think about and develop a process to balance my work and life but do not use it rigorously.	I am trying to participate fully and authentically at work and in my personal life guided by my personal balanced scorecard and according to the Plan-Do-Act-Challenge cycle.	I bring my whole self (physical, mental, emotional and spiritual aspects) to work. I consciously and continuously seek to balance my work and personal life guided by my personal balanced scorecard and the Plan-Do-Act-Challenge cycle, and I use my time more effectively.
1.5 Personal leadership.	Improving (Plan-Do-Act-Challenge)	I don't know what motivates/drives me. I don't understand myself.	I am not sure what motivates/drives me. I don't completely understand myself.	I partly know what motivates/drives me. I understand myself partly and have not balanced all aspects of my life.	I know what motivates/drives me. I understand myself and have balanced almost all aspects of my life based on my PBSC.	I am absolutely clear on what motivates/drives me. I understand myself based on my personal ambition and there is harmony between my personal ambition and my behavior. I have balanced all aspects of my life based on my PBSC.

Table continues on next page.

Table 12.2. TPS-Lean Six Sigma Life Cycle Scan Matrix Continued

TPS-Lean Six Sigma Cycle	Basic Performance	Improving Performance	Moderate Performance	Advanced Performance	Total Performance
1.6 Serving leadership.	[ ] My peers or employees see me as authoritative and directive. I do what my organization asks of me.	[ ] I try to help my peers and employees.	[ ] I try to put myself at the service of my peers or employees and occasionally I am successful.	[ ] I am learning to be there for my colleagues and employees and how to serve them so that they can achieve their objectives.	[ ] As a leader, I continuously put myself at the service of my colleagues and employees in a trustful manner; I spontaneously respect, inspire, stimulate, help, and encourage them, listen to them, and appreciate their contributions.
2. Strategic management					
2.1 Shared ambition.	Formulating	[ ] There is an organizational strategy but no mission, vision or core values.	[ ] There is an organizational strategy and a mission, vision and core values, but they are not linked. The mission, vision and core values are not meaningful to the employees.	[ ] The organization has a collective mission, vision and core values reflecting the aspirations of the senior management, but not individual employees.	[ ] The organization has a collective mission, vision and core values reflecting the aspirations of the senior management, and individual employees contribute to it.	[ ] The organization has a collective mission, vision and core values reflecting the aspirations of the stakeholders. I identify with the shared ambition and it provides guidance and focus for me.

2.2 Business strategy road mapping.	Deploying	[ ] The organization has a business plan but this is not shared across the organization.	[ ] The organization has a business plan that is shared across the organization, but has little input from employees.	[ ] Some parts of the organization have developed an organizational balanced scorecard. This has been cascaded to departmental managers, at least. Performance is tracked.	[ ] The entire organization has formulated an organizational balanced scorecard and it has been cascaded to departmental managers, at least. Performance is tracked.	[ ] The organization has formulated organizational balanced scorecard (OBSC) effectively; with shared ambition translated strategically into organizational critical success factors, objectives, performance measures, targets, and creative strategies. Progress is tracked and the OBSC is constantly used as a reminder of organizational priorities.
2.3 Customer centric strategies.	Deploying	[ ] Hardly any attention is given to the opinions or satisfaction of our customers.	[ ] The customer is important. We survey our customers about customer satisfaction.	[ ] We recognize the value and opinions of our customers. We solicit feedback and occasionally act on it.	[ ] We recognize the value and opinions of our customers. We actively solicit feedback and build them into creative strategies as reflected in our OBSC.	[ ] The needs to add value to customers are reflected in actionable business strategies set out in the OBSC. We are using Customer Relationship Management (CRM) techniques to understand customer's needs and desires and to continuously improve customer satisfaction.

Table continues on next page.

Table 12.2. TPS-Lean Six Sigma Life Cycle Scan Matrix Continued

TPS-Lean Six Sigma Cycle	Basic Performance	Improving Performance	Moderate Performance	Advanced Performance	Total Performance
2.4 Continuous organizational improvement.	Improving (DMAIC)	[ ] Hardly any attention is given to systematic organizational improvements.	[ ] Organizational improvements are designed and implemented yearly but no formal ongoing structure exists to manage this.	[ ] The corporate balanced scorecard (OBSC) is implemented in some parts of the organization, to measure business performance against key metrics. Organizational improvement, based on the OBSC, is still sporadic.	[ ] The corporate balanced scorecard is implemented in the most important parts of the organization, to measure business performance against key metrics. Organizational improvement based on the OBSC and according to the Plan-Do-Check-Act cycle is occurring in some parts of the organization.	[ ] The corporate balanced scorecard is implemented systematically across the organization. Organizational improvement is a continuous learning process based on the OBSC and according to the DMAIC process, in order to achieve desired results.
2.5 Strategy communication.	Deploying	[ ] Business results are infrequently communicated to middle management and employees.	[ ] The business plan is communicated to middle management on an ad hoc basis.	[ ] The scorecard is communicated to middle management quarterly, and there is an opportunity for them to discuss progress with senior executives.	The organizational balanced scorecard is communicated to employees from time to time, and there is an opportunity for them to discuss progress with senior executives.	[ ] The corporate balanced scorecard is communicated timely, honestly, clearly, frequently and face-to-face with all stakeholders to renew ownership and commitment at all organizational levels. Two-way communication is encouraged.

2.6 Scorecard deployment	Deploying	[ ] The organization has a cloudy business plan but this is not shared nor cascaded across the organization. There is no OBSC.	[ ] The organization has a business plan that is shared across the organization, but not cascaded. There is no OBSC.	[ ] Where the organizational balanced scorecard exists, it is cascaded to the departments only. The OBSC is not yet reflected in team scorecards or in individual performance plans.	[ ] The organizational balanced scorecard is cascaded to the departmental and team scorecards only. My individual performance plan is not related to my team scorecard.	[ ] The organizational balanced scorecard is systematically cascaded through the whole organization using departmental scorecards (tactical level), team scorecards (operational level), and individual performance plans (individual level).
3. Business values management					
3.1 Personal integrity	Improving (Plan-Do-act-challenge) Developing & learning	[ ] I don't pay attention to moral values and principles at work. I don't have a personal mission, vision and key roles identified. I take each day as it comes.	[ ] I am aware of inconsistencies between my beliefs and behaviors.	[ ] I am striving to attain consistency between my beliefs and behavior.	[ ] I take personal responsibility, but I am not always successful at achieving a balance between my personal ambition and my behavior.	[ ] I take personal responsibility to act in accordance with my conscience creating a continuous balance between my personal ambition and my behavior. I strive to live authentically and it is a continuous learning process.

Table continues on next page.

Table 12.2. TPS-Lean Six Sigma Life Cycle Scan Matrix Continued

	TPS-Lean Six Sigma Cycle	Basic Performance	Improving Performance	Moderate Performance	Advanced Performance	Total Performance
3.2 Business integrity	Formulating	[ ] Some policies and disciplinary measures against unethical behavior exist, but are not enforced.	[ ] Policies and disciplinary measures against unethical behavior are formalized, communicated and sometimes, enforced.	[ ] A code of ethics has been developed for the organization. We have a growing awareness of business integrity.	[ ] There is a well-defined corporate governance program that sets guidelines, practices, actions, and reporting, which are linked to regulations. We strive to act ethical towards our stakeholders. Ethical awareness and behavior are encouraged.	[ ] Trust is at the core of our company and it is easy to recognize. We act ethically towards all stakeholders and we treat others with professional respect and courtesy, regardless of differences, positions, titles, ages, or other types of distinctions. Ethical awareness and behavior are valued and encouraged and is integrated into our policies, practices and decision-making.
3.3 Corporate social responsibility	Improving (DMAIC) Formulating	[ ] Hardly any attention is given to the economic, social and environmental impacts of our activities.	[ ] We are not aware of the economic, social and environmental impacts of our activities.	[ ] We have a growing awareness of the economic, social and environmental impacts of our activities.	[ ] We care about most of the economic, social and environmental impacts of our activities.	[ ] We continuously consider the economic, social and environmental impacts of our activities and have formal structures in place to sustain the effort.

3.4 Transparency and accountability	Improving (DMAIC) Developing & learning	[ ] No information is available that can be used to measure the performance and to guard against any possible misuse of powers. We don't accept responsibility and are not accountable for our actions.	[ ] Hardly any information is available that can be used to measure the performance and to guard against any possible misuse of powers. We partly accept responsibility and are not always accountable for our actions.	[ ] We have a growing awareness of the availability of information that can be used to measure the performance and to guard against any possible misuse of powers. There is growing acceptance of the responsibility and accountability of our actions.	[ ] Some information is available that can be used to measure the performance and to guard against any possible misuse of powers. We accept responsibility and are accountable for most of our actions.	[ ] We ensure that all information is available that can be used to measure the performance and to guard against any possible misuse of powers. We accept responsibility and are accountable for all our actions. Our business is a responsible community contributor.
3.5 Regulatory compliance	Improving (DMAIC) Developing & learning	[ ] There is little recognition of the protection of the privacy, integrity and accessibility of critical information, which comply with all local, state and federal regulations.	[ ] The organization is beginning to recognize the protection of the privacy, integrity and accessibility of critical information, which comply with all local, state and federal regulations.	[ ] A corporate governance program is emerging which includes the protection of the privacy, integrity and accessibility of critical information, which comply with local, state and federal regulations.	[ ] There is a formal corporate governance program in place, to protect the privacy, integrity and accessibility of all critical information, which comply with local, state and federal regulations.	[ ] We protect the privacy, integrity and accessibility of all critical information and comply with all local, state and federal regulations. This is reinforced through an effective corporate governance program.
3.6 Branding and trust	Improving (DMAIC) Developing & learning	[ ] Internally, the importance of a brand name to the external world has not yet been recognized.	[ ] The organization is aware of the value of a brand name. Some effort has been made to address this.	[ ] The organization's brand name is emerging and is beginning to be recognized.	[ ] The organization's brand name is known and is associated with trust and integrity.	[ ] We take pride in having a brand name that is synonymous with trust in the eyes of our stakeholders. Our integrity is recognized by our competitors and all stakeholders.

Table continues on next page.

Table 12.2. TPS-Lean Six Sigma Life Cycle Scan Matrix Continued

TPS-Lean Six Sigma Cycle	Basic Performance	Improving Performance	Moderate Performance	Advanced Performance	Total Performance
4. Talent management					
4.1 Individual competencies	Developing & learning	[ ] Observable and measurable skill, knowledge, performance behavior and personal attributes that contribute to enhanced employee performance and organizational success are not defined.	[ ] Observable and measurable skill, knowledge, performance behavior and personal attributes that contribute to enhanced employee performance and organizational success are defined for some positions at some levels.	[ ] Observable and measurable skill, knowledge, performance behavior and personal attributes that contribute to enhanced employee performance and organizational success are defined for most employees.	[ ] Assessment of the observable and measurable skill, knowledge, performance behavior and personal attributes that contribute to enhanced employee performance and organizational success are being held annually.	[ ] The line-Manager regularly assesses the individual competencies to ensure that employees have the opportunity to identify both their areas of strength and opportunities for improvement. Individual competencies entail a combination of observable and measurable skill, knowledge, performance behavior and personal attributes that contribute to enhanced employee performance and organizational success.

4.2 Individual capability and performance planning	Developing & learning	[ ] The employee does not have a mechanism that guides capability development and performance planning.	[ ] The Manager and employee informally discuss priorities for performance.	[ ] The Manager and employee follow a formal process for performance planning. The emphasis of this process focuses on the tasks to be executed, instead of the results to be obtained.	[ ] Annually the Manager and employee jointly formulate an Individual Performance Plan. The emphasis of the Individual Performance Plan focuses on the results to be obtained.	[ ] Annually the Manager and employee jointly formulate an Individual Performance Plan, in which it is indicated which job-oriented performance objectives; the employee is expected to fulfill. The emphasis of the individual performance plan focuses on the results to be obtained and the related performance measures, and targets. Continuous improvement choices are made on a desired path toward incorporating employee aspirations, organizational opportunity, growth path and a fit of employee capabilities with role and performance requirements.

Table continues on next page.

Table 12.2. TPS-Lean Six Sigma Life Cycle Scan Matrix Continued

	TPS-Lean Six Sigma Cycle	Basic Performance	Improving Performance	Moderate Performance	Advanced Performance	Total Performance
4.3 Review and mentoring	Developing & learning	[ ] Managers hold goal-setting and review meetings on performance sporadically.	[ ] Managers hold annual goal-setting and review meetings on employee performance. Management guidance is limited.	[ ] Managers hold annual goal-setting and review meetings on employee performance. Management guidance occurs from time to time.	[ ] Managers and employees review the agreed upon results and competencies at least once a year. Guidance is given on how the employee can improve performance.	[ ] Managers effectively guide employees continuously in optimizing their performance and competencies. Formal interim reviews of employee's progress take place, assessing employee's areas for further development.
4.4 Talent development	Developing & learning	[ ] Training of employees has a low priority in the organization. Employees are not often supported in acquiring new skills or knowledge.	[ ] Some job-related training is available and supported.	[ ] Training of employees takes place on a regular basis. A wide variety of job-related courses are available.	[ ] Training is emerging as a priority for the organization. Guided "learning by doing" and "on the job" principles are practiced.	[ ] Training is a high priority for all employees to obtain new insights and acquire new skills. Guided "learning by doing" and "on the job" principles enable employees to work smarter and fulfill their role effectively.

4.5 Reward and recognition	Developing & learning	[ ] Hardly any attention is given to fair principles in compensation, recognition, and job-related rewards based on job responsibilities, capabilities and experience.	[ ] Some positions, in some parts of the organization, only are founded on fair principles in compensation, recognition, and job-related rewards based on job responsibilities, capabilities and experience.	[ ] Each position, in some parts of the organization, only is founded on fair principles in compensation, recognition, and job-related rewards based on job responsibilities, capabilities and experience.	[ ] Each position across the company and from top to bottom is founded on fair principles in compensation, recognition, and job-related rewards based on job responsibilities, capabilities and experience.	[ ] The organization values every position regardless of level. Every position is value-linked with the organizational ambition. Fair and equitable treatment of employees in our code of conduct can only exist if we are successful in defining the importance of every position. Each position across the company and from top to bottom is founded on fair principles in compensation, recognition, and job-related rewards based on job responsibilities, capabilities and experience.

Table continues on next page.

Table 12.2. TPS-Lean Six Sigma Life Cycle Scan Matrix Continued

	TPS-Lean Six Sigma Cycle	Basic Performance	Improving Performance	Moderate Performance	Advanced Performance	Total Performance
4.6 Succession planning	Developing & learning	[ ] Little knowledge exists about the capability and experience required for any position other than what the employee currently has.	[ ] The organization has some understanding of experience and capabilities required to fill various positions. Vacant positions are sometimes filled based on employee career planning.	[ ] Within certain pockets, the organization understands the experience and capabilities required for all positions. Within these pockets, a map of open positions is known and available. Employees have a difficult time changing job paths due to many barriers.	[ ] Generally the organization has qualified people within most positions. A limited set of individuals is identified for key positions within the company. These may or may not be qualified and accepted by all.	[ ] There are highly qualified people in all positions within the organization. They are recruited effectively and developed for future higher level and broader responsibilities and to fulfil each key role within the company. They are prepared for advancement.
5. Process management						
5.1 Customer definition	Improving (DMAIC) Formulating	[ ] We don't know our external customers.	[ ] Specific criteria define our external customers. The organization is not aware of the importance of recognizing internal customers.	[ ] External customers are defined according to our strategic focus. The organization is beginning to realize the importance of recognizing internal customers.	[ ] External customers are defined according to our strategic focus. The organization has begun to define internal customers.	[ ] Internal and external customers are defined according to the principles of TPS-Lean Six Sigma, reflecting the strategic focus of the organization. They are systematically re-evaluated for fit and redefined or expanded according to changes in process and strategic focus.

		Level 1	Level 2	Level 3	Level 4	Level 5
5.2 Customer needs	Improving (DMAIC) Formulating	[ ] We don't know what our customers need and what their expectations are. Customer needs are not taken into account in designing product and processes.	[ ] There is some awareness about customer needs but processes do not reflect them.	[ ] Customer needs are surveyed at a high level, leading to segmentation of product or service offers, but processes are only changed to handle different offerings.	[ ] Customer needs are surveyed and understood, sometimes leading to processes changes to reflect segments' different needs.	[ ] We know what our customers need and what their expectations are. Their needs and expectations are continuously surveyed, understood and fed back into product and process improvement.
5.3 Customer value and process definition	Improving (DMAIC) Formulating	[ ] Customer value is not a high priority.	[ ] There is some awareness about the importance of customer value. Business processes involved in adding value have not been defined.	[ ] Customer value is recognized as important and some business processes involved in adding value have been defined.	[ ] The organization has defined which business processes are adding value to the customer and which related key metrics are affecting the process effectiveness.	[ ] Every step in the process of engineering, producing and delivering the product or services has been defined and designed to contribute to customer value. Key metrics monitor process performance and reflect the organization's commitment to delivering customer value.
5.4 Process evaluation and standardization	Improving (DMAIC) Deploying	[ ] Critical business processes are not evaluated and described.	[ ] Some critical business processes are evaluated and described.	[ ] The most important critical business processes relating to customer satisfaction are evaluated and described.	[ ] All critical business processes are evaluated, described and standardized in order to fulfill the customer's desires.	[ ] All critical business processes are described, evaluated, understood and standardized in order to continuously fulfill the customer's desires. The standard procedures are being used routinely and spontaneously to fulfill the customer's desires.

Table continues on next page.

Table 12.2. TPS-Lean Six Sigma Life Cycle Scan Matrix Continued

	TPS-Lean Six Sigma Cycle	Basic Performance	Improving Performance	Moderate Performance	Advanced Performance	Total Performance
5.5 Process performance measurement	Deploying	[ ] The effectiveness of critical business processes is not being measured.	[ ] The effectiveness of some critical business processes is being measured on ad-hoc basis.	[ ] The effectiveness of the most important critical business processes is being measured through key performance indicators.	[ ] The effectiveness of all critical business processes is being measured through key performance indicators.	[ ] The effectiveness of all critical business processes is being measured and monitored continuously through key performance indicators in order to delight external customers.
5.6 Continuous process improvement	Improving (DMAIC)	[ ] Hardly any attention is given to process improvement.	[ ] Some attention is given to improving processes when a crisis occurs.	[ ] There is a formal quality program that includes process improvement.	[ ] All critical business processes are improved using lean techniques.	[ ] All critical business processes are continuously and pro-actively improved using a project approach and TPS-Lean Six Sigma techniques according to the DMAIC process, reflecting both internal and external customer needs.

6. Knowledge management

	(Plan-Do-Act-Challenge)					
6.1 Self-knowledge	Improving (Plan-Do-Act-Challenge)	[ ] Employees pay little or no attention to self-knowledge.	[ ] Some employees are aware of the need to develop their self-knowledge and strive to capture what they know.	[ ] Some employees strive to develop their self-knowledge, based on the formulation and implementation of their Personal Ambition and through thinking and doing.	[ ] Employees strive to develop their self-knowledge and to get a better self-image, based on the formulation and implementation of their Personal Ambition and through thinking and doing.	[ ] Employees continuously strive to develop their self-knowledge and to get a better self-image, based on the formulation and implementation of their Personal Ambition and through thinking and doing.
6.2 Self-learning	Improving (Plan-Do-Act-Challenge)	[ ] Fear of reprisal limits employee risk taking and learning. Making mistakes is punished.	[ ] There are some obstacles to employee risk-taking, in taking on new challenges, taking action, making new informal contacts, gaining experience, and taking initiative. Making mistakes might be punished.	[ ] Employees are encouraged to challenge process, get more room to take on challenges, to take action, to make informal contacts, to gain experience, and to take initiatives.	[ ] Employees reflect on their personal balanced scorecard. They have the freedom to challenge existing processes, take on new challenges, taking action, making new informal contacts, gaining experience, and taking initiative.	[ ] Employees continuously reflect on their personal balanced scorecard according to the Plan-Do-Act-Challenge cycle. They have the freedom to challenge existing processes, take on new challenges, taking action, trying new things, making new informal contacts, gaining experience, and taking initiative, experimenting and taking risks. Making mistakes is valued as learning.

Table continues on next page.

Table 12.2. TPS-Lean Six Sigma Life Cycle Scan Matrix Continued

	TPS-Lean Six Sigma Cycle	Basic Performance	Improving Performance	Moderate Performance	Advanced Performance	Total Performance
6.3 Shared knowledge	Developing & learning	[ ] People don't know what knowledge exists in the organization and it is not clear who has what knowledge. Knowledge is not being shared with each other.	[ ] Only top management has knowledge that is important to the success of the organization, and this knowledge is sporadically being spread to employees.	[ ] We share knowledge with each other on an ad-hoc basis. Relevant knowledge is available to everyone.	[ ] Relevant knowledge is systematically being generated, cultivated, updated, mobilized and made applicable. Individuals, teams and departments share this knowledge with each other.	[ ] Knowledge within our organization is managed in such a way that we, spontaneously and intensively, share knowledge with each other and the knowledge flow is being managed effectively. The continuous and intensive generation, cultivation, updating, mobilization, application and sharing of relevant knowledge is a way of life in the organization.
6.4 Shared learning	Developing & learning	[ ] Shared learning is not recognized as having value in my organization.	[ ] The organization has recognized that shared learning is important but there is no formal program for it.	[ ] We are learning together and from each other from time to time. Our organization does not facilitate this process adequately.	[ ] We are learning together and from each other. Our organization facilitates this process in some divisions.	[ ] We are learning together and from each other spontaneously, and knowing one another thoroughly. Our organization facilitates this process in all their divisions and based on this, we continually transform ourselves.

6.5 Problem solving	Improving (DMAIC)	[ ] There is no formal recognition of problem solving in my organization.	[ ] Problem solving is sporadically done and on ad-hoc basis, even when there is a problem.	[ ] We solve common problems in a structured way only when there is a problem.	[ ] We solve common problems in a structured way, based on some problem solving tools and techniques.	[ ] Problem solving is a pro-active part of each person's daily work and a structured approach to creativity. We solve common problems routinely and systematically in multidisciplinary teams, based on consistent application of problem solving tools and techniques.
6.6 Knowledge infrastructure	Developing & learning	[ ] There is no formal knowledge infrastructure in my organization.	[ ] Our knowledge infrastructure is very poor. My colleagues and I retain documents and share them on request, but it is very hard to know what exists.	[ ] Our knowledge infrastructure is inadequate. The IT department has created a central document repository and keeps it updated on a regular basis.	[ ] We have a knowledge infrastructure of tools, systems and training. A knowledge manager has been appointed to create and manage the knowledge infrastructure and organize communities to put this into practice.	[ ] We have an effective knowledge infrastructure of tools, systems, continuous training, brainstorm sessions, and review meetings that supports and facilitates all facets of the organizational learning process and which continuously stimulates creativity, systems thinking, self-confidence, innovations, and a conducive learning environment.

Table continues on next page.

Table 12.2. TPS-Lean Six Sigma Life Cycle Scan Matrix Continued

	TPS-Lean Six Sigma Cycle	Basic Performance	Improving Performance	Moderate Performance	Advanced Performance	Total Performance
7. Team management						
7.1 Team balance	Developing & learning	[ ] There is no formal recognition of team balance.	[ ] My team recognizes that a range of competencies and personalities produces better higher team performance, but finds it difficult to put this into practice.	[ ] There is combined action between complementary competencies and personalities and a balance of learning styles on my team only.	[ ] There is combined action between complementary competencies and personalities and a balance of learning styles on some of our teams.	[ ] There is a balance between the team role and the job of individual team members and a balance of learning styles within and across all teams. Team members know what their own roles, capacity and capability are, as well as, those of other team members and accept these.

7.2 Team development	Developing & learning	[ ] My team behaves like a very loosely coupled work. Team members work independently.	[ ] My team behaves like a beginning group where there is a lack of unity and where team members spend more time talking instead of taking action.	[ ] My team behaves like an advanced group, where there is a limited feeling of unity and where team members spend more time doing work and less time on talking.	[ ] My team is a mature group. There is a feeling of unity inside my team and there's constructive collaboration.	[ ] My team is a mature group. Our team leader take serious notice of the team development phases—forming, storming, norming, and performing. He/she facilitates us by collaboratively setting goals challenging to all team members, looking for ways to enhance the team's ability to excel, developing an on-going assessment of the team, recognizing individual contributions, and developing members' full potential through coaching and feedback.

Table continues on next page.

Table 12.2. TPS-Lean Six Sigma Life Cycle Scan Matrix Continued

	TPS-Lean Six Sigma Cycle	Basic Performance	Improving Performance	Moderate Performance	Advanced Performance	Total Performance
7.3 Team learning	Developing & learning	[ ] Team learning is not recognized as having value in my team.	[ ] We recognize that team learning is important but there is no formal program for it.	[ ] Some team members share their PBSCs with each other.	[ ] Most team members share their PBSCs with each other and continuously seek out new learning opportunities through creative problem-solving vigorous and healthy conflict.	[ ] All team members share their PBSCs with each other spontaneously establishing the basis of team learning through trust and respect. We continuously seek out new learning opportunities through creative problem solving, vigorous and healthy conflict, taking risks, and forgiving and learning from mistakes.
7.4 Team diversity	Developing & Learning	[ ] Culturally diverse team members don't work well together.	[ ] Team members are becoming aware of diversity in members. Discussions are held occasionally on diversity issues.	[ ] Team members acknowledge each other's diversity. Respect governs interactions.	[ ] Team members acknowledge and accept each other's diversity. Respect and seeking to understand govern interactions.	[ ] Team members unconditionally acknowledge and accept each other's diversity. Respect and seeking to understand constantly govern our interactions. The team relies on diversity to be creative and continuously channels this into robust outcomes.

7.5 Team measurement and performance	Improving (DMAIC) Developing & learning	[ ] The effectiveness of my team is not being measured. Team members don't feel responsible for the team results.	[ ] The effectiveness of my team is sporadically being measured. Most team members don't feel responsible for the team results.	[ ] The effectiveness of my team is being measured on an ad-hoc basis. Team results sometimes stay behind compared to the sum of individual results. Some team members don't feel responsible for the team results.	[ ] The effectiveness of my team is being measured frequently. Most team members feel responsible for the team results.	[ ] The effectiveness of my team is constantly being measured and evaluated, in order to continuously improve team performance. The team results are a combined effort of all team members and are more important than individual results. All team members feel responsible for the team results and continuously understand progress towards goals.
7.6 Team communication	Developing & learning	[ ] There is no open communication among my team members. My team doesn't ensure communication on the team's ambition and progress to stakeholders.	[ ] There is communication among my team members but it is not open. My team ensures communication on the team's ambition and progress to some team member only.	[ ] There is open communication among some of my team members. My team ensures communication on the team's ambition and progress to team member only.	[ ] There is open communication among most of my team members. My team ensures communication on the team's ambition and progress to stakeholders.	[ ] There is open communication among my team members. My team ensures adequate communication on the team's ambition and progress to all stakeholders. Feedback from stakeholders is constantly sought and acted upon to improve contribution and enrich learning.

Table continues on next page.

Table 12.2. TPS-Lean Six Sigma Life Cycle Scan Matrix Continued

	TPS-Lean Six Sigma Cycle	Basic Performance	Improving Performance	Moderate Performance	Advanced Performance	Total Performance
8. Change management						
8.1 Change infrastructure	Improving (DMAIC) Developing & learning	[ ] Employees make changes in their own way or not at all. Changes are being avoided.	[ ] Organizational changes are being dealt with in an ad-hoc manner.	[ ] Organizational changes are being dealt with in a structured manner and may, or may not, be visible to affected employees.	[ ] Organizational changes are systematically being dealt with in a structured manner, based on improvement teams only and visible to most of the affected employees.	[ ] Organizational changes are integrally and systematically being dealt with in a structured manner, based on a steering group, project group, sponsorship and improvement teams, which are known to all affected employees.
8.2 Change circumstances	Improving (DMAIC) Developing & learning	[ ] Employees are closed to change. They are satisfied with the status quo.	[ ] Employees are beginning to recognize the need for change.	[ ] In some pockets employees are fairly open to change. They accept the fact that they, too, must change.	[ ] Many of the employees are open to and embraces change. They accept the fact that they, too, must change.	[ ] Employees are open to and embrace change. It is regarded as a challenge. They exhibit an attitude of mutual trust, commitment, dedication, willingness to learn, and inner involvement, realizing that change begins with them.

		Level 1	Level 2	Level 3	Level 4	Level 5
8.3 Managing change	Improving (DMAIC) Developing & learning	[ ] There is a lot of opposition to change. There is no way to deal with this opposition effectively.	[ ] Many employees are skeptical about change and resist. Most departments have no way to deal with this opposition.	[ ] Resistance to change is considered by the appropriate team and steps are taken to mitigate the resistance.	[ ] Resistance to change is recognized and is discussed and addressed by the appropriate team with the employee(s) who may oppose the change.	[ ] Resistance to change is recognized and openly discussed with all stakeholders and addressed by executives. The different phases in the responses of employees are recognized early and moved through to the phase of acceptance.
8.4 Change behavior	Improving (DMAIC) Developing & learning	[ ] There's a climate of fear and distrust inside the whole organization.	[ ] There's a climate of fear and distrust inside certain departments in the organization.	[ ] Fear and distrust are not sufficiently dispelled from the organization.	[ ] Fear and distrust are sufficiently dispelled from the organization.	[ ] Fear and distrust are completely dispelled from the organization.
8.5 Implementing change	Improving (DMAIC) Developing & learning	[ ] Key persons are not involved in the decision-making about change. Information about the what, why, how and the consequences of change are being held back. Employees don't know what managers know.	[ ] Certain key persons are sporadically involved in the decision-making about change. Managers communicate on ad hoc basis, briefly, and unclear about the what, why, how and the consequences of change.	[ ] Certain key persons are frequently involved in the decision-making about change. The what, why, how and the consequences of change are being communicated by managers.	[ ] All key persons are involved in the decision-making about change. The what, why, how and the consequences of change are consistently and decisively being communicated by executives to all key persons.	[ ] All key persons are involved as change leaders throughout the organization. Executives, managers and all employees are committed to supporting change. The what, why, how and the consequences of change are constantly, honestly, timely, consistently, decisively and face-to-face being communicated by executives to all stakeholders.

Table continues on next page.

Table 12.2. TPS-Lean Six Sigma Life Cycle Scan Matrix Continued

	TPS-Lean Six Sigma Cycle	Basic Performance	Improving Performance	Moderate Performance	Advanced Performance	Total Performance
8.6 Change sustainability	Improving (Plan-Do-Act-Challenge) Developing & learning	[ ] Employees are not being encouraged to change themselves. There is no formal structure for this.	[ ] Employees are sporadically being encouraged to change themselves.	[ ] Employees are frequently being encouraged to change themselves first.	[ ] Employees are continuously being coached to change themselves according to their PBSC and the PDAC-cycle.	[ ] Employees accept personal responsibility for changing themselves according to their PBSC and the PDAC-cycle. This forms the starting point for durable organizational change.

EPILOGUE

Quality is not an act. It is a habit.

—Aristotle 384 BC–322 BC, Greek philosopher and scientist, student of
Plato, and teacher of Alexander the Great

*The man who will use his skill and constructive imagination to see how much he can
give for a dollar, instead of how little he can give for a dollar, is bound to succeed.*

—Henry Ford

By way of this book, we are launching a revolutionary, holistic concept
called TPS-Lean Six Sigma which actively has human capital embedded
in Lean Six Sigma in a manner that not only stimulates commitment,
integrity, work-life balance, passion, enjoyment at work, and employee
engagement but also stimulates individual and team learning in order to
develop a motivated workforce and sustainable performance improvement and quality enhancement for the organization. We want to provide
project team members with some new tools, tested in practice, so that they
can master the tools themselves, gain more understanding for self-
responsibility, create a stable basis for their growth, and execute TPS-Lean
Six Sigma projects successfully.

Also, we want Executives and project leaders/Champions/Master Black
Belts to understand that they can improve the quality of life of their cus-

*TPS-Lean Six Sigma: Linking Human Capital to Lean Six Sigma: A New Blueprint for
Creating High Performance Companies,* pp. 337–345
Copyright © 2007 by Information Age Publishing
All rights of reproduction in any form reserved.

337

tomers and make them happy, if they improve the quality of life of their coworkers/project members and make them happy first. We want them to understand that a healthy family situation of the coworkers/team members has an important impact on their functioning at work and they should not ignore this fact. They can encourage their team members/ employees to systematically use their Personal Balanced Scorecard within their family and to help improve their home situation on the basis of the Plan-Do-Act-Challenge cycle. With this book, we want to drive fear out of organizations and to create a way of life within organizations, which is characterized by freedom, trust, enjoyment, motivation, self-awareness, ethical behavior, and learning, so that project team members/employees and organizations can deliver sustainable top performance and enhance their value. Our aim with this new revolutionary TPS-Lean Six Sigma^{TM} concept is to realize the benefit of human capital, and understand that a motivated workforce is like turbo fuel for their company engine, and that it is possible for both company and employee to realize their goals and ambitions concurrently.

We believe this book differs in a number of essential points from most other books in the field. It is up to you, the reader, to judge whether this is true. We gladly welcome any reactions and suggestions from you regarding this book. Please send your feedback by e-mail to h.rampersad@TPS-LeanSixSigma.com   or   a.el-homsi@TPS-LeanSixSigma.com.   The development of the TPS-Lean Six Sigma concept and the writing of this book has been a continuous learning process. If you want to keep track of the new developments in this field, visit our Web site: www.TPS-LeanSixSigma.com. TPS-Lean Six Sigma^{TM} is a worldwide registered trademark. We are devoted to helping individuals and organizations become more successful. We provide integrated and sustainable professional services (certification, coaching, consulting, and training) based on the proven TPS-Lean Six Sigma^{TM} principles. The results are individual and organizational effectiveness and a related unique competitive advantage. For more information about the TPS-Lean Six Sigma concept, our certification programs, our TPS-Lean Six Sigma Project BSC software, our TPS-Lean Six Sigma Personal BSC software, or if you are interested in a customized pocketsize TPS-Lean Six Sigma booklet for your company, please write to one of our international offices closest to you;

TPS-Lean Six Sigma LLC

Linking Human Capital
to Lean-Six Sigma

United States
TPS-Lean Six Sigma Inc. (New York)
144 Village Landing, #303
Fairport, NY 14450
Voice: 585-750-8203
Fax: 585-425-8931
E-mail: info@TPS-LeanSixSigma.com
Web: www.TPS-LeanSixSigma.com

TPS-Lean Six Sigma Inc. (Florida)
P.O. Box 601564
North Miami Beach
Florida 33160
Phone: 786-537-7580
Fax: 714-464-4498
E-mail: info@TPS-LeanSixSigma.com
Web: www.TPS-LeanSixSigma.com

Caribbean
TPS Solutions Caribbean
L.G. Smith Boulevard 162,
Oranjestad. Aruba
Phone: +297-588-7296/+297-594-0005
Fax: +297-588-7295
info@tps-solution-caribbean.com
www.tps-solution-caribbean.com

TPS-Lean Six Sigma LLC

Linking Human Capital to
Lean-Six Sigma

Impacto Consultores, Inc.
Global Partner of TPS, International, Inc.
638 Aldebarán St.
Banco Desarrollo Económico Bldg.
Suite HQ-12B
San Juan, Puerto Rico 00920
Tel. (787) 775-0244
Fax (787) 783-9011
info@impactoconsultores.com
www.impactoconsultores.com

Canada
TPS-Lean Six Sigma Canada
509 Commissioners Rd. W.
Suite 360
London, Ontario, Canada N6J-1Y5
info@TPS-LeanSixSigma.com
www.TPS-LeanSixSigma.com

Europe
TPS Consulting Netherlands
Riet Blom-Mouritsstraat 27
3066 GL Rotterdam
Netherlands
Tel: +31645584607
Fax: +17144644498
info@total-performance-scorecard.com
www.Total-Performance-Scorecard.com

Middle East
VTC-TPSI Middle East
Saad Bin Abdurrahman St
Riyadh
P.O. Box 50385
Riyadh 11523, Saudi Arabia
Telephone: 96612411125
Fax: 96612709919
vtc.center@yahoo.com

Golden Trust Business Consultancy
P.O. Box 33388, Isa Town
Bahrain
Phone: +973-17532771/+973-39657666
Fax: +973-17532773
lmutlaq@gtconsultancy.net

Step-Up Consultancy and Training
Iman El Kaffass, PhD.
100 West Golf, New Cairo, Egypt
Cell Phone: (2-010)200-1227
Phone: (202)797-5532
Fax: (202)795-7565
E-mail: Kaffass@aucegypt.edu

Asia
Kairos International Corp.
Jl. Mojo Klanggru Kidul Block G - No 22 , Surabaya - 60285
Indonesia
Phone/Fax: 031-5910223 / 081 330 505161
Oongko_djaja@yahoo.com.sg

PT Panglima Performa Maksima
Jakarta, Indonesia
Phone: +62-8881868587
edirghantara@panglimapm.co.id

TPS-Asia
4th Floor Seoul Finance Center
84 Taepyengno 1-ga, Jung-gu,
Seoul, South Korea, 100-768
Tel: 82.2.752.8032
Fax: 82.2.752.8041
jungjs@wesleyquest.com

Russia
TPS Russia
454080, Chelyabinsk
Lenin Ave, 76
Russia
Phone:+73512689684/+791289
gor@if.susu.ac.ru
www.tps-russia.ru

South and Central America
TPS - PERFORMANCE DO BRASIL
Av. Brig. Faria Lima 1931, 10 andar
01451-917 - São Paulo - SP - Brasil
Tel: 55-11-3816-3144
Fax: 55-11-3816-9621
jorge@ml.com.br
www.tpsbrasil.com.br

THUOPER
Calle 90 N. 11A - 34 of. 101
Bogotá - Colombia
Phone: 571 - 6100625
jcrthuoper@cable.net.co
www.thuoper.com

Our Company Brand

Our Mission
　We are devoted to serve organizations to achieve their full potential
and to link human capital to Lean Six Sigma.

Our Vision

- To be the best at helping organizations to realize their dreams. We will accomplish our mission by:
- Achieving excellent financial results through the successful introduction of our unique TPS-Lean Six Sigma concept.
- Providing excellence in performance and quality management for our customers and offer them opportunities to realize sustainable competitive advantage.
- Creating organizations where human spirit thrives and help build organizations which model the best practices in business ethics, quality, and performance.
- Fostering a mutually supportive, inspiring, and learning environment within our organization and working with talented people who care for the needs of the society.

Our Core Values

We are guided by the following core values:

Integrity: We keep commitments, deliver at al time the promised quality, and are responsible and accountable for our results.
Passion: We thoroughly enjoy our work and are passionate in everything we do.
Professionalism: We foster personal leadership, strive for perfection and innovate wisely and continuously.
Excellence: Excellence is the hallmark in all of our business associations with suppliers, independent consultants and most importantly our clients.

Our People

TPS-Lean Six Sigma is a group of experts from both academia and industry with advanced degrees and certifications as Six Sigma Black Belts and Master Black Belts. Our talents come from careers at companies including Becton Dickinson, Corning, DuPont, Eaton Corp, Eastman Kodak, Ford, General Electric, General Motors, Harris RF, Heidelberg, Honda, Panasonic Consumer Electronics, Pepsi, Rockwell Automation, Xerox Corporation, Philips Electronics.

Our Core Activities

(A) Consulting

- Advising and implementation of solutions for complex management issues on the basis of our unique TPS-Lean Six Sigma concept. Sustainable organizational change plays here a central role.
- Executing TPS-Lean Six Sigma Projects; Implementing TPS-Lean Six Sigma.

TPS-Lean Six Sigma Implementation Steps

1. Assessment of the organization based on the TPS-Lean Six Sigma Life Cycle Scan—understand gaps and to determine "areas of opportunities."
2. Developing/fine tuning the Organizational Balanced Scorecard on strategic level.
3. Cascading/deploying the company BSC to lower levels in the organization.
4. Identifying TPS-Lean Six Sigma projects based on the company BSC.
5. Establishing the project organization for each selected project.
6. Coaching Executives, Champions and Master Black Belts to build their Personal Balanced Scorecard and to implement this successfully based on the PDAC cycle.
7. Blending of their personal ambition with the shared company and project ambition to create commitment and engagement.
8. Providing tailor made TPS-Lean Six Sigma training and certification programs to the project members: Executive "Platinum Belt," Champion, Master Black Belt, Black Belt, and Green Belt Certification Programs.
9. Coaching project team members to build their Personal Balanced Scorecard and to implement this successfully based on the PDAC cycle.
10. Blending of their personal ambition with the shared company and project ambition to create commitment and engagement.
11. Training Executives, Champions, Master Black Belts, Black Belts, and Green Belts to coach their employees/project team members based on the TPS-LSS Coaching framework.
12. Formulating and executing the Project Balanced Scorecard of each identified TPS-LSS project.

13. Monitoring the project execution continuously with the help of the TPS-LSS project BSC software.

14. Linking the Company BSCs, Project BSCs and Personal BSCs to effective Talent Management (appraisal system); Integrate this in the current HR system.

15. Technical project support.

(B) Training

- TPS-Lean Six Sigma "Belt" training; we offer five types of "Belt" training programs; Executive, Champion, Master Black Belt, Black Belt, and Green Belt. Each of the belts programs has their own advantages and targeted participants.
- Public and in-house training and workshops.

(C) Coaching

We coach executives, managers, "Belts," and consultants to develop their personal leadership and effectiveness. We help them to be more proactive, more self-conscious, action orientated and smarter. This program focuses on leaders and consultants who would like to develop their personal leadership and effectiveness; improve employee performance; enhance employee engagement; empower their employees and team members; create trust and a real learning organization; increase employee's self-responsibility and a happy work force; and ultimately, enhance sustainable organizational and project effectiveness.

(D) Tailor Made TPS-Lean Six Sigma Certification Programs:

- Executive "Platinum Belt" Certification Program.
- Champion Certification Program.
- Master Black Belt Certification Program.
- Black Belt Certification Program.
- Green Belt Certification Program.
- TPS-Lean Six Sigma Consultant Certification; This entails a program through which senior consultants can apply to receive the designation of Certified TPS-Lean Six Sigma Consultant. It is based on standards and criteria to distinguish practitioners who have proven they can produce results through the holistic TPS-Lean Six Sigma process.
- TPS-Lean Six Sigma Coaching Certification; This program is based on our unique Ten-Phase PBSC coaching framework, which focuses

on personal effectiveness and growth in life. We certify Executives, managers, "Belts" and consultants to coach others successfully based on the PBSC system. Our related PBSC coach training program is certified by the International Coaching Federation (ICF) for Continuing Coach Education credits.

- TPS-Lean Six Sigma Company Certification.

(E) Implementing TPS-Lean Six Sigma Project BSCsoft and TPS-Lean Six Sigma Personal BSCsoft.

APPENDIX

Appendix A summarizes some of the TPS-Lean Six Sigma tools referred to in the improving phase of the TPS-Lean Six Sigma Life Cycle (see Figure 4.1) throughout the book. Definitions, methods, and applications of each of these tools are presented for each of the define, measure, analyze, improve, and control (DMAIC) model introduced in chapter 3 and 4. Table A.1 summarized these tools. Later in this Appendix, we will cover an overview of Minitab. Minitab is a statistical data analysis software used in our training and some of the tools listed below. We will also cover an overview of TPS-Lean Six Sigma Personal BSCsoft, an interactive software system that will assist you with the successful formulation and implementation of your Project Balanced Scorecard (Project BSC), and finally, TPS-Lean Six Sigma Personal BSCsoft, an interactive software system that will assist you with the formulation and implementation of your Personal Balanced Scorecard (PBSC). Appendix B covers extra tools for Effective Interpersonal Communication and for team evaluation. Appendix C describes the TPS-Lean Six Sigma Team Evaluation which can be used to enhance the performance of TPS-Lean Six Sigma meetings. Appendix D describes the TPS-Lean Six Sigma Knowledge Management Quick Scan to be used to increase the learning ability of organizations.

Table A.1.   Summary of TPS-Lean Six Sigma Tools

Phase	Tools
Define	TPS-Lean Six Sigma Life Cycle Scan, covered in chapter 12
	Quality Function Deployment (QFD), covered in chapter 5
	Brainstorming
	Kano Model, covered in chapter 7
	Benchmarking
	SIPOC
	Flowchart
Measure	Value Stream Map
	Force Field Analysis
	Pareto-diagram
	Tree diagram
	Measurement System Analysis (MSA)
	Process Capability Studies
	Check sheet
	Affinity diagram
Analyse	Why-Why Diagram
	Seven W and IS/IS-not Questions
	Hypothesis Testing
	Regression Analysis
	Process Failure Mode and Effect Analysis
	Histogram
	Scatter diagram
	Line graph
Improve	Design of Experiments (DOE)
Control	Run chart
	Control chart

A.1 TPS-LEAN SIX SIGMA TOOLS—DEFINE PHASE

TPS-Lean Six Sigma Life Cycle Scan

The TPS-Lean Six Sigma Life Cycle Scan is a performance excellence model that will help both public and private sector organizations to increase individual and organizational quality and performance in the direction of Total Performance. The TPS-Lean Six Sigma Life Cycle is covered in detail in chapter 12.

Quality Function Deployment (QFD)

Quality Function Deployment is a tool that helps design engineers translate customer needs and wants into engineering metrics. QFD is covered in detail in chapter 5.

Brainstorming

What is it?

Brainstorming encompasses the systematic and structured generation of possible ideas, on the basis of the creative thinking of a group of people.

Four game rules:

1. Criticism is prohibited.

The participants of a brainstorming session should try not to think of usefulness, importance, feasibility and relevance, and may certainly not comment on these. Therefore, the review of ideas has to be postponed. This rule must not only lead to many but also to unexpected associations. Strictly upholding of this rule is also essential to prevent team members from feeling attacked.

2. Generate ideas freely.

The purpose is for team members to express each idea. Each idea that surfaces has to be shared without fear for criticism. Therefore, in a brainstorming session, a sphere has to be created that gives team members a feeling of security and freedom.

3. Build upon ideas of others.

The team members have to generate ideas by building on ideas of others. One should look for combinations and improvements of ideas.

4. Try to generate as many ideas as possible.

In this case, quantity is more important than quality. The more ideas, the greater the chance of good solutions. The idea behind this is that quantity leads to quality.

When do you use it?

This technique can be used in all phases of the problem-solving discipline to obtain a good idea of problems, causes, results, and solutions.

The goal of brainstorming is to generate as many ideas as it takes to solve a problem.

How do you use it?

Steps in the brainstorming process:

Preparation:

1. Formulate the problem accurately. Complex problems should be divided into subproblems if needed.
2. Form a group of five to eight members. Experts from various disciplines with the same status.
3. Select a team leader who coaches, steers, helps, and guides.
4. Some time before the session, send a note to the team members with the formulation of the problem and some background information.

The formulation of the problem has to be clear to everyone, just like the delimitation of the problem. Defining the problem will often take longer than the brainstorming session itself and should end in a formulation of the problem in the form of a question, such as: *How can we improve the efficiency of the purchase process? How can we shorten the throughput time of the production process?*

Execution of the Brainstorming Process:

1. Problem formulation. Write the formulation of the problem and the four game rules on a blackboard or flip-over in such a way that it is visible for everyone. Bring the problem up for discussion once again.
2. Generate and write ideas down. Ask the team members to generate as many ideas as possible and let them raise their hands if they want to share an idea. If necessary, allow them to share their ideas by turn. Every member should be given the same opportunity to share ideas in the group (as concrete and concise as possible). These ideas have to be written down immediately on a flip chart or blackboard, in clear sight of all team members. The facilitator should make sure that every member gets a chance to speak. It is not allowed to criticize, discuss or judge ideas. Nobody should be allowed to dominate. While writing down ideas, they should not be

amended. Respect for each other's ideas is necessary. Privacy should be guaranteed in such a way that every member could openly share his/her ideas. Stimulate building on ideas of others. Therefore, give preference to members who have an idea that builds upon an already mentioned idea. Continue this process until everyone has "passed." Often, this process lasts up to 45 minutes.

3. Cluster several similar ideas.

4. Establish selection criteria, for example, feasibility, costs, and relevance.

5. Appoint a group for each cluster of ideas to evaluate the ideas after ending the brainstorming session. Let the groups organize separate follow-up meetings to eliminate unusable ideas themselves on the basis of the selection criteria.

6. Let separate teams work out the selected ideas and report this to management.

Benchmarking

What is it?
Benchmarking is the systematic and continuous process of determining what the best performances and underlying skills of leading organizations are in their strive for excellence, and based on this, stimulate the organization's own strive for excellent performances at all organizational levels (Camp, 1995). It is a strategy to stimulate changes and optimize performances.

When do you use it?
Benchmarking is mostly used to compare processes and performances against those of recognized leaders. Based on this, the performance gap between the organization and the best competitor is evaluated. Organizational processes usually used for benchmarking are: marketing, sales, purchasing, technology development, product development, and logistics. Depending on the chosen subject, several types of benchmarking can be identified: *Internal, competitive, process, and strategic benchmarking.*

Internal Benchmarking

Internal benchmarking involves a comparison of internal units (activities and processes) within the own company. This is usually of interest to large organizations where it is determined in how far other departments and divisions execute similar activities within their own department more efficiently and effectively.

Competitive Benchmarking

During competitive benchmarking, a comparison is made with direct competitors. Operations processes of these competitors are measured and compared against its own situation. Based on what is done by the competitor and what is lacking within the own organization, the own processes can be adjusted to improve efficiency, and thus produce a better and cheaper product. For example; a software producer who wants to improve his competitive position can try to figure out what Microsoft has done to become the market leader.

Process Benchmarking

Process benchmarking involves a search for the best in class of a certain process, regardless if it is a competitor or not and in which industrial branch it is applicable. In this way, for example, the logistical activities of a chemical company can be compared with an electronics company with an excellent logistical process.

Strategic Benchmarking

Strategic benchmarking is used to obtain sweeping breakthroughs in the areas of productivity and distinctive capacity, in order to strengthen its competitive position. This implies big leaps, which are hard to realize on your own. This type of benchmarking can support the strategic planning process by determining the relative competitive position of all business activities and accordingly, suggest the best course to follow. This form of benchmarking can be done in several ways, for example by:

- Comparing your own strategy and financial performance against those of the competitors.
- Determining from the strengths and weaknesses of the competitors in which areas your organization can outdo these competitors, and which improvements are best contributed to its own core competencies.

How do you use it?

Steps for executing the benchmark process (Figure A.1):

1. Determine what should be benchmarked. During this stage, it is determined which functions, tasks, processes, or activities within the own organization will be subjected to benchmarking. Based on the critical success factors (factors that are of decisive importance to the organization) one or more processes will be selected for benchmarking. Chapter 5 shows how this can be done. Appoint a team that will map these processes in details: identify process stages and determine the process flow, the procedure for each process stage, relevant performance indicators, inputs and outputs of the process, and customer requirements. In this stage, the project goals will also be formulated, the data to be collected will be determined, and a tentative list of questions will be prepared.

2. Identify the benchmark partners. Against whom should benchmarking be done? Important criteria for the selection of benchmark partners are for instance: the partners should be outstanding (best in class) regarding the benchmark subject, competitiveness of activities, availability of reliable information about the partners. Identifying benchmark partners requires consultation of several information sources such as databases, professional magazines,

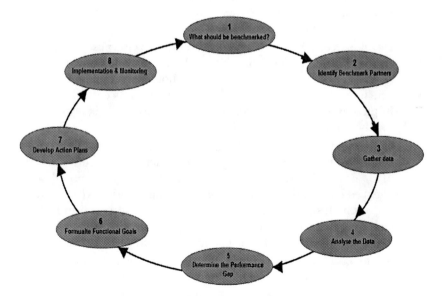

Figure A.1. The Benchmark Process.

newspapers, bank reports, annual reports of competitors, seminars, consultancy bureaus, universities, and so forth. In addition,
interviews with customers, suppliers, employees, and bankers can
be a valuable contribution.

3. Gather data. Data about the process performances of partners are
gathered based on interviews, surveys, and consultation of contacts
and technical magazines. The process and underlying working
methods of partners are examined thoroughly, performance indicators are measured and qualitative and quantitative data are gathered.

4. Analyze the data.

5. Determine the gap between the performance level of the organization and that of its benchmark partner. After the data is gathered,
measured, and analyzed, these will be compared to the data of the
own organization. Based on this, the current performance gap
between the own organization and that of the benchmark partner
is determined. The differences in underlying working methods
and the causes of the differences in performance will also be documented. The main question is: Why are the efficiency and effectiveness of the own process lagging behind that of the best in class?

6. Formulate functional goals. Based on the results of the bench-
mark-study, new functional goals will be formulated to close the
performance gap. The benchmark results should also be integrated into the company's policy to facilitate the implementation
of the improvement possibilities.

7. Develop action plans. The goals should now be transformed into
concrete action plans. These plans should provide an explanation
about the following questions: When should which action with
which goal is implemented? How can changes successfully be
implemented? Who does what? In which way? Who is responsible
for the implementation of the different actions?

8. Implement specific actions and monitor the progress. This step
relates to the execution of improvement actions and introduction
of changes. The continuation of the implementation should be
checked constantly for successful execution, verified whether the
actions are executed as planned, whether the process is in fact
changing (with which results), and if the benchmark goals are
being met. Based on this, possible adjustments will be made.

9. Start again. Benchmarking is not a one-time activity, but a process
of continuous improvement. There are always other and better
improvement methods. Competition is not standing idle, in due
time new best practices are developed.

SIPOC

What is it?

SIPOC stands for Supplier-Input-Process-Output-Customer. It is mapping diagram that gives a snapshot of process flow. It helps specify boundaries and understand the scope of the process. It also help identifies relationships between suppliers, inputs and the process and determine key customers (internal and external).

When do you use it?

The purpose of SIPOC analysis is to provide a quick perspective of process steps in conjunction with key suppliers, inputs, outputs, and customers. It is used early in the define phase to help specify the project scope.

How do you use it?

The followings are the steps to use the SIPOC:

1. Start with mapping the process.
2. Identify the outputs of this process.
3. Identify the customers that will receive the outputs of this process.
4. Identify the inputs that are required for the process.
5. Identify the suppliers of the inputs that are required by the process.

Example

Figure A.2 shows an example of SIPOC for a product development test.

Flowchart

What is it?

A flowchart clearly shows the steps of a process, by using standard symbols. It allows you to examine and understand relationships in a process.

When do you use it?

A flowchart is used to document and analyze the connection and sequence of events in a process. It is used to create an integrated understanding of the activities that are performed and the relationship between the different process steps.

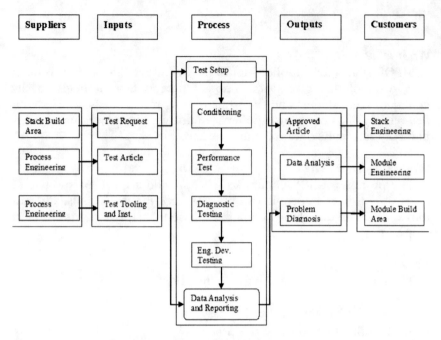

Figure A.2.   SIPOC for a product development test.

How do you use it?

Steps for drafting a flowchart:

1. Decide which process should be mapped.
2. Clearly define the borders of this process.
3. Define the start and end of the process.
4. Define the steps in the process (subactivities); determine the sequence of the activities, the decisions to be made, and the inputs and outputs of the activities.
5. Map the process using standard symbols (see Figure A.3). Make sure that this indicates the sequence of the activities, using arrows and eventual feedback loops.
6. Compare the flowchart with the actual process.
7. Date the flowchart for future reference and use.

Example

Figure A.4 illustrates a flowchart of the process "answering the telephone."

A.2 TPS-LEAN SIX SIGMA TOOLS—MEASURE PHASE

Value Stream Map

What is it?

It is a pictorial presentation of a product's production path from beginning to end.

When do you use it?

It is used in the measure phase to help you to see and understand the flow of material and information as a product makes its way through the value stream. More importantly it helps you see the source of waste.

Symbol	Explanation	Inscriptions, clarifications
	Opening or closing symbol of a diagram	"Initial" or "final"
	Process function; action which causes change in the form composition, physical properties or place of a product	An infinitive (mix, cut off) that indicates what happens, if necessary with explanation (Eg. sanding pulverization, the name of the device used).
	Indicates that a decision must be made at this point as to what must happen based on the observed facts	(Eg. t = 230 ℃?)
	Administrative data; specifications; registration of data on forms, in data files, log books, etc.	Name of the form, verification card, etc.
	Here, the task is indicated, Eg. "adjust pace", "block product", "stop process", etc.	Command (Eg. check temperature)
	Here, the variables which can be observed with a process or products are stated and assessed in relation to specified values	Variables (Eg. end concentration)
	Input or output; start and end product or output of a process	A noun (if necessary, plus a distinctive adjective. Eg. unpolished axles)
	Connector to another process on another sheet	A number

Figure A.3. Standard symbols used for drafting flowcharts (Akzo Nobel, 1994)

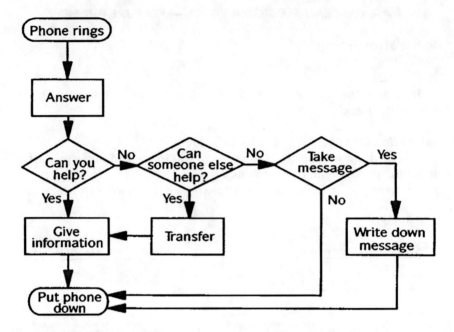

Figure A.4.   Flowchart of the Process "Answering the Telephone."

How do you use it?

Follow a product's production path from customer to supplier, and carefully draw a visual representation of every process in the material and information flow.

Example

Figure 3.3 shows an example of value stream map.

FORCE FIELD ANALYSIS

What is it?

Force field analysis is a management technique for diagnosing situations. In any situation there are both driving and restraining forces. Driving forces affecting a situation that are pushing in a particular direction. Pressure from a supervisor, incentive earnings, and competition may be examples of driving forces. Restraining forces decrease the driving forces. Apathy and hostility may be examples of restraining forces against change. The analysis involves looking at which driving forces may be strengthened and which restraining forces may be eliminated or counter-acted.

When do you use it?

Force field analysis is useful when looking at the variables involved in determining effectiveness of a change program. It is a useful technique for looking at all the forces for and against a change. By executing the analysis you can plan to strengthen the forces supporting a decision, and reduce the impact of opposition to it. Force Field Analysis is a useful technique for looking at all the forces for and against change. It helps you to weigh the importance of these forces and decide whether a plan is worth implementing.

How do you use it?

1. To carry out a force field analysis, follow these steps (Manktelow, 2003): List all forces for change in one column, and all forces against change in another column.
2. Assign a score to each force, from 1 (weak) to 5 (strong).
3. Draw a diagram showing the forces for and against change.

Example

Imagine that you are a manager deciding whether to install new manufacturing equipment in your factory. You might draw up a force field analysis like the one in Figure A.5. Based on these results, you might suggest the following changes to the initial plan (Manktelow, 2003):

- By training staff (increase cost by 1) you could eliminate fear of technology (reduce fear by 2)
- It would be useful to show staff that change is necessary for business survival (new force in favor, +2)
- Staff could be shown that new machines would introduce variety and interest to their jobs (new force, +1)
- You could raise wages to reflect new productivity (cost +1, loss of overtime -2)
4. Slightly different machines with filters to eliminate pollution could be installed (environmental impact -1)

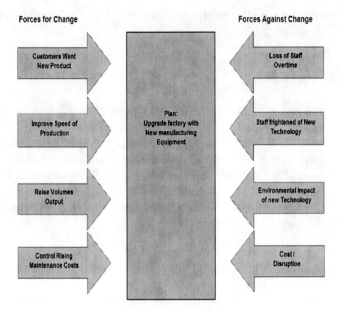

Figure A.5.   Force Field Analysis Example (Manktelow, 2003).

These changes would swing the balance from 11:10 (against the plan), to 8:13 (in favor of the plan).

PARETO-DIAGRAM

What is it?

A Pareto-diagram is a graphical tool to gain insight into the most important causes of a problem. It is a bar chart in which the data are arranged in descending order of their importance; the diagram displays the relative contribution of each item to the total effect in decreasing order. Based on this, the most important problems can be distinguished from the less important ones and the greatest improvement can be realized with the least effort. The diagram is based on the Pareto-principle, which states that just a few of the defects account for most of the effects. This pattern is called the 80/20-rule and is applicable to all sorts of situations; thus, it is likely that only 20% of your equipment problems account for 80% of the downtime. The issue here is that of many problems, only a limited number are essential and should be solved immediately. The rest can be solved later. A Pareto-diagram clearly indicates which problems belong to this small number. Interpretation of the diagram should be done with care, because the most frequent occurring problems are usually not the most expensive ones.

When do you use it?

A Pareto-diagram is used to systematically organize collected data. Based on this, the most important causes of a problem and priorities can be identified. It aids the decision-making process because it puts the most critical issues into an easily understood framework.

How do you use it?

Steps for drafting a Pareto-diagram:

1. Formulate the problem.
2. Select the time-period during which an inventory of its causes should be made.
3. Design a check sheet for registering the gathered data.
4. Make an inventory of the causes. Count the number of times each cause occurs and write it down on the check sheet.
5. Calculate the total.
6. Rank the causes in decreasing order. If necessary, the category "others" can be used here.
7. Draw a bar chart with two vertical axes. Along the left vertical axis, mark the measured values for each cause, starting from zero till the total number of causes. The right vertical axis should have the same height and should go from 0 to 100%. This axis displays the cumulative percentages. List the different kinds of causes along the horizontal axis, from left to right in decreasing order of frequency or costs.
8. Draw a bar above each item whose height represents the number for that cause.
9. Construct the cumulative frequency line. First draw the cumulative bars by adding the number of each cause from left to right. Then draw a cumulative curved line from zero till the 100% level on the right vertical axis, by connecting the top right hand corner of the bars with each other.

10.   Draw a horizontal line from 80% (on the right vertical axis) to the left till the point of intersection with the cumulative line, and then draw a vertical line from this intersection downwards till the horizontal axis. Left from this intersection point, 20% of the causes are located (the most essential bottlenecks) causing 80% of the damages. Thus, causes which require immediate attention.

Example

The manager of a hotel is concerned about the amount of complaints he receives from customers. That's why he has decided to study the most important problems, in order to take the right measures. With the help of his employees, he drafts a check sheet with all known problems for each separate department. During the following four weeks, the employees register the complaints. They use the check sheets shown in Table A.2 (PA Consulting, 1991). The corresponding Pareto-diagram is shown in Figure A.6. During the period studied, 40 complaints were registered. From the Pareto-diagram, it appears that ample 80% of the complaints relate to only 5 of the 23 possible causes. These are, ranked according to priorities: "slow service in the restaurant," "coffee arrives too late in the conference room," "bedrooms are not clean," and "restaurant personnel are impolite," "noisy rooms." These complaints should thus be solved first.

Table A.2.   Data Sheets Collection

Restaurant			Conference room	
Types of complaints	Number of complaints			
Cold food				
Slow service	‖‖‖ ‖‖‖		Types of complaints	Number of complaints
Expensive			Defective equipment	
Cork parts in the wine			Coffee too late	‖‖‖ ‖‖‖
Overcooked food			Too few provisions	
Impolite personnel	‖‖‖‖		Too cold	│
			Impolite personnel	│
Recreation center			Bedrooms	
			Types of complaints	Number of complaints
Types of complaints	Number of complaints		Beds not made	
Hygiene			Too cold	
Unavailable facilities	‖		Not clean	‖‖‖ │
Cold swimming water			TV's not working	
Too crowded			No towels	│
Defective equipment			Noisy	‖‖‖‖
Impolite personnel	│			

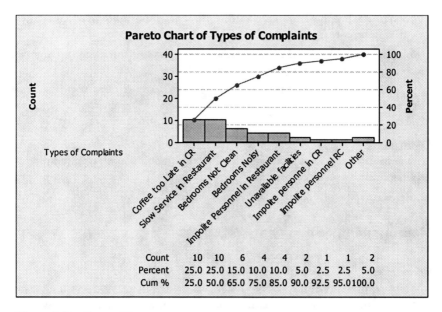

Figure A.6.   Pareto-Diagram.

Tree Diagram

What is it?

A tree diagram systematically breaks down a topic into its component elements. It shows the logical and sequential links between these elements.

When do you use it?

A tree diagram is used to show the relationships between a topic and its component elements.

How do you use it?

Steps for drafting a tree diagram (NEN-ISO, 9004-4, 1993):

1. Clearly and simply state the topic to be studied.
2. Define the major categories of the topic. Brainstorm or use the header cards from the affinity diagram.
3. Construct the diagram by placing the topic in a box on the left-hand-side. Branch the major categories laterally to the right.

4. For each major category, define the component elements and any subelements.
5. Laterally branch the component elements and subelements for each major category to the right.
6. Review the diagram to ensure that there are no gaps in either sequence or logic.

Example

Figure A.7 shows a tree diagram which represents a telephone answering machine.

Measurement System Analysis (MSA)

What is it?

Measurement system analysis (MSA) is an experimental method used to determine how much variation within the measurement process contributes to overall process variability. There are five parameters to investigate in an MSA: bias, linearity, stability, repeatability and reproducibility.

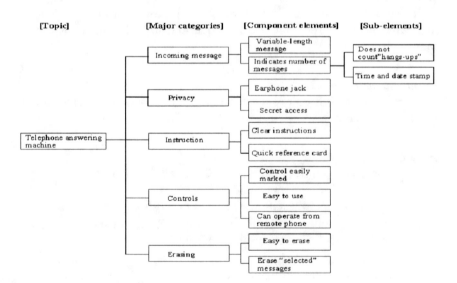

Figure A.7.   Tree Diagram.

Bias:

Bias is the difference between the observed average of measurements and the true average.

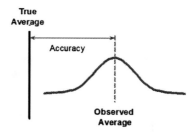

Figure A.8.   Gage bias.

Linearity:

Linearity is the difference in the accuracy values through the expected operating range.

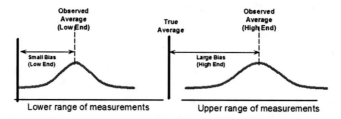

Figure A.9.   Gage linearity.

Stability:

Stability refers to the difference in the average of at least two sets of measurements obtained with the same Gage on the same parts taken at different times.

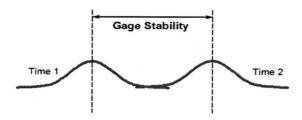

Figure A.10.   Gage stability.

Repeatability:
Repeatability is the variation between successive measurements of the same part, same characteristic, by the same person using the same instrument.

Reproducibility:
Reproducibility is the variation in the average of measurements made by different operators using the same Gage when measuring identical characteristics of the same parts.

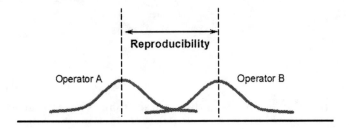

Figure A.11.   Reproducibility.

When do you use it?
It is used in the measure phase to help project leader quantify the amount of observed process variation that is due to error in the measurement system. It also helps answer the following questions: Does the measurement system have an adequate discrimination? Is the measurement system stable over time? Is the measurement variation is small relative to process variation or specifications?

How do you use it?
The following are the steps to conduct Gage R&R study:

1. State the study objectives
2. Determine number of appraisers, samples, and repeat readings
3. Chose appraisers who normally operate the instrument
4. Use samples that represent the process
5. Assure instrument discrimination at least 1/10 of the expected process variation
6. Assure measurement study is following the normal measurement procedures

7. Use at least two operators
8. Select at least 10 units to be measured
9. Measure each unit at least two times by each operator
10. There should be a strategy for qualifying new operators and new equipment.

Example

Figure A.12 is the results of an example of Gage R&R study. It shows that most of the variation is coming from the process or part-to-part.

Process Capability Study

What is it?

Process capability is a measure of process performance. Capability refers to the ability of a process to meet customer requirements. A pro-

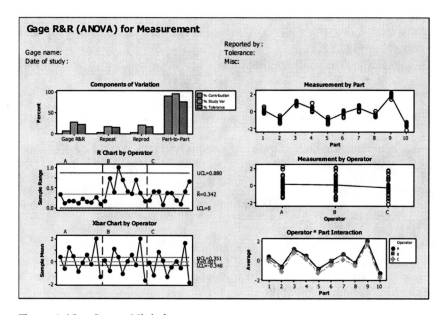

Figure A.12.   *Source:* Minitab.

cess is considered to be capable when its natural variation is equal to or less than the total tolerance of the specification.

When do you use it?
It is used in the measure phase to asses if the process meets customer requirements. Process capability study helps answer the following questions:

1. Does the process need to be improved?
2. How much improvement does it need?

Usage for process capability study:

- Estimate percentage of defective parts
- Evaluate new equipment purchases (machine capability)
- Predicting whether design tolerances can be met
- Track improvement of process over time
- Identify process for improvement
- Assessing suppliers

How do you use it?
The capability of a process is most often expressed by two capability indices C_p and C_pk:
C_p stands for capability of a process

$$C_p = \frac{USL - LSL}{6S}$$

C_pk is an index which takes into account both the spread of the distribution and its location:

$$C_pk = \min(USL\text{-Mean}/3S, \text{Mean-LSL}/3S)$$

Example
Figure A.14 shows the results of process capability study. The process seems to be barely capable and is not centered within the specification. It has $C_p = 1.16$ and $C_pk = 0.90$.

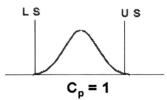

$C_p = 1$

Process just meets specs
Any shift in the mean will
result in out-of-spec
product – Marginal
Capability

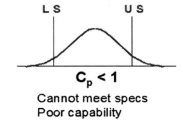

$C_p < 1$

Cannot meet specs
Poor capability

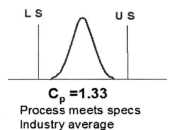

$C_p = 1.33$

Process meets specs
Industry average

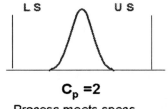

$C_p = 2$

Process meets specs
Best in class companies

Figure A.13. C_p for differnt process.

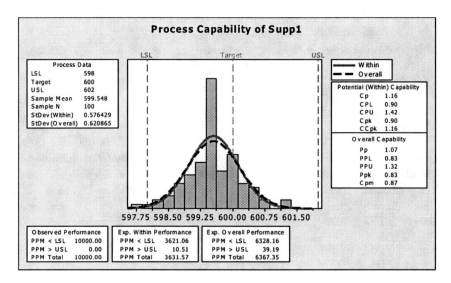

Source: Minitab.

Figure A.14.   Process capability study.

Check Sheet

What is it?

A check sheet is a form for systematic data gathering and registering to get a clear view of the facts. It is used to keep track of how often something occurs. A check sheet offers the possibility to register similar data in the same way.

When do you use it?

A check sheet is used to indicate the frequency of a certain occurrence.

How do you use it?

Steps for drafting a data sheet:

1. Formulate the objective for collecting data.
2. Decide which data is necessary.
3. Determine who and how the data will be analyzed.
4. Develop a list on which everyone participating with the study can record the collected data.
5. Start counting by tallying on the list; |, ||, |||, ||||, and ||||| represent the numbers 1, 2, 3, 4, and 5, respectively.
6. Indicate on the list the total number of facts, which were noticed.

Example
A copying company notices a sudden increase in complaints about poor quality photocopies. Management decides to analyze these complaints by using a check sheet to trace the causes (see Table A.3).

Affinity Diagram

What is it?

An affinity diagram is a tool to group a large amount of similar or related ideas generated by means of brainstorming.

Table A.3. Management Check Sheet

Causes of Defects	Missing Pages	Muddy Copies	Pages out of Sequence	Show Through	Data Collected by: John Adams Date: August 11, 2003 Total
		Types of Defects			
Humidity	||	|||| |||		|	11
Machine jams		Ӽ		|	3
Toner	|||	||	|	||	8
Conditions of originals	|	||	ЖІ |	|	10
Total	6	14	7	5	32

When do you use it?

An affinity diagram is used on the one hand to group a large amount of ideas based on existing relationships between these ideas, and on the other hand to stimulate creativity and teamwork during the brainstorming process. It is used when it is necessary to find the major themes from a large number of ideas and when chaos exists.

How do you use it?

Steps for drafting an affinity diagram:

1. Assemble the right team; four to six open-minded team members with varied qualities.
2. Formulate the problem broad, neutral, clearly, and well understood. Write down the problem formulation on a blackboard or flip chart in such a way, that it is visible to everyone.
3. Generate and record ideas. Allow everyone to formulate their ideas in random order (clearly and concretely in four to seven words, consisting of at least a noun and a verb), and record each idea on a note card (post-it note). Follow the guidelines for brainstorming.
4. Randomly layout completed note cards. Place the note cards in random order on the blackboard, wall, table, or flip chart.
5. Sort the note cards into related groupings. When all the note cards have been placed on the board, all team members should come in front to group or categorize the note cards around certain themes without discussion or comments (in silence). Group the note cards

by assumed associations and limit these to ten. If you disagree,
move the note cards. Don't agonize over sorting.

6.   Place a header above each grouping. Keep the total number of
     headers between four and eight.

Example
In processing customer claims, it is discovered that customers are dissatisfied with the time it takes to respond to their claims. To improve the efficiency of this claim process, a brainstorming session was organized using the affinity diagram. Since more than one department is involved in this process, the department managers consulted and reviewed all the process steps. Figure A.15 shows the results of this exercise.

A.3 TPS-LEAN SIX SIGMA TOOLS - ANALYZE PHASE

Why-Why Diagram

What is it?
The Why-Why diagram is a variation of the Fishbone diagram. This technique helps you to get a specification of a problem's cause, by asking the question "Why?" three to five times. For example if someone suggests that your product is poorly, the question "Why?" is immediately raised. If the person gives an answer, the question "Why?" is raised again, and so forth.

When do you use it?
The Why-Why diagram is used to systematically expose a problem's root cause.

Example
Figure A.16 shows a Why-Why diagram which represents the root causes of the problem "*product sales disappointing.*"

Seven W and IS/IS-not Questions

What is it?
There are two kinds of questions that can be used to specify a problem; seven W questions and "Is/Is-not" questions. The seven W questions is a tool to describe a problem more clearly by asking the following questions: Who, What, Where, When, What … with, in What way, to What extent. By asking questions like "who does it concern?",

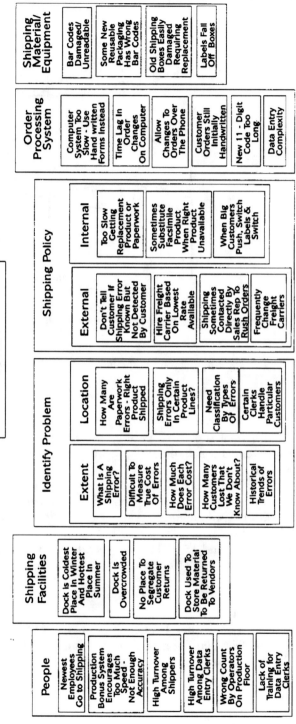

Figure A.15.   Affinity Diagram Missed Promised Delivery Dates (Akzo Nobel, 1994).

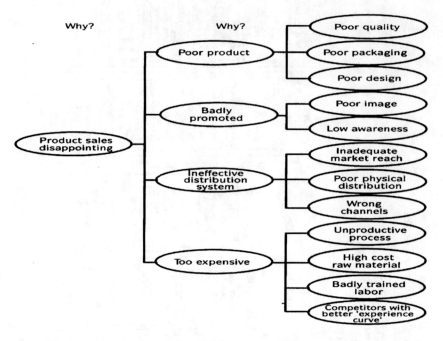

Figure A.16.   Why-Why Diagram of the Problem "Product Sales Disappointing" (Akzo Nobel, 1994)

"what happened exactly?", "where did it happen?", "when did it happen?", "with what did it happen?", "in what way did it happen?", and "to what extent did it happen?" you will get a clear specification of the problem.

You will get a sharper picture and clear definition of problems by systematically describing what the problem could have been, but is not. The seven W and Is/Is-not questions can be asked at the same time. For example: "what did happen?", "what did not happen?" and so forth. The contrast between IS and IS NOT also provides information about possible causes. Kepner-Tregoe (1998) provides a framework for these two questions (see Table A.4.)

When do you use it?

The seven W and the "Is/Is-not" questions are used to get a sharper picture and clear definition of problems, and obtain information about possible causes.

Table A.4.   The Contrast Between IS and IS NOT

Is	*Is Not*
What?	
Which specific object has a defect?	Which similar object could most likely show the same defect, but is not?
What is the defect exactly?	Which other defects could most likely be discovered, but are not?
Where	
Where is the geographic location of the defect?	Where could the defect possibly be detected, but is not seen?
Where does the object's defect occur?	Where else on the object could the defect also occur, but has not?
When?	
When was the defect first observed (date and time)?	When could the defect further be discovered for the first time, but has not?
When was the defect observed again?	At which other times could the defect have been detected, but was not?
When was the defect first seen, measured to the object's lifespan?	At which other moment in the object's lifespan could the defect have been first observed, but has not?
How many? How large?	
How many objects show the defect?	How many other objects could also display the defects, but did not?
How large or serious is such a single defect?	How large could the defect be, but is not?
How many defects per object?	How many defects could be on one object, but are not?

Example

Some years ago, the Fiberfix Company developed a new type of yarn for introduction to the carpet industry (Akzo Nobel, 1994). In the process development phase of the yarn some serious problems occurred; the number of thread breakages on processing the yarn from the spinning process to the winding coils was higher than commercially acceptable. A problem-solving team was formed that attacked the problem systematically; using the W and Is/Is-not questions (see Table A.5.).

Table A.5.   The W and Is/Is-not Questions, Used for Attacking the Problem "Broken Threads" (Akzo Nobel, 1994)

	Is	Is Not
What	Thread breakages	Wear or machine failure
Where	Spinning process	Finishing/winding process
Who	Certain shifts	All process shifts
When	Certain time periods	Occasional incidents
What with	All raw materials	Some raw materials
How	Suddenly	Not gradual
How much	Number of breakages causes unacceptable down time	Number of breakages makes "fixing" feasible

Hypothesis Testing

What is it?

Hypothesis testing is the process of using a variety of statistical tools to analyze data and, ultimately, to fail to reject or reject the null hypothesis. Hypothesis testing refers to the process of using statistical analysis to determine if the observed differences between two or more samples are due to random chance (the null hypothesis) or to true differences in the samples (the alternate hypothesis). A null hypothesis (H_0) assumes that there is no difference in parameters (mean, variance, proportion, etc.) for two or more populations. The alternate hypothesis (H_a) is a statement that the observed difference or relationship between two populations is real and is not the result of an error in sampling.

When do you use it?

Hypothesis testing is used in the analyze to test the theories (or hypotheses) regarding the inputs (Xs) that have an effect on the output (Y). It helps answer which inputs (Xs) really impact the output(Y) or outputs(Ys).

How do you use it?

Below are the steps necessary to conduct Hypothesis testing:

1. Define the Problem.

2. State the Objectives.
3. Establish the Hypotheses.

   - Null Hypothesis (H_0).
   - Alternative Hypothesis (H_a).

4. Decide on appropriate statistical test (assumed probability distribution, Z, t, F, etc.).
5. State the Alpha level (usually 5%).
6. State the Beta level (usually 10-20%).
7. Establish the Effect Size (Delta).
8. Establish the Sample Size.
9. Develop the Sampling Plan.
10. Select Samples.
11. Conduct test and collect data.
12. Calculate the test statistic from the data.
13. Determine the probability of that calculated test statistic occurring by chance = *P*-Value.
14. If *P*-Value is less than, reject H_0 and accept H_a. If *P*-Value is greater than, don't reject H_0.

Example

A production manager is interested to know if there is a difference in performance between two machines. He collected 10 samples from each machine and measured a critical to quality characteristics. He used hypothesis testing tool in Minitab to test his theory. He used 2-sample *t*-test. Here are the results:

Difference = mu (Machine 1) - mu (Machine 2)
Estimate for difference: -2.99442
95% CI for difference: (-3.18593, -2.80291)
T-Test of difference = 0 (vs not =): *T*-Value = -32.85 *P*-Value = 0.000
DF = 18
Both use Pooled *StDev* = 0.2038

Since the *P* value is 0.00 which is smaller than Alpha (0.05), he rejected the null hypothesis and concluded that the two machines perform differently.

Regression Analysis

What is it?

Regression analysis is a method of analysis that enables you to quantify the relationship between two or more variables (X) and (Y) by fitting a line or plane through all the points such that they are evenly distributed about the line or plane. Regression analysis generates an equation/model used to predict one variable from another.

When do you use it?

Regression analysis used in the analyze phase. It calculates a "prediction equation" which can mathematically predict Y for any given X. The primary objective of regression analysis is to make predictions.

How do you use it?

1. Identify the response/output variable need to be predicted.
2. Identify the input variables.
3. Collect data.
4. Plot the data.
5. Perform linear regression analysis.
6. Create the regression equation.
7. Diagnose the equation.
8. Use the equation to predict the response performance.

Example

Figure A.17 shows the equation and relationship between independent variable (X) and the response variable (Y).

Failure Mode and Effect Analysis / TPS-Lean Six Sigma Risk Management

What Is It?

TPS-Lean Six Sigma Risk Management (FMEA) is a preventive approach for systematically mapping the causes, effects, and possible actions regarding observed bottlenecks. This method is usually used to analyze products and processes. The emphasis here is on the analysis of processes, whereby answers to the following questions are sought in advance for each process step: How can the process execution fail? What

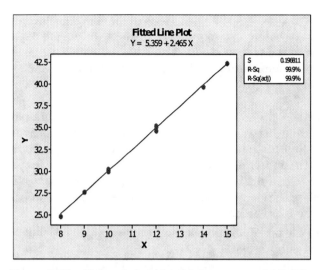

Fitted Line Plot
Y = 5.359 + 2.465 X

S	0.196811
R-Sq	99.9%
R-Sq(adj)	99.9%

Figure A.17.　Shows the relationship between variable (*X*) and the response variable (*Y*).

are the possible causes of this? What happens if the process execution fails? How can we prevent this? How important is this prevention? Who is responsible for the implementation of the solution? When will this be executed?

When Do You Use It?

TPS-Lean Six Sigma Risk Management is used for systematically identifying failures in critical business processes and then eliminating them. This results in a list of critical points with instructions on what should be done to minimize the chance of process failure.

How Do You Use It?

TPS-Lean Six Sigma Risk Management is executed as a team. The chairperson is responsible for forming the team, gathering relevant information, organizing and planning the analysis session(s), leading the discussions, documenting the results, and providing feedback regarding the continuation of the actions. To identify as many potential bottlenecks as possible, the team should have a broad, multidisciplinary composition with team members who have extensive subject matter experience. A session should take no more than 2 hours, depending on the problem formulation, knowledge, and experience of the team members, and on the preparation of the session.

The steps for executing TPS-Lean Six Sigma Risk Management are displayed in Figure A.18:

1. Form a multidisciplinary, expert team of five to eight participants and call a brief kickoff meeting. Make relevant information available to team members in advance, so that it can be studied by the team members before the meeting. At the meeting, explain the objective of the session, the approach, and the role of the team members. Select the most critical process; in other words, define the problem area.

2. Map the process and make an inventory of all relevant process steps (subprocesses).

3. Determine for each process step the possible failure modes. Anticipate possible failures in the process in relation to the rest of the process steps.

4. Indicate what the cause of each failure mode is and what the effects of the failure modes are on the controllability of the process.

5. Judge the risks; quantify the weak points in the process by estimating the probability of occurrence (P) and the severity of failure (S) for each failure mode (see Table A.6). The multiplication of these two factors is the risk factor (R). The chance of discovering the error on time is expressed in the factor (S). The more difficult it is to discover the error in advance, the higher this factor will be.

6. Determine for each failure mode the actions necessary to improve the weak points in the process. The failures with the highest R factors have the highest priority (for instance R-values > 20). Appoint a responsible problem solver to resolve the highest risk cases.

7. Report and review the results. Give feedback to the team members about the status of executed actions.

Example 1

Immediately after the September 11, 2001, Business Jet (Airline Company which OBSC is described in chapter 4) decided to implement extra strong safety measures in addition to the existing safety precautions at the airports. Thus, several improvement actions regarding safety and security were formulated, such as: equipping cockpits with an impermeable (bulletproof) door; putting in two air marshals (military trained and armed

Figure A.18. TPS-Lean Six Sigma Risk Management Model.

Table A.6. Factors *P* and *S*

Factor P (Probability of Occurrence)		*Factor S (Severity of the Failure)*	
Factor P can be determined with the following scale:		*Factor S can be scaled as follows:*	
0 =	Impossible/ hardly ever	0 =	Not a problem
1 =	Very low	1 =	Very low/hardly a problem
2 =	Low	2 =	Low/to be solved through employee intervention
3 =	Not as low	3 =	Less serious
4 =	Less than average	4 =	Less than average
5 =	Average	5 =	Average
6 =	Above average	6 =	Above average
7 =	Rather high	7 =	Rather serious
8 =	High	8 =	High
9 =	Very high	9 =	Very high
10 =	Certain	10 =	Catastrophic/Dangerous to people

guards) on each flight; making scans of the irises of passengers; encouraging, through communication, the alertness and involvement of passengers regarding public safety; and other measures. It was also decided to sharpen the safety measures at the Business Jet gates of the airports.

Amsterdam Airport received a high priority. During the past three years several safety incidents, such as an attempted hijacking, fights between aggressive passengers and cabin personnel, confiscated weapons, and others, had been recorded onboard Business Jet flights departing from this airport. These were also accompanied by long delays. Consequently, Business Jet decided last year to place their own scanner and a metal detector at gate B–4 (where most of its flights originate) and to perform additional controls in order not to damage its *safe and reliable* image. One of the Business Jet security teams at the airport executed a TPS-Lean Six Sigma Risk Management of this process. For this purpose a team of six Business Jet volunteers was assembled under the leadership of John Johnson. The other team members were Rita Reeves, Rodney Harisson, Warren Jackson, Robert Dean, and Danny Job, who were selected based on their knowledge and expertise in this problem area as well as their social and communicative skills. In this improvement team, Rita and Rodney played a facilitating role in the fields of human resources management and maintenance, respectively. The other group members belong to the Security team. John was in charge of preparing the sessions.

Three sessions were organized, each lasting 1.5 hours. During the first session the team formulated the following project mission: *The systematic identification and elimination of safety problems in order to secure the safety of our airline company.* The team members also defined the sub-processes related to the primary process "Supervision of Gate B–4 at Amsterdam Airport." The process was displayed with flowcharts, whereby the following process steps were identified:

1. Passenger places hand luggage on scanner conveyor belt.
2. Hand luggage is scanned.
3. At the signaling or detecting of a suspicious item, search hand luggage and take measures if warranted.
4. Passenger passes through the metal detector gate.
5. If metal detector alarm sounds, search passenger and take measures if warranted.
6. Passenger removes hand luggage from the conveyor belt and boards the airplane.

The other process steps, such as passport check, handing over airline ticket, receiving torn ticket stub, and taking a seat in the airplane, are left out here for the sake of brevity. The executed risk analysis resulted in several recommendations for flight safety improvement of Business Jet at Amsterdam Airport, which were put into operation within 6 months. Table A.7 shows the results of the analyses from the fist session.

Example 2

SUCCESSFULLY AVOIDING MEDICAL ERRORS IN ROTTERDAM EYE HOSPITAL AND THE HAGUE MEDICAL CENTRE IN THE NETHERLANDS BASED ON THE TPS-LEAN SIX SIGMA RISK MANAGEMENT MODEL; TWO REAL-LIFE CASE STUDIES

Submitting the wrong medicine, amputating the wrong leg, operating on the wrong eye, and other issues could be prevented with an effective application of risk analysis process, these could have been prevented, and considerable cost as well as a lot of suffering would have been avoided. By including preventive actions in the process execution in a routine way and making this a way of life in the organization, the number of medical errors can be drastically decreased. In this section we will describe the application of the TPS-Lean Six Sigma Risk Management model applied at two large hospitals in the Netherlands.

Rotterdam Eye Hospital (*Oogziekenhuis Rotterdam*) and The Hague Medical Centre (*Medical CentreHaaglanden*–MCH) in the Netherlands applied the TPS-Lean Six Sigma Risk Management model successfully in order to reduce the risk of medical errors. This section describes the results of these very successfully executed risk management analyses in both hospitals. The results were very positive; using a team approach over three sessions of one hour, more than 30 improvement points were generated. Using this process, a stable basis was created for an efficient and manageable process. Cost control and implementation time are positively influenced through this process.

Results of the TPS-Lean Six Sigma Risk Analyses at Rotterdam Eye Hospital

The critical process at *Oogziekenhuis Rotterdam* that was assessed according to the risk management model was "operating the correct, planned eye." When the analysis of the eye that needs to be operated was done, the entire process was mapped and a number of critical process steps were identified and correspondingly valued. This was done in

Table A.7. TPS-Lean Six Sigma Risk Management at Business Jet

Date: October, 2001
Page: 1
Primary Process: Supervision of Gate B–4 at Amsterdam Airport

Organization: Business Jet
Business Unit: Safety
Team: Security

Participants: John Johnson, Rita Reeves, Rodney Harisson, Warren Jackson, Robert Dean, and Danny Job
Prepared by: John Johnson

Subprocess	Failure Mode	Cause	Effect	P	S	R	Action	Responsible	Date
Passenger places hand luggage on scanner conveyor belt	Hand luggage of passenger gets entangled in the scanner with that of fellow passengers	Passengers arbitrarily stack hand luggage on top of each other on the conveyor belt	Passengers take wrong hand luggage with them	6	5	30	Develop working instructions for effective scanner use	Danny	November 2001
							In consultation with Airport Maintenance examine adjustment of scanner conveyor system	Warren	December 2001
Scanner scans hand luggage	In certain cases scanner does not identify suspicious items	Curtains in x-ray equipment allow too much artificial and sun light to enter the scanner	Increase of safety risks	2	10	20	No action	-	-
If suspicious item is signaled/detected, search hand luggage and take measures if warranted	Hand luggage is searched superficially	Large stream of passengers, great handling speed (time pressure)	Increased chances of successfully committed attacks	9	10	90	Investigate installation of a second scanner (and additional personnel) next to the existing one	Robert	December 2001
Passenger passes through metal detector gate	The detection gate does not identify metal items	Metal sensor is damaged	Increase of safety risks	7	10	70	Consult with Airport Maintenance regarding this and replace sensors	Rodney	January 2002

Process step		Cause	Effect				Action	Responsible	Deadline
	Plastic explosives (such as Semtex and C4) are not detected	Limited functioning of metal detector	Increased chance of success of committed attacks	10	10	100	Develop and implement preventive maintenance system	Rodney	February 2002
							Investigate use of tracker dogs specially trained to detect plastic explosives at airplane entrance	Warren en Danny	March 2002
When alarm of metal detector sounds, search passenger and take measures if warranted	Searching passengers is progressing with difficulty	Aggressive behavior of passengers	Long waiting lines in font of metal detectors	8	7	56	Instruct and train security personnel in dealing with and searching of aggressive passengers	John	March 2002
		Insufficient searching skills of security employees	Increase of safety risks	6	10	60	Organize passenger search training for security employees in question	John	February 2002
Passenger removes hand luggage from conveyor belt and boards the airplane	There is no final check at the entrance of the airplane	Do not belong to the assigned tasks of security employees	Increase of safety risks	4	8	32	Analyze and adjust tasks, responsibilities, and authorities of security personnel	Rita	December 2001

three sessions of one hour by a project team composed of two ophthal-mologists, one operation assistant, the quality executive, and the head of the operation theatre. Table A.8-1 was filled in based on consensus. In this table, a number of process steps are recorded as an example. It was decided not to take action when the risk factor was less than 15. The analysis shows that the most important causes for errors are human behavior/failure, carelessness, lack of concentration and so forth, unclear written reports and deficient communication with patients. Using the risk factors, improvement actions have been determined that are being implemented on the basis of the TPS-Lean Six Sigma con-cept. A number of these improvement actions are given in Table A.8-1 According to Mr. Frans Hiddema (CEO of Oogziekenhuis *Rotterdam*): *To implement improvements in health care is a laborious process. Proven good practice is not automatically copied. Also, risk management does not attract a lot of interest, even though the benefits that can be obtained are large. It appears that the* TPS-Lean Six Sigma Risk Management model *method creates enthusiasm with the participants. The brainstorming on possible failures in a team setting has a positive effect on the motivation of the participants. The cho-sen method of analysis is simple, prioritizing is easy, and the method is efficient. In a short period of time a list of improvement actions can be compiled. Accep-tance and buy-in for improvements are created because the participants have dis-covered and suggested these improvements themselves."*

Results of the TPS-Lean Six Sigma Risk Analyses at The Hague Medical Centre (MCH)

The most critical process that was chosen at this hospital was: *submis-sion of medicines in the nursing department*. The combined Orthopedics/ trauma/ neurology/neurosurgery department currently has 27 beds. There are approximately 200 different types of medicine in stock. This process was selected because the possibility that errors could occur, and the risks related to these errors within MCH, are both relatively large. A team was formed consisting of seven experienced people (volunteers) coming from various disciplines involved in the process on a daily basis: two nurses, one pharmacist, and so forth. Three sessions of approxi-mately one hour each were held, with one of the authors acting as the external facilitator. Looking at the final results in Table A.8-2, there are a number of issues identified that certainly need action to improve the process of medicine submission at MCH. These results (with an *R* fac-tor of > 15) were reported to the director care of MCH as follows:

Table A.8-1. TPS-Lean Six Sigma Risk Management at Rotterdam Eye Hospital (Oogziekenhuis Rotterdam) in the Netherlands

Secondary Process	Failure	Cause	Consequence	P	S	R	Action
Intake	Not checking which eye needs to be operated.	Checking is not included in the working instructions of the intake nurse.	No correction in operation files.	3	8	24	Include check in intake interview. Adapt working instructions, ask actively, determine next steps in case of confusion (note for eye surgeon/contact eye surgeon).
Screening	No checking which eye needs to be operated.	Checking is not included in the working instructions of the intake nurse.	No correction in operation files.	3	8	24	Include check in instructions interview.
	Medicinal drops are given to wrong eye.	Inattentiveness/ reading error.	Confusion when screened by eye surgeon, risk of wrongly filling in preoperational plan.	3	8	24	Adapt working instructions, actively ask, determine next steps in case of confusion.
Screening ophthalmologists: filling in preoperational plan.	Incorrect filling in of preoperational plan.	Inattentiveness/ reading error/communication error.	Planning wrong eye for operating theatre.	3	9	27	Investigate installation of a second scanner (and additional personnel) next to the existing one. 1. OT checklist / recovery nurse verifies actively which eye with patient. 2. In the case of confusion always stop procedure. Address behavior.

Table continues on next page.

Table A.8-1. TPS-Lean Six Sigma Risk Management at Rotterdam Eye Hospital (Oogziekenhuis Rotterdam) in the Netherlands Continued

Secondary Process	Failure	Cause	Consequence	P	S	R	Action
							3. Check files on OT when screening is uniquely done on basis of file.
							4. Determine at later stage if pre-operational plan has to be entered in the process at an earlier stage, or possibly the introduction of an integrated multi-disciplinary operation form.
Recovery nurse checks pre-operational plan with patient and completes report pre-operational care	Report on preoperational care filled in incorrect or insufficiently	Communication problems (language/mental state of patient in supposing other eye)	Procedure will be terminated, consult ophthalmologists	2	9	18	• Periodically repeat instructions to recovery nurses. • Point out responsibilities and importance of complete check. • Make accountable for behavior. • Give insights, occurrences and risk analyses. • When confused always terminate procedure.

Table A.8-2. TPS-Lean Six Sigma Risk Management at MCH (Medical Centre Haaglanden Hospital) in the Netherlands

Secondary Process	Failure	Cause	Consequence	P	S	R	Action
Doctor prescribes medication.	Unreadable	Bad writing.	Wrong dosing. Wrong medicine. Delayed start medication.	7	9	63	Implement "Medicator" (in operation) Extra checks by nurse (now 2 times a week).
	Gets lost.	Disappears in nurse's pocket.	No medication Delayed start of medication.	2	9	18	Extra checks by nurse (now 2 times a week).
	Wrong medication order.	Lack of knowledge.	Wrong medicine.	3	7	21	Structural development knowledge doctor on medicines/consulting pharmacist / provide clinical lessons.
Nurse receives medication prescription and checks if medication is on stock.	Accepting wrong prescription.	Lack of knowledge Too busy distracted.	Wrong medicine Delayed start medication.	3	7	21	When in doubt check.
	Forgets to order.	Too busy/distracted.	Delayed start medication	2	5	10	No action.
	Note wrong times.	Lack of knowledge.	Suboptimal effects.	2	2	4	No action.
	Prescription filed for wrong patient.	Human error:	Double error (two patients may receive wrong medication)	2	10	20	Extra checks by nurse (now 2 times a week).
Night shift prepares medication for all patients for next 24 hours.	Error at planning / preparation	Human error	Delays, extra work colleagues and through wrong preparation increased risk for wrong submission	2	4	8	No action.
Nurse prepares the medication for a patient without submitting a standard form.	Dosing/preparation error.	Wrong calculation. Wrong concentration in solution. Wrong pack.	Wrong dose. Wrong solution. Wrong medication.	3	9	27	Use of calculation tables/calculator. Supplementary instructions.
	Wrong label.	Human error/distraction.	Wrong medication.	2	9	18	Optimize process (prepare and share medication per patient) Develop plan for adaptation pharmacy room.

Cause of failure:	Action
Unreadable prescriptions.	Full implementation of "Medicator."
Dosing / preparation error.	Extra instructions/purchase and use of calculator.
Wrong dosing speed.	Better controls/optimizing process.
Wrong labeling.	Optimizing process/develop plan for adaptations pharmacy room.
Wrong selection.	Optimizing process/automated input.
Not signed off.	Reconfirm importance signing off.
Medication not stopped.	Implementation of Medicator in all departments/input of termination date in Medicator by doctor/position checklist of stopped medication next to the Cardex for extra checks/arrange virtual patient visit using the computer, in which the termination order is applied directly by the doctor (application for PC in assistants' room).

According to the team members, the actions need to be implemented as soon as possible, to improve the department's process efficiencies and to avoid serious medical problems. From the analysis, an important lesson has been learned: brainstorming in a team setting about what could possibly go wrong in the normal daily processes improves the efficiency of process execution. It is valuable to share knowledge among the team in this way. It generates acknowledgement and buy in for the improvement actions generated by the team, because these have been formulated by the team members themselves. The analysis is very simple and only asks for a minimum financial resource. The return is relatively high because a way of life is being instituted centrally that is characterized by routine, preventive reflection and action, effective team work, and coaching and team learning.

Because of the good results and success of these two pilot projects, both hospitals have decided to implement the TPS-Lean Six Sigma Risk Management model on full scale in other departments within the hospitals.

Fishbone Diagram

What is it?

A Fishbone diagram or cause and effect diagram (also called Ishikawa-diagram) is a graphic representation of the relationship between a given effect and its potential causes (Ishikawa, 1985). The potential causes are divided into categories and sub-categories so that the display resembles a skeleton of a fish.

When do you use it?

A Fishbone diagram is used to analyze cause-and-effect relationships and based on this, facilitate the search for solutions of related problems. It is a useful tool in brainstorming, process evaluation, and planning activities.

How do you use it?

Steps for drafting a Fishbone diagram:

1. Define the effect clearly and concisely. Place a short description of this in a box and draw from this box a long line to the left.
2. Determine during brainstorming sessions the most important categories of causes. Possible categories of causes are:

   - Equipment;
   - Working methods;
   - Environment;
   - Organization;
   - Materials; raw materials, semi-manufactured articles, energy, data, and information.
   - People; knowledge, skills, attitude, style, and behavior.
   - Means; facilities.
   - Management; knowledge, skills, attitude, style, and behavior.
   - information;
   - Measurements.

3. Place these categories with some distance between them along the main line (see Figure A.19)
4. Draw skew lines from these categories to the main line.
5. Look during brainstorming for a couple of possible causes and place these on the diagram by the corresponding category; doing this also for the subsequent levels, will result in branching. A good rule of thumb is to repeat the question "why" five times.
6. Judge and analyze the possible causes.
7. Select a small number (3 to 5) of highest-level causes that are likely to have the greatest influence on the effect.
8. Look for possible solutions for these causes.
9. Introduce the changes.

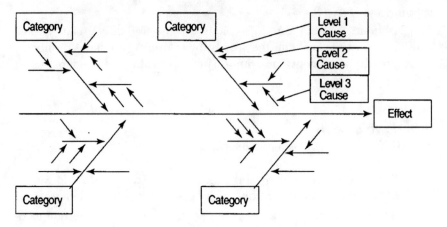

Figure A.19.   Development of a Cause-and-Effect Diagram.

Example

A copying company receives a lot of complaints about poor quality photocopies. Management decides to analyze this problem through a Fishbone diagram. Figure A.20 shows the different causes that are identified (NEN-ISO 9004-4, 1993).

Histogram

What is it?

A histogram is a bar diagram, which indicates how data is divided in a group of values. Such a display is also known as a frequency distribution. The data are displayed as a series of rectangles of equal width and varying heights. Examination of the patterns of varying heights offers insight into process behavior.

When do you use it?

A histogram is used to clearly show where the most frequently occurring values are located and how the data is distributed. It is also a tool for determining the maximum process results. Based on the visual information about process behavior, priorities can be set about the improvement efforts.

How do you use it?

Steps for drafting a histogram:

1. After the necessary measurements are taken, count how many data values you have gathered.
2. Determine the range of the data by subtracting the lowest values from the highest.
3. Divide the data values in groups or classes and count the number of values in each class. Follow the guidelines that are shown in Table A.9.

Thus, if you have gathered 110 data values, you can distribute those over a minimum of 7 and a maximum of 12 classes.

4. Then, determine the width of the classes by:

    *   dividing the range by the minimal number of classes;
    *   dividing the range by the maximal number of classes;
    *   choose a class width that is somewhere between the two results.

5. Make a frequency table for all values.
6. Draw a histogram based on the frequency table. Mark the class limits on the horizontal axis and the frequency on the vertical axis.

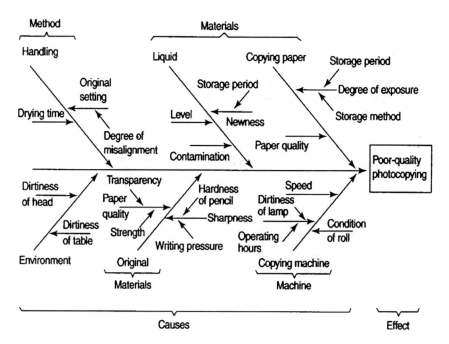

Figure A.20.   Fishbone Diagram.

Table A.9.   Guidelines

Number of Values	Number of Classes
Less than 50	5–7
50-100	6–10
100-250	7–12
More than 250	10–20

7.   Write the title and number of values in the empty spaces of the diagram.

Example

The Human Resource manager of an organization decides to study how long it takes to recruit administrative employees, from the moment the vacancy is known till the day the new employee is hired. He studies the files of his department and registers how many working days the procedure took (PA Consulting, 1991).

Time spent recruiting new employees (in working days):

32 27 27 36 31 31 19 38 12 28 25 33 48 44 16 34 21 28 27 59 31 31 39 36 57 53 29 36 47 39 26 41 34 38 42 41 13 22 37 21 27 31 21 29 24 29 17 18 26 22 19 33 26 32 21

Next, he makes the following calculations:
Number of data values = 55 (the number of classes = 6–10)
Range = 59–12 = 47
The class width lies between 7.8 (47 divided by 6) and 4.7 (47 divided by 10). The choice is a class width of 5. Next, he drafts a frequency table, Table A.10. Based on this, he draws the corresponding histogram (see Figure A.21).

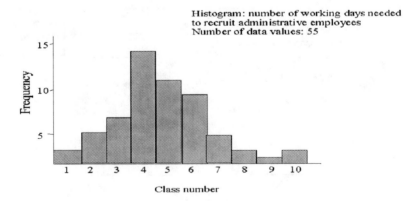

Figure A.21.   Histogram.

Table A.10.   Frequency Table

Class	Limits	Counts	Frequency
1	10 – 14	||	2
2	15 – 19	₦|	5
3	20 – 24	₦| ||	7
4	25 – 29	₦₦|| || ||	13
5	30 – 34	₦| |||||	11
6	35 – 39	₦| ||||	8
7	40 – 44	||||	4
8	45 – 49	||	2
9	50 – 54	|	1
10	55 – 59	||	2
		Total :	55

The histogram indicates that most recruitment procedures take 25 to 29 days (class 4) (see Figure A.21).

Scatter Diagram

What is it?
A scatter diagram is a graphical technique for studying relationships between two variables (which occur in pairs); to figure out if there is a connection between the variables and how strong this relationship is. The diagram displays the paired data as a cloud of points. Relationships between the two variables are inferred from the shape of the clouds. The density and direction of the cloud indicate how the two variables influence each other. If the value of one variable seems to influence the other, then there is a correlation between these two variables. A positive relationship between two variables means that increasing values of one variable are associated with increasing values of the other. A negative relationship on the other hand, means that increasing values of one variable are associated with decreasing values of the other. Six commonly occurring shapes of clouds are shown in Figure A.22 (NEN-ISO 9004-4, 1993).

Figure A.22.   Six commonly occurring shapes of clouds.

When do you use it?

A scatter diagram is used after a cause and effect analysis to determine whether a certain cause is related to a certain effect. This can be used to determine what will happen to the one variable if the other is changed.

How do you use it?

Steps for drafting a scatter diagram:

1. Collect 30 to 50 paired data of two associated sets of variables (cause and effect) whose relationship is to be studied.
2. Draw a horizontal (X) and a vertical (Y) axis. Usually the values related to the cause are marked on the X-axis and those related to the effect on the Y-axis. Both axes should approximately be of equal length.
3. Label the axes, give the diagram a title and register the data source, date and the responsible persons.
4. Plot the paired (x, y) data in the diagram, by marking each point. When pairs of data have the same values, draw a concentric circle round these points.
5. Examine the shape of the cloud of points in the diagram to determine the type and strength of the mutual relationships.

Example

The manager of Florence Ice Cream in New York receives an interesting offer from an ice cream supplier. The supplier introduces a new kind of ice cream on the market, which was tested on the market with positive results. The profits from the new ice cream seem promising. If Florence orders a sufficient amount of the new ice cream, a new freezer must be installed. It is known that the tests were done during warm weather and Florence is afraid that the new ice cream will not sell as well when it is cold. That is why the company decided to study the relationship between the sale of ice cream and the maximum daily temperature. Each day during 4 weeks, the company registered the sales data and compared these with the temperature measured that day. The scatter diagram derived from this is shown in Figure A.23.

From the diagram, it appears that there is hardly any relationship between the amount paid for ice cream and the maximum daily temperature. Based on this, Florence can decide to install a second freezer and to purchase the new ice cream, possibly after also studying the effects of other factors on sales. Thus, decision making was made possible with the help of the scatter diagram.

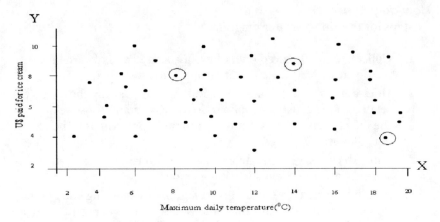

Figure A.23.   Scatter Diagram.

Line Graph

What is it?

A line graph is a graphic representation of the relationship between two variables. It is a communication tool, which represents data in simple graphical form that is quickly and easily understood.

When do you use it?

A line graph is used to visualize the relationship between two variables and to study fluctuations in time. Line graphs are particularly used to identify trends in a certain process.

How do you use it?

Steps for drawing a graph:

1.   Draw a vertical (Y) and a horizontal (X) axis and label both axes. Usually, the time sequence is indicated on the horizontal axis (year, weak, hour, etc.).
2.   Choose a scale so that most of the available space is filled by the graph. Both axes usually start at zero.
3.   Plot the different points in the graph and draw straight lines in the correct sequence between the points.
4.   Give the graph a clear descriptive title.

Example

Figure A.24 shows a line graph illustrating the number of complaints from customers over the last 8 months. This shows that most of the complaints were received in month 4 and the least in month 5.

A.4 TPS-LEAN SIX SIGMA TOOLS—IMPROVE PHASE

Design of Experiments (DOE)

What is it?

Design of Experiments is a series of structured and organized tests where deliberate, simultaneous changes are conducted on the process input variables (temperature, pressure, etc.) to evaluate the effect of these changes on the process output variables or responses (strength, surface roughness, etc.). These tests are analyzed as whole.

When do you use it?

Design of Experiments method is used in the design phase to help determine the relationship between factors (Xs) affecting a process and the output of that process (Y). It assists in identifying which inputs (Xs) that have the largest effect on the output (Y).

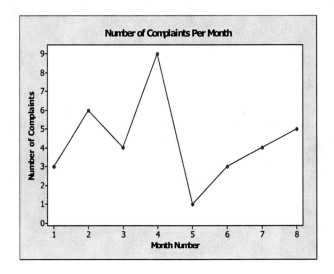

Figure A.24.   Line Graph.

How do you use it?

The following are the necessary steps to conduct Design of Experiment:

1. Identify the problem.
2. Define the experiment objective.
3. Select the response variables (Y's)(has to be meaningful).
4. Select the independent variables (X's).
5. Choose the independent variable levels.
6. Select the experimental design.
7. Perform the experiment.
8. Collect and analyze data.
9. Draw statistical conclusions.
10. Confirm results.
11. Implement solutions.

Example

A scientist is interested to test the hypothesis that the lens surface roughness is a function of polymer viscosity, cure type, post bake temperature, post bake time, Etcher, and etcher power. Table A.11 shows the variables and their levels to be tested.

Table A.12 shows the experimental design matrix.

Figure A.25 shows the results of the experiment. The graphs indicates that post bake temperature has the biggest impact on surface roughness.

Table A.11.   Variables and Their Levels

Responses:
Surface Roughness

Factors	Levels	
Polymer Viscosity	High	Low
Cure type	Thermal	UV
Post bake temperature	High	Low
Post bake time	Short	Long
Etcher	ICP	Oxford
Etcher power	Low	High

Table A.12. Surface Roughness Design Matrix

Run #	Polymer Viscosity	Cure Type	Post Bake Temp.	Post Bake Time	Etcher	Etcher Power	Surface Roughness
1	Low	Thermal	Low	Short	ICP	Low	
2	High	Thermal	Low	Short	Oxford	Low	
3	Low	UV	Low	Short	Oxford	High	
4	High	UV	Low	Short	ICP	High	
5	Low	Thermal	High	Short	Oxford	High	
6	High	Thermal	High	Short	ICP	High	
7	Low	UV	High	Short	ICP	Low	
8	High	UV	High	Short	Oxford	Low	
9	Low	Thermal	Low	Long	ICP	High	
10	High	Thermal	Low	Long	Oxford	High	
11	Low	UV	Low	Long	Oxford	Low	
12	High	UV	Low	Long	ICP	Low	
13	Low	Thermal	High	Long	Oxford	Low	
14	High	Thermal	High	Long	ICP	Low	
15	Low	UV	High	Long	ICP	High	
16	High	UV	High	Long	Oxford	High	

Main Effects Plot for Surface Roughness

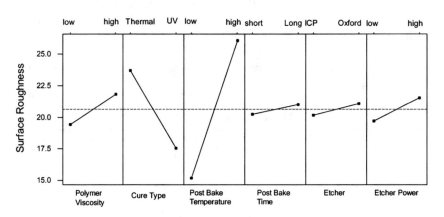

Figure A.25. Surface roughness Main effects plot.

A.5 TPS-LEAN SIX SIGMA TOOLS—CONTROL PHASE

Run chart

What is it?
A run chart encompasses a kind of time series graph to monitor a process.

When do you use it?
A run chart is used to identify trends and significant changes in a process.

How do you use it?
Steps for drawing a run chart:

1. Collect the necessary data.
2. Draw a vertical (Y) and a horizontal (X) axis; usually the points of time are marked out on the X-axis.
3. Plot the data in the graph and draw a straight line between these points.
4. Check if there are developments, trends and changes. A trend is a series of points, which display an upward or downward slope.

Example
The manager of a delicacy shop in Brussels notices that there are periods where he cannot handle the demand and customers have to wait in line outside the shop. There are also periods in which he hardly has anything to do. He decides to study which fluctuations in sales occur during one year, to identify the peaks and lows. He hopes to forecast the queue in the shop better with this tool. To do this, he collects the following data (see Table A.13), which he marks out on a run chart (see Figure A.26).

Table A.13.   Collected Data

Month	Sales (x $5,000)	Month	Sales (x $5,000)
January	2	July	4
February	6.5	August	3
March	4.5	September	5.5
April	9	October	6
May	5.5	November	6.5
June	4	December	11

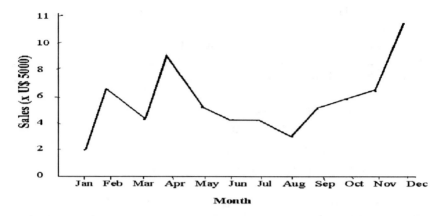

Figure A.26.   Run Chart.

The run chart displays an interesting pattern, which is not immediately noticeable from the table. There are peaks in February (Valentines Day), April (Easter) and December (Christmas). The least are sold in January because people have to be conscious about expenses after the holidays and in August when many are on vacation.

Control Chart

What is it?
Statistical Process Control is one of the underlying principles of the Six Sigma program (Monhemius, 2001). The basics are developed in the twenties of the previous century (Shewart, 1931). But the concepts are still applicable and up to date. The key concept is that a process cannot be improved by imposing narrow specifications. The management is responsible to supply an organization with a process that can produce according to the customer's expectations and specifications. Once this step is made, the process must be monitored. If the process is OK ("in control," or variation from "common cause") it will perform according to a stable statistical distribution. The function of the monitoring is no longer the inspection of products; monitoring only checks if the process is still OK. And a good process can only produce good products. If the process is disturbed, the monitoring will signal this as an alarm ("out of control" or variation from "special cause"). The process should be stopped and the cause must be repaired. This seems logical but it also means that the process must be left alone if there is not an "out of control" condition. In practice employees, responding to not significant variations, cause many

disturbances. This results in so called "tampering" of the process and increases variation and reduces quality.

The control chart is a Statistical Process Control technique to evaluate a process and to achieve and maintain a state of control. It indicates what a process can do. It helps you answering the questions:

- Can we do the job correctly?
- Are we doing the job correctly?
- Have we done the job correctly?
- Could we do the job more consistently and on target?

A control chart is the statistical tool that filters the special cause from common cause. In its most simple form the control chart is a trend chart for a certain parameter. In the trend chart the common cause variation is used to calculate "control limits." When the measured value exceeds the control limits, there must be a special cause. It is essential that the graph is drawn and judged real time with the process. In the typical application the employee will monitor his own process. Direct after completion of each production series, he will plot a data point and see if the next series can start. If an out of control is found, the problem-solving process can start immediately without interference with superiors.

When do you use it?

A control chart is used to show the most important sources of variations (destabilizing factors) and to eliminate them in order to statistically control the process; to check whether the process is being controlled statistically. It allows you to distinguish between measurements which are predictable (related to the inherent capability of the process) and measurements, which are unpredictable (produced by special causes). The chart is used to evaluate process stability and to decide when to adjust the process. Once Statistical Process Control is implemented, problems are signaled and documented in a stable and reliable way. SPC forms the starting point for improvement teams. Adopting the philosophy of process control can even be considered a necessary condition for further improvement with Six Sigma or other programs.

How do you use it?

Steps for making a control chart:

1. Select the characteristics for applying a control chart.
2. Select the appropriate type of control chart.
3. Collect the data.

4. Draw a vertical axis (Y-axis) with the value of the quality character-istic (e.g., time, length, etc.). The position (spread) of the quality parameters of the process is shown on this axis.

5. Draw a horizontal axis (X-axis) with the time of measurement or samples taken at random.

6. Draw the central line (CL) which is the average of the process, *or the target line if the process is adjustable.* On each side *of the central line* (see Figure A.27):

   • the Lower Control Limit (LCL);
   • the Upper Control Limit (UCL). These limits describe the nat-ural variation of the process.

7. Plot the data in the chart.

8. Examine the plot for points outside the control limits. Points under the Lower Control Limit or above the Upper Control Limit signal that something has occurred which requires special attention. The circled point on the chart in Figure A.27 is out-side the Upper Control Limit. This point is a sign for a correc-tive action.

9. If out of control is detected: follow the "Out of Control Action Plan" (OCAP). An OCAP is a predetermined troubleshooting flowchart. It empowers the employee to take action on the pro-cess. It removes the most frequent special causes, and keeps the employee responsible for the corrective actions (Sandorf & Bas-sett, 1993).

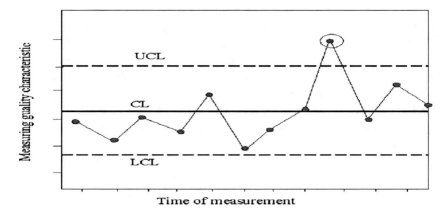

Figure A.27.   Example of a Control Chart.

Example Individual Measurements: The Formula's

The individual measurements X_1, X_2, X_3, and so forth, form the basis of the *Individuals* control chart. Thus, X_1 is the value of the first measurement. The central line (CL) or the average of k measurements can be calculated as follows:

$CL = (X_1 + X_2 + X_3 + \ldots\ldots + X_k) / k$ or CL = target, if the process can be adjusted.

The Upper Control Limit en the Lower Control Limit (for more than 25 measurements) can be calculated as follows:

$$UCL = CL + 2{,}66 \; MR$$

$$LCL = CL - 2{,}66 \; MR$$

$$MR = [\Sigma \, |X_i - X_{i-1}|] / k\text{-}1 \; (\text{for } i \geq 2) \; (\text{for } k \geq 25)$$

MR is the average Moving Range; a measurement for the spread of the average random samples. The constant figure 2,66 is used here to determine the distance between the central line and the control borders. The value 2.66 is a statistical constant that turns the average into an estimate of three sigma.

A.5 MINITAB OVERVIEW

Minitab® is powerful statistical software packed used by TPS-Lean Six Sigma for virtually all tools described in the book and in this Appendix. Minitab remains the ideal choice for Six Sigma and other quality initiatives worldwide. Minitab's powerful data management capabilities, unparalleled ease of use, a comprehensive set of methods, and compelling graphics help quality professionals identify and target the best opportunities for business improvement. Draw valuable insights from your data and easily illustrate and interpret the results of your analyses. Minitab is backed by exceptional, free technical support and is used by distinguished companies such as 3M, DuPont, Toshiba, Honeywell International, and leading Six Sigma consultants.

TPS-Lean Six Sigma uses Minitab exclusively in all the tools described in this book. While there are a variety of statistical tools on the market, we found Minitab fits all the needs for TPS-Lean Six Sigma deployment and has excellent reference manuals, specialized training, and service. Additionally, Minitab is available in most any language desired.

A.5.1 Minitab Multiple Graphing Options

In Minitab, you have the option of looking at a single graph or several graphs at once. In the Figure A.28 below, there is a variety of chart options shown on a single screen. This allows the user to look visually at the data from several different vantage points. Figure A.29 shows a graph on a single page.

Minitab is simple to use for the beginning or occasional user, but also contains the depth and breadth of tools and guidance to satisfy even the most rigorous quality improvement projects. Table A.14 outlines the many features you'll find in Minitab:

A.6 TPS-LEAN SIX SIGMA PROJECT BSCSOFT

TPS-Lean Six Sigma Project BSCsoft is an interactive software system that will assist you with the successful formulation and implementation of your Project Balanced Scorecard (Project BSC). It offers TPS-Lean Six Sigma Champions/Master Black Belts/Black Belts/Green Belts/Project Managers the possibility to execute their project effectively. This software system consists of the following functions:

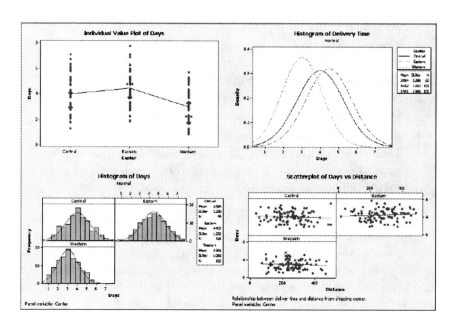

Figure A.28.   Multiple Graph Option.

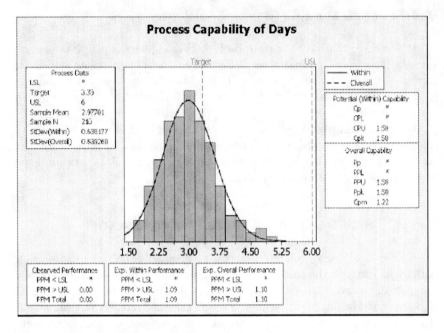

Figure A.29.   Single Graph Option.

1. Formulating the Project BSC.
2. Implementing and tracking the project; to confirm the project is progressing through each of its defined tollgates and to assure the project and team members are staying on course.
3. Aligning the Project BSC with project member's Personal BSC (PBSC) and with the Organizational BSC (OBSC).
4. Monitoring the performance of the project continuously
5. Effectively communicating the project results to Upper Management, Executives, and Champions, and to keep the TPS-Lean Six Sigma initiatives visible to them.

The first step is the formulation of the project vision, mission, values, and the related objectives, performance indicators, targets and improvement actions. Possibilities are available to make use of a predefined set of project performance measures or numerous examples in the system. The TPS-Lean Six Sigma Project BSCsoft is related to the OBSC. Using this software, Champions/Master Black Belts/Black Belts/Green Belts will have the opportunity to manage their project successfully, and project members will obtain an improved understanding of the project actions and

Table A.14.   Minitab Features Overview

Easy to Use

Minitab's logical interface makes it simple to use, and its outstanding support features make it easy to get results.

State of the Art Graphs and Graph Editing

Clear, bold graphs are simple to create for any application, with intuitive point and click editing.

Data and File Management

Minitab accepts data in many file formats and keeps your work tidy in a single, automatically organized project file.

General Statistics

A broad range of simple yet powerful tools to help you to make quick assessments and comparisons.

Regression Analyses

Linear, polynomial, logistic, PLS and more detect and define relationships.

Statistical Process Control

Take control of your processes with this suite of control charts and more.

Measurement Systems Analysis

Gage analyses and related tools to ensure the quality of your data.

Analysis of Variance

A comprehensive set of tools including ANOVA, GLM, Analysis of Means, and more.

Quality Tools

Ensure your processes meet your expectations with Process Capability analyses, Pareto charts, and other powerful tools.

Design of Experiments

A wide variety of available designs – now including D-optimal and distance based designs.

Table continues on next page.

Table A.14.   Minitab Features Overview Continued

Reliability/Survival Analysis

Calculate the lifespan of the products you use or sell, predict failure rates, establish warranty parameters, and more.

Power and Sample Size

Collect the right amount of data for your situation – use power curves to visualize the relationship between the sample size and power.

Multivariate Analysis

Principal component analysis, cluster analysis, and other multidimensional tools.

Time Series and Forecasting

Large collection of time-related analyses, like trend analysis and decomposition. Now with auto, partial, and cross correlations.

Nonparametric

Perform critical analyses even without normally distributed data.

Tables

Chi-square, Fisher's exact and other table-based tools.

Simulations and Distributions

Generate random numbers, pick random samples, and more.

Macros and Customizability

Automate the analyses you perform regularly, customize menus and settings, even integrate with Minitab COM objects.

results. The status of the project improvement actions and results is made visible through unambiguous indicators at any given moment and is communicated online to top-management, Executives, and Champions. Targets that have been achieved can also be brought up-to-date immediately. A dashboard is part of the software. This is a visual status of all open and closed projects and is strongly related to the Project BSC. Dashboards are a common tool used by today's managers to provide quick reference to key objective data. Figure A.30 is an example of a TPS-Lean Six Sigma Dashboard.

The alignment of the Project BSC with project member's PBSC and with the OBSC is achieved by comparing the project targets and objectives with the project member's targets and objectives as formulated in the PBSC and with the organization' targets and objectives as formulated in the OBSC. Other contributions to this match are given through the filling-in of interactive questionnaires and the recording of results of the ambition meetings (between Champion/Master Black Belt/Black Belt/ Green Belt/Project Manager and his/her project members). The result is a clear overview of the similarities and differences between the project's shared ambition and the project member's and organization's ambition. These results contain valuable information for Champions/Master Black Belts/Black Belts/Green Belts/Project Managers to be able to effectively manage their TPS-Lean Six Sigma project and the talents within their project team. Please visit www.TPS-LeanSixSigma.com *for* further details and the latest information about TPS-Lean Six Sigma Project BSCsoft.

For further information regarding TPS-Lean Six Sigma Project BSCsoft:

TPS-Lean Six Sigma ᴸᴸᶜ

Linking Human Capital to
Lean Six Sigma

TPS-Lean Six Sigma Inc. (New York)
144 Fairport Village Landing, #303
Fairport, NY 14450
Voice: 585-750-8203
Fax: 585-425-7381
E-mail: info@TPS-LeanSixSigma.com
Web: www.TPS-LeanSixSigma.com

TPS-Lean Six Sigma, Inc. (Florida)
P.O Box 601564
North Miami Beach
Florida 33160
Phone: 786-537-7580
Fax: 714-464-4498
E-mail: info@TPS-LeanSixSigma.com
Web: www.TPS-LeanSixSigma.com

A.7 TPS-LEAN SIX SIGMA PERSONAL BSCSOFT

TPS-Lean Six Sigma Personal BSCsoft is an interactive software system that will assist you with the formulation and implementation of your Per-

Finacial Impact

DMAIC Tollgate Status

Project #	Business Unit	Project Name	Approval Status	D	M	A	I	C	Projected Savings	Actual Savings	Percent Acheived
1	SLS01	Increase share by 20%	Approved				■	■	$250,000	$111,000	44%
2	MKT01	Develop tri-fold	Approved		■				$1,000,000	$0	0%
3	MFG11	Reduce cycle time shift 2	Pending						$200,000	$0	0%
4	PRO10	Shorten MG12 antenna by 2 ft	Pending				■	■	$1,500,000	$1,650,000	110%
5	SLS01	Increase net margin 3%	Pending						$500,000	$0	0%
6	MKT01	Reduce database pct by 30	Approved		■				$550,000	$0	0%
7	FIN03	Open sub-dept	Approved						$1,380,000	$1,250,000	91%
8	FIN03	Eliminate 10% waste control	Draft						$3,400,000	$0	0%
9	SHP04	Increase throughput mech #4	Closed						$1,675,000	$1,675,000	100%
10	TST15	Double prober speed	Approved				■	■	$1,200,000	$1,325,000	110%
11	CUS20	Resolve CTQ 5 on PN 09-SBT	Closed						$850,000	$950,000	112%

| Totals | 11 | | | | | | | | $12,505,000 | $6,961,000 | |

Figure A.30. TPS-Lean Six Sigma Project Dashboard.

sonal Balanced Scorecard (PBSC). It offers individuals to coach themselves, TPS-Lean Six Sigma coaches to coach others, Champions/Master Black Belts/Black Belts/Green Belts/Project Managers to coach their project members and Executives/HR to effectively steer their organization on performance, happiness, joy and motivation. This software system consists of the following parts:

1. Formulating the PBSC.
2. Implementing the PBSC based on the Plan-Do-Act-Challenge cycle.
3. Aligning the PBSC with the OBSC and project BSC.
4. Effectively managing of talents within the project and the organization.

Every employee owns responsibility for the filling-in of his/her own PBSC. The first step is the creation of an employee's profile. Subsequently, the employee/project member formulates from every perspective, his/her personal ambition and the related objectives, performance indicators, targets and improvement actions. Possibilities are available to make use of a predefined set of data or numerous examples in the system. Doing this, and using these possibilities, the employee/project member will obtain an improved understanding of him/her self and have the opportunity to manage and coach him/her self in a goal-oriented way. The status of his/ her improvement actions is made visible through unambiguous indicators at any given moment. After being authorized by the employee/employee, others can provide feedback on his/her actions at any moment. Targets that have been achieved and challenges that have been taken up can also be brought up-to-date immediately. The TPS-Lean Six Sigma Code of Ethics is being applied here; this implies that the system respects the individual employee's privacy and that no personal information can be shared with unauthorized others. Another benefit of the system is that any employee can benchmark him/her self against any other employee with the same profile, from inside and from outside the own organization. The PBSC database also contains demographic data so that the possibility exists to compare with other like-minded individuals. The PBSC is connected to a knowledge database that gives feedback and advice to further improve oneself. The match between personal and organizational/project ambition is also achieved by comparing the personal targets and objectives of the employee/project member with the organizational/project targets and objectives as formulated in the OBSC/project BSC. Other contributions to this match are given through the filling-in of interactive questionnaires and the recording of results of the ambition meetings. The result is a clear overview of the similarities and differences between the PBSC of the employee/project member and the OBSC/project BSC. These results contain valuable information for Champions/Master Black Belts/Black Belts/Green Belts/Project Managers, and Executives/HR to be able to effectively manage the talents that exist within the organization and within their TPS-Lean Six Sigma project team. Please visit www.TPS-LeanSixSigma.com *for* further details and the latest information about TPS-Lean Six Sigma Personal BSCsoft.

For further information regarding TPS-Lean Six Sigma Personal BSCsoft:

TPS-Lean Six Sigma Inc.
144 Fairport Village Landing, #303
Fairport, NY 14450
Voice: 585-750-8203
Fax: 585-425-7381
E-mail: info@TPS-LeanSixSigma.com
Web: www.TPS-LeanSixSigma.com

TPS-Lean Six Sigma Inc.
P.O. Box 601564
North Miami Beach
Florida 33160
Phone: 786-537-7580
Fax: 714-464-4498
E-mail: info@TPS-LeanSixSigma.com
Web: www.TPS-LeanSixSigma.com

TPS-Lean Six Sigma LLC

Linking Human Capital to
Lean Six Sigma

APPENDIX B: TOOLS FOR EFFECTIVE INTERPERSONAL COMMUNICATION

In this section we will describe the TPS-Lean Six Sigma tools related to Interpersonal communication, which are based on Rampersad (2003). Interpersonal communication is an essential element of teamwork and acts as the glue that binds elements of the TPS-Lean Six Sigma concept. Differences in style in interpersonal communications between colleagues, friends, and others are the source for lack of understanding, conflicts, disappointments, and missed opportunities. These are all wasted opportunities that have no place in the TPS-Lean Six Sigma philosophy. As discussed before, reducing/eliminating waste is one of the targets of this concept. The primary goal of interpersonal communication is the creation of mutual understanding. Apart from that, the following communication goals also play a role (Rampersad, 2003):

- Stimulating collective learning; updating, sharing, and exchanging knowledge; keeping employees updated and creating transparency.
- Stimulating mutual organizational cooperation and commonality (we-feeling) and urging people into action.
- Articulating organizational norms and values; influencing people's views and attitudes; and cultivating an understanding of change and improvement.
- Developing skills such as the ability to listen well, set priorities, plan activities, and other abilities.
- Giving and receiving feedback.

Thus, interpersonal communication is concerned with broadening knowledge (learning) and, as a result, changing people's attitude and behavior. The following statement of top manager Robert Staubli illustrates the importance of interpersonal communication and related social skills:

> There are well-founded reasons to place more emphasis—some say perhaps a disproportionate emphasis—on the development of social skills. For an average company the estimated loss of potential business performance varies from 30 to 50% due to mutual problems, unresolved conflicts, barriers, disrupted relations, not enough personal space, and lack of development possibilities. I think that this is a cautious estimation.

The Communication Process

Learning requires controlling the communication process. This learning process consists of a sender who transmits a message to a receiver, who interprets this message, and, in turn, the reaction to this message from the receiver. This feedback gives the sender the opportunity to ascertain that the message has been received and understood. Communication is therefore a continuous cycle of action and reaction. It is a constant process of two-way traffic. When people communicate with each other, they are alternately the sender and receiver of messages. Communication is only successful when the receiver interprets the message according to the intention of the sender. According to Evans and Russell (1991) communication gains depth and value when we can create a sphere of openness, trust, and mutual respect in such a way that we can also share our thoughts, feelings, emotions, sensitivity, intuitions, excitement, happiness, ideals, and truths with each other. This process can be hampered by differences in the mindsets of the sender and receiver. This mindset, or the personal way we look upon things, is created by things such as upbringing, education, experience, norms, and values.

In the context of a team, interpersonal communication entails a process of the exchange of messages between team members. This may occur via talking or writing. The following list outlines key elements of oral communication:

- *Spoken language (verbal).* This includes the ways in which words are used, such as in long, complex sentences or short, easy ones; the language (as in French or Spanish) in which someone speaks; if someone speaks in the "I" or "we" form. Spoken language conveys, among other things, a person's level of education and intelligence.
- *Sound variations.* These are the sound elements that do not belong to the spoken language itself, such as volume, accent, clearness, pitch, speed of speech, laughing, crying, and so forth. From these elements we are able to deduce people's feelings. Nervousness, for example, is identified by high speed of speech and a quivering voice.
- *Visible information (nonverbal).* This concerns body language, such as blushing out of shyness, turning pale out of fear, frowning, laughing, head movements, crossing of arms, hand signals, clothing, and personal care, scratching, playing with objects during lengthy stories, and so on. Research shows that more than 70% of all communication is nonverbal.

Nonverbal communication can be divided among the following categories:

- *Posture.* This includes postural indicators such as shoulders hanging (weak, sense of inferiority); head up (self-assured, proud); crossed legs (confident); feet under the chair (suspicious); slouching (not interested); leaning toward conversation partner (interested, enthusiastic); and other forms of body language.
- *Facial expressions.* These are facial expressions such as eyes wide opened (amazed, startled); eyes blinking (nervous); looking someone straight in the eyes (interested, attentive); avoiding eye contact (insecure); firmly closed mouth (determined); blushing (shyness, excitement); turning pale (fright, fear, rage); and other expressions.

- *Gesticulating*. These include actions involving the hands, such as hand on the hips (superior); hands on the back (pensive, passive); closed fist (angry, excited); hand on the mouth (shy, insecure); head resting in hands (pensive); movements with the index finger (drawing attention to); arranging ones glasses (hesitating); cleaning glasses (saving time); and others.
- *Distance*. The actual space between people during communication. Most interpersonal contact takes place at approximately an arm's length. Strangers usually keep a greater distance, while people who know each other well usually stand at half an arm's length.

Table B.1 shows how negative nonverbal messages can lead to negative reactions (Barton, 1990).

**Table B.1. Nonverbal Messages That can
Produce Negative Reactions (Barton, 1990)**

Nonverbal Message/Expression	Signal Received/Emanation	Reaction Receiver
Manager looks away when he is speaking to an employee.	I do not have this person's attention.	My superior is too busy to listen to my problem or simply does not care.
Failure to acknowledge greetings from a colleague.	This person is unfriendly.	This person is unapproachable.
Angry glance; that is, look at the person angrily.	I am angry.	Reciprocal anger, fear, or avoidance depending on who is sending the signal.
Rolling of eyes.	I am not being taken seriously.	This person thinks he or she is smarter or better than I am
Deep sighing.	Annoyance/aversion or displeasure	My opinions do not count. I must appear stupid or boring to this person.
Heavy breathing (sometimes accompanied by hand waving).	Anger or heavy stress	Avoid this person at all costs.
Eye contact not maintained during communication.	Suspicion and/or uncertainty	What does this person have to hide?
Manager crosses arms and leans back.	Indifference and difficult to persuade.	This person has already made up his or her mind; my opinions are not important.
Manager peers over his glasses.	Skepticism or distrust.	He or she does not believe what I am saying.
Continues to read a report while employee is speaking	Lack of interest/attention.	My opinions are not important enough to get my supervisor's attention.

Comprehension of the message from the *sender* can be improved by:

- *Simplicity of style*; comprehensible formulation, easy words, and short sentences.
- *A recognizable structure*; a clear argument with a clear direction.
- *Conciseness*; stick to the essentials, be brief;
- *A stimulating style*; such as frankness, asking questions, joking, regarding the other person as valuable and equal.

Effective interpersonal communication is therefore an important aid for the successful implementation of TPS-Lean Six Sigma projects. Communication skills are also a part of the competency profile of managers and employees. Interpersonal communication involves, among other things, asking the right questions, listening to the answers you get, and then responding to these answers. To achieve effective mutual communication *the receiver* should listen intently by, for example, questioning, summarizing, explaining, and being alert. It is the responsibility of the manager to create a working environment where effective communication can be developed. This can be done with the following methods:

- Be honest and open and give everyone the necessary information.
- Speak about *we* and not about *me* and *you*.
- Don't ignore your employees.
- Ask them about their opinions and views.
- Explain in advance why certain measures will be taken.
- Listen attentively and give constructive feedback.
- Put yourself in the other person's place.
- Understand your employees and meet them halfway.
- Avoid egotistical remarks such as, "My years of experience show that...," "I know what I'm talking about...," and so on.
- Emphasize the objectives.
- Don't look for a scapegoat.

Interpersonal Communicative Skills

The most important interpersonal communicative skills may be summarized as *listening, questioning, building on the ideas of others, constructive arguing, clarifying, summarizing, involving others, showing appreciation, giving and receiving feedback, constructive negotiating,* and *conflict handling* (PA Consulting Group, 1991; Rampersad, 2003). These skills will be briefly described in this section.

Listening

What Is It?

Listening is the beginning of all wisdom; learning is listening effectively. Interpersonal communication starts with good listening. Listening is more important than speaking. There is a difference between listening and hearing. When someone listens, the words are actively registered and processed in the brain and then used. On the other hand, when someone hears, the words are registered in the brain but nothing is done with them. Listening can thus be summarized as hearing, understanding, remembering, and doing something with it. Thus, good listening is effective learning. Table B.2 displays the difference between good and bad listeners. As a result of bad listening, billion of dollars are wasted annually due to: letters that have to be retyped, postponed appointments, labor conflicts, failed sales presentations, and so on (Evans and Russell, 1991).

Some other bad listening habits are (Rampersad, 2003; Thomas, 1996):

- Not paying attention, thinking of something else, playing with papers on your desk or interrupting the conversation by answering the phone.
- Acting as if you are listening.
- Listening until you have something to say, then not listening and bracing yourself to interrupt the other person when the next opportunity arises.
- Emotional oversensitivity and prejudice.
- Hearing what you expect, thinking that you hear what you expected, or refusing to hear what you don't want to hear.

Table B.2. Good Listeners Versus Bad Listeners

Good Listeners	Bad Listeners
Are quiet when someone else is expressing his or her opinions, tries to understand what the other person means and asks questions for clarification.	Interrupts the speaker before he or her is finished.
Display nonverbal behavior such as nodding or looking straight at the person and leaning forward.	Display nonverbal behavior such as playing with objects, rocking or looking at the time.

- Focusing on points of disagreement, looking for a chance to attack, listening intensively for something you don't agree with instead of concentrating on positive aspects.
- Being turned off by the other person and therefore being disinterested.
- Listening only to the facts, as opposed to listening to the whole message.
- Dropping out when something is boring and not interesting.

How Do You Use It?

Be quiet, make eye contact, relax and concentrate on listening when the other person is expressing an opinion. Allow the other person to finish, because people usually come to their point at the end of their story. Stay in tune with the speaker by using the "listening thought time" to review what has been said. The listening thought time is the gap between thinking speed and speaking rate, which gives you time to think while listening. In general, listeners think at a rate of about 500 words per minute, but the typical speaker talks at a rate of about 125 to 150 words per minute (Miller, Catt, & Carlson, 1996). Therefore, we mentally process words almost four times as quickly as people normally talk. Some other recommendations for effective listening are (Rampersad, 2003):

- Listen critically and intently to the whole message; listen for ideas, feelings, intentions, and facts, and extract the most important themes.
- Postpone your opinion; don't jump to conclusions before the other person has finished speaking.
- Don't be distracted by external disturbances and the manner of presentation; concentrate on what is said, pay attention to the speaker, and show that you are listening intently by making eye contact and showing through verbal and nonverbal means show that you understand what is being said.
- Concentrate on the contents and not on the "packaging."
- Wait before reacting; if you react too soon, you are liable to listen less intently and therefore to assimilate insufficient information. Don't be tempted to interrupt at the first opportunity.
- Be prepared to react to ideas, suggestions, and remarks without putting them down.

- Don't concentrate on what you expect to hear; don't anticipate what the other person is going to say; and let the other person finish talking.
- Don't listen impatiently, defensively, or aggressively.
- Suppress your prejudices.
- Suppress the need to react emotionally to what is said or to what you think is said.
- Try to organize what you hear.
- Take notes occasionally, but don't be distracted by constantly taking notes.
- Prepare yourself mentally to start listening.

Remarks That Show You Are Really Listening

- From your words I understand that ... Is that correct?
- As I listen to you, it seems that you are very disappointed about...
- Do you mean to say that...?
- If this is the case, then we must...

Questioning

What Is It?

Questioning gives you the opportunity to pursue factual information from the other person, or to find out what someone's opinion is about a certain subject. Two basic types of questions can be distinguished: *open* and *closed questions*. *Open questions* are meant to invite someone to give elaborate information about, for example, opinions and feelings. They are also used to involve people in a conversation. Open questions usually start with the words *what, when, why, who, which, where,* or *how*. Open questions invite and stimulate participation and involvement. By asking an open question, all possibilities for answering the question are available, which can result in broadening and deepening the contact. These questions are meant, for example, to ask for clarification and to stimulate one's own discovery. *Closed questions* are used to place emphasis on something or to get a *yes* or *no* answer. With these questions you can guide the conversation in a certain way. They can also be used to obtain specific information quickly. Unfortunately, they are less useful than open questions because the answer to them is usually only *yes* or *no*. To obtain a complete picture, it is important to ask mostly open questions.

Open and closed questions can be subdivided as the following types of questions:

- *Informative questions*; questions to receive actual information.
- *Specific questions*; questions that invite a person to think in a certain direction. This limits the answer possibilities, which means that limited information is obtained. With this questioning you prove your professional skill.
- *Multiple choice questions*; questions with alternatives.
- *Suggestive questions*; questions in which the answer is already suggested; these are based on the expectations and perceptions of the questioner.
- *Chain questions*; these are composed of several questions.
- *Opinion questions*; questions used to ask the opinion of the other person.

How Do You Use It?

Ask as many open questions as possible in order to increase involvement, prevent uncertainties, reveal valuable information and ideas, and correct outdated views. The results of such questioning are, for instance, more focused discussions, better supported decisions, and evidence of respect and interest. Questions to be avoided when coaching teams are (Pareek & Rao, 1990):

- *Critical and sarcastic questions*; to rebuke the other person or to call his or her ability in question, which develops a gap between leader and employees. These questions may lead to grudges, hostility, and the suppression of ideas. For example, "Why didn't you meet the deadline for this assignment?" contains criticism, whereas "Could you explain to me why it is that you did not meet the deadline?" is an invitation to search for the causes of the delay.
- *Annoying questions*; to check if the other person is right or wrong; this type of interrogation suggests a superior attitude on the part of the leader.
- *Suggestive questions*; to put the wrong answer in the employee's mouth and try to tempt the employee to give an answer. For instance, "Were you not able to meet the deadline because of other problems in the company?" This only leads to those answers the leader wants to hear and, consequently, hinders a closer examination of the problem.

Examples of Various Types of Questions

- Open questions: Can you tell me something about this? What do you mean? How does that work? What do you think? What is your vision on that? Why is it done this way?
- Closed questions: Did you or did you not receive the book? Is the work environment in our organization good or bad? Would you like a green or a blue one?
- Informative question: Since when have you been working there?
- Direct question: Are you satisfied with the delivery timeframe? What do you think about the work environment in our organization?
- Choice question: Do you want a red or a black pen?
- Suggestive question: Is it also your opinion that...? Don't you also think that...? You approve of the work environment, don't you?
- Chain question: How do you execute the process? Did you approach Frank about this? What does he think?
- Opinion question: Do you find this work meaningful?

Building on the Ideas of Others

What Is It?
People continuously generate ideas. It is important that you are able to build on the ideas of others; this results in an increase in the number and quality of ideas. Building on the ideas of others means that you adopt someone's suggestion and add something of your own to it.

How Do You Use It?
Give credit to the other person's idea and then suggest improvements and supplements. This way, fewer ideas are lost and more solutions that are thought through are obtained. Giving credit also produces a feeling of appreciation from the person who had the idea in the first place. The goal of building on someone's ideas is to elaborate, improve, and convert this person's idea into successful action. It is therefore important to always take ideas seriously. An internal reward given to the best idea may produce useful suggestions.

Examples of Building on Ideas

- Yes, because in the meantime we will have a chance to prepare ourselves better and analyze a few things more carefully.
- Good idea, Arnold. This gives us the opportunity to create the buy-in for …

Constructive Arguing

What Is It?

Constructive arguing makes differences in opinion known in a positive and constructive way; this results in a productive contribution to a discussion. The conversation is thus broadened, whereby new ideas and opinions can be created.

How Do You Use It?

Object in a positive and constructive manner. State another viewpoint and explain why, according to you, the first idea should not be accepted. Thus, correct inaccurate statements and offer different views. In doing so, you will obtain greater clarity, better involvement, and improved decision making.

Examples of Constructive Arguing

- That can be true, but look at it from the point of view of …
- In my opinion, it may not be such a good idea, because it is coupled with …

Clarifying

What Is It?

Interpret and repeat clearly and distinctly in your own words what the other person has said. Experience indicates that in approximately 50% of all cases misunderstandings occur because the other person's statement has not been clarified.

How Do You Use It?

Ask a question to be sure that you understood what the other person meant. Thus, interpret what the other person said, repeat this in your own words, and check if it is correct. This way you will have fewer misunderstandings, greater clarity, more objective discussions, and a better understanding of personal feelings.

Examples of Clarifying

- So as to leave no doubt, you say that ...
- Thus, in other words, you mean that ...
- If I understand what you've said correctly, this means that...

Summarizing

What Is It?

By summarizing what is said and repeating what is agreed on, you create order, clarity, structure, progress, peace, and more depth in the discussion. Clarifying involves a particular point in the discussion, whereas a summary encompasses an entire conversation.

How Do You Use It?

At the beginning of a meeting summarize the most important points of the previous meeting. From time to time during the meeting, give an impartial, none-critical review of the connection between the different items of the meeting. Ask as often as necessary whether your summary corresponds with what participants meant. Also, give a summary before going on to the next item on the agenda.

Example of Summarizing
- Okay, let's start. During the previous meeting, we discussed a couple of possible solutions and eliminated a few others, so that in the end three solutions remained. Rhoda was going to research the feasibility of the remaining solutions. Does this match with what we already discussed? Rhoda, could you please give us the results?

Involving Others

What Is It?
Involve the participants in a discussion in such a way that their active participation is encouraged and supported.

How Do You Use It?
See to it that no one is excluded from the discussion. Bring people who have been silent for a long period of time into the discussion by asking them a question. This way active participation is stimulated and a feeling of self-worth and strong motivation is created as well.

Examples of Involving Others

- John, we have not heard from you yet. What do you think of this solution?
- Frank, you're out of the spotlight. What is your plan regarding to …?

Showing Appreciation

What Is It?
Show appreciation during a discussion in such a way that you stimulate improved performance, stronger motivation, and a feeling of self-worth.

How Do You Use It?

One method to encourage employees to improve performance is by expressing your honest appreciation every time someone endeavors something and gets results. Indicate clearly what you're showing your appreciation for and for whom it is meant. Do this when others are present and shortly after the delivered performance. Appreciation can be a word of thanks or a compliment for something someone has done or said correctly. The objective of this is to show that you have noticed someone's efforts, to stimulate people to repeat the effort, and to encourage others to deliver similar efforts. Don't focus exclusively on what employees do wrong. Catch them red-handed doing a good job and give them the benefit of the doubt.

Examples of Showing Appreciation

- Very good, Jane. That was a terrific speech. Thanks a lot.
- Finally, I would like to thank Fred for all the work he has done.

Giving and Receiving Feedback

What Is It?

Feedback is a form of communication whereby the receiver of the message lets the sender know how the message came across. As a result, the person will know the effect that his or her behavior has on others. Annoying behavior can be corrected and shaped into the required behavior. Giving and receiving feedback involves redirecting, correcting, and complimenting. As a result, group cooperation becomes more open and effective. This skill also fits within the framework of 360° feedback, an important means to improve the functioning of individual employees.

How Do You Use It?

Here are some general guidelines to follow. Feedback:

- Describes the behavior that has led to the feedback; it does not make a description about the person.
- Is not given to judge the person, it is just something that is mentioned in order to achieve improvement.
- Is specific and not general; it is clear so that the receiver understands its message.
- Is in the interest of both receiver and sender.
- Is only meaningful if and when the receiver is open to it.
- Should be given within 5 minutes.
- Is not a discussion.

Apart from these guidelines there are certain rules for the sender as well as for the receiver. The most important rules for the *feedback provider* are (Rampersad, 2003):

- Clarify to yourself beforehand what you want to say and collect the necessary data.
- Start out with positive points.
- Present feedback in such a way that it is seen as an opportunity and not a threat.
- Be specific; make clear what effects the other's behavior has had on you: for instance, "The remark you just made irritated me, because I felt that I did not do my utmost to solve the problem adequately."
- Be open and honest.
- Make your observation of the other person's behavior descriptive (what you see) and not judgmental (giving assessments): "During

the meeting you were not very talkative, why?" Not: "Your participation in the meeting was not up to par, were you not interested?"

- Convey what you observe in terms of specific behavior, not personal attacks or generalized judgments: "The remark you just
made irritated me." Not: "You're someone who always wants to be
in the spotlight with your off-the-wall remarks."
- Refer to events that occur now or have happened recently, such as:
"Your absence today was very annoying." Not: "In previous years
you have frequently been absent too."
- Give the other person the opportunity to react; listen intently and
keep an open mind to his or her opinion.
- Show that you trust the other person and end the conversation with
some positive remarks about the future.
- Appreciate people for who they are, not only for their accomplish-
ments.
- Be selective in giving feedback; only give feedback if the other per-
son can benefit from it at this time.
- Draw conclusions and give specific examples.

The most important rules for the *receiver of feedback* are (Rampersad,
2003):

- Listen attentively and closely before you accept the feedback; ask or
clarification when something is not clear.
- Don't go into a defensive mode or start attacking; don't look for
explanations; feedback is a learning process.
- Accept the feedback and analyze why you're acting in the way that
has been addressed.
- Know that the feedback giver is kindly disposed toward you; don't
feel that you are being attacked.
- Don't express negative feelings; study the feedback with the
sender.
- Don't try to be humorous or smart; concentrate on a change for the
better.
- Summarize the feedback to be able to formulate your observations.
- Ask questions to clarify the feedback.
- Carefully evaluate the usefulness of the feedback.
- Don't react vehemently and aggressively toward negative feedback;
get information from it.
- Don't consider the feedback to be criticism.

- Show appreciation to the feedback sender because he or she had the courage to help you.

Constructive Negotiating

What Is It?

Constructive negotiating is a process in which interdependent people with conflicting needs, interests, or objectives try to find a compromise through a good and tactical negotiation that will be acceptable to everyone. Such a negotiation is also characterized by recognition of disputes, mutual benefits, possible use of pressure by the negotiating parties, and a willingness to bargain. Constructive negotiation is an essential part of teamwork. In fact, although team members have the same team objective, sometimes differences in opinion, contrarieties, and conflicts of interest can still develop. Through constructive negotiation team members can agree on how to reach the team objective.

How Do You Use It?

With constructive negotiation it is necessary to take into consideration the following rules, so that negotiating partners can enter into a good process that favors everyone (Rampersad, 2003):

- Adequately prepare the conversation.
- Look for the golden mean between hard negotiating (winning at the expense of mutual understanding) and soft negotiating (personal objectives are abandoned to maintain friendship with the other party). Continue to keep your own objectives in perspective, even if you make concessions.
- Attend to maintaining a balance in power and don't be completely dependent upon the other person; negotiations are not necessary when one party has more power than the other.
- Listen actively and put yourself in the other's shoes; try to understand his or her interests and perception on things. Say: "*I understand fully that you....*" Nevertheless, don't forget your own interests. Ask open questions and, when necessary, direct questions to find out the other person's interests. Also provide adequate information. Don't answer questions before you fully understand them; ask for an explanation.
- Strive for a compromise that benefits both parties; look for similarities in interests (mutual benefits) and combine them in a flexible way. Say: "*Can we share the work in such a way that everyone...*"

- See to a positive environment and good mutual relationship; separate the people from the problem. Be businesslike, not personal and emotional. Don't focus on the behavior of the other person. Focus on issues to which both parties are committed.

- Don't negotiate about positions and from one person's point of view but on the basis of interests; don't put your objective first, as if you are not about to give in an inch. A fighting attitude seldom rewards you, and forcing a point through does not lead to good results.

- Make choices from different alternatives, and use independent and objective criteria accepted by both parties to test these alternatives.

- Avoid a direct rejection of a proposal from the other person; get positive points out in the open, and express appreciation for these. If the other person proposes something, do not immediately make a counterproposal. React to the proposal by asking questions, and then try to present your proposal as an addition.

- Look for verbal and nonverbal signals from the other person, because these can be an indication of what the other person finds important or not.

- Be patient, optimistic, and friendly; have respect for the other person, and strive for a positive feeling in both of you.

- Give a summary; in this way any confusing or difficult situations or differences of opinion can be made transparent. In addition, summaries entail making concrete agreements, which creates continuity and order in the discussion.

Conflict Handling

What Is It?

If the differences between people are considerable, negotiations are generally useless and conflict arises. A conflict is a clash between people that is revealed by their behavior and attitude. Team conflicts arise when, due to irritation or differences of opinion, two or more team members are not willing to cultivate positive cooperation. Differences in speaking styles, conflicting objectives, differences in personal style, personal egos, differences in values and norms, differences in personal interest, lack of clarity, working under time constraints, and claims about scarce resources can all be the cause of conflict. Conflict handling, or the way in which we deal with differences, can sometimes be more harmful than the conflicts themselves. Conflicts can be positive in certain cases, however, because they force employees to reassess their own ideas and thus develop new knowledge. If we were always to agree with each other, there would be no reason to challenge the status quo and benefit from the change. In conflict handling there must always be a continuous search for a balance between learning and escalation.

How Do You Use It?

In a conflict three phases of escalation can be distinguished:

1. *Rational phase.* The case is still negotiable; the cause of the irritation is separate from the matter at hand; parties often reach a solution without outside help, provided that the conflict is recognized and there is willingness for constructive cooperation.
2. *Emotional phase.* Parties blame each other for the conflict, and efforts are undertaken to form coalitions.
3. *Fighting phase.* The relationship between the parties is in grave danger of being irreparably damaged. The parties try as much as possible to inflict damage, even at their own expense.

To effectively handle a conflict it is important to know the sensibility of those involved and in which phase the conflict is. Five styles of coping with conflicts have been outlined by Kor (1998):

1. forcing or enforcing your own solution if you are sure that you are right ("*stand firm*");
2. putting up with the other's ideas ("*keep the peace*");
3. reaching a compromise ("*pacification*");
4. denying that something is happening ("*play dumb*"); and
*   putting the problem on the table and together looking for acceptable solutions to benefit the team results ("*be open and above board in one's dealings*").

There is no ideal style for handling conflict. The preference for a certain style has more to do with your own personality and depends on the situation and the phase in which the conflict is. Good conflict handling requires application of all the aforementioned interpersonal skills as well as good negotiating. Some important rules for conflict handling include:

*   Voice any irritations as soon as possible.
*   If there are differences of opinion, discuss them quietly; do not react emotionally and become angry.
*   Listen and evaluate before drawing conclusions.

- Search for points of agreement as soon as possible.
- Prevent the conflict between two persons from escalating into a team problem.
- Prevent emotional reactions; don't get angry, don't start crying, don't become jealous, and don't show hate. If necessary, go home to cool off.
- Don't make demands, and don't have an intractable standpoint.
- Don't linger too long on the past; look ahead.
- Be nice.
- Negotiate constructively.

A summary of the interpersonal skills discussed in the preceding sections is provided in Table B.3.

APPENDIX C: TPS-LEAN SIX SIGMA TEAM EVALUATION

In the scope of the TPS-Lean Six Sigma, the meeting process should be reviewed continuously, so that we can learn from it, control this process and reduce waste of ideas. To accomplish this aim, an evaluation form may be used, which is introduced and illustrated in Table C.1 (Rampersad, 2003). The interpersonal skills discussed in the preceding section are included in this form. After the TPS-Lean Six Sigma meeting each project team member should score the assertions in the Teamwork Evaluation Form (see scoring key in Table C.1 for guidelines) then add the scores in this form. The closer the total score is to 100, the more effective the teamwork process. The closer your score is to 30, the more inefficient the meeting process. After you and others have completed this evaluation form individually, discuss your scores in the team. Indicate what could have been done better. For this purpose a team of six Business Jet volunteers was assembled under the leadership of John Johnson's security team at Business Jet evaluated the meeting process during the execution of the risk analyses (see previous section in this Appendix and OBSC of this company in chapter 4) with the aid of the evaluation form presented in Table C.1. In this table the shared evaluation results are marked with black bullet marks. The total score came to 77 points, which implies that the meeting process went reasonably well. Nevertheless, there are a number of improvement points to be addressed, which are indicated by the statements with a score of 1 or 2 (see the bottom of Table C.1).

Table B.3. Summary of Interpersonal Skills

Goal	Result	Technique
	Listening	
Gather information.	Better understanding and being informed.	Be quiet, make eye contact, relax, and listen attentively when the other person gives his opinion. Listen until the other person has finished speaking, reply only then. Try to imagine yourself in the other's position; this allows you to understand the subject of discussion better. Show the other person that he is being taken seriously and you are trying to understand him. Ask questions for clarification, repeat what has been said literally or in your own words, and look for common interests.
	Questioning	
Obtain valuable information and ideas, increase involvement.	Better decisions and focused discussions.	First, decide what you want to achieve with your question and then ask the right question. Second, ask questions in such a way that the other person feels comfortable and involved in the discussion.
	Building on Ideas of Others	
Develop and shape ideas.	More solutions that are thought out, hence better, and a greater feeling of appreciation.	Express your appreciation for the other person's idea and then add something of your own.
	Constructive Arguing	
State other views of the other person and correct wrong statements.	Transparency, better decision making, and involvement.	Analyze the other person's ideas and give an alternative view. Furnish reasons for why the idea cannot be accepted or explain why it would fail.

Table continues on next page.

Table B.3. Summary of Interpersonal Skills Continued

Goal	Result	Technique
Clarifying		
Be certain that you have interpreted what the other said correctly.	More transparency, fewer misunderstandings, and better listening skills.	Interpret what the other person has said and check if it is correct. Repeat the other person's words according to your understanding.
Summarizing		
Create insight on the most important points from the previous discussion.	Clarity and structure in the discussion.	Repeat the most important decisions and agreements from a previous meeting.
Involving Others		
Stimulate greater involvement and active participation.	Create better listening skills as well as self-esteem and stronger motivation.	Address the respective person by name and ask a question to involve him in the meeting.
Showing Appreciation		
Encourage someone to deliver the same effort and urge others to do the same.	Motivation and self-esteem- inspire higher performances.	Show your appreciation for good performance immediately and clearly. Preferably show appreciation in the presence of others and state clearly whom it is meant for.
Giving and Receiving Feedback		
Correct annoying behavior and adjust it to encourage the required behavior. Cooperation in the group becomes more open and effective.	More effective cooperation and open communication.	Decide for yourself if you will give the feedback or not and what you and the other will gain from it. If you will give and receive feedback, use the aforementioned rules. use the rules more open and listed in the section on giving and receiving feedback, such as be specific, open, and honest; appreciate people for who they are; don't express negative feelings; don't consider the feedback to be criticism; and so forth.

Constructive Negotiating

After positive deliberation come to an understanding on conflicting wishes, interests, and goals; find a compromise that is acceptable to all parties.	More clarity, less irritations, and differences of opinion, higher team performance, and a good relationship between the negotiating parties.	Provide good preparation, power balance and positive climate. Be patient and apply the rules mentioned, such as don't be completely depended upon the other person; strive for a compromise that benefits both parties; be patient, optimistic, and friendly; and so forth.

Conflict Handling

Reduce conflicts that result of irritations and differences of opinion.	More clarity, fewer misunderstandings, greater involvement, effective cooperation, and higher team performance.	Check in which phase the conflict is and acknowledge the sensibility of those involved. Then, apply the mentioned rules, such as listen and evaluate before drawing conclusions, search for point of agreements, prevent emotional reactions, be nice, and so forth.

Table C.1. TPS–Lean Six Sigma Team Evaluation Form, Used on Business Jet

	1	2	3	4
We know our own team roles and learning styles as well as those from the other project team members. These were accepted, appreciated, and respected.	1	2	3	•4
We received support for our personal development and help with the generation of new ideas.	1	2	3	•4
Everyone listened attentively to each other. They listened to everyone's opinion, including minority points of view.	1	•2	3	4
Mostly open questions were asked.	1	2	•3	4
The ideas of others were built on.	•1	2	3	4
There was constructive arguing.	1	•2	3	4
The remarks of others were clarified.	1	2	•3	4
Previous conversations were summarized.	•1	2	3	4
People who did not participate in the meeting were asked to become involved.	1	•2	3	4
Appreciation was expressed.	1	2	•3	4
Constructive feedback was given.	1	2	3	•4
There were no serious conflicts; there was no power struggle among project team members.	1	2	•3	4
We exchanged knowledge spontaneously; we did not keep it to ourselves.	1	2	•3	4
The opinions of the team members were clearly expressed.	1	2	3	•4
We were in agreement and spoke the same language; we understood and complemented each other.	1	2	3	•4
We devoted ourselves to the shared project team mission and the Project BSC.	1	2	3	•4
The project vision, and mission were clear to us, and everyone found it valuable and approved of it.	1	2	3	•4
We each got the chance to openly express our opinions and ideas; we could say the things we wanted in a frank discussion and through open communication.	1	2	3	•4
There was no gossip in smaller groups.	1	•2	3	4
We respected and trusted each other; we felt comfortable, equal to each other; and responsible.	1	2	•3	4
Everyone had his own clearly defined task: time keeper, process keeper; minute taker, data collector; and so forth.	1	2	3	•4
We followed the TPS–Lean Six Sigma method and had the opportunity to think and act creatively.	•1	2	3	4

What we were working on was transparent, and our discussions were purposeful.	1	•2	3	4
We stuck to the points on the agenda.	1	•2	3	4
We were clear about our responsibilities for the points of action taken; we committed ourselves to the project team decisions.	1	•2	3	4
The Chairperson was well prepared.	1	2	•3	4
We worked together harmoniously toward generating new ideas; we continuously looked for fresh points of views to tackle problems.	1	2	•3	4

Total Score: 77 points

Circle the correct number: 1 = never/no/not correct 2 = once in a while/hardly ever 3 = frequent/usually 4 = always/yes/correct

Remarks/Recommendations: improve listening skills; build more on ideas of others; argue constructively; give more summaries; encourage those who are silent to participate more in the group; apply brainstorming techniques more systematically; communicate meeting objectives more clearly; follow the agenda during the meeting, and clearly communicate responsibilities regarding points of action.

APPENDIX D:
TPS-LEAN SIX SIGMA KNOWLEDGE MANAGEMENT QUICK SCAN

In order to increase organizational learning ability, insight into the present knowledge and learning situation and related organizational barriers is also needed. For this purpose we introduce here a knowledge management quick scan, shown in Table D.1, which consists of 50 statements regarding your organizational *knowledge and learning orientation*, which are divided into the following five dimensions: *general*, *leadership style*, *strategic vision*, *internal processes*, and *human resources*. As TPS-Lean Six Sigma is implemented in your organization, judge the learning ability of your organization based on this checklist, and, as a team, check why this is characteristic for your organization. To this end, complete the survey in Table D.1 by circling the number that best reflects the accuracy of the assertions in your organization. Use the scoring key (1 to 4) in Table D.1; 1 = never/no/not correct, 2 = once in a while/a little/less, 3 = frequent/ usually, and 4 = always/ yes/correct. Add these scores vertically. The closer your total score gets to 200, the more knowledge intensive your company is. A comparably high score is related to a learning organization with a large learning ability. The closer your total score is to 50, the smaller the organizational learning ability. Discuss your scores in your team and indicate, what could have been done better in your organization.

Business Jet's executive team also completed this quick scan in order to comply with the corporate knowledge and learning perspective in the corporate scorecard. The shared evaluation results are marked (with black bullets) in Table D.1. The total score was 138 points; this implies that, in the area of knowledge management, something needs to be done for Business Jet to be classified as a full-fledged learning organization. Statements with a score of 1 and 2 in Table D.1 suggest areas where improvement actions may be taken (see bottom of Table D.1). These are part of the result area *knowledge and learning* in Business Jet's OBSC (see chapter 4).

The following boxed text, shows the TPS-Lean Six Sigma Strategies to Increase the learning ability of organizations.

TPS-Lean Six Sigma Strategies to
Increase the Organizational Learning Ability

- Creating conditions whereby people are willing to apply their knowledge, and share and intensively exchange it with each other.
- Establishing the organizational structure in such a way that people get sufficient space and opportunities to gain experiences and think.

Table D.1. TPS-Lean Six Sigma Knowledge Management Quick Scan

Circle the correct number: 1 = never/no/not correct, 2 = once in a while/a little/less, 3 = frequent/usually, 4 = always/yes/correct

General

	Statement	1	2	3	4
1.	Making mistakes is allowed; failures are tolerated and not penalized. People learn from each other's mistakes, and errors are openly discussed.	1	2	•3	4
2.	Managers and employees know where particular knowledge can be found in the organization, and who knows what is transparent to everyone.	•1	2	3	4
3.	Employees get the space to think, learn (consciously as well as subconsciously), act, make informal contacts, gain experience, experiment and take risks.	1	2	•3	4
4.	Management information systems are integrated and continually updated.	1	2	3	•4
5.	The necessary knowledge for important decisions is usually readily available and easily accessible.	1	•2	3	4
6.	There are no barriers for the use and exchange of knowledge.	1	2	3	•4
7.	Managers and employees have the skills to adequately categorize, use, and maintain knowledge.	1	2	•3	4
8.	The organization has a network of knowledge workers.	1	2	•3	4
9.	The organizational structure is simple, has few hierarchical levels and consists of autonomous units.	•1	2	3	4
10.	The organization is characterized by diversity (people with different cultural backgrounds and learning styles), a planned as well as intuitive approach, people with different team roles, etc.	1	2	•3	4
11.	There is an active program for developing ideas. Based on this, new knowledge is continually generated.	1	2	3	•4
12.	There is no competition between colleagues. Internal competition is not reinforced.	1	•2	3	4
13.	An atmosphere of fear and distrust does not exist in the organization.	1	2	3	•4

Leadership Style

	Statement	1	2	3	4
14.	Upper management is committed to enlarging learning ability and creating a learning organization.	1	2	3	•4
15.	Employees are continually stimulated and encouraged to identify and solve shared problems as a team, to brainstorm, to generate creative ideas, and to share these with each other.	1	2	3	•4
16.	Managers and employees have the knowledge important for organizational success	1	2	•3	4

Table continues on next page.

Table D.1. TPS-Lean Six Sigma Knowledge Management Quick Scan Continued

Circle the correct number: 1 = never/no/not correct, 2 = once in a while/a little/less, 3 = frequent/usually, 4 = always/yes/correct

Leadership Style

	1	2	3	4
17. Executives, Champions and Belts fulfill the styles of coaching, inspiring and serving leadership in an optimal mix. They stimulate a fundamental learning attitude, intensive knowledge exchange and internal entrepreneurship, and they promote individual as well as team learning.	1	•2	3	4
18. Managers and employees are continually focused on developing and mobilizing the knowledge of employees/project team members and regularly give constructive feedback about attempted improvement, development, and learning actions.	1	•2	3	4
19. Managers and employees use simple oral and written language, are action oriented, and facilitate the process "learning by doing."	1	2	•3	4
20. Management knows which employees are the carriers of valuable and scarce knowledge. Sources of internal expertise have been mapped out.	•1	2	3	4
21. A knowledge manager, one who coaches and facilitates the learning processes, has been appointed. His or her most important skills are: understanding, processing, communicating, and sharing knowledge.	1	2	3	•4

Strategic Vision

	1	2	3	4
22. Knowledge management is a strategic theme that is part of the shared organizational ambition.	1	2	3	•4
23. There is continuous collective learning in order to develop the core competences of the organization.	1	•2	3	4
24. There are a minimum of five knowledge and learning objectives and related performance measures formulated in the corporate scorecard.	1	2	3	•4
25. Managers and employees have formulated a minimum of three knowledge and learning objectives and related performance measures in their Personal Balanced Scorecard that are aligned to the shared organizational and project ambition (OBSC and Project BSC).	1	2	3	•4
26. Customer information is considered strategically valuable.	1	2	•3	4

Internal Process

	1	2	3	4
27. Managers and employees do not hoard knowledge but share it spontaneously with each other. Individuals, teams, and business units systematically and intensively exchange knowledge with each other.	•1	2	3	4
28. Knowledge growth is promoted through the organizational culture. This is a culture characterized by simplicity, open-communication, and doing instead of talking too much.	•1	2	3	4
29. Problems are tackled holistically by a systems approach. For this purpose, procedures are drafted and used routinely.	1	•2	3	4
30. Knowledge gaps are systematically and continually mapped out and measures are taken to narrow and eliminate them.	1	•2	3	4
31. Relevant implicit knowledge is made explicit through images and metaphors, reviewed, spread throughout the organization and intensively exchanged.	•1	2	3	4
32. User friendly communication and information systems are used to broadly spread knowledge among all employees.	1	•2	3	4
33. Obtained and developed knowledge is continually documented and made available to everyone in the organization.	1	•2	3	4
34. Employees with valuable and scarce knowledge rotate among different business units and participate in a variety of project teams.	1	2	•3	4
35. There is a learning environment characterized by positive thinking, self-esteem, mutual trust, willingness to intervene preventively, taking responsibility for business performances, openness, enjoyment, and passion. Employees and project team members are urged to continually study how they work and to adjust their work if needed.	1	•2	3	4
36. The learning processes are initiated and guided by existing or expected problems. Problems are seen as a chance to learn or change. Conflicts are seen as unresolved challenges.	1	2	•3	4
37. People work and learn together harmoniously in self-guiding teams. Here team members have knowledge that overlaps; a balance of personalities, skills and learning styles; and knowledge about their own favorite learning style and that of their colleagues.	1	2	•3	4
38. Knowledge is constantly being implemented and incorporated into new products, services and processes.	1	2	•3	4
39. Benchmarking is done systematically to gain knowledge. Best practices within and outside the organization are identified and propagated internally. That which is learned is generalized.	1	2	3	•4
40. Knowledge and learning indicators are measured constantly and used as the starting point for process improvement.	1	2	3	•4

Table continues on next page.

Table D.1. TPS-Lean Six Sigma Knowledge Management Quick Scan Continued

Circle the correct number: 1 = never/no/not correct, 2 = once in a while/a little/less, 3 = frequent/usually, 4 = always/yes/correct

Internal Process

	1	2	3	4
41. Organizational knowledge is shared through informal contacts, internal lectures, conferences, problem solving and project review meetings, dialogue sessions, internal rapports, memos, etc.	1	•2	3	4
42. Knowledge sharing is facilitated through Internet, intranet, library, comfortable meeting rooms, auditorium, computerized archive and documentation system, etc.	1	•2	3	4
43. Employees and project team members have varied and challenging work. There is task rotation.	1	2	3	•4

Human Resources

	1	2	3	4
44. Job appraisal and competence development are explicitly linked to the personal ambition of individuals and the shared ambition of the organization.	1	2	3	•4
45. Managers and employees are judged by what they do, not on how smart they seem and how much they talk.	1	2	•3	4
46. Employee knowledge is developed constantly and kept up-to-date by means of training, coaching, and talent development programs.	1	2	•3	4
47. There is a proactive competence development policy, which includes internal and external training, courses, working conferences, symposia, and seminars.	1	•2	3	4
48. Knowledge and learning competences are part of every employee's competence profile.	1	2	3	•4
49. The knowledge of departing employees is passed on to successors.	•1	2	3	4
50. Managers and employees who deliver collective learning performances for the sake of the entire organization's well-being and constantly share their knowledge with colleagues are rewarded more than others and have more promotion opportunities.	1	2	•3	4

Total Score:	138 points

Remarks /Suggestions: improve localizing of knowledge; improve availability and accessibility of knowledge; improve leadership skills; create more insight with management about those who carry valuable and scarce knowledge; increase learning efforts; stimulate employees to share knowledge with each other and exchange it intensively; stimulate knowledge exchange between teams and business units; systematically map out and remove knowledge gaps; make relevant implicit knowledge explicit; improve user-friendliness of information and communication systems; improve the learning climate; develop competence policy; and convey knowledge of departing employees to successors.

- Stimulating employees to formulate their own Personal Balanced Scorecard and through this cultivate a positive attitude toward improvement, learning, and developing.
- Letting employees reflect on the balance between their own personal ambition and the shared organizational and project ambition.
- Making an inventory of your learning style and aligning it to your personal ambition. Reviewing this periodically; aligning it to the planning, coaching, and appraisal meetings and the 360°–feedback system.
- Establishing improvement teams in which a balance of personalities, skills, and learning styles is present.
- Developing and accepting self-knowledge regarding your own favorite learning style and those of other project team members.
- Giving people a sense of direction based on the shared organizational and project ambition and connecting them with each other.
- Working with teams where team learning is central—teams that think and act from a synergetic perspective, are well coordinated, and work with a feeling of unity.
- Using images, metaphors, and intuitions to share and exchange implicit knowledge.
- Working with self-directing project teams in an organizational network that uses generalists with ample responsibilities and competences and in which there are knowledge overlaps and task rotations between employees/project team members.
- Stimulating employees and project team members to think about, identify, and solve common problems as a team, let go of traditional ways of thinking, constantly develop their own skills, acquire experience, and feel responsible for company and team performances.
- Having Executives, Champions, and Belts who coach, help, inspire, motivate and stimulate, are action-oriented, and constantly evaluate processes based on performance measures.
- Having people who continually learn from their mistakes and openly communicate with each other, and who constantly apply TPS-Lean Six Sigma in their actions.
- Systematically working with problem-solving methods (brainstorming, problem-solving cycle, risk management, etc.) included in this book.
- Giving feedback about improvement actions undertaken.
- Applying an integral and systems approach.

- Implementing a knowledge infrastructure; Internet, intranet, library, evaluation sessions, and so forth.
- Stimulating informal employee contacts.
- • Driving out fear and mistrust from the organization and project teams
- Simplifying the organizational structure and the language of managers.
- Allowing mistakes; without mistakes, there is no learning.

LIST OF ACRONYMS

ANOVA–Analysis of Variance

BOM–Bill of Materials

BSC–Balanced Scorecard

BSCsoft–Balanced Scorecard Software

CFR–Critical Functional Responses

COPQ–Cost of Poor Quality

CM–Commodity Manager

CRM–Customer Relationship Management

CSFs–Critical Success Factors

CTF–Critical to Functions

CTQs–Critical to Quality Characteristics

DFSS–Design for Six Sigma

DMAIC–Define, Measure, Analyze, Improve, and Control

DOE–Design of Experiment

DPMO–Defects Per Million Opportunities

DPO–Defect Per Opportunities

DPU–Defect Per Unit

EOQ–Economic Order Quantity

FMEA–Failure Modes and Effects Analysis

ICF–International Coaching Federation

IDOV–Identify, Design, Optimize, and Verify

ISO–International Organization for Standardization
MRO–Multiple Response Optimization
MSA–Measurement System Analysis
MSF–Management by Fact
OBSC–Organizational Balanced Scorecard
PA–Personal Ambition
PB–Personal Behavior
PBSC–Personal Balanced Scorecard
PD–Product Development
PDAC–Plan-Do-Act-Challenge
PDCA–Plan-Do-Check-Act
PET–Project Evaluation Template
PM–Performance Measures
QFD–Quality Function Deployment
ROI–Return on Investment
RSM–Response Surface Methodology
SA–Shared Ambition
SIPOC–Supplier Input Process Output-Customer
SPC–Statistical Process Control
SWOT–Strengths, Weaknesses, Opportunities, and Threats
TPS–Total Performance Scorecard
TPS–Lean Six Sigma–Total Performance Scorecard Lean Six Sigma
TQM–Total Quality Management
TRIZ–Inventive Problem Solving
VOC–Voice of the Customer

REFERENCES AND RECOMMENDED READINGS

Akzo, Nobel. (1994). *Managing total quality*. Netherlands: Author.

Barton, G. M. (1990). *Communication: Manage words effectively*. Costa Mesa, CA.

Besterfield, D. H. (1995). *Total Quality Management*. Upper Saddle River, NJ: Prentice Hall.

Boyett, J. H., & J. T. Boyett. (1998). *The guru guide: The best ideas of the top management thinkers*. New York: Wiley.

Camp, R. C. (1995). *Benchmarking: Searching for the best working methods that will lead to superior performances* Deventer: Kluwer Business Information.

Covey, S. R., (1990) *The 8th habit*. New York: Simon & Schuster.

Cryer, B. (2003). *Pull the plug on stress*. Harvard Business Review.

Deming, W. E. (1985). *Out of the crisis*. Cambridge: Massachusetts Institute of Technology.

Evans, R., & P. Russell. (1991). *De creatieve manager*. Cothen, the Netherlands: Servire.

Genco, F (2007). *ROI INFORMATION FOR YOUR CFO*. Retrieved from, http://www.lovethewayyouwork.com/roi.php

Harry, M. J., & Schroeder, R. (2005). *Six Sigma: The breakthrough management strategy revolutionizing the world's top corporations*. Bantam Dell Pub Group.

Hauser, J. R., & D. Clausing. (1988). The house of quality. *Harvard Business Review, 66*(3).

Imai, M. (1986). *Kaizen*. New York: Random House.

Ishikawa, K. (1985). *What is Total Quality Control? The Japanese way*. Englewood Cliffs, NJ: Prentice-Hall.

Juran, J. M. (1974). *Quality control handbook*. New York: McGraw-Hill.

Kano, N. (1996, April), Attractive quality and must-be quality. *The Journal of the Japanese Society for Quality Control*, 39-48.

Kaplan, R. S., & D. P. Norton. (2003). *Strategy maps: Converting intangible assets into tangible outcomes*. Boston: Harvard Business School Press.

Kepner-Tregoe. (1998). *Probleemanalyse en Besluitvorming*. Princeton: Kepner-Tregoe.

Kor, R. (1998). *Werken aan Projecten*. Deventer, the Netherlands: Kluwer Bedrijfsinformatie.

Kotter, J. P. (1996). *Leading change*. Boston: Harvard Business School Press.

Krueger J., & Killham, E. (2005, December 8). At work, feeling good matters. *Gallup Management Journal*. Retrieved from, http://gmj.gallup.com

Manktelow J., (2003). *Force field analysis*, West Sussex, England: Mind Tools.

McCall, M. W. (1998). *High flyers: Developing the next generation of leaders*. Boston: Harvard Business School Press.

Miller, D. S., Catt, S. E., & Carlson, J. R. (1996). *Fundamentals of management: A framework for excellence*. Minneapolis, MN: West.

Monhemius, L. (2001). *Six Sigma and Baldrige, Malcom, Engine and Roadmap*. The Netherlands: Sigma Number 4, 2001, pp. 0–24

NEN-ISO 9004-4. (1993). *Guidelines for Quality Improvement*. Retrieved from, http://www.iso.ch/en

Ohno, T. (1990), *Toyota production system: Beyond large-scale production:* University Park, IL: Productivity Press.

O'Tool, J. (1996). *Leading change: The argument for values-based leadership*. New York: Ballantine Books.

PA Consulting Group. (1991). *TQM Manual*. London: PA Consulting Group.

Pareek, U., & T. V. Rao. (1990). Performance coaching. In T. W. Pfeifer (Ed.), *Development human resources* (pp. 52-60). San Diego, CA: Academic Press.

Pasmore, W. (1994). *Creating strategic change: Designing the flexible high-performing organization*. New York: Wiley.

Pfeffer, J., & Sutton, R. I. (2002). *De Kloof tussen Weten en Doen*. Schiedam, the Netherlands: Scriptum Management.

Rampersad, H. K. (1994). *Integrated and simultaneous design for robotic assembly*. New York: Wiley.

Rampersad, H. K. (2003). *Total Performance Scorecard; Redefining management to achieve performance with integrity*. Elsevier Science, MA: Butterworth-Heinemann Business Books,

Rampersad, H. K. (2005). *Managing total quality; Enhancing personal and company value*. New Delhi, India: Tata McGraw-Hill.

Rampersad, H. K. (2006). *Personal personal balanced scorecard; The way to individual happiness, personal integrity, and organizational effectiveness*. Greenwich. CT: Information Age Publishing.

Rampersad, H. K. (2007). *Personal brand management: The way to powerful and sustainable personal branding*. Greenwich. CT: Information Age Publishing.

Roozenburg, N. F. M., & J. Eekels. (1995). *Product design, structures and methods*. New York: Wiley.

Rucci, A. J., Kim, S. P., & Quinn, R. T. (1998). The employee-customer profit chain at Sears. *Harvard Business Review, 76*(1), 83-97.

Senge, P. M. (1990). *The fifth discipline: The art and practice of the learning organization*. New York: Doubleday.

Shewart, W. (1931). *Economic control of quality of manufactured product*. Reprint ASQ 18090.

Montgomery, D. C. (1997). *Design and analysis of experiments*. New York: Wiley.

Morita, A. (1994). *Made in Japan*. New York: HarperCollins

Pande, P., Neuman, R., & Cavanagh, R. (1980). *The Six Sigma Way*. New York: McGraw-Hill.

Philips Electronics. (1994). *Customer surveys*. Eindhoven, the Netherlands: Corporate Quality Bureau.

Pyzdek, T. (2001). *The Six Sigma Handbook*. New York: McGraw-Hill.

Rother, M., & Shook, J. (2003). *Learning to see*. Cambridge, MA: Lean Enterprise Institute.

Salary.Com Research. (2006). *Poor Performers can drag a company down*. Retrieved from, http//www.motivationstrategies.com

Salary.Com Research. (2007). *Wasting time at work. You're not alone*. Retrieved from, http://news.yahoo.com/s/nm/20070726/wr_nm/work_time_tech_dc

Schonberger, J. (1996). *World class manufacturing: The next decade: Building power, strength, and value*. Columbus, OH: The Free Press.

Thomas, A. (1996). *Coaching van Teamleden*. Baarn, the Netherlands: Nelissen.

Towers Perrin. (2005). *Winning strategies for a global workforce: Attracting, retaining and engaging employees for competitive advantage*. Retrieved from, www .towersperrin.com

Womack, J. P., Jones, D. T., & Roos, D. (1990). *The machine that changed the world*. Scribner.

Womack, J. P., & Jones, D. T. (1996). *Lean thinking: Banish waste and create wealth in your corporation*. Riverside, NJ: Simon & Schuster.

ABOUT THE AUTHORS

HUBERT RAMPERSAD'S
PERSONAL BRAND/AMBITION

Personal Vision

To live life completely, honestly, and compassionately and to serve the needs of mankind to the best of my ability. I want to realize this in the following way:

- Enjoy physical and mental health.
- Inspire others, earn their respect, and always serve out of love.
- Create organizations where human spirit thrives and which model the best practices in business ethics and performance.
- Experience enjoyment in my work by being full of initiative, accepting challenges continuously, and to keep on learning.
- Achieve financial security.

451

Personal Mission

Enjoy the freedom to develop and share knowledge, especially if this can mean something in the life of others.

Personal Key Roles

- In order to achieve my vision, the following key roles have top priority:
- Spouse: My wife is the most important person in my life.
- Father: Guide my two sons on the road to independence.
- Coach: Serve people and organizations to realize their dreams.
- Student: Learn something new every day and always be a scholar.

About Myself

I was born in Suriname (a former Dutch Colony in South America) in 1957. My father worked as policeman and had little money to raise 10 children (I was number 7). We were living in a very old house in Paramaribo, almost in poverty. Life was quite hard and we lived from week to week. So my parents decided to migrate to the Netherlands in 1971 in order to create better learning opportunities for us. They used all their savings to finance this migration. I was 12 years old when we moved to the Netherlands. At that time, I had a dream to make people happy and to serve the needs of mankind. This was my higher calling, my inner assignment. I remember this. I looked up at factories and buildings and said, I want to make the people that go to those factories and buildings lives a happy life. I was also very eager to learn and I knew that life is short, so I chose to work hard and to grasp all opportunities to educate myself and to make my parents proud of me and not to disappoint them.

I decided to study mechanical engineering at Enschede Polytechnic Institute, where I got my bachelor of science degree. After this, I received a master's of science in robotics from Delft University of Technology, and a PhD in management from Eindhoven University of Technology. I was the first person at this university in the Netherlands who got his doctorate within 2 years. My dissertation was published by John Wiley, Inc. in the United States. I was also the first person from my family, friends, and relatives to receive these advanced degrees.

During this time, I married and had two sons. In order to support my growing family and pay for tuition, I worked in the evenings and during the weekends as a laborer in a factory. While doing this, I noticed that many employees were unhappy. I also noticed that executives contributed to this unhappiness by their disrespectful and often unethical behavior toward their employees. These practices certainly harmed the productivity of the organization. In 1987, I had my first consulting job in the high-tech industry and taught part-time at the Rotterdam School of Management focusing on improving management techniques. After 5 years, I started my own consulting firm serving industrial companies. I also became author of four Dutch books and 50 articles in the field of technology and reengineering business processes within factories.

In 2001, I started thinking about people in a more holistic way; about what would make them engaged and more happy at work, as well as, in their private life and spare time, about how to create work-life balance, how to reduce the gap between company life and private life, how to create more enjoyment and passion at work, how to help executives act in a more ethical manner, how to create a climate of trust and real learning, and how to eliminate fear and distrust. I wanted to humanize companies and to stimulate love and happiness in organizations. In doing all of this, I knew that greater productivity would then emerge.

During this time of inner reflection, I developed my own spirituality— something had changed within me. I discovered that my higher calling was to help people live a higher quality of life by developing and sharing knowledge of themselves with others.

During this time, I reformulated my dream into this vision "To live life completely honestly, and compassionately and to serve the needs of mankind to the best of my ability" and this related mission "Enjoy the freedom to develop and share knowledge, especially if this can mean something in the life of others." Based on my vision and mission, I wrote the book *"Total Performance Scorecard (TPS); Redefining Management to Achieve Performance With Integrity"* which was published by Butterworth-Heinemann in the United States in 2003. I realized that I wrote the book in order to help humanize companies, to stimulate greater enjoyment and happiness at work, to tackle lack of employee engagement, to develop a workforce of committed employees and managers, and to reinforce honesty and trustworthiness in the workplace.

This became my first international best selling book and was translated in 22 languages, which changed my life forever. Based on this success, I began to build an international Total Performance Scorecard movement/network in 2004, which has resulted in strategic alliances in more than 30 countries within 2 years. Padmakumar Nair (professor in

Organization, Strategy, and International Management at the University of Texas School of Management) said the following about this in 2004: "I am amazed with the fact that the Total Performance Scorecard concept is spreading like gospel. Dr. Hubert Rampersad's innovative and pragmatic approach to combine organizational and personal performance agendas into one line of thinking helps organizational participants to come up with tangible solutions to current performance and leadership issues."

Feeling the desire to introduce this process into the United States, in 2006, I decided to move with my family to the United States in order to establish TPS International Inc. and to launch this new business management concept globally from here. In the same year, I published "*Personal Balanced Scorecard; The Way to Individual Happiness, Personal Integrity and Organizational Effectiveness*" (Information Age Publishing, Inc.) which now also has been translated in 15 languages. My related article was awarded in the United Kingdom with "*The most outstanding paper.*" The Total Performance Scorecard and Personal Balanced Scorecard are now worldwide registered trademarks. Based on this, I have established a global business, with strategic alliances in more than 60 countries within 3 years, getting professorships all over the world, conducting keynote speeches and seminars almost weekly somewhere in the world, and coaching executives in many countries about how to master themselves and to become more ethical and effective. I am a member of the editorial advisory board of the journal *Training and Management Development Methods* (UK), member of the editorial advisory board of the journal *Measuring Business Excellence* (UK), member of the editorial advisory board of the *TQM Magazine* (UK), member of the editorial advisory board of the *Journal of Knowledge Management Practice* in Canada, and editorial advisor to *Singapore Management Review*. I am also a member of Marshall Goldsmith's prestigious Thought Leader Advisory Board (www.MarshallGoldsmithLibrary.com) and selected by The Marshall Goldsmith School of Management as one of the 35 distinguished thought leaders in the United States in the field of leadership development. Our related Personal Balanced Scorecard course (as part of our certification program) has been certified by the International Coach Federation (ICF), the world's largest coaching organization. I am currently working on my fifth new book (*Personal Brand Management; The Way to Powerful and Sustainable Personal Branding*) to be published globally and I am living happily with my wife and my two sons in Miami, Florida. This success is based on my higher calling, and my authentic dream in life. I was aware of my Personal Brand/Ambition and responded to it with love and passion, had the courage to pursue it, have faith in myself, and live according to this dream and higher calling. I took the responsibility to identify my authentic dream and genius and to keep it at the forefront of my mind each day. I knew very clearly what I wanted, asked for it, wished it, dreamt it, formulated it in my PBSC, fixed it in my mind, visualized it, felt it, allowed it, enjoyed it, accepted my responsibility for everything in my life, determined what to give in return, and gave it all my positive energy. I hope you will do the same. I dedicate my portion of this book to my wife Rita and my sons, Rodney and Warren. I can be reached at h.rampersad@tps-international.com and www.total-performancescorecard.com. Our new TPS-Lean Six Sigma company (established in partnership with my friend and co-author Anwar El-Homsi) is devoted to helping individuals and organizations become more successful. We provide integrated and sustainable professional services (consulting, coaching, certification, and training) based on the proven TPS-Lean Six Sigma principles. The results are individual and organizational effectiveness and a related unique competitive advantage. Call or write us for information on our international office closest to you, or for a free catalogue of TPS-Lean Six Sigma products and programs.

TPS-Lean Six Sigma Inc. (Florida)
P.O. Box 601564
North Miami Beach
Florida 33160
Phone: 786-537-7580
Fax: 714-464-4498
E-mail: info@TPS-LeanSixSigma.com
Web: www.TPS-LeanSixSigma.com

TPS-Lean Six Sigma LLC

Linking Human Capital to
Lean Six Sigma

ANWAR EL-HOMSI'S PERSONAL BRAND/ AMBITION

Personal Vision

To be happy with my personal life and career, grow professionally, and help others by sharing knowledge and experience, and make a great contribution to society. I would like to accomplish this by:

- Balancing family, business, and personal interests.
- Continually learn and utilize knowledge to teach others.

- Assuring my work will contribute to helping organizations and society.
- Attain financial security.

Personal Mission

Contribute to society by sharing knowledge with others and help them achieve their professional goals.

Personal Key Roles

In order to achieve my vision, the following key roles have top priority:

- Spouse: Provide love and support and have a satisfying relationship that is build on mutual respect and trust.
- Father: Provide my son with love and financial security.
- Manager: Treat my employees fairly and with respect and a spirit of partnership.
- Consultant: Educate individuals and corporations to be more efficient and effective.

About Myself

I was born in Tripoli, Lebanon in 1959. My father, who I dedicate my portion of this book to, was great man, excellent father, an educator and politician, and he wanted his children to be raised with good morals and values and receive a higher education. We lived a happy and prosperous life. My father died at the age of 36. Our lives were then changed forever. My wonderful mother never got remarried and dedicated her life to her children. I am the oldest among four siblings—a brother and three sisters and at 13 years old, it was my responsibility to take care of my family. I always remembered my father's wishes for me to pursue a higher education and realized how hard life is without an education. I promised myself and was determined to never give up on my dream of furthering my studies and acquiring a good education. Two years after my father's death, I met a man, Salam Izzedine and he took me under his wing and treated me just like his own son. When I was 15 years old, the Lebanese civil war began and it was difficult to attend school and study but I continued my education at a French private school and one of my dreams was to eventually attend University. This dream became reality when I enrolled at the Lebanese University. During the war, I witnessed many people suffering and I wished that I could alleviate all their pain and make them happy. I promised myself then, to do my best to assist people and be a peaceful and loving person. At the age of 25, I was granted a full scholarship to come to the United States to study from the Hariri Foundation, which was founded by the former Lebanese Prime Minister, Rafik Hariri, who was unfortunately assassinated on February 14, 2005. It was a sad day for me. I looked to him as a father who assisted me to begin obtaining my educational goals and helped me become, who I am today.

I came to the United States in August 1985. I studied material-ceramic engineering at Alfred University in Alfred, New York, where I received my bachelor of science degree. After graduation, I married and had a son. I worked at Becton Dickinson for 3 years and decided to go back to university. I received my master's of science degree in applied statistics from the Rochester Institute of Technology and completed a 2 year program in one year.

I have over 17 years of quality and statistics experience in a variety of industries. I have held many positions in engineering and management positions at many reputable companies such Eastman Kodak Company, Heidelberg, Xerox Corporation, and Corning Corporation.

In July 2002, I started my own consulting and training company, Transformation Partners Company, in which, I am the president. As a consultant, I have coached hundreds of companies to improve the quality of their product and services with Six Sigma deployment and philosophy and these companies have documented millions of dollars in savings.

I have a passion to share knowledge and my philosophy with others and I am an Instructor, coach, and trainer. I currently teach Lean Six Sigma's Concepts, Tools and Philosophy at three colleges—at Monroe Community College in Rochester, New York, at Erie Community College in Buffalo, New York and at Bucks County Community College in New Town, Pennsylvania. I have trained more than a thousand engineers, managers, directors, and scientists, and mentored and trained many Black Belts, Green and White Belts, and Champions. I am a Lean Six Sigma Master Black Belt and I have also mentored many professionals to become Master Black Belts.

I have been active in many professional societies such as the American Society for Quality and Society of Reliability Engineers. I was a member of the advisory council for Rochester Institute of Technology's Center for Quality and Applied Statistics. I am one of the originators and served as president of the Society of Reliability Engineers, Rochester Chapter. Also, I served as a member of and president of the Rochester Alliance Business

Group. I have given many presentations on Lean Six Sigma at workshops, conferences, summits, forums and seminars.

I can be reached at www.ael-homsi@tpcompany.com. Our new TPS-Lean Six Sigma Company (established in partnership with my friend and coauthor Hubert Rampersad) is devoted to helping individuals and organizations become more successful. We provide integrated and sustainable professional services (consulting, coaching, certification, and training) based on the proven TPS-Lean Six Sigma principles. The results are individual and organizational effectiveness and a related unique competitive advantage. Call or write us for information to our international office, or contact us for a free catalogue of TPS-Lean Six Sigma products and programs.

Anwar El-Homsi
CEO, TPS-Lean Six Sigma $_{LLC}$
144 Fairport Village Landing, #303
Fairport, NY 14450
Voice: 585-750-8203
Fax: 585-425-7381
E-mail: a.el-homsi@TPS-LeanSixSigma.com
Web: www.TPS-LeanSixSigma.com

TPS-Lean Six Sigma LLC

Linking Human Capital to
Lean Six Sigma

More Advance Praise for TPS-Lean Six Sigma:

The major difference between two companies in the same industry lies not with the machines they use, not with their locations, not with their advertising campaigns, and not with their buildings, but rather with the people who work there—their skills, their talents, the processes they carry out, and especially with the motivation they bring to the job. TPS-Lean Six Sigma provides a guidepost for executives to craft an organization that both celebrates individual differences while molding disparate individuals into an efficient team executing the right processes smartly. It was once said of a great sports coach (Bum Phillips) that "he could take 'hissen' and beat 'youren' or he could take 'youren' and beat 'hissen.'" TPS-Lean Six Sigma will teach you how to do that: how to build upon widely ranging individual strengths so as to combine them into a set of efficient and effective performers who deliver value with no waste and target precisely what customers desire. —**Professor Francis D.Tuggle, PhD, Argyros School of Business and Economics, Chapman University, California.**

Aligning personal goals with organizational goals in the deployment of Lean Six Sigma is brilliant! This book will help many organizations whose deployment of Lean Six Sigma was not as they had anticipated and will make the journey much more rewarding for those just starting. — **Reginald Stewart, Quality Officer and Six Sigma Master Black Belt, University of Rochester, Strong Memorial Hospital, USA.**

TPS-Lean Six Sigma is a wonderful, thought provoking concept that we will incorporate into all of our quality training. Lean Six Sigma has helped many of our customers improve their product or service. It is my hope that with TPS-Lean Six Sigma, we can now begin to address how these quality tools affect the most important part of any organization, its people. —**Charles J. Caples, Program Director Workforce Development, Monroe Community College, USA.**

The TPS-Lean Six Sigma book is a synergetic approach and business perspective for leading companies; a major contribution in the cohesive development of organizations. By aligning and combining human and organizational interests Hubert Rampersad and Anwar El-Homsi created a thorough concept for successful improvement of organizational and human behavior. Enjoy the richness of the content and you will understand that implementing TPS-LSS generates self propelling engagement and related results. —**Ad Rutten, Executive Vice President & COO, Schiphol Group, Amsterdam Airport Schiphol, the Netherlands.**

TPS-Lean Six Sigma is an excellent book on a topic that is so important in today's business climate. It describes in a very pragmatic and structured way how to improve company performance and personal satisfaction of employees by aligning company- and personal objectives. Optimizing business processes and enhancing personal engagement does not only result in an enhanced performance but also addresses sustainability of realized improvements over time. A highly readable and useful book. — **Paul Stuyvenberg Vice President Corporate Quality Management, ASML, the Netherlands.**

Printed in the United States
91679LV00001B/25-30/A